50 YEARS OF CLASSIC Cars

50 YEARS OF

CLASSIC Cars

A celebration of the world's greatest motor cars

JONATHAN WOOD

CLB

Colour Library Books

THE AUTHOR

Jonathan Wood is a writer who has specialized in the motor industry for more than 30 years. He served his journalistic apprenticeship on the *Reading Chronicle* and *Mercury* newspapers, and then became assistant editor of *Car Mechanics* magazine in 1967. He was a founder member of the team that created *Classic Car* magazine in 1973, and spent eight years as its features editor. In 1977 he was awarded Renault's Pierre Dreyfus Award for "outstanding journalistic effort" for a series of articles on the history of the Austin Seven. He became a freelance writer in 1981, and now has some 26 highly acclaimed books to his credit. In 1988 he was awarded the Montagu Trophy for his history of the British motoring industry, *Wheels of Misfortune*. He has twice been awarded the American Society of Automotive Historians' highest accolade, the Gugnot Award, firstly for *Wheels of Misfortune* in 1989, and again in 1993 for his largest published work to date, *Bugatti: The Man and The Marque*.

CLB 4225
This edition published 1995 by Colour Library Books
© 1994 Colour Library Books Ltd,
Woolsack Way, Godalming , Surrey GU7 1XW, UK

ISBN 1-85833-252-4

Credits

Editor
Philip de Ste. Croix

Designers
Richard Hawke
Barry Savage

Line artwork
Richard Hawke

Index
Brian Jones

Production
Ruth Arthur
Sally Connolly
Neil Randles
Karen Staff
Jonathan Tickner

Director of production
Gerald Hughes

Typesetting
SX Composing Ltd, Essex

Colour reproduction
Advance Laser Graphic Arts, Hong Kong

Printed and bound in Italy
New Interlitho SpA

CONTENTS

INTRODUCTION   6

SPORTS CARS   10

MG TC, TD, TF (1945-1955)   12
JAGUAR XK120, XK140, XK150 (1948-1961)   14
HEALEY SILVERSTONE (1949-1950)   16
PORSCHE 356 (1948-1965)   18
TRIUMPH TR2, TR3, TR3A (1953-1961)   20
AUSTIN-HEALEY 100/4, 100/6, 3000 (1953-1968)   22
CHEVROLET CORVETTE (1953-1962)   24
JAGUAR XK SS (1957)   26
MGA (1955-1962)   28
LOTUS SEVEN/CATERHAM SEVEN (1957 to date)   30
AUSTIN-HEALEY SPRITE/MG MIDGET (1958-1979)   32
JAGUAR E-TYPE SERIES I AND II (1961-1971)   34
TRIUMPH TR4, 4A, 5, 6 AND 7 (1961-1981)   36
LOTUS ELAN (1962-1974)   38
MGB (1962-1980) MGC (1967-1969) MGB GT V8 (1973-1976) 40
AC COBRA (1962-1969, 1983 to date)   42
CHEVROLET CORVETTE STING RAY (1962-1967)   44
PORSCHE 911 (1963 to date)   46
ALFA ROMEO SPIDER (1966-1993)   48
MORGAN PLUS 8 (1968 to date)   50
CHEVROLET CORVETTE (1967-1982)   52
DATSUN 240Z (1969-1973)   54
PORSCHE 911 TURBO (1974 to date)   56
CHEVROLET CORVETTE (1983 to date)   58
TOYOTA MR2 (1984-1990)   60
BMW Z1 (1988-1991)   62
MAZDA MX-5 MIATA (1988 to date)   64
LOTUS ELAN (1989-1994)   66
DODGE VIPER (1992 to date)   68
MG RV8 (1992 to date)   70
TVR GRIFFITH (1992 to date)   72

GRAND TOURERS   74

HEALEY ELLIOT (1946-1950)   76
CISITALIA 202 GRAN SPORT (1947-1952)   78
BRISTOL 400 FAMILY (1947-1961)   80
FERRARI 166 INTER (1948-1950)   82
ASTON MARTIN DB2, DB2/4 (1950-1959)   84
PEGASO Z102 (1951-1958)   86
LANCIA AURELIA B20, 2500GT (1951-1958)   88
FERRARI 340, 342, 375 AMERICA (1951-1954)   90
FACEL VEGA (1954-1964)   92
FERRARI 250 GT (1954-1964)   94

ALFA ROMEO GIULIETTA/GIULIA SS (1957-1965)	96
MASERATI 3500 GT (1957-1964)	98
LOTUS ELITE (1957-1963)	100
ASTON MARTIN DB4, DB5, DB6 (1958-1971)	102
VOLVO P1800, 1800S, 1800E (1961-1972)	104
FERRARI 250 GT BERLINETTA LUSSO (1962-1964)	106
STUDEBAKER AVANTI (1962-1965)	108
BUICK RIVIERA (1962-1965)	110
MERCEDES-BENZ 230, 250, 280SL (1963-1971)	112
LAMBORGHINI 350GT AND 400GT (1963-1967)	114
FORD MUSTANG (1964-1967)	116
AC 428 (1965-1973)	118
FERRARI 330 GTC AND 365 GTC (1966-1970)	120
JENSEN INTERCEPTOR AND FF (1966-1976)	122
(FERRARI) DINO 206 GT AND 246 GT (1967-1974)	124
ASTON MARTIN V8 (1969-1989)	126
FORD CAPRI (1969-1987)	128
CITROËN SM (1970-1975)	130
BMW 3.0 CS, CSL, CSi (1971-1975)	132
JAGUAR E-TYPE SERIES III (1971-1975)	134
FERRARI 365 GT4 2+2, 400, 412 (1972-1989)	136
JAGUAR XJS (1975 to date)	138
LOTUS ESPRIT (1975 to date)	140
PORSCHE 928 (1977 to date)	142
MAZDA RX-7 (1978-1985)	144
AUDI QUATTRO (1980-1991)	146
PORSCHE 944 (1981-1992)	148
NISSAN 300ZX (1989 to date)	150
MERCEDES-BENZ SL300, SL500, SL600 (1989 to date)	152
HONDA NSX (1990 to date)	154
FERRARI 456 GT (1992 to date)	156
ASTON MARTIN DB7 (1993 to date)	158
TOYOTA SUPRA (1993 to date)	160

SUPERCARS

162

BENTLEY CONTINENTAL (1952-1959)	164
MERCEDES-BENZ 300SL (1954-1957)	168
CADILLAC ELDORADO BROUGHAM (1956-1958)	172
ASTON MARTIN DB4GT ZAGATO (1960-1963 and 1991)	176
FORD GT40 (1966-1968)	180
LAMBORGHINI MIURA (1966-1972)	184
FERRARI DAYTONA (1968-1973)	188
LAMBORGHINI COUNTACH (1971-1990)	192
LANCIA STRATOS (1972-1975)	196
ROLLS-ROYCE CAMARGUE (1975-1985)	200
ASTON MARTIN LAGONDA (1976-1990)	204
FERRARI TESTAROSSA AND 512TR (1984 to date)	208
PORSCHE 959 (1983-1988)	212
ASTON MARTIN V8 VANTAGE ZAGATO (1986-1990)	216

FERRARI F40 (1987-1992)	220
ASTON MARTIN VIRAGE (1988 to date)	224
LAMBORGHINI DIABLO (1990 to date)	228
JAGUAR XJ220 (1991-1994)	232
BENTLEY CONTINENTAL R (1991 to date)	236
BUGATTI EB110 GT (1991 to date)	240
McLAREN F1 (1993 to date)	244

SALOONS

248

CITROËN TRACTION AVANT (1934-1957)	250
VOLKSWAGEN BEETLE (1945 to date)	252
MORRIS MINOR (1948-1971)	254
CITROËN 2CV (1948-1990)	256
CADILLAC SERIES 60, 61, 62 (1948-1953)	258
JAGUAR MARKS VII, VIII, IX (1950-1961)	260
ROLLS-ROYCE SILVER CLOUD (1955-1965)	262
JAGUAR MARKS I AND II (1955-1969)	264
CITROËN DS (1965-1975)	266
FIAT 500 (1957-1975)	268
CADILLAC ELDORADO SEVILLE (1958-1959)	270
MINI (1959 to date)	272
CHEVROLET CORVAIR (1959-1969)	274
BMW 1500, 1600, 1800 (1961-1968)	276
FORD CORTINA (1962-1966)	278
RENAULT R16 (1965-1979)	280
ROLLS-ROYCE SILVER SHADOW (1965-1980)	282
NSU Ro80 (1967-1977)	284
JAGUAR XJ6, XJ (1968-1986)	286
ALFA ROMEO ALFASUD (1972-1983)	288
RENAULT 5 (1972 to date)	290
VOLKSWAGEN GOLF (1974 to date)	292
CADILLAC SEVILLE (1980-1985)	294
MERCEDES-BENZ 190 (1982-1993)	296
BENTLEY TURBO R (1985 to date)	298
JAGUAR XJ6 (1986 to date)	300
BMW 7 SERIES (1986 to date)	302
ALFA ROMEO 164 (1987 to date)	304
CITROËN XM (1989 to date)	306
LEXUS LS400 (1989 to date)	308
MERCEDES-BENZ S-CLASS (1991 to date)	310
FORD MONDEO (1993 to date)	312
RENAULT TWINGO (1993 to date)	314
ROVER 600 (1993 to date)	316

INDEX

318

INTRODUCTION

The myriad of firms that constitute the world's motor manufacturers have sprung from a wide and diverse range of origins. Sometimes they developed from simple bicycle makers; in other instances from engineers fascinated by the mysteries of the internal combustion engine; some produced totally unrelated products such as manufacturing looms for the weaving industry; another (Buick) was a maker of bathroom fittings before turning to the motor car!

Germany was the birthplace, in 1886, of the automobile with Gottlieb Daimler and Karl Benz sharing the credit for their respective vehicles which appeared in that year. They established their own car companies which, in 1926, merged to form Daimler-Benz. Today this concern enjoys an enviable reputation as the maker of Mercedes-Benz cars. Its undisputed German rival is BMW, a firm with very different origins. The Bavarian Motor Works, formed in 1916, began by producing aero engines and its badge is a representation of the blur of a turning propeller. BMW switched to motor cars in 1928 when it took over the Dixi company, which was building the British Austin Seven under licence. Ironically, in 1994, BMW bought the British Rover Group that was the custodian of the by-then moribund Austin marque. The industry is full of such historical coincidences.

Across the Rhine in France both Peugeot and Renault were market leaders before World War I. Peugeot was a prosperous bicycle manufacturer, and Louis Renault a talented self-taught engineer. After hostilities had ceased, both were challenged by the mercurial Andre Citroën who had made his name by mass producing France's munitions. He was to emerge as the country's largest car maker until he gambled all on his revolutionary front-wheel-drive Traction Avant model of 1934 and lost control of his company to Michelin, his largest creditor.

Similarly, most of the principal components of the Italian motor industry were in place before World War I. By far and away the largest of them, Fiat, was established at the turn of the century in Turin while Lancia was also based, from 1906, in the city. Alfa Romeo, by contrast, hailed from nearby Milan.

However, it was Britain which dominated European production in the years between 1932 and 1955 when it ceded pole position to Germany. By the 1930's, Britain's industry was dominated by the Big Six car makers. Largest of them was Morris, which by then included MG, Wolseley and Riley. The group was to be known as the Nuffield Organisation and had its origins in Morris Motors established by garage proprietor, William Morris, in 1913. Herbert Austin's car business, Morris's great rival of the interwar years, also dates

from the pre-World War I days. Standard began building cars in 1903 while Rootes were distributors which purchased the bankrupted Hillman, Humber and Sunbeam companies in the 1930's.

The American-owned sector in Britain was represented by Ford, with a manufacturing presence established in 1912 and General Motors which, in 1926, bought the insolvent Vauxhall company.

Across the Atlantic, the massive American market was dominated by the Big Three motor manufacturers. By the 1930's these were headed by General Motors with its bevy of makes which embraced the Chevrolet, Buick, Oldsmobile and Cadillac names. Up until the late 1920's Ford had been the market leader and also owned the prestigious Lincoln marque. Chrysler, the last of the Three to be established, had Plymouth as its high volume, low cost arm.

There were some flickerings of a motor industry in Japan. Datsun's origins reach back to 1912 while Toyota is the firm that began by making looms and diversified into cars in 1936. It was destined to become the country's premier car maker and one of the world's largest motor manufacturers. In 1939 the entire Japanese industry produced just 856 cars; it was otherwise preoccupied with building trucks and other vehicles for the military.

In the 50 or so years since the ending of World War II, the industry's epicentre has switched, in global terms, from America to Japan and, in the European arena, Germany has emerged as the Continent's largest and most powerful industry. This was at the expense of Britain, which of all the world's car makers experienced the greatest realignment of its motor manufacturing base.

The early post-war years saw the pre-war SS marque renamed Jaguar, and the arrival of the Bristol, Healey (later Austin Healey) and Lotus makes, while Standard took over Triumph. In 1952 Austin merged with Nuffield to form the British Motor Corporation, which became the country's largest car maker. But it was destined to survive for just 16 years because it too was absorbed, in 1968, by Leyland Motors which had, in the meantime, taken over the rival companies Standard Triumph and Rover.

The outcome was that almost the entire indigenous industry was contained within British Leyland Motor Corporation. In 1975, it was nationalized in the wake of the ongoing world depression triggered by the oil price hike of '73. By this time Austin Healey, Riley and Wolseley had disappeared and in 1986 the business was renamed the Rover Group. In 1988 it was taken over by British Aerospace and by the time that it sold the greatly slimmed-down and profitable business to BMW in 1994, only two marque names, those of Rover and MG, survived. This means that only two main-

stream car makers, Rolls-Royce and Morgan, remain in British hands.

Of the other members of the much depleted Big Six, Rootes was swallowed up in the 1960's by Chrysler and its British operations were, in turn, absorbed into Peugeot Citroën. The take-over of Citroën by Peugeot had, incidentally, been effected in 1975.

Ford consolidated its position and in 1968 merged with the business's German arm to produce the integrated Ford of Europe. It has since purchased two British automotive institutions, Aston Martin in 1987 and Jaguar in 1988.

General Motors continued as custodian of the Vauxhall name and in 1986 it bought sports car maker Lotus, an association that was only destined to survive for six years. In 1993 GM sold the business to the revived Italy-based Bugatti company.

Like Britain, Italy has also undergone some realignment of its industry but the post-war years have also seen some emergence of some new marques, of which Ferrari, dating from 1947, is the best known. These are years in which Fiat has absorbed practically all the country's car makers, namely Ferrari and Lancia in 1969, Alfa Romeo in 1984 and Maserati in 1993. One of the country's newest makes, Lamborghini, was bought by Chrysler in 1987, but in 1994 the American corporation disposed of it to an Indonesian-based group.

The post-war years also saw the growth and establishment of the international standing of the Italian styling houses, namely Pininfarina, Bertone and Ghia along with, in more recent years, Ital Design. Not only did they work closely with the indigenous car makers but their services are retained by motor manufacturers the world over.

Across the Alps in Germany, another new make, Volkswagen with its seemingly evergreen Beetle, emerged as by far and away the country's largest car maker. This German People's Car had been designed pre-war by Porsche which, in 1948, introduced a new VW-based sports car under its own name. The partitioning of Germany after the war meant that BMW's car business, previously based at Eisenach in the east, was re-established in Munich and revitalized under new ownership from 1960 to become a major force within Germany and the world. Similarly Audi, whose factory was previously located behind the Iron Curtain, was reformed in the West and since 1964 has been owned by Volkswagen. The American presence in Germany, consisting of Opel and Ford, had existed since the 1920's, and continued as a significant force there.

In America itself, the Big Three continued to hold sway in the booming 1950's, but it was a decade in which European imports, in the shape of the British sports cars and, secondly and more significantly, the Volkswagen Beetle, began to make their respective presences felt. But this was nothing compared with the impact that the Japanese began to make there from the 1960's onwards.

It will be recalled that before the war Japan's car makers consisted, in essence, of Toyota and Nissan, which produced the Datsun. From 1960 the Nissan name appeared on some models sold on the home market. Those built for export were called Datsun, but this practice only lasted until 1983. Since then, the company has only manufactured Nissan cars.

After that excursion into terminology, back to the 1950's and 1960's! It was then that Toyota and Nissan were joined by a further four makes and today these six names constitute the essential elements of the Japanese motor industry. One of the earliest new recruits was Daihatsu which had, since 1930, built vans and in 1954 extended its range to include automobiles. This remained an independent company until it was absorbed, in 1968, by the burgeoning Toyota concern. Later in the decade, in 1959, came the first Mitsubishi car from a firm which could trace its lineage back to that of a late 19th century ship builder.

In 1960 came Mazda from Toyo Kogyo which had started its life in the 1920's producing cork products. The company introduced its first rotary-engined car in 1967 and is today the world's sole manufacture of a device which was once thought would overturn the reciprocating engine in popularity.

The 1950's saw Japan emerge as the world's largest manufacturer of motor cycles and, in the following decade, two of its principal manufacturers diversified into car production. Suzuki had begun building two wheelers in 1936 and entered the car market in 1960. Incredibly, Honda only started production in 1948, yet within a decade it dominated the market and added cars to its portfolio in 1962.

With a ferocious export drive first targetted at America and then Europe, Japan has emerged as the international community's major manufacturing force. In 1980 it toppled America from its perch as the world's largest car maker – a position it had held since 1904 – although the US has subsequently redressed the balance.

Not only are Japan's products seen on almost every road on the globe, its car makers have also taught the rest of the motoring world how to build its automobiles more efficiently. And all this has come from a country which produced no cars at all in the first two years after the war and, in 1947, built just 110 vehicles! Such are the ironies of this fascinating industry.

Sports Cars

The sports car, a vehicle in which its owner can delight in driving fast, is almost as old as the automobile itself. These invariably stylish models were almost exclusively produced in Britain and Continental Europe; it was not until after World War II that the delights of open air motoring were enthusiastically embraced by the American public.

Up until the 1960's, with a few notable exceptions, such cars were of mostly British origin and typified by the ultra traditional T Series MGs of the late 1940's with their wheel tracks firmly placed a decade earlier. They paved the way in 1955 for the more modern MGA and later, in 1962, for the even more successful MGB that endured for 18 years and of which over half a million were built.

More expensive and faster was Jaguar's lovely XK120 of 1948, powered by an advanced twin-overhead-camshaft engine, which ensured that the model was capable of 120mph (193km/h). This, in turn, led to the sensational E-Type, unquestionably the most memorable of Jaguar's sports cars. Other British car makers soon followed MG and Jaguar's lead. Triumph's TR series appeared in 1952 so engendering a family that lasted until 1980. By contrast, the seemingly indestructible but dated Morgan happily survives to this day.

These were all established car makers, but the British Motor Corporation's Austin Healey marque was a post-war creation and was conceived with the American market very much in mind. It lasted until 1970. Another new make was Lotus, the brainchild of the talented Colin Chapman. The glass-fibre-bodied Elan of 1962 found appreciate owners on both sides of the Atlantic.

By contrast, AC's Cobra of 1962 was a truly Anglo-American creation in which a Ford V8 engine was shoehorned into a British-designed body and chassis. The outcome was one of the world's fastest cars which was capable of over 160mph (257km/h).

While Britain initially dominated the sports car market, on the European mainland two new makes, the Italian Ferrari and Porsche from Germany, were to attain legendary status. Ferrari was in the vanguard of the Grand Touring movement and it thus belongs in that section of this book, but the Porsche marque, which appeared in 1948, was both new and idiosyncratic. This was a company which had been responsible for designing the Volkswagen Beetle in pre-war days, and its first car, the 356, echoed the VW tradition by adopting a rear-mounted, air-cooled, horizontally opposed engine. This theme was perpetuated in the 911 of 1963, which is one of the great sports cars of the post-war years and is still in production, 31 years on, at the time of writing (1994).

These Porsches acquired a dedicated American following and their impact, along with the more plentiful British imports, resulted in the mighty General Motors Corporation unveiling, in 1953, its own sports car in the shape of the glass-fibre-bodied Chevrolet Corvette. After getting off to an uncertain start, the model grew in stature and refinement, an advance which is maintained in the current version of the design.

Sports cars usually rely for components on those developed for their saloon counterparts and, as Britain's motor industry stumbled and stuttered into 1970's, the growing impact of the Japanese car makers made their presence felt in that sector with the 1969 arrival of the Datsun 240Z coupé. Targetted at the vast American market, it proved to be an instant success and so paved the way for the Z car family which endures to this day. There could now be no doubt that the Japanese were able to take on the best of the world, and this was underlined, in 1982, when Toyota, which had previously only manufactured mass-produced saloons, unveiled its mid-engined MR2 which set new standards for such a configuration. More recently, Mazda has produced its acclaimed MX5 Miata which, ironically, echoes the no-nonsense specification of British sports cars of the 1960's.

Despite the success of the Japanese, today the tradition of the open-topped British two-seater is being maintained by such cars as the stylish TVR Griffith, another post-war make, and the MGB-based MG RV8 of 1992. This car is to pave the way for a revival of the MG marque which, conveniently, brings us back to where we came in!

MG TC, TD, TF (1945-1955)

The sports car that re-introduced America to the pleasures of open air motoring was British and yet delightfully outdated when it entered production in 1945. Although the TC Midget's transatlantic impact was considerable, it sold in relatively small numbers there but paved the way for the updated and numerically more successful TD of 1950 and this, in turn, led to the (by then) archaic TF of 1953, which soldiered on until production finally ended in 1955.

The TC's origins were rooted in the MG TA Midget of 1936 with its double humped scuttle, cutaway doors and slab petrol tank. The Abingdon-built two seater was, in essence, a modestly updated version of the TB of 1939, powered by a 1.2 litre, Morris 10-related engine which would be employed in every MG sports car until 1955. In line with its pre-war ancestry, the TC used a simple box section chassis, underslung at the rear, with all-round, half elliptic springs. The car was, accordingly, stiffly sprung but handling was well balanced; top speed approached the 75mph (121km/h) mark but, with the hood lowered, it felt considerably more!

Although the car sold for £479 on its introduction, it was in short supply in its native land, because the government was directing car makers to export their products and nearly 65 per cent of the 10,000 TCs built found overseas customers. The majority went to Australia and the Antipodes; only 2001 were sold in the United States, some of which were brought home by GIs serving in Britain. However, its influence there was considerable and it made way, in 1950, for the TD.

TD Takes The Stage

This retained the lines of the TC but the body was slightly wider and it used a new chassis, overslung at the rear, independent front suspension and rack-and-pinion steering, all of which were related to the MG Y Series saloon of 1947. It was available with left-hand steering (unlike the TC) and, despite the fitment of rather unappealing disc wheels in place of the traditional knock-off wires, the car was a great success. Nearly 80 per cent of the 29,664 cars built found American customers. In the USA, many racing drivers, most notably Phil Hill and Richie Ginther, began their careers at the wheels of British MGs.

Charming as they were, time was running out for these latter day Midgets. In 1952 MG's Morris Motors

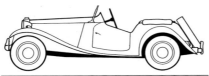
parent company was absorbed into the British Motor Corporation and the newly minted Austin Healey 100 became its corporate sporting flagship. So MG was left with an ageing model range. The final generation of the T Series family was the TF of 1953 with a lowered body line, handsome, sloping radiator grille and faired-in headlamps. Wire wheels were, significantly, available as an optional extra. Heavier than its predecessor, the TF's performance was consequently inferior to the TD's and an increase in engine capacity to 1.5 litres in 1954 did little to boost sales. The TF was discontinued in 1955, to make way for the new and thoroughly modern MGA, after 9600 examples had been built. Ironically, today the TF is the most sought-after of these memorable MG two seaters.

RIGHT: *Charming but unashamedly pre-war in concept with handsome lines, the TC arrived in 1945 and was widely exported. This is a 1946 car.*

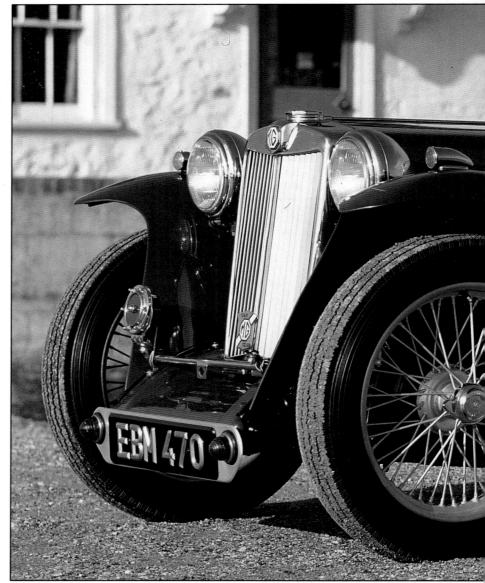

MG T Series

1.3 litre MG TA roadster 1936

1.1 litre Morris
Series M saloon 1938

1.2 litre TB 1939

1.2 litre TC 1945

1.2 litre MG Y type
saloon 1947

1.2 litre TD 1950

1.2 litre TF 1953

1.5 litre TF1500 1954

LEFT: *A 1952 TD. Independent front suspension contributed to it being the best-selling T Series model.*

RIGHT: *A 1955 TF easily identifiable by its inclined radiator grille and faired-in headlamps.*

JAGUAR XK120, XK140, XK150 (1948-1961)

The XK120 re-established Jaguar as one of the world's leading manufacturers of sports cars although, ironically, this Coventry company has actually always built more saloons. The 120, one of the fastest, best looking and most refined performance cars of its day, was in turn succeeded by the XK140 in 1955 and, finally, by the XK150 of 1957.

During World War II, Jaguar planned to produce a 100mph (161km/h) saloon to be powered by an advanced 3.4 litre six cylinder engine with, adventurously, twin overhead camshafts, a configuration that had hitherto been reserved for high performance, and sometimes temperamental sports cars. The Mark VII saloon finally appeared in 1951 but, three years earlier at the 1948 Motor Show, the engine made its debut in Jaguar's new sports car, named the XK120 to reflect its almost unprecedented top speed. The appropriateness of the designation was underlined, in 1949, when a factory-prepared example attained 132mph (212km/h) at Jabbeke in Belgium.

As ever, the sensational two-seater roadster was styled by Jaguar's talented chairman, William Lyons. The equally handsome XK engine was mounted in a chassis with torsion bar independent suspension related to that fitted to the Mark V saloon.

Such was the 120's allure that demand for the car caught Jaguar by surprise. The bodies of the first 240 examples were built using traditional aluminium/wood construction, but, thereafter, all-steel bodies were the norm. Well priced on its announcement at £1273, this cost was of only academic interest in Britain because practically all 120s were exported, mostly to America. The car did not reach the home market until March 1950. The following year saw the introduction of an elegant fixed head coupé version and this was followed, in 1953, by a drophead coupé variant.

The XK140, an updated version of the 120, arrived in 1954. It had heavier bumpers and radiator grille and a medallion on the boot lid, indicating that Jaguar had won Le Mans in 1951 and 1953. However, unlike its predecessor, the model number did not reflect the car's top speed for the 140, in closed form, was only capable, flat out, of nearly 130mph (209km/h). Body options followed the 120 precedent and the new car was otherwise mechanically similar, although the 3.4 litre engine was moved 3in (76mm) forward in the chassis to permit the fitment of two small occasional rear seats on all but the roadster version. In addition, rack-and-pinion steering was a welcome driver refinement.

In the spring of 1957 the model gave way to the XK150 with similar but wider bodywork, enlarged radiator grille and disc brakes. It was also available in faster S form with a race breed "straight port" cylinder head. From 1959, the 150 followed the example of Jaguar saloons by listing an optional 3.8 litre engine, which meant that the most potent version was capable of 135mph (217km/h). Automatic transmission, an option on some late 140s, was available on the 150 from the outset.

The XK150 lasted until 1961, but it and the 140 never quite attained the popularity, and impact, of their illustrious progenitor. XK120 production totalled 12,078 cars, which compared with 8884 examples of the 140 and the XK150's 9395 customers.

BELOW: *The XK120 even looks good with the hood raised. This roadster dates from 1953 and left-hand-drive indicates that it is one of many to have been exported to America.*

Length:	14ft 6in (4420mm)
Width:	5ft 1in (1549mm)
Height:	4ft 4in (1321mm)
Wheelbase:	8ft 6in (2590mm)
Track:	front 4ft 6in (1372mm), rear 4ft 5in (1346mm)
Unladen weight:	2912lb (1320kg)
Engine: Six cylinder, twin overhead camshaft, 83x106mm, 3442cc. Compression ratio, 8:1. Max power, 160bhp at 5000rpm. Max torque, 195lb/ft at 2500rpm.	
Transmission:	Four-speed manual
Drive:	Rear
Suspension (front):	Independent, torsion bars, wishbones
Suspension (rear):	Live axle, half-elliptic springs
Top speed:	120mph (193km/h)
0-60mph (96km/h):	8.4 seconds
Production (total XK):	30,357

ABOVE: *A 1954 Jaguar XK140 roadster with optional wire wheels. The bumpers are more substantial than those of its 120 predecessor and a medallion on the boot lid records Jaguar's Le Mans racing triumphs.*

BELOW: *A 1959 XK150 fixed-head coupé; last of the XK line and identifiable by the wide radiator grille.*

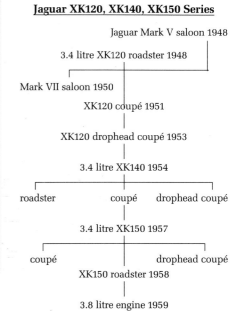

Jaguar XK120, XK140, XK150 Series

Jaguar Mark V saloon 1948

3.4 litre XK120 roadster 1948

Mark VII saloon 1950

XK120 coupé 1951

XK120 drophead coupé 1953

3.4 litre XK140 1954

roadster — coupé — drophead coupé

3.4 litre XK150 1957

coupé — drophead coupé

XK150 roadster 1958

3.8 litre engine 1959

HEALEY SILVERSTONE (1949-1950)

The functional and distinctive Warwick-built Silverstone was the most memorable of the cars produced by the Donald Healey Motor Company in its formative era. Donald Mitchell Healey was a tough minded Cornish rally driver, who had won, among many other events, the 1931 Monte Carlo Rally. During World War II he decided to build cars under his own name. In 1946 came the Elliot saloon and Westland roadster, powered by the potent (though heavy) 2.4 litre twin carburettored Riley engine which was mounted in a robust box section chassis fitted with trailing arm independent front suspension. These Healeys were some of the fastest cars of their day, although their respective prices, in open and closed forms, of £1566 and £1597, reflected their hand-built status.

In 1947, Healey was distressed when the Labour government doubled the purchase tax on cars selling for over £1000. This policy pushed the price of the top-line Elliot to an eyebrow-raising £2232. Healey responded by introducing, in 1949, a low cost model based on his existing engine and chassis aimed at the small but popular club racing market. The car was named the Silverstone after Britain's new motor racing circuit, opened in 1948. It carefully did not breach the £1000 ceiling. The model, announced in July 1949, sold for a basic price of £975 which, with purchase tax added, came to a total of £1246.

As cost was the overriding consideration, the open, two-seater body, essayed by Healey's Len Hodges, was simple and distinctive. Detachable cycle wings were fitted, the Silverstone's nose was positioned well to the fore and the headlamps mounted, in the manner of the pre-war Peugeot 402, behind the Healey kite-shaped grille. For the same financial limitations, there were no bumpers. Ingeniously, the horizontally located spare wheel did double duty as a rear bumper. A further novelty was that the windscreen lowered into the scuttle although sufficient still projected to form a low 'screen for competition use. Unlike earlier cars which used the traditional wooden frame, the all-metal aluminium body was built for Healey by Abbey Panels of Coventry.

Further Refinement

Like its predecessors, the Silverstone was a 100mph- (161km/h)-plus car and was soon proving its worth in club racing, sprints and hill climbs. After 51 examples had been built, the model was refined, from April 1950, with the arrival of the E type version, the original model having carried the D designation. This had a slightly wider body than hitherto; a bench took the place of bucket seats and leg room was improved. In addition, the windscreen was enlarged, while the most noticeable difference was the introduction of an air intake in the bonnet.

In an effort to pep up performance, Healey experimented with a Wade supercharger and later tried a 5.4 litre Cadillac V8 engine. This led to the restyled Nash Healey of 1951. Silverstone production, therefore, ceased in 1950. Today the car is avidly sought by collectors; a curious state of affairs for such a sparsely equipped model.

Healey Silverstone

Riley 2.4 litre
saloon 1937

2.4 litre Healey 1946

Westland roadster   Elliot saloon

2.4 litre Silverstone 1949

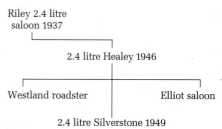

LEFT: *A 1950 E type, chassis E57, Silverstone with simple though distinctive body lines. Just 54 examples of the series were built.*

ABOVE: *On the Silverstone the spare wheel does double duty as a bumper.*

RIGHT: *1950 Silverstone with costly hiduminium trailing-arm independent front suspension readily apparent.*

Specifications: Healey Silverstone

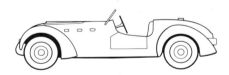

Length:	14ft 1in (4293mm)
Width:	5ft 3in (1600mm)
Height:	3ft 7in (1092mm)
Wheelbase:	8ft 6in (2591mm)
Track:	front 4ft 6in (1372mm), rear 4ft 5in (1346mm)
Unladen weight:	? 2072lb (940kg)
Engine: Four cylinder, overhead valve, 80x120mm, 2443cc. Compression ratio, 6.8:1. Max power, 104bhp at 4500rpm. Max torque, 132lb/ft at 3000rpm.	
Transmission:	Four-speed manual
Drive:	Rear
Suspension (front):	Independent, coil springs, trailing arms
Suspension (rear):	Live axle with torque tube, coil springs
Top speed:	100mph (161km/h)
0-60mph (96km/h):	11 seconds
Production:	105

PORSCHE 356 (1948-1965)

The 356 sports car, the first of the famous Porsche line, was inspired by the concept of the Cisitalia (see page 78) which used proprietory Fiat parts. Similarly, the 356 initially relied heavily on Volkswagen components, the Porsche bureau having designed the German People's Car (*Volkswagen*) before the war. The 356's most distinctive feature is, therefore, its VW-related, rear-mounted, horizontally opposed, air-cooled engine, an approach which survives today in its 911 successor.

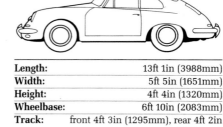

Specifications: Porsche 356B Super 75 coupé

Length:	13ft 1in (3988mm)
Width:	5ft 5in (1651mm)
Height:	4ft 4in (1320mm)
Wheelbase:	6ft 10in (2083mm)
Track:	front 4ft 3in (1295mm), rear 4ft 2in (1270mm)
Unladen weight:	1932lb (876kg)
Engine:	Rear-mounted, air-cooled flat four cylinder, overhead valve, 82x74mm, 1582cc. Compression ratio, 8.5:1. Max power, 75bhp at 5000rpm. Max torque, 88lb/ft at 3700rpm.
Transmission:	Four-speed manual
Drive:	Rear
Suspension (front):	Independent, torsion bars, trailing arms
Suspension (rear):	Independent, transverse leaf spring, torsion bars, swing axle.
Top speed:	105mph (169km/h)
0-60mph (96km/h):	11.2 seconds
Production (total 356):	77,509

The car took shape at Gmünd, Austria, where Porsche, which had been based in Stuttgart, Germany since 1930, had established itself during the war to be out of range of enemy bombers. The 1131cc VW engine (some units were reduced to 1086cc so as to be eligible for 1100cc events) was mounted in a simple platform chassis. The all-round, Porsche-patented, torsion-bar-sprung independent suspension similarly followed VW precedent. The intention was to produce this first Porsche in mainly aerodynamically efficient coupé form, although some open cars were also to be built. The lines were, therefore, based on a special closed, two-seater VW, created by Porsche in 1939 for an aborted Berlin to Rome road race. However, the 356 was, technically, a four-seater with occasional accommodation in the rear.

A Nimble Creation

Aluminium bodywork was used and the outcome was a light, sure footed car which, Ferry Porsche later recalled, "climbed mountains like a chamois and touched 80mph (129km/h) easily." A batch of 50 was laid down but then, from 1950, production was transferred to Stuttgart. These cars had steel bodies and, so as to offset the increased weight, from 1951 the flat-four engine was enlarged to a bigger bored 1286cc unit. For 1952, capacity was once again increased, this time to an optional 1488cc. Inevitably, as the model evolved, the VW ingredients steadily declined and purpose-designed Porsche components took over.

In 1955, 1290 and 1582cc engines were available for the revised 356A, identifiable by a panoramic windscreen which replaced its predecessor's divided one. There was also a 100mph (161km/h) Super version which was continued as the top line model. In 1953, Porsche had introduced the Speedster convertible, initially for its American westcoast customers. It had bucket seats and the

Californian climate only demanded a rudimentary hood. This model lasted until 1958 when it was replaced by the D-type convertible, built for Porsche by Drauz of Heilbronn.

Another 1955 arrival was the potent but noisy Carrera. Outwardly similar to the 356A, it was powered by a formidable, race-breed 112bhp 1498cc engine, with gear-driven twin overhead camshafts per cylinder bank, twin sparking plugs, a roller-bearing crankshaft and dry sump lubrication. It was based on the unit which had powered Porsche's 550, its first purpose-designed sports racer, that had run at Le Mans in 1953. This made the Carrera a 120mph (193km/h) car; capacity was upped to 1587cc in 1958 and the model discontinued in 1959.

That year saw the introduction of the mainstream 356B with 1582cc power. This was replaced, in 1963, by the more refined 356C with all-round disc brakes. This feature was also extended to Carrera 2 which had evolved from its formidable forebear in 1960. Like the 356C, it endured until 1965, so overlapping with its legendary 911 successor by one year.

RIGHT: *Porsche exported most of 356 production to America. These US-registered cars are, left, a Super 1600 version of the famous Speedster of 1953-58 vintage, and right, a 356A coupé which was built between the years of 1955 and 1959.*

Porsche 356

1.1 litre Type 64 coupé 1939
|
1.1 litre Porsche 356 1948
|
coupé   roadster
1.3 litre 1951
|
1.5 litre 1952
|
1.5 litre 550 coupé
1953
356A 1955   1.5 litre Carrera
coupé 1955
1.6 litre 1958
|
356B 1959   1.6 litre Carrera 2
1960
356C 1963

RIGHT: *A 1949 aluminium-bodied 356 coupé, built at Gmünd, Austria.*

LEFT: *A 356A with detachable hardtop and flat-four engine still betraying its Volkswagen origins.*

TRIUMPH TR2, TR3, TR3A (1953-1961)

The Triumph TR2, like its Austin-Healey 100 and MG TD contemporaries, was created specifically for the enormous potential of the American sports car market. It was followed in 1956 by the TR3 which, in turn, made way for the most popular of this generation of TRs, the 3A, that arrived for 1958 and endured until 1961.

Based in the Canley district of Coventry, Standard, which owned Triumph, had first tried to buy Morgan in 1950. When these overtures were rebuffed, its managing director, the formidable Sir John Black, decided that Standard should develop its own sports car. However, the Triumph Roadster, that appeared at the 1952 London Motor Show, was really the starting point of the idea rather than a fully evolved finished product. Retrospectively titled the TR1, the design used a modified pre-war Standard Flying Nine chassis, and Triumph Mayflower front suspension, while the sturdy and economical 1991cc engine, in twin carburettored form, was courtesy of the Standard Vanguard.

During the winter of 1952/53, the design was extensively modified, following an intensive development programme orchestrated by BRM engineer, Ken Richardson. The outcome was the greatly improved two-seater TR2, a no-nonsense, reliable car which was announced at the 1953 Geneva Motor Show in March. It entered production in August of that year. Top speed had risen from 90mph (145km/h) to beyond the magic 100mph (161km/h), while a stripped works car achieved a well publicized 124mph (199km/h) at Jabbeke, Belgium in May 1953. The TR2 sold for a competitive £787 and production was, initially, modest with a total of 8628 examples built. During this period, some useful extras arrived in the shape of a hardtop, wire wheels as an option to the standard discs, and overdrive.

New Car, New Grille
Its 1956 replacement was the TR3, an improved version of the TR2, outwardly similar to it but identifiable by a new Ferrari-inspired, egg-crate type grille. Engine power was boosted to 95bhp and there was also a very occasional rear seat. For 1957 front disc brakes were offered, which was a notable "first" for a series production British sports car. Once again, output was relatively modest with 13,378 cars being built over a two year period before it made way for the popular

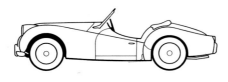

Specifications: Triumph TR3A

Length:	12ft 7in (3835mm)
Width:	4ft 7in (1397mm)
Height:	4ft 2in (1270mm)
Wheelbase:	7ft 4in (2235mm)
Track:	front 3ft 9in (1143mm), rear 3ft 9½in (1156mm)
Unladen weight:	2050lb (930kg)
Engine: Four cylinder, overhead valve, 83x92mm, 1991cc. Compression ratio, 8.5:1. Max power, 100bhp at 5000rpm. Max torque, 117lb/ft at 3000rpm.	
Transmission:	Four-speed manual
Drive:	Rear
Suspension (front):	Independent, coil springs, wishbones
Suspension (rear):	Live axle, half-elliptic springs
Top speed:	102mph (164km/h)
0-60mph (96km/h):	12.3 seconds
Production (total TR2, 3, 3A&B):	83,573

TR3A. Incidentally, this model designation – TR3A – was never used officially by Triumph.

Announced in Britain in January 1958, the model had, in fact, been available on the American market from the autumn of the previous year. It was instantly identifiable by a new, full width radiator grille. The faithful four was, once again, boosted in power, this time to 100bhp and, from 1959 it was available with an enlarged 2138cc engine. Demand from America was considerable, so British sales were modest and accounted for a mere 1896 cars sold of the total of 58,236 examples built before the model ceased production in 1961.

Mention should also be made of the similarly unofficially titled TR3B of 1962. It was destined for the all important American market. Outwardly a TR3A, it was fitted with the larger capacity 2.1 litre engine and a new all-synchromesh gearbox earmarked for its contemporary TR4 replacement. This is a relatively rare and coveted TR: just 3331 were built.

ABOVE: *A 1959 Triumph TR3A, which differed from its predecessor by the fitment of a full-width radiator grille. Note that it is badged a TR3.*

RIGHT: *This beautifully restored 1956 TR3 is a former works car and ran in the 1958 Monte Carlo Rally. Most were exported to America.*

Triumph 2, 3, 3A, 3B

2 litre Standard Vanguard saloon 1948

2 litre TR1 roadster 1952

2 litre TR2 1953

2 litre TR3 1955

2 litre TR3A

2.1 litre engine 1959

TR3B 1962

AUSTIN-HEALEY 100/4, 100/6, 3000 (1953-1968)

Originally conceived as the 2.6 litre, four cylinder Healey 100 in 1952, the car, exhibited at that year's London Motor Show, was spotted by the British Motor Corporation's chairman, Leonard Lord, and therefore the *Austin*-Healey became BMC's corporate sports car for the burgeoning American market. In 1956 BMC replaced the original four with its 2.6 litre, six cylinder engine and the renamed 100/6 endured until 1959. That year the unit was enlarged in capacity to 3 litres and the car became the 3000. This lasted until 1968 when BMC was absorbed into the British Leyland Motor Corporation, an amalgamation that spelt the end for the by-then ageing Big Healey.

ABOVE: *The 100, the first Austin-Healey, perpetuated the Healey's kite-shaped radiator grille. Designated BN2 by the works, this is a 1956 car.*

BELOW: *A 1961 Austin-Healey 3000 Mark II. This is a BN7 series car with room for two very occasional rear passengers.*

After five years of producing cars at Warwick under his own name, Donald Healey recognized that, unless he produced a lighter, cheaper and faster model than the ones he had hitherto manufactured, he would go out of business. He, therefore, initiated the Healey 100, its title reflecting its 100mph (161km/h) top speed. It was powered by Austin's redundant 2.6 litre, four cylinder engine used in its ill-fated Atlantic model. The Healey featured a new box-section chassis and the coil-and-wishbone independent front suspension and steering were also Austin units. The handsome, open two-seater body was nicely styled by Healey's own Gerry Coker.

Following the model's overnight transformation into the Austin-Healey, production began at the Austin factory at Longbridge. This was in mid-1953 and, inevitably, the majority of cars were sold on the American market.

The 100M Version

Austin-Healey 100 owners were also offered the option of converting their cars to what was termed 100M specifications. This took the form of a kit which upped engine power from a standard 90 to 110bhp in the manner of cars prepared by Healey for the 1953 Le Mans race; both finished, being placed 12th and 14th. There was also a louvred bonnet, with leather strap and anti-roll bar. Some 100Ms were converted at Warwick, which made a total of 1159 cars so modified. Rarer still was the more potent, Healey-built 100S competition version with aluminium body panels, 132bhp engine using an aluminium cylinder head and all-round disc brakes. Just 50 were made in 1955.

No doubt recognizing the limitations of a four cylinder unit on the big engined American market, in 1956 BMC replaced it with the corporate 2.6 litre six. The car's wheelbase was also lengthened, so as to accommodate occasional rear seats but a strictly two-seater option was reintroduced in 1958. In all, this resulted in a heavier car and the 100/6 lacked the performance of the fours, although the situation was improved, to some extent, by the fitment from 1957 of a six-port cylinder head, which boosted output from 102 to 117bhp.

In 1957 Austin-Healey production was transferred from Longbridge to the MG factory at Abingdon and, in 1959 the model benefitted from an increase in capacity to 3 litres, and power to 132bhp. This was called the Austin-Healey 3000. Further refinements followed in the Mark II version of the 3000 in 1961 which, adventurously, employed no less than three SU carburettors, although, because of tuning difficulties, it reverted to the customary two in 1962. In 1963 came the Mark III 3000 which was the best of the breed, with a 148bhp engine, servo-assisted brakes and wood-panelled dashboard. Production ceased in 1968 after a total of 72,022 cars had been built, the vast majority, no less than 57,360, being sixes, compared with a relatively modest 14,662 fours.

Austin-Healey 100/4, 100/6, 3000

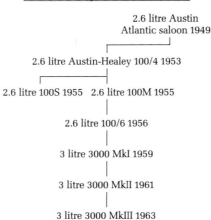

2.6 litre Austin Atlantic saloon 1949

2.6 litre Austin-Healey 100/4 1953

2.6 litre 100S 1955   2.6 litre 100M 1955

2.6 litre 100/6 1956

3 litre 3000 MkI 1959

3 litre 3000 MkII 1961

3 litre 3000 MkIII 1963

Specifications: Austin-Healey 3000 Mark III

Length:	13ft 1in (3988mm)
Width:	5ft (1524mm)
Height:	4ft 2in (1270mm)
Wheelbase:	7ft 8in (2337mm)
Track:	front 4ft (1219mm), rear 4ft 2in (1270mm)
Unladen weight:	2550lb (1155kg)
Engine: Six cylinder, overhead valve, 83x88mm, 2912cc. Compression ratio, 9:1. Max power, 148bhp at 5200rpm. Max torque, 165lb/ft at 3500rpm.	
Transmission:	Four-speed manual
Drive:	Rear
Suspension (front):	Independent, coil springs, wishbones
Suspension (rear):	Live axle, half-elliptic springs
Top speed:	120mph (193km/h)
0-60mph (96km/h):	7 seconds
Production (total):	72,022

RIGHT: *1961 Mark I which was the first of the 3 litre sixes. These disc wheels were the standard fitment; wires could be had at extra cost.*

CHEVROLET CORVETTE (1953-1962)

In 1953 the mighty General Motors conglomerate responded to the British MGs, Jaguars and Austin-Healeys by producing its own sports car. In creating the Chevrolet Corvette roadster, it established a motoring legend, even if the first cars did leave something to be desired. Significantly, a V8 engine was fitted in 1955 with restyling and refinement following. Yet production remained modest, output did not exceed the 10,000 mark until 1960 but, from there on, the Corvette's future was assured.

As introduced in June 1953, the Corvette, named after a small, fast naval gunboat, looked like no other GM product. As this was a low production model, it was decided to use glass fibre – then a relatively untried material – for the body. Although the chassis was purpose-made, most of the other components, inevitably, came from the corporate parts bin. The engine was a tuned version of Chevrolet's 235cid (3.8 litres), in-line, overhead valve six while transmission, surprisingly for a sports car, was the automatic, two-speed Powerglide system.

In its original form, the Corvette was capable of a rather uncertain 100mph (161km/h), handling left much to be desired, while the body leaked water and let in dust. In its inaugural year of 1953, just 300 examples were built. Production began at Flint, Michigan and, in 1954, transferred to a purpose-designed assembly line at St. Louis, Missouri. That year output rose to 3640 cars but this was a mere drop in the ocean by General Motors standards. The Corporation considered dropping the model at this stage but, in the event, decided to persevere.

For 1955 there was an eggcrate-type grille concealing Chevrolet's new 265cid (4.3 litres), overhead valve V8 engine, which was destined to transform the Corvette's performance. Top speed was now approaching the 120mph (196km/h) mark and 60mph (96km/h) came up in less than nine seconds. A three-speed manual gearbox came as a further late '55 option and, from thereon, only around 20 per cent of cars continued to be fitted with automatic transmission.

For 1956 the Corvette benefitted from a revised body on which distinctive concave side panels, inherited from the LaSalle II and Biscayne showcars, were evident. The V8 was enlarged to 283cid (4.6 litres) for 1957 and a Rochester fuel injection system arrived as an option. It proved to be unreliable and a mere 240 examples of the so-called "fuelie" were built.

Fashionable "quad", double headlamps appeared in 1958 but GM's styling supremo, Harley Earl, retired that year and his place was taken by the talented William Mitchell, who was much more influenced by the lines of European cars than his predecessor. The first fruits of his labours were not apparent on the Corvette until the 1961 model year. There was a neater radiator grille and, more significantly, a stylish new tail while the model's distinctive scooped side panels were downplayed.

In 1962 came a further engine capacity increase, to 327cid (5.3 litres), which saw the Corvette's top speed leap to around the 150mph (241km/h) mark. The same year, production hit a high of 14,531 cars but the Chevrolet would receive its most radical facelift later in 1962 with the appearance of a completely new body. The Sting Ray had arrived (page 44)!

Chevrolet Corvette

235cid six cylinder
Corvette roadster 1953

265cid V8 1955

LaSalle II and
Biscayne show cars
1955

Revised body 1956

283cid V8 1957

327cid V8 1962

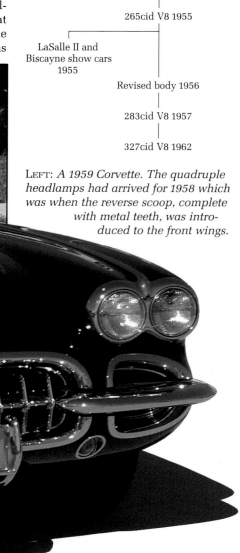

LEFT: *A 1959 Corvette. The quadruple headlamps had arrived for 1958 which was when the reverse scoop, complete with metal teeth, was introduced to the front wings.*

RIGHT: *This body style arrived for 1956, with only the concept of the vertical barred radiator grille carried over. This is a 1957 car.*

Specifications: Chevrolet Corvette (1962)

Length:	14ft 9in (4496mm)
Width:	5ft 10in (1778mm)
Height:	4ft 2in (1270mm)
Wheelbase:	8ft 6in (2591mm)
Track:	front 4ft 9in (1448mm), rear 4ft 11in (1499mm)
Unladen weight:	2900lb (1315kg)
Engine:	V8, overhead valve, 4x3.25in (101x82mm), 327cid (5358cc). Compression ratio, 10.5:1. Max power, 250bhp at 4400rpm. Max torque, 350lb/ft at 2800rpm.
Transmission:	Three-speed manual
Drive:	Rear
Suspension (front):	Independent, coil springs, wishbones
Suspension (rear):	Live axle, half-elliptic springs
Top speed:	150mph (241km/h)
0-60mph (96km/h):	5.9 seconds
Production (total 1953/62):	68,817

RIGHT: *The influence of GM stylist William Mitchell is apparent on this 1962 Corvette. The revised rear end arrived for 1961 and anticipated that of the Sting Ray era.*

Jaguar XK SS (1957)

Based on the legendary Le Mans-winning D-Type, the XK SS road car was capable of speeds approaching 150mph (241km/h) but was expensive and impractical. Only 16 were built. This has ensured that today it is the rarest and most sought-after of all Jaguar's sports cars. The Coventry company won the Le Mans 24-hour race for the first time in 1951 with its sports racing C-type and repeated the feat in 1953. Jaguar again took the chequered flag in 1955 with its D-Type, which had appeared in the previous year. This triumph was repeated in 1956, after which Jaguar withdrew from competition racing and, towards the end of that year, it began work on a roadgoing version of the design, which it called the XK SS.

A precedent for this course of action already existed as, earlier in 1956, former Jaguar works driver Duncan Hamilton had converted his ex-works 1954 Le Mans team car for the road. More significantly, the Sports Car Club of America suggested that a D-Type might be suitable for production sports car racing. With the USA as Jaguar's most lucrative market, the factory felt obliged to respond, particularly as it still had 29 unsold D-Types in stock.

The XK SS name was no doubt used to underscore its connection with the XK120/140 family of road cars even though the only mechanical similarity between the two was the essentials of the 3.4 litre XK engine. For the D-Type had no chassis, as such, but was built up around a monocoque tub to which was attached a triangulated front subframe containing the engine and independent front suspension.

The conversion of the D-Type to road use meant that the division between the driver and his theoretical passenger was dispensed with, the cockpit area comfortably reupholstered and a nearside door introduced. A large windscreen was fitted, while token quarter bumpers offered little more than a decorative contribution. A mohair hood was provided, along with side screens to keep the elements at bay. As there was no boot, luggage could only be carried externally, on a chromium-plated rack thoughtfully provided on the tail.

Virtually no changes were made to the 3.4 litre, triple carburettored, dry sump 250bhp engine. This imbued the 2016lb (914kg) car with a sensational performance as 100mph (161km/h) came up in just under 14 seconds, which was precisely half that of its contemporary open XK140, itself no sluggard.

The XK SS was priced at $6900 in America and £3878 in Britain, which compared with £1741 for the 140 roadster. The first example was dispatched to America on 18th January 1957, and the model officially launched three days later, on the 21st. However, its production life was destined to be curtailed after a mere three weeks. On 12 February, a fire broke out in the part of Jaguar's Browns Lane factory where the first few cars were being made. It destroyed some of the remaining D-Type shells, and although production restarted in March, when four cars were delivered, output continued only intermittently until November 1957 when the final example was completed. So production was a mere 16 cars, of which 12 went to America and two to Canada, while two D-Type owners had their cars converted to XK SS specifications. The true roadgoing version of Jaguar's most famous sports racer would not appear until 1961 in the shape of sensational E-Type. That one endured until 1975.

ABOVE: *The XK SS's 3.4 litre dry sump engine was much the same as the D-Type's. Note oil tank in foreground.*

ABOVE LEFT: *The SS's cockpit, apart from the passenger's seat, is pure D-Type. The speedometer reads up to 180mph (290km/h).*

LEFT: *This car began life as D-Type XKD540 and was so converted by the factory in the winter of 1958-59 for hill climb champion Phil Scragg.*

Specifications: Jaguar XK SS

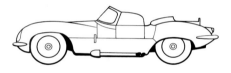

Length:	12ft 10in (3912mm)
Width:	5ft 5in (1651mm)
Height:	2ft 7in (787mm)
Wheelbase:	7ft 6in (2286mm)
Track:	front 4ft 2in (1270mm), rear 4ft (1219mm)
Unladen weight:	2016lb (914kg)

Engine: Six cylinder, twin overhead camshaft, 83x106mm 3442cc. Compression ratio, 9:1. Max power, 250bhp at 5750rpm. Max torque, 242lb/ft at 4000rpm.

Transmission:	Four-speed manual
Drive:	Rear
Suspension (front):	Independent, torsion bars, wishbones
Suspension (rear):	Live axle, torsion bars, trailing links
Top speed:	149mph (240km/h)
0-60mph (96km/h):	5.2 seconds
Production:	16

Jaguar XK SS

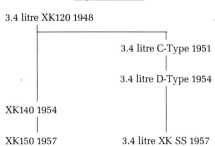

3.4 litre XK120 1948

3.4 litre C-Type 1951

3.4 litre D-Type 1954

XK140 1954

XK150 1957   3.4 litre XK SS 1957

MGA (1955-1962)

The MGA was as modern as the T Series MGs that it replaced were archaic. The A was destined to become the world's best selling sports car of its day and by the time that production ceased in 1962, over 100,000 had been built. Like its immediate predecessors, the vast majority were exported to America.

The MGA's origins date back to 1952 when Sydney Enever, MG's unofficial chief engineer, created EX 175, a prototype two-seater roadster which outwardly resembled the finished product of three years later. But BMC, which was MG's parent company, opted instead for the Austin-Healey (see page 24) and the new MG was temporarily sidelined.

Fortunately, in June 1954 BMC gave MG permission to reopen the drawing office which had closed in 1935 and, at long last, Syd Enever was officially appointed chief engineer. He wasted little time in reactivating the EX 175 concept although, unlike the original, the production version used the BMC 1488cc four cylinder engine of Austin ancestry. The new model was impressively launched, in EX 182 guise, at Le Mans in 1955 when three cars were entered. Although one crashed, the other two MGs finished, coming in 12th and 17th.

MGA Coupé
The MGA proper did not appear until three months later, in September 1955. The modern body lines concealed a substantial box-section chassis while the independent front suspension was essentially carried over from the T Series cars. But it was, inevitably, considerably faster, being capable of over 95mph (153km/h). For 1957 the open car was joined by a supplementary coupé model which, because of its superior aerodynamics, was just capable of hitting the 100mph (161km/h) mark.

In the summer of 1959, the capacity of the pushrod four was upped to 1588cc. This version, which was titled the MGA 1600, also benefitted from the introduction of front disc brakes. The roadster's top speed was accordingly taken over the 100mph (161km/h) mark. In June 1961 came a further capacity increase to 1622cc, this Mark II model being identified by its recessed radiator grille. Production ceased in June 1962, by which time a total of 98,970 cars had been built.

These MGAs were, like their predecessors, pushrod-engined but in 1958

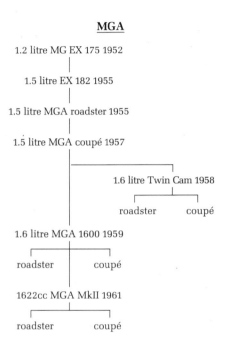

MGA

1.2 litre MG EX 175 1952
|
1.5 litre EX 182 1955
|
1.5 litre MGA roadster 1955
|
1.5 litre MGA coupé 1957
|
              1.6 litre Twin Cam 1958
              roadster   coupé
|
1.6 litre MGA 1600 1959
|
roadster   coupé
|
1622cc MGA MkII 1961
|
roadster   coupé

MG announced an exciting derivative, powered by a twin overhead camshaft, 1588cc, B Series-based engine developing 108bhp which compared with 79bhp for the 1600 model. The MGA Twin Cam, as it was titled, was outwardly identical to its stablemates, apart from the fitment of handsome centre-lock Dunlop disc wheels which concealed all-round disc brakes. It was, inevitably, faster than its pushrod contemporaries, both through the gears and in its top speed, which was in excess of 110mph (177km/h). Uncharacteristically for an MG, however, there were reliability problems. The 9:1 compression ratio required high octane fuels, burnt-out pistons were not uncommon and the engines of early examples developed an alarming thirst for oil. Eventually, only 2111 cars were built before the model was discontinued in 1960. Some Twin Cam bodies were left over and these were fitted with the 1588cc pushrod engine and sold as De Luxe models.

The grand total MGA production, therefore, stood at an unprecedented 101,081 cars. In 1962 MG's most successful model gave way to its replacement in the shape of the even more popular MGB.

BELOW: *A 1959 MGA Twin Cam with its handsome knock-off Dunlop wheels and discreet badge on upper front wing. Also available in coupé form, of the 2111 cars built, 1801 were roadsters.*

Specifications: MGA open two seater (1955)

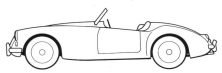

Length:	13ft (3962mm)
Width:	4ft 9in (1448mm)
Height:	4ft 2in (1270mm)
Wheelbase:	7ft 10in (2388mm)
Track:	front 3ft 11in (1194mm), rear 4ft (1219mm)
Unladen weight:	1988lb (901kg)
Engine: Four cylinder, overhead valve, 73x88mm, 1488cc. Compression ratio, 8.3:1. Max power, 72bhp at 5500rpm. Max torque, 77lb/ft at 3500rpm.	
Transmission:	Four-speed manual
Drive:	Rear
Suspension (front):	Independent, coil springs, wishbones
Suspension (rear):	Live axle, half-elliptic springs
Top speed:	95mph (153km/h)
0-60mph (96km/h):	15.4 seconds
Production (total pushrod):	98,970

ABOVE: *This MGA dates from 1962 with the recessed radiator grille identifying a Mark II 1600 car.*

BELOW: *The A had a shallow boot and many owners fitted a luggage rack on its lid to carry suitcases.*

The stark, distinctive and potent Lotus Seven is a car that has refused to die. In its day it was the Lotus company's longest running model, having been produced between 1957 and 1973. In that year it was taken over by Caterham Cars of Caterham, Surrey which maintained production and has kept the spirit of the original car alive in the still formidably fast Caterham Seven.

The model's origins are rooted in the Lotus Mark VI model of 1953 which was the firm's first production sports car, although it was only available in kit form. A popular choice for club racing, the VI was built up around a multi-tubular space frame, reinforced by aluminium panels, with the engine of the constructor's choice. This was usually the faithful side valve 1172cc Ford.

The VI was replaced in 1957 by the outwardly similar, improved Seven which Lotus built as a complete car. It was also available in kit form and continued to be so until April 1973 when the advent of Value Added Tax in the United Kingdom cancelled out the financial advantages to the do-it-yourself constructor. The low, doorless, open two-seater body only measured 27.5in (698mm) to the top of the windscreen, ground clearance was a meagre 5in (127mm), and the Lotus turned the scales at a mere 1008lb (457kg). The space frame chassis was related to the contemporary Mark XI sports racer. Engines were, once again, Ford units but now the options included overhead valve BMC A Series and single overhead camshaft Coventry Climax fours. The coil and wishbone front suspension was courtesy of Lotus's Formula 2 racer. The Seven's progress was arrested by hydraulic brakes. In its Ford-powered form, the Seven was capable of a spirited 75mph (121km/h).

A Lighter Series

In 1960, a lightened version of the design, with fewer chassis tubes, was introduced. This Series 2 version lasted until 1968. It had been joined in 1964 by the better equipped 1.3 litre, Ford-engined Super Seven, identifiable by its more substantial glass-fibre wings. In 1962 the Cortina GT-powered Super Seven 1500 with front disc brakes appeared. There was also a more powerful Cosworth-tuned 95bhp version powered by a twin Weber carburettored engine, which helped the Seven attain the magical 100mph (161km/h) mark.

Nineteen-sixty-eight saw the arrival of the interim Series 3 cars; the top of the range model was the Super Seven Twin Cam with a 1.6 litre, Ford-based Lotus unit. It was replaced in 1970 by the Series 4 cars which incorporated the most radical change to the Seven since its 1957 inception. The chassis was redesigned as a tubular and ladder frame; the body was wholly of glass-fibre. The engine range remained essentially the same as the Series 3 models, but the Super Seven name was dropped.

Limited production continued at Lotus's Hethel factory but in 1973, by which time some 3,000 cars had been sold, the manufacturing rights were transferred to Graham Nearn's Caterham Cars. The Seven could no longer be badged a Lotus. A further 40 examples of what had become the Caterham Seven were completed in 1974. The same year, the Surrey company decided to revive the Series 3 Seven, discontinued by Lotus in 1970, and this remains in production at the time of writing. Today the original Ford-engined Sprint and Super Sprint have been joined by the 1.3 litre, Rover Metro-powered Super K which still holds the road like a leech, is capable of an earth shattering 100mph (161km/h) and can reach 60mph (96km/h) in a mere 6.7 seconds.

Lotus Seven/Caterham Seven

Lotus Mark VI 1953

Lotus XI 1956

Lotus Seven 1957

Series 2 1960

Series 3 1968

Series 4 1970

Caterham Seven 1974

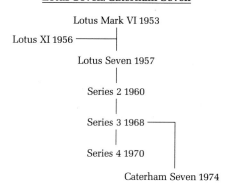

RIGHT: *The stark two-seater Caterham Seven has the minimum of creature comforts. This 1980 car weighs just 1200lb (544kg).*

Specifications: Lotus Seven Series 4

Length:	12ft 2in (3708mm)
Width:	5ft (1524mm)
Height:	3ft 6in (1067mm)
Wheelbase:	7ft 6in (2286mm)
Track:	front 4ft (1219mm), rear 4ft 3in (1295mm)
Unladen weight:	1310lb (594kg)
Engine: Four cylinder, overhead valve, 81x77mm, 1598cc. Compression ratio, 9:1. Max power, 84bhp at 5800rpm. Max torque, 96lb/ft at 3600rpm.	
Transmission:	Four-speed manual
Drive:	Rear
Suspension (front):	Independent, coil springs, wishbones
Suspension (rear):	Live axle, coil springs
Top speed:	90mph (145km/h)
0-60mph (96km/h):	8.9 seconds
Production (Series 1-4 total):	approx. 3,000

LEFT: *A 1971 Series 4 Lotus Seven with glass fibre body. It was longer and wider than its predecessors.*

RIGHT: *A 1991 Caterham HPC Seven powered by a 2 litre, 16 valve Vauxhall engine, tuned to 284bhp.*

AUSTIN-HEALEY SPRITE/MG MIDGET (1958-1979)

Created as a spiritual successor to the pre-war Austin Seven Nippy, the cheeky 948cc Sprite, with its distinctive "Frogeye" headlamps, followed on from the success of the Austin-Healey 100 as BMC's corporate sports car. A Mark II version, though lacking the distinctive lamps, followed in 1961, which also saw the introduction of an MG Midget version of the design. But the Sprite, like its 3000 big brother, was destined for oblivion when BMC was taken over by Leyland. The last example was built in 1970, but the Midget continued until 1979.

Commissioned by BMC's Leonard Lord, the Sprite, designed by Donald Healey's son, Geoffrey and styled by Gerry Coker, was built from its introduction by the MG factory at Abingdon. Priced at a competitive £678, it was a cost-conscious concept with non-opening boot (access was via the interior of the cabin when the seats were folded down), lack of external door handles and sidescreens, a detachable hood and, out of sight, quarter-elliptic rear springs. The one-piece bonnet hinged forwards to permit access to BMC's A Series engine. The car's most memorable feature was undoubtedly its protruding headlamps. When viewed in conjunction with the mouth-like radiator grille, the Sprite seemed to sport an instant smile and the public smiled back. An impressive 48,987 "Frogeyes" were built between 1958 and 1961.

Capable of speeds approaching the 85mph (136km/h) mark, the Sprite made way in 1961 for its more conventional Mark II successor. Its opening boot was a plus but there was some dilution of personality in the redesign. The rear of the body resembled that of the in-house MGB, then a year away, and there was also, significantly, a badge-engineered MG version for which the Midget name was revived. An enlarged 1098cc engine and front disc brakes were fitted for 1963.

In 1964 came the outwardly similar Sprite III with wind-up windows, external door handles and half-elliptic rear springs. Wire wheels became available as an option. Engine output was boosted from 56 to 59bhp to cope with the extra weight. This version endured until 1966. Its Mark IV replacement was powered by a detuned version of the 1275cc Mini Cooper S engine, while the hitherto detachable hood was now fixed.

For 1970, the Mark IV Sprite appeared with Rostyle wheels and black sills. A commonized radiator grille was shared with the similarly revised Mark III MG Midget, with only the badges differing. From January 1971, the final 1029 cars were named Austin Sprites; production ceased in July of that year.

The Mark III MG Midget, however, continued. Demand held up well, as did exports, and a total of 86,623 units were built by 1974. Its successor for 1975, which perpetuated the Mark III designation, was fitted with energy absorbing bumpers, like the car's MGB stablemate. Ride height was, similarly, increased. By now BMC's A series engine, that had powered the model since its inception, had reached the limit of its development, a problem which was exacerbated by increasingly stringent emissions regulations imposed by the all-important American market. It was, therefore, replaced by the corporate 1493cc Triumph Spitfire engine which made the Midget, for the first time, a 100mph (161km/h) car. The increasingly outdated model survived until 1979, by which time a further 73,899 cars had been built, so ending a 21 year run of production.

Austin-Healey Sprite/MG Midget

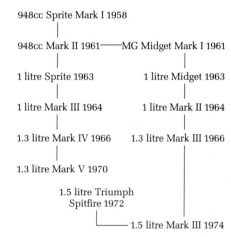

948cc Sprite Mark I 1958	
948cc Mark II 1961	MG Midget Mark I 1961
1 litre Sprite 1963	1 litre Midget 1963
1 litre Mark III 1964	1 litre Mark II 1964
1.3 litre Mark IV 1966	1.3 litre Mark III 1966
1.3 litre Mark V 1970	
1.5 litre Triumph Spitfire 1972	
	1.5 litre Mark III 1974

LEFT: *A 1969 MG Midget Mark III. The model was destined to endure until 1979, nine years after its Austin-Healey Sprite progenitor had been discontinued.*

RIGHT: *A 1958 Austin-Healey "Frogeye" Sprite that was built in this form until 1961. The forward hingeing wing/bonnet structure was inspired by that of the D-Type Jaguar.*

Specifications: Austin-Healey Sprite Series I

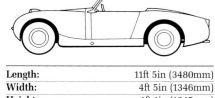

Length:	11ft 5in (3480mm)
Width:	4ft 5in (1346mm)
Height:	4ft 1in (1245mm)
Wheelbase:	6ft 8in (2032mm)
Track:	front 3ft 9in (1143mm), rear 3ft 8in (1118mm)
Unladen weight:	1327lb (602kg)
Engine: Four cylinder, overhead valve, 62x76mm, 948cc. Compression ratio, 8.3:1. Max power, 48bhp at 5000rpm. Max torque, 52lb/ft at 3300rpm.	
Transmission:	Four-speed manual
Drive:	Rear
Suspension (front):	Independent, coil springs, wishbones
Suspension (rear):	Live axle, quarter-elliptic springs
Top speed:	85mph (137km/h)
0-60mph (96km/h):	20.8 seconds
Production (total, Series I to IV):	129,354

RIGHT: *Rear view of 1974 Midget shod with the usual Rostyle wheels. The rounded rather than angular rear wheel arches arrived for 1972.*

JAGUAR E-TYPE SERIES I AND II (1961-1971)

The E-Type was one of the fastest sports cars of its day and, as such, is the most memorable and charismatic British car of the post-war era. Essentially a road-going version of Jaguar's Le Mans-winning D-Type, it appeared in two-seater roadster and coupé forms in 1961. Originally produced with a 3.8 litre engine, for 1965 its capacity was enlarged to 4.2 litre, while in 1966 came a longer wheelbase, 2+2 coupé version. Nineteen-sixty-eight saw the arrival of the Series II cars specifically geared to the requirements of the American market, which was where most E-Types were sold. Here, however, emissions regulations took the edge off the car's formidable performance and in 1971 the six cylinder E-Type bowed out to make way for a V12-powered version (see page 134).

The first prototype E-Type, designated E1A, had been running in 1957, a further car followed in 1958 and the sports racing E2A, which came closest to the final concept, competed – albeit unsuccessfully – at Le Mans in 1960. Four years in the making, the E-Type was finally unveiled at the Geneva Motor Show of March 1961, and it had been well worth the wait. Chief engineer William Heynes had created an outstanding sports car, which looked like no other, and sold for only £2097 in open form. A key ingredient in this impressive package was the fact that Jaguar's aerodynamicist, Malcolm Sayer, who had the lines of the C and D-Types sports racers to his credit, produced a breathtakingly elegant and distinctive body which still delights the eye today.

The car's structure followed, in essence, that of the D-Type, being built up around a central monocoque tub with a triangulated front sub-frame. The E-Type also had the distinction of being the first Jaguar sports car to employ all-independent suspension and its rear system was shared with Jaguar's Mark X saloon, announced five months later. The 3.8 litre, triple-carburettored XK engine was essentially carried over from the XK 150S along with, less desirably, the Moss gearbox with its notchy change and lack of synchromesh on bottom gear.

Although Jaguar claimed a top speed of 150mph (241km/h) for the E, in truth only the factory-prepared press cars were capable of that figure. Nevertheless, most examples could comfortably exceed 140mph (225km/h). Not sur-prisingly, the car was in instant demand. Sales were evenly balanced between roadsters and coupés and, as ever, the vast majority of cars, over 80 per cent, went to the USA; a mere 750 examples of the 3.8 litre roadster stayed at home. The arrival in 1965 of the 4.2 litre engine with better torque saw the simultaneous introduction of an all-synchromesh gearbox, also shared with the Mark X.

A Longer 2+2

In its original form, the E-Type was essentially a two seater but in 1966 came the 2+2 coupé, which was only available in closed form. Its wheelbase was lengthened by 9in (229mm) which permitted the introduction of two small seats for children at the rear. There was also an automatic option.

As so many E-Types were exported to America, Jaguar, like MG, could not afford to ignore newly introduced safety and emissions requirements. For 1969 came the Series II E-Types with the original headlamps, which had been contained behind perspex covers, replaced by exposed units. There were also larger bumpers. Inside, the dashboard was remodelled for the same reasons and optional power steering introduced. More significantly, beneath the forward-hingeing bonnet, legislation demanded that the engine was detoxed. This regulation would progressively stifle the car's performance until, by 1970 its top speed had been reduced to around 130mph (209km/h). Such a state of affairs could not be allowed to continue and in 1971 the six-cylinder E-Type was replaced by the V12-powered Series III cars, which gave this respected model a new lease of life (see page 134).

Jaguar E-Type Series I and II

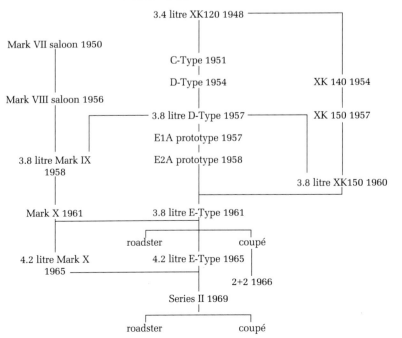

Mark VII saloon 1950

3.4 litre XK120 1948

C-Type 1951

D-Type 1954 — XK 140 1954

Mark VIII saloon 1956

3.8 litre D-Type 1957 — XK 150 1957

E1A prototype 1957

E2A prototype 1958

3.8 litre Mark IX 1958

3.8 litre XK150 1960

Mark X 1961 — 3.8 litre E-Type 1961

roadster — coupé

4.2 litre Mark X 1965 — 4.2 litre E-Type 1965

2+2 1966

Series II 1969

roadster — coupé

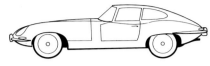

Length:	14ft 7in (4445mm)
Width:	5ft 5in (1651mm)
Height:	4ft (1219mm)
Wheelbase:	8ft (2438mm)
Track:	front and rear 4ft 2in (1270mm)
Unladen weight:	2520lb (1143kg)
Engine: Six-cylinder, twin overhead camshaft, 87x106mm, 3781cc. Compression ratio, 9:1. Max power, 265bhp at 5500rpm. Max torque, 260lb/ft at 4000rpm.	
Transmission:	Four-speed manual
Drive:	Rear
Suspension (front):	Independent, torsion bars, wishbones
Suspension (rear):	Independent, coil springs, lower wishbone/drive shaft
Top speed:	140mph (225km/h)
0-60mph (96km/h):	7.5 seconds
Production (total six cylinder E-Type):	57,250

BELOW: *An American registered 1966 4.2 litre Series I E-Type coupé. The car was marketed there as the XK-E.*

ABOVE: *What other drivers got used to seeing: the elegant rear view of a 1964 3.8 litre E-Type roadster.*

The established TR sports car line received a fillip in 1961 with the arrival of the Michelotti-styled TR4 roadster, although the mechanicals were essentially carried over from its TR3 predecessor. In 1965 the model received independent rear suspension and was renamed the TR4A, while in 1967 the TR5, powered by a 2.5 litre six cylinder engine appeared. The TR6 of the 1969/76 period was updated with a new Karmann-styled front but the TR7 coupé of 1975 was a completely new design and reverted to the four cylinder theme. Intended as British Leyland's corporate sports car, the wedge-shaped styling of the model proved controversial, and it was plagued with production and reliability problems. It was dropped in 1981, despite 112,368 having been built; a record for the TR range.

British versions retained the fuel-injected engine, those cars destined for trans-Atlantic customers were fitted with less powerful but "cleaner" twin Stromberg-carburettored engines.

The TR6, in turn, made way for the TR7 coupé which owed nothing to its predecessors. It was of monocoque construction with strut front suspension and live rear axle. The 2 litre, slant four cylinder, single overhead camshaft engine was related to that of the Triumph Dolomite as was, initially, its gearbox, although this was replaced from 1979 by a five-speed unit. But performance was inferior to that of the TR6 and the cars were also unreliable. Production was transferred from Liverpool to Canley and then to Solihull. In 1979 came a better looking and better mannered roadster version and in 1980 the supplementary TR8, with Rover's proven 3.5 litre V8 engine. This was, perhaps, what the TR7 should have been in the first place. Nevertheless, both cars were discontinued in 1981 after TR8 production had accounted for a mere 2722 cars.

The TR4 was, in essence, a rebodied TR3A/B with the added refinement of rack-and-pinion steering. It was also available with a "Surrey" hardtop which, in concept, anticipated the Porsche Targa top by two years. A great improvement on what had gone before, it was – if anything – let down by its rigid suspension, the engineering of which was rooted in the previous decade. This was rectified, to a great extent, by the TR4A of 1965 with trailing-arm, independent rear suspension shared with Triumph's new 2000 saloon. By this time top speed was nudging 110mph (177km/h), but the faithful 2.1 litre Standard Vanguard-based four was showing its years and this was dropped in 1967 when the outwardly similar TR5 was fitted with a 2.5 litre, fuel-injected version of the 2000's six cylinder unit. A 115mph (185km/h) car, it was also available in a lower powered, TR250-carburettored version for the American market.

The TR5 was only destined for a 15 month life when in 1969 it was replaced by the TR6 with its body competently facelifted by the German company Karmann. Destined for an eight year production life, it was the best selling TR of its day with 94,619 produced. As before, the vast majority were sold in America and although the

Triumph TR4, 4A, 5, 6 and 7 Family

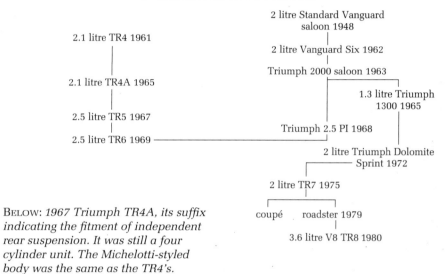

```
2.1 litre TR4 1961                                    2 litre Standard Vanguard
                                                         saloon 1948
                                                              |
                                                      2 litre Vanguard Six 1962
                                                              |
                                                      Triumph 2000 saloon 1963
                                                              |
2.1 litre TR4A 1965                                                  1.3 litre Triumph
                                                                       1300 1965
                                                              |
2.5 litre TR5 1967                                                    |
                            |                         Triumph 2.5 PI 1968
2.5 litre TR6 1969 ─────────                                   |
                                                              2 litre Triumph Dolomite
                                                                  ── Sprint 1972
                                                              |
                                                      2 litre TR7 1975
                                                              |
                                                      ┌───────┴───────┐
                                                   coupé        roadster 1979
                                                                      |
                                                              3.6 litre V8 TR8 1980
```

BELOW: *1967 Triumph TR4A, its suffix indicating the fitment of independent rear suspension. It was still a four cylinder unit. The Michelotti-styled body was the same as the TR4's.*

RIGHT: *The TR6 as bodily revised by Karmann. This is a 1974 car and the black plastic air dam beneath the front bumper, intended to reduce lift, arrived for the 1973 season. Production ceased in July 1976.*

TYA 373M

Specifications: Triumph TR6

Length:	13ft 3in (4039mm)
Width:	4ft 10in (1473mm)
Height:	4ft 2in (1270mm)
Wheelbase:	7ft 4in (2235mm)
Track:	front 4ft 2in (1270mm), rear 4ft 1in (1245mm)
Unladen weight:	2475lb (1121kg)
Engine: Six-cylinder, overhead valve, 74x95mm, 2498cc. Compression ratio, 9.5:1. Fuel injection. Max power, 104bhp at 4700rpm. Max torque, 132lb/ft at 3000rpm.	
Transmission:	Four-speed manual
Drive:	Rear
Suspension (front):	Independent, coil springs, wishbones
Suspension (rear):	Independent, coil springs, semi-trailing arms
Top speed:	118mph (190km/h)
0-60mph (96km/h):	8.3 seconds
Production (total TR4 to 7):	287,136

RIGHT: *The TR7 as it originally appeared in 1975. Its lines were controversial from the outset.*

HOE 59S

LOTUS ELAN (1962-1974)

With the arrival of the open, two-seater Elan, Colin Chapman's Lotus company came of age as a manufacturer of sports cars. A characteristically advanced model, it featured a glass-fibre body with backbone chassis, 105bhp, twin overhead camshaft engine, all-independent suspension, and disc brakes. It was destined for a long production run. Available from 1962 until 1973, from 1965 the roadster was joined by a coupé version and they were followed in 1967 by the longer wheelbase Elan +2 coupé which remained available until 1974.

The Elite, the Elan's ingenious but loss-making predecessor, was a glass-fibre monocoque. This meant that it was only available in closed form, a limitation that was rectified in the case of the Elan, which was initially only built as an open car. The glass-fibre bodywork followed previous practice and the concealed, pop-up headlamps, fitted in the interests of aerodynamic efficiency, were a novel feature at the time. The car's clever backbone chassis was splayed at the front to receive Lotus's Ford-based, 1.6 litre engine. Like the Elite, suspension was all-independent with coils and wishbones at the front, and Chapman struts with exposed driveshafts at the rear.

Do-It-Yourself

From the outset, the Lotus Elan could be bought in kit form from £1095, although Lotus would also produce it in a completed state for £1499. As expected, performance was impressive and the nimble 1290lb (585kg) car was capable of 110mph (177km/h); road holding was up to Lotus's demanding standards. For 1965 came the Series 2 Elan with large front-brake callipers, while the interior benefitted from a new wood veneer dashboard.

The Series 3 Elan, of September 1965, was a coupé version of the design although the S2 open car continued in production. Early in 1966 a 115bhp Special Equipment version of the convertible was introduced and a Series 3 car followed in mid-1966. The Series 4 version of the Elan is identifiable by its wider wheels and enlarged arches to accommodate them. The final Elan, the Sprint, appeared in 1973 with distinctive two-tone paintwork and 126bhp "Big Valve" version of the twin cam four. Although the two-seater Elan came to an end in 1973, by then approximately 8900 had been built. Since 1967 it had been joined by the longer wheelbase Elan +2 coupé.

As originally conceived, the Elan

Specifications: Lotus Elan Series I

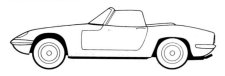

Length:	12ft 1in (3683mm)
Width:	4ft 8in (1422mm)
Height:	3ft 9in (1143mm)
Wheelbase:	7ft (2134mm)
Track:	front and rear 3ft 11in (1194mm)
Unladen weight:	1290lb (585kg)

Engine: Four-cylinder, twin overhead camshaft, 82x72mm, 1558cc. Compression ratio, 9.5:1. Max power, 105bhp at 5500rpm. Max torque, 102lb/ft at 4000rpm.

Transmission:	Four-speed manual
Drive:	Rear
Suspension (front):	Independent, coil springs, wishbones
Suspension (rear):	Independent, damper struts, lower wishbones
Top speed:	110mph (177km/h)
0-60mph (96km/h):	9.1 seconds
Production (total Elan/+2):	12,200 (approx)

was a genuine two-seater but the wheelbase of the Lotus Elan +2 for the family man was 12in (305mm) longer to permit the introduction of two occasional rear seats. Track was also wider and the car was only available in closed form. Weight, inevitably, was 448lb (203kg) greater, so the Special Equipment engine was a standard fitment. In 1969 came the +2S, which was the first Elan not to be offered in kit form. In consequence, the interior trim was an improvement on the original. The final +2 Elan was the 126bhp Sprint version, identifiable by its silver roof. There was also the concurrent 2S/130-5 of 1972 which had a five-speed gearbox. By the time that the model ceased production in 1974, a total of 3300 Elan +2s had been built.

RIGHT: *A 1968 Elan S4 with glass fibre bodywork and then novel concealed headlamps. Under the bonnet is a Ford-based, 1.6 litre, twin-overhead-camshaft engine.*

Lotus Elan

Ford Cortina 1962 ─┐
│
1.5 litre Cortina engine
│
Lotus Elan 1962 ──────── 1.6 litre Lotus engine
│
Cortina Lotus 1963 ─┘

roadster   coupé 1965

Elan +2 coupé 1967

LEFT: *Rear view of the S4 Elan. The new tail lights were shared with the +2 Elan and Europa.*

RIGHT: *A closed version of the Elan, the +2 coupé with a longer wheelbase arrived in 1967.*

In 1962 MG replaced the MGA with the MGB which was intended to have a production life of eight or so years. But the turmoil that successively engulfed MG's parent companies meant that the B was destined to remain in production for no less than 18 years with its manufacture ceasing in 1980. But this was not the end of what had become Britain's best loved sports car. Incredibly, in 1992 its spiritual successor, the limited edition MG RV8, appeared (see page 70). It is intended to have a two year life.

The RV8's origins, therefore, reach back to 1958 when MG's chief engineer, Syd Enever, began work on what became the MGB. It perpetuated the MGA concept although its successor had a unitary hull and a new body, styled by MG's Don Hayter. The BMC B Series engine was carried over and enlarged to 1798cc, a unit which was unique to the MGB until the arrival of the in-house Austin 1800 saloon in 1964. This ensured that the car, in its original open form, could exceed 100mph (161km/h). Independent front suspension and leaf-sprung rear were essentially carried over from the A. Like the A also, the car would be exported to the USA in large numbers; eventually over a third of a million MGBs found American owners.

The B was, in truth, more of a high speed tourer than a sports car. Two people could be accommodated in comfort but there was room for two children on a ledge behind the seats. Also wind-up windows were a welcome improvement on the MGA's sidescreens.

A Closed GT

Three years after the open car had appeared, it was joined late in 1965 by the closed GT version with a useful opening tailgate and improved passenger seating. There was some Pininfarina input to the handsome body lines. However, the GT's top speed was slightly less than that of the roadster, on account of its greater weight. Despite the open car being the more popular body option, the GT remained in production throughout the model's manufacturing life and eventually accounted for around 25 per cent of total production.

The cars remained essentially unchanged, although overdrive was available from 1963, a stronger five bearing crankshaft followed for 1965 and Rostyle wheels appeared in 1970. But the 1975 model year cars differed radically from their predecessors in the shape of the energy absorbing polyurethane bumpers demanded by American safety regulations, which MG could only ignore at its peril. The

ABOVE LEFT: The bonnet bulge caused by a larger radiator is the only apparent difference between the MGC and the MGB. This is a 1968 car.

LEFT: The MGC was also produced in GT form with the badge on the tailgate as the only giveaway.

ride height was also increased to the detriment of handling, although this was rectified, to some extent, by a revision of spring rates in 1977.

Such was the soundness of the design, the MGB continued to sell long after it should have been replaced. Output peaked in 1972 and continued at a respectable rate until 1979. Then the car began to be hit by the rising exchange rate value of the pound sterling. MG's parent company – BL Cars – calculated that it was losing £900 on every car it sold in America. In the face of much public outrage, in 1980 the MGB ceased production after over half a million had been built. Its Abingdon factory, which had been MG's home since 1929, was closed down.

During this period two variations on the B theme were introduced, although neither was particularly successful. The first came in 1967; called MGC, it was a 3 litre, six cylinder version of the design. Only destined for a two-year manufacturing life, a mere 8999 were built. Handling was controversial, caused by the heavy engine, which also required the fitment of a unique torsion bar, independent front suspension system. By contrast, the MGB GT V8 of the 1973-76 era required far less mechanical modification. Under the bonnet was Rover's fine alloy 3.5 litre V8 engine. Only available in closed form, its arrival coincided with the post-1973 oil price rise and only 2591 examples of this 120mph (193km/h) car were built.

Specifications: MGB Tourer	
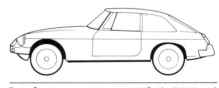	
Length:	12ft 9in (3886mm)
Width:	4ft 11in (1499mm)
Height:	4ft 1in (1245mm)
Wheelbase:	7ft 7in (2311mm)
Track:	front 4ft 1in (1245mm), rear 4ft 1¼in (1251mm)
Unladen weight:	2030lb (920kg)
Engine: Four cylinder, overhead valve, 80x88mm, 1798cc. Compression ratio 8.8:1. Max power, 95bhp at 5400rpm. Max torque, 110lb/ft at 3000rpm.	
Transmission:	Four-speed manual
Drive:	Rear
Suspension (front):	Independent, coil springs, wishbones
Suspension (rear):	Live axle, half-elliptic springs
Top speed:	102mph (164km/h)
0-60mph (96km/h):	12.1 seconds
Production (total):	512,112 (GT 125,323)

MGB/MGC Family

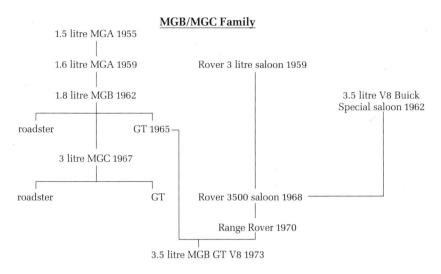

```
1.5 litre MGA 1955
        |
1.6 litre MGA 1959          Rover 3 litre saloon 1959
        |
1.8 litre MGB 1962                          3.5 litre V8 Buick
        |                                   Special saloon 1962
   ┌────┴────┐
roadster   GT 1965 ┐
        |          |
3 litre MGC 1967   |
   ┌────┴────┐     |
roadster    GT   Rover 3500 saloon 1968 ─┘
        |          |
        |   Range Rover 1970
        └────┬─────┘
   3.5 litre MGB GT V8 1973
```

BELOW: *The MGB acquired its so-called rubber bumpers in 1975. They were demanded by American safety regulations, but all B's had to have them. This GT dates from 1979.*

RIGHT: *The MGC was powered by a 3 litre six-cylinder engine shared with the Austin 3 litre saloon. The power unit of this left-hand-drive car has been prepared for rally use.*

AC COBRA (1962-1969, 1983 to date)

The Cobra, a happy liaison of an English chassis and body with an American V8 engine was, in its day, one of the world's fastest sports cars. This charismatic classic is still in production, more than three decades after it first appeared on the street.

The model's origins are rooted in the open two-seater AC Ace of 1954, with its tubular chassis and all-independent suspension. Engines were either AC's own six, by Bristol or, latterly, Ford. In truth, the model was coming to the end of its life when, in September 1961, American racing driver Carroll Shelby wrote to AC with the audacious idea of transforming the Ace's performance by fitting an American V8 engine and selling the resulting car in the USA. Shelby followed up this overture with a visit to the AC factory at Thames Ditton, Middlesex and the Cobra (he had literally dreamed up the name) was born.

Hands Across The Ocean
The cars would leave the AC works in unpainted form, less their engines and gearboxes, and then be transported to the USA and thence to Shelby American in California to have their internals installed. The power unit was Ford's small block, thin walled, 260cid (4.2 litres) engine. The first car was completed in the autumn of 1962. The car was marketed as the Shelby-AC Cobra but, as time went by, AC's involvement became less and the name was, in due course, dropped; the car being known as the Ford Shelby, which reflected the Texan's close involvement with the American automotive giant.

At the end of 1962, after 75 cars had been built, the engine capacity was increased to 289cid (4.7 litres) and rack-and-pinion steering introduced. Externally, the car was unchanged. The renamed 289 Cobra was built until 1965, by which time 576 examples had been completed. As Shelby had anticipated,

the car's performance was sensational. The 289 could reach 100mph (161km/h) in just 14 seconds and was capable of a raucous 138mph (222km/h) flat out. But there was even more to come!

Nineteen-sixty-five saw the arrival of the Mark III Cobra, which incorporated the latest Ford thinking and relegated AC to the role of sub-contractor. The chassis was widened and strengthened, and the by-then outdated, transverse leaf suspension was replaced by all-round coils and wishbones. Power was once again increased, to 427cid (6.9 litres), and this muscular 165mph (265km/h) car was the definitive Cobra with its flared wings and new wider Halibrand wheels of the Ford GT 40 type. In Britain, AC, which had no rights to the Cobra name, also produced the Mark III for the European market as the AC 289 using the earlier 289 V8 engine.

Latterly in America, the Cobra was

fitted with a 428cid (7 litres) engine and the last car off the line was built in 1969. The model had enjoyed competition success. In 1964, on the race track, Shelby had broken Ferrari's hold on the GT Category of the Manufacturers Championship with his Cobra-based Daytona coupé.

But this was not the end of the story. In 1983, CP Autokraft, based at the old Brooklands motor racing circuit in England, which had hitherto supplied spares to Cobra owners, announced (after an 18 year hiatus) the arrival of the 4.9 litres AC Mark IV. This was built using the original tooling, although it could not, at that stage, be called a Cobra. In 1982 AC had agreed that Autokraft could call its car an AC, and then in 1986 the company was permitted by Ford to use the Cobra name. Today the AC Cobra remains in production, only 10 miles (16km) or so from its original home.

AC Cobra

AC Ace 1954

Ford V8 260cid ———— 4.2 litre AC Cobra 1962

Ford V8 289cid ———— 4.7 litre Mark II Cobra 1962

6.9 litre Mark III 1965 ———— Ford V8 427cid

Ford V8 302cid ———— 428cid engine

4.9 litre Mark IV 1983

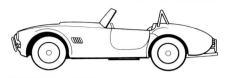

Length:	12ft 7in (3835mm)
Width:	5ft 1in (1549mm)
Height:	4ft 1in (1245mm)
Wheelbase:	7ft 6in (2286mm)
Track:	front 4ft 3in (1295mm), rear 4ft 4in (1330mm)
Unladen weight:	2020lb (916kg)
Engine: V8, overhead valve, 96x72mm, 260cid (4261cc). Compression ratio, 9.2:1. Max power, 260bhp at 5800rpm. Max torque, 269lb/ft at 4500rpm.	
Transmission:	Four-speed manual
Drive:	Rear
Suspension (front):	Independent, transverse leaf spring, wishbones
Suspension (rear):	Same as front
Top speed:	153mph (246km/h)
0-60mph (96km/h):	5.9 seconds
Production (total to 1969):	1052

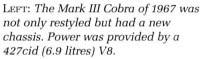

LEFT: *The Mark III Cobra of 1967 was not only restyled but had a new chassis. Power was provided by a 427cid (6.9 litres) V8.*

ABOVE: *The AC Cobra lives! This 1992 Mark IV Lightweight was built by Autokraft and uses the still current 5 litre Ford V8 Mustang engine.*

BELOW: *A right-hand-drive 1966 Cobra 427 with appropriate number plate. Instrument layout is essentially that of the AC Ace.*

CHEVROLET CORVETTE STING RAY (1962-1967)

After getting off to a hesitant start in 1953, Chevrolet's Corvette sports car reached maturity with the arrival of the Sting Ray. Today it has acquired a legendary status on account of its handsome and distinctive body lines, essayed by General Motors' styling supremo, William Mitchell. Once again glass-fibre was employed but for the first time in the Corvette's history, the roadster was joined by a coupé.

With the exception of the 327cid (5.3 litres) V8 engine, which was carried over from the previous year, practically everything about this fourth generation Corvette was new. Work on the project had begun in 1960 and the starting point for those finely executed memorable lines was an experimental coupé, titled XP-720, completed by Mitchell in 1959. This, in turn, had been based on an open two-seater racer he had created in 1958, which he had called Stingray. A distinctive aspect of the XP-720 design was its fastback styling with a rear profile dominated by a divided rear window, a feature of which designer William Mitchell was particularly proud.

E-Type Echoes

Using this 1960 car as his starting point, he proceeded to produce a closed car of considerable beauty. Mitchell had by then been exposed to the influence of Jaguar's sensational 1961 E-Type, and echoes of it were to be apparent in the new Corvette. A notable feature was the fitment of concealed headlights which were actuated by electric motors. In addition to his prized coupé, Mitchell also perpetuated the concept of the open-topped Corvette roadster.

The Belgian-born engineer, Zora Arkus-Duntov, who had been involved with the Corvette since soon after joining GM in 1953, had from 1957 been responsible for the model's design and evolution. His objectives for the new 'Vette included better driver and passenger accommodation and improved handling. With this in view, a new, reinforced, box-section chassis was designed and, for the first time, the model was endowed with independent rear suspension. This employed a transverse leaf spring used in conjunction with control arms and radius rods.

The new Corvette was announced in January 1962 for the 1963 season and the general opinion was that it represented an enormous improvement over its predecessor, both in terms of looks and roadholding. Mitchell and Arkus-Duntov had every reason to be delighted with this verdict.

Minor changes were made for the 1964 model year when the coupé's divided rear window was deleted in the interests of better visibility and slotted wheels discs introduced to improve brake cooling. Much needed, all-round disc brakes finally arrived on the Corvette for the 1965 season.

In its original 1963 form, the model was powered by Chevrolet's proven 250bhp, 327cid V8. A top line 360bhp, fuel-injected version was also available until 1965. A three-speed manual gearbox was fitted although there was the option of an automatic. With this sort of power available, the Sting Ray was capable of over 140mph (225km/h). In 1965 came the option of a new, more powerful, 396cid (6.5 litres), 425bhp V8, while for 1966 its capacity was upped to 427cid (7 litres).

The Sting Ray lasted until mid-1967. Its success can be gauged by the fact that over four years' production accounted for nearly 118,000 cars, compared with some 69,000 Corvettes built in the nine years between 1953 and 1962.

Chevrolet Corvette Sting Ray

Stingray open racer 1958
|
XP-720 coupé 1959
|
Corvette 327cid 1961
|
Corvette Sting Ray 327cid 1962
|
roadster   coupé
|
396cid engine 1965
|
427cid engine 1966

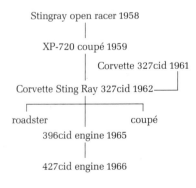

RIGHT: A 1967 Sting Ray convertible looking good even with the hood raised. The fitment of a 390bhp 427cid (7 litres) V8 engine required a special bonnet. This was the final year of Sting Ray production and is regarded as one of the best.

Specifications: Corvette Sting Ray

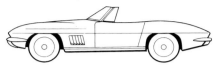

Length:	14ft 7in (4445cm)
Width:	5ft 9in (1753mm)
Height:	4ft 1in (1245mm)
Wheelbase:	8ft 2in (2489mm)
Track:	front 4ft 8in (1422mm), rear 4ft 9in (1448mm)
Unladen weight:	2860lb (1297kg)
Engine: V8, overhead valve, 101x82mm, 327cid (5346cc). Compression ratio, 11.2:1. Max power, 360bhp at 6000rpm. Max torque, 352lb/ft at 4000rpm.	
Transmission:	Three-speed manual
Drive:	Rear
Suspension (front):	Independent, coil springs, wishbones
Suspension (rear):	Independent, wishbones, transverse leaf spring
Top speed:	142mph (229km/h)
0-60mph (96km/h):	6 seconds
Production:	117,964

LEFT: *The Sting Ray coupé with its distinctive divided rear window, which was only available in 1963.*

RIGHT: *A 1965 Sting Ray convertible. The 357cid (5.8 litres) V8 was offered in 250, 300 and 365bhp forms.*

One of the great sports cars of the post-war era, the 911 perpetuated the theme of the rear-mounted, air-cooled, horizontally opposed engine that equipped its 356 predecessor. This unconventional but potent mechanical specification, coupled with an individualistic, wind-cheating coupé body, endowed the car with its own distinctive persona. Combined with the undoubted allure of the Porsche name, this has meant that the endlessly refined 911 still remains the mainstay of the Stuttgart company's model range.

The body was the work of Ferry Porsche's son, Butzi, and its lines have remained essentially intact ever since. Unlike the 356, the 2 litre, 130bhp, six cylinder engine, essayed by Porsche family engineer, Ferdinand Piech, employed chain-driven single overhead camshafts instead of pushrods. Suspension incorporated the established, Porsche-patented torsion bars which were longitudinally located at the front and used in conjunction with wishbones and telescopic dampers with transverse bars and semi-trailing arms at the rear.

Extended Options
In its original form, the model was capable of 135mph (217km/h). However, early examples suffered from unpredictable handling as the low-mounted, rear-located engine caught new owners unawares. Power was upped to 160bhp for the higher performance 911S of 1967 which remained available until 1975. For 1968, it was joined by a cheaper T model, which only lasted until 1969, and by the Weber-carburettored L. Four-speed gearboxes were initially the norm although, late in 1966, the semi automatic Sportomatic 'box was introduced and this option continued until 1979. The 1969 cars had a lengthened wheelbase, with the wheels moved back 2.2in (56mm) to improve weight distribution and handling. For that year the L model was replaced by the fuel-injected E variant, which lasted until 1973, when the system was extended to the entire 911 range. The 1970 cars saw the first of many engine capacity increases, with a 2.2 litre engine which was, again, stretched to 2.3 litres for 1972.

The coupé had remained the sole 911 body option until the 1966 model, when it was joined by the Targa which featured a detachable roof panel and, later, a fixed rear window. The 1973 model year saw the top line Carrera version, introduced on the 356, extended to the 911. Engine size was upped, once again, to 2.7 litres, which resulted in a 210bhp, 150mph (241km/h) car. This enlarged engine was fitted to the mainstream models until 1977. For 1978 the flat six was further extended to a full 3 litres and a five-speed gearbox was standardized. At this point the Carrera, along with the standard 911, was discontinued and the range reduced to just two models: the 180bhp 911SC and 911SC Sport, the latter identifiable by a front air dam and rear spoiler.

New Pretenders
The mid 1970's saw the 911's influence on the wane as a new management at Stuttgart envisaged that the projected generation of front-engined, water-cooled 924, 944 and 928 Porsches would move centre stage. The 911, therefore, seemed destined for oblivion; the intention was to discontinue it in 1984. On a more positive front, 1975 saw the arrival of the 911 Turbo, which is described on page 56.

Then, in 1981 the corporate pendulum swung back in the 911's favour and 1982 saw the appearance of a long-awaited cabriolet version. In 1984 roles were reversed, with the SC cars being replaced by the Carrera which was revived in 3.2 litre form. Ironically, a near-record 14,000 examples of the 911 were built in that year, which had originally been earmarked for its demise. The 3.2 litre engine continued to power the 911 throughout the decade. Then, in 1989, the four-wheel-drive Carrera 4, that was actually designated the Porsche 964, came on the scene. It was powered by a new 3.6 litre, 250bhp engine and there were revised body lines with deformable front and rear sections. The long running torsion bars were finally dispensed with and replaced by coils and wishbones at the front and semi-trailing rear arms. A new Speedster convertible with Turbo running gear appeared at the same time and, in 1990 the 911 was only available in 3.6 litre Carrera 2 and Carrera 4 forms. These models remain in production in 1994, along with the Turbo, and a rebodied 911 (coded 993) with new chassis and six-speed gearbox is intended for 1994. Over 30 years on, the 911 looks set to take Porsche into the 21st century.

BELOW: *Halfway between a convertible and coupé, the so-called Targa top with detachable roof panel has been a popular 911 option since the 1966 season. This is a 1975 car.*

Porsche 911

```
2 litre Porsche 901 1963
         |
  Porsche 911 1964
         |
              Targa 1969    coupé
         |
  2.2 litre 911 1970
         |
2.7 litre Carrera coupé 1972    2.3 litre 911 1972
         |                            |
3 litre Carrera RS 1974        2.7 litre 911 1974
         |
  3 litre Carrera 1976
                               3 litre 911 1978
cabriolet 1982
                      3.2 litre Carrera 1984
3.6 litre Carrera 4 1989
                      3.6 litre Carrera 2 1990
```

RIGHT: *This is the first right-hand-drive 911, a 1965 car owned by English concessionaires AFN Ltd. Note the appropriate number plate. The Fuchs-forged alloy wheels were standardized on the more powerful 911S for 1967.*

Specifications: Porsche 911 1964 coupé

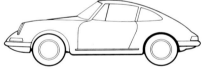

Length:	13ft 6in (4114mm)
Width:	5ft 2in (1575mm)
Height:	4ft 2in (1270mm)
Wheelbase:	7ft 2in (2184mm)
Track:	front 4ft 4in (1321mm), rear 4ft 3in (1295mm)
Unladen weight:	2183lb (990kg)
Engine: Rear-mounted, air-cooled, flat six, single overhead camshafts, 80x66mm, 1991cc. Compression ratio, 9:1. Max power, 130bhp at 6200rpm. Max torque, 120lb/ft at 4600rpm.	
Transmission:	Four-speed manual
Drive:	Rear
Suspension (front):	Independent, torsion bars, MacPherson struts
Suspension (rear):	Independent, torsion bars, trailing arms
Top speed:	135mph (217km/h)
0-60mph (96km/h):	8.1 seconds
Production to date:	352,000 (approx)

RIGHT: *The Carrera name had been applied to the most powerful car in a Porsche range since the 356 of 1956. It was revived for the 911 in 1973 and the model was easily recognizable by the fitment of this distinctive rear spoiler.*

ALFA ROMEO SPIDER (1966-1993)

Timeless good looks combined with the potency of a generation of fabled twin overhead camshaft engines has ensured that the Spider has been a steady seller for an impressive 27 years. It has been in production for longer than any other Alfa Romeo. The model, introduced at the 1966 Geneva Show, was the open version of the Giulia saloon of 1962. The two-seater body was the last designed by Battista Pininfarina, founder of the styling house that bore his name, who died in 1966.

It says much for the competence of Pininfarina's work that its lines had first appeared in prototype form in 1961, five years before the Spider entered production. Also built by Pininfarina, the Spider (open sports) line had began with the 1955 Giulietta and that body was carried over to the 1.6 litre Giulia, discontinued in 1965. The new Spider was lower and wider than its predecessor with a low nose, faired-in headlights, sculptured side panels and a gently tapering tail. Top speed was an impressive 115mph (185km/h), on account of the Giulia's 109bhp, 1.6 litre, twin-carburettored engine. All-round disc brakes were fitted, while the live rear axle was coil sprung. The model was available with a substantial hardtop.

Name That Car
When it came to nomenclature, the car was first known as the 1600 Spider but, perversely, Alfa Romeo decided to stage an international competition for the public to make its own suggestions. This produced an unlikely crop of names which included Patrizia, Edelweiss, Sputnik and ... Hitler. The winner was a certain Guidobaldi Trionfi of Bari, who suggested *Duetto*, which is Italian for duet.

Despite this unusual precedent, in 1967 when the model was revised after 6325 cars had been built, the Duetto name was dropped and the car was simply known as 1750 Spider Veloce (fast sports) on account of the engine having been enlarged to 1.8 litres. Externally, it was similar to its predecessor, although the tapering tail was cut off at right angles and it looked none the worse for that.

The model soon established a dedicated following in America and was perhaps best remembered for being the car that was spiritedly driven by Dustin Hoffman in the celebrated 1967 film, *The Graduate*. Spiders sold there sported a different nose from the European models in deference to the country's safety regulations. From 1984 onwards those cars destined for the US market were fitted with lower powered, 115bhp, emissions-conscious, fuel-injected engines.

The Spider was a modest though consistent seller and a further 8722 cars were built in 1970, when the model's engine was once again enlarged. Extended to 2 litres, with 132bhp on tap and featuring a five-speed gearbox, the 2000 Spider Veloce was, incredibly, to endure until 1993. However, this version was destined for export only; those cars intended for the Italian market were still powered by the long running 1600 units. From 1978 onwards, only left-hand-drive cars were built. The car's lines remained unsullied until 1990 when the nose and tail were revised. Despite its years, the Spider could still attain 119mph (191km/h). Production finally ceased in June 1993, an impressive 27 years after this stylish Alfa Romeo was first announced.

Specifications: Alfa Romeo 2000 Spider Veloce

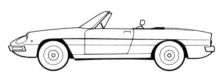

Length:	13ft 11in (4242mm)
Width:	5ft 4in (1626mm)
Height:	4ft 2in (1270mm)
Wheelbase:	7ft 4in (2235mm)
Track:	front 4ft 4in (1321mm), rear 4ft 2in (1270mm)
Unladen weight:	2293lb (1040kg)
Engine: Four cylinder, twin overhead camshaft, 84x88mm, 1962cc. Compression ratio, 9:1. Max power, 128bhp at 5400rpm. Max torque, 131lb/ft at 4000rpm.	
Transmission:	Four-speed manual
Drive:	Rear
Suspension (front):	Independent, coil springs, wishbones
Suspension (rear):	Live axle, coil springs
Top speed:	119mph (191km/h)
0-60mph (96km/h):	9.4 seconds
Production:	123,000 (approx)

Alfa Romeo Spider

Pininfarina prototype 1961
|
                   1.6 litre Giulia saloon 1962
                       |
1.6 litre Duetto 1966 —————— Giulia Sprint GT 1966
|
1750 Spider Veloce 1967 —————— 1750 GT Veloce 1967
|
2000 Spider Veloce 1970 —————— 2000 GT Veloce 1970
| to 1977
to 1993

LEFT: *A 1974 Spider. Its front remained unchanged until 1990.*

RIGHT: *The model's revised tail appeared in 1967. This is a 1976 Spider Veloce and still looking good.*

BELOW: *The timeless lines of a British-registered 1976 Spider Veloce.*

MORGAN PLUS 8 (1968 to date)

If old fashioned looks combined with a modern V8 engine is a recipe for immortality, then the Plus 8 is a prime candidate. With its body lines firmly rooted in the 1930's, the 8 was effectively a re-engined version of Morgan's long running Plus 4 model, the introduction of which revitalized the concept. Although introduced in 1968, demand shows no signs of abating.

The Morgan company of Malvern, Worcestershire began in 1910 by producing three-wheelers and all their vehicles, the Plus 8 included, have employed its founder's sliding pillar, independent front suspension. From the outset, Morgan relied on proprietary engines. The first four-wheelers were built in 1935 and produced exclusively from 1952. The four-cylinder, Standard Vanguard-engined Plus 4 had arrived in the previous year. In 1954 the model's original flat radiator was replaced by a new cowled one, while headlamps were now faired into the front wings. Simultaneously, the Plus 4 was offered with the related but more potent TR2 engine, which transformed the car's performance and sales. The Plus 4 continued to benefit from updates in the TR range until 1967, which was when the TR4A engine was discontinued to make way for the six-cylinder TR5.

This presented Morgan with a dilemma. To install the six would have required extensive reworking of the design, which opened the door to selecting the shorter but wider V8 engine. Thankfully, in view of its later unreliability, Morgan decided against using Triumph's new V8, then under development for the Stag, and ceased to rely on Standard Triumph, its engine supplier of 30 years standing. It opted, instead, for Rover's ex-Buick, 3.5 litre, alloy V8 which was already powering that company's 3.5 litre and 3500 saloons.

Hitherto, the Plus 4 had struggled to reach 100mph (161km/h) but with the V8 under the handsome louvred bonnet, the renamed Plus 8 could comfortably exceed 120mph (193km/h). The car otherwise appeared little changed. This was, in fact, deceptive because the handcrafted, wood-framed body was slightly wider than

50

its predecessor's and the car's wheelbase 2in (51mm) longer. Archaically, the Moss gearbox continued to be located separately from the engine and the design of the similarly antiquated, Z-section chassis was retained. The only outward manifestation of the new unit was the fitment of handsome, cast-magnesium wheels. Demand for the new car was instantaneous but, sensibly, Morgan decided to keep its customers waiting and production did not exceed the 15 cars a week figure throughout the 1970's.

Today's cars appear similar to the first Plus 8 but some modifications have taken place below the surface. From 1973 the Moss gearbox was replaced by the four-speed, all-synchromesh, unit construction 'box used on the Rover 3500S saloon. This was subsequently changed for 1977 with the five-speed unit used on its SD1 replacement. The power unit has similarly benefitted from updates; the option of fuel injection was offered from 1985 and standardized in 1990 when the V8's capacity was increased to 3.9 litres. This has ensured that the Morgan Plus 8 is still a 120mph (193km/h) car, although one with its wheel tracks firmly placed in the 1930's.

LEFT: *Outwardly a pre-war sports car but with performance provided by a modern Rover V8 engine. This is a 3.5 litre 1990 model.*

Morgan Plus 8

Morgan 4-4 1935
|
1.2 litre Plus 4 1951
|
TR engine 1954
| Rover 3500 1968
3.5 litre Plus 8 1968 ——
|
3.9 litre Plus 8 1990

ABOVE: *A 1970 Plus 8. The model is easily distinguishable from the four cylinder Morgans by the fitment of these handsome alloy wheels.*

BELOW: *The Rover V8 engine in a Plus 8. It is available in standard 3.9 and optional 4.2 litre forms, the latter arriving for 1994.*

Specifications: Morgan Plus 8

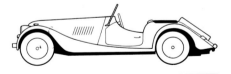

Length:	12ft 2in (3708mm)
Width:	4ft 9in (1448mm)
Height:	4ft 4in (1321mm)
Wheelbase:	8ft 2in (2489mm)
Track:	front 4ft (1219mm), rear 4ft 2in (1270mm)
Unladen weight:	1876lb (851kg)
Engine: V8, overhead valve, 89x71mm, 3528cc. Compression ratio, 10.5:1. Max power, 184bhp at 5200rpm. Max torque, 266lb/ft at 3000rpm.	
Transmission:	Four-speed manual
Drive:	Rear
Suspension (front): Independent, sliding pillar	
Suspension (rear):	Live axle, half-elliptic springs
Top speed:	120mph (193km/h)
0-60mph (96km/h):	6.8 seconds
Production to date:	4000 (approx)

CHEVROLET CORVETTE (1967-1982)

The fifth generation Corvette, which arrived in 1967, had a hard act to follow. Its predecessor, the William Mitchell-styled Sting Ray, had been universally acclaimed and was the design by which the model came of age. The replacement arrived to mixed reviews but, before long, the old magic was working and by 1969 the new car was selling in record numbers. In that year it was christened and badged "Stingray".

The Muscle Car era of the 1960's gave way to a more safety and fuel conscious decade and the Corvette reflected this shift in attitudes by becoming relatively slower but more refined. This was clearly in tune with the public mood and, in 1979, annual output broke the 50,000 barrier for the first time. Although there were then thoughts of replacing it, the car continued to be built until 1982 when it was discontinued after a 15-year production life which was another record for the model.

Work on the new car had started in 1963, soon after the launch of its Sting Ray predecessor. Mechanically, it was essentially unchanged, but the bodywork was inspired by a General Motors' show car, built in 1965 and named Mako Shark II. Like the Sting Ray Corvette, its lines were the inspiration of GM's chief stylist, William Mitchell. When David Holls, Chevrolet's styling supremo, began work on the Corvette, Mako Shark was his starting point. But its excesses were toned down, although the distinctive droop snoot was retained and vacuum-activated concealed headlamps introduced. The result was a clean cut, uncluttered body which Holls succeeded in imbuing with an elusive, timeless quality.

A New Stingray

Introduced in mid-1967 for the 1968 model year, the new Corvette, like its immediate predecessor, was available in coupé and convertible forms but the latter was discontinued in 1975. This was, in part, due to the fact that, from the outset the coupé was fitted with a detachable roof panel in the manner of the Porsche 911 Targa top. The glass fibre bodywork was mounted on a chassis which was unchanged since 1962. All-independent suspension therefore followed previous practice. Similarly, there was a choice of no less than nine engines and transmission teams with a line-up of three V8 engines; a 350bhp 327cid (5.4 litres) and its 427cid (7 litres) stablemate, along with a fearsome top-line race-bred 560bhp unit. Assorted rear axle ratios were specified. A host of optional extras included power brakes and steering, along with air conditioning and tinted windows.

Performance was, by any standards, impressive and the Corvette with the lowest capacity 327 had a top speed nudging the 130mph (209km/h) mark. However, the 427 with 435bhp on tap was good for a sparkling 160mph (257km/h).

Seventies Styles

For 1969 the Stingray name was revived and was badged on the car – as a single word – above the air vents on the front wings. The 1970's were dominated first by emissions and safety regulations, and then by the oil price hike of 1974. As a result, from 1975 until 1980, the Corvette was only available with its bottom-line 350 engine, which had replaced the 327 in 1969.

In 1978 came the first radical alteration to the body when the "sugar scoop" rear, a feature of the model from its outset, was replaced by a wrap-around, glassback, opening tailgate. Simultaneously the Stingray name, which had been almost continuously applied to the Corvette since 1962, was dropped. In addition to the mainstream coupé, two celebrated versions of the 'Vette were produced for 1978. There was the appropriately silver and grey Silver Anniversary model to celebrate 25 years of America's most famous sports car. Chevrolet also built replicas of the black and silver Corvette used as a pace car for the 1978 Indianapolis 500 Mile race.

A record 53,807 Corvettes were produced in 1979. The following year saw the arrival of a lower capacity 305cid (4.9 litres) V8 to join the 350s. The long running model endured until 1982. There were no '83 model year cars, and it was finally replaced by the sixth generation Corvette for 1984.

LEFT: *The Corvette convertible was built until 1975. This car dates from that year and is therefore one of the last examples. A 350cid (5.7 litres) V8 engine is fitted.*

BELOW: *The David Holls-styled Corvette was a worthy successor to the Sting Ray. This 1968 car was named the Corvette for one year; the Stingray name reappeared in 1969.*

ABOVE: *Chevrolet celebrated the 25th anniversary of the Corvette with a commemorative Silver Anniversary edition for 1978 with special paintwork. Note the Porsche-inspired Targa roof.*

Chevrolet Corvette

Corvette Sting Ray 1962

Mako Shark II 1965

Corvette 1967

Stingray roadster   Stingray coupé

Specifications: Chevrolet Corvette (1976)

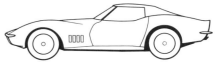

Length:	13ft 9in (4704mm)
Width:	5ft 9in (1752mm)
Height:	4ft (1219mm)
Wheelbase:	8ft 4in(2489mm)
Track:	front, 4ft 10in (1490mm), rear, 4ft 11in (1511mm)
Unladen weight:	3445lb (1562kg)
Engine: V8, overhead valve 101×88mm, 350cid (5736cc). Compression ratio, 8.5:1. Max power, 180bhp at 4000rpm. Max torque, 270lb/ft at 2,400rpm.	
Transmission: Four-speed manual or automatic	
Drive:	Rear
Suspension (front):	Independent, coil springs and wishbones
Suspension (rear):	Independent, wishbones, transverse semi-elliptic spring
Top speed:	132mph (212km/h)
0-60mph (96km/h):	8.2 seconds
Production:	525,749 (total, all models)

Datsun 240Z (1969-1973)

The multifarious troubles that beset the British motor industry in the 1970's were felt across the Atlantic where the American market continued to be offered a variety of sound but ageing open sports cars. Then the Austin Healey disappeared and, while MGs and Triumphs continued to sell, there was clearly a demand for a more modern, better value for money performance car. The breach was filled by Japan in the shape of the Datsun 240Z coupé, which went on to spawn a generation of best-selling Z cars that continues successfully in production to this day.

Despite the fact that the 240Z was a Japanese car, its parentage was, essentially, European. The starting point was a stillborn Nissan project completed in 1964 by a German-born, but usually American-domiciled Count, Albrecht Goertz. His profession was that of automobile stylist and, after the war and while still US based, he was responsible for the lines of the BMW 503 cabriolet and 507 sports coupé of the 1950's.

In 1961 Goertz decided to go to Japan and, as a result, he was recruited by Nissan as a design consultant. Two years later, in 1963, he began work on a sports car which Nissan was targeting at the American market which he knew so well. Jaguar's sensational E-Type had appeared only two years previously and Goertz's starting point was the coupé version. He decided to scale down its dimensions to echo those of the Porsche 911. As originally conceived, the car would have been powered by a sophisticated six-cylinder, twin overhead camshaft engine but, when this proved troublesome, the concept was shelved and Goertz returned to America.

Taking On Toyota

It was the rival Toyota company that was, indirectly, responsible for the re-activation of the idea, because, in 1965, it introduced a very similar 2000GT. This triggered a revival of the Nissan project and the 240Z made its debut, appropriately in America, in October 1969. Unlike British sports cars, which were usually open, the new Datsun was a two-door, two-seater coupé. Its 2.3 litre engine was unique to the model and was a six-cylinder version of the overhead camshaft four used in the 1967 Datsun 510 Bluebird saloon.

The 240Z had a useful opening tailgate but was strictly a two-seater. There was, however, plenty of room for luggage. The Datsun also progressively employed all-independent suspension

with MacPherson struts at the front, and also MacPherson struts used in conjunction with lower wishbones at the rear.

Mechanically, the 240Z's closest rival was the 2.5 litre, six-cylinder Triumph TR6 but it accelerated better and was faster flat out than the British car, being capable of 125mph (201km/h) compared with the TR's 120mph (193km/h). Well priced at $3500, the 240Z was a strong seller from the outset and an impressive 50,000 examples were sold in the first two years of production. It proved to be a robust performer with good road-holding and enviable reliability, qualities that were to prove their worth on the demanding East African Safari rally, which, to the surprise of many, a 240Z won in 1971 and again in 1973. By the time the model was discontinued in 1973, no less than 156,076 examples had been built. It made way for the 260Z, which was a more refined product than the no-frills 240.

ABOVE: This 1972 right-hand-drive 240Z has been beautifully rebuilt by a British enthusiast. He found the 240's handling predictable and neutral while the car returned a creditable 25mpg (11.3 litres/100km).

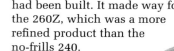

RIGHT: *The first of the Z cars, the Datsun 240Z was only available in three-door hatchback form. The lines are distinctive yet they have more than a hint of the E-Type Jaguar coupé about them.*

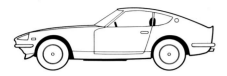

Specifications: Datsun 240Z

Length:	13ft 6in (4115mm)
Width:	5ft 4in (1626mm)
Height:	4ft 2in (1270mm)
Wheelbase:	7ft 6in (2286mm)
Track:	front 4ft 5in (1346mm), rear 4ft 5in (1346mm)
Unladen weight:	2260lb (1025kg)
Engine: Six cylinder, single overhead camshaft, 83x73mm, 2393cc. Compression ratio, 9:1. Max power, 161bhp at 5600rpm. Max torque, 146lb/ft at 4400rpm.	
Transmission:	Four- or five-speed manual
Drive:	Rear
Suspension (front):	Independent, MacPherson strut, lower trailing arms
Suspension (rear):	Independent, MacPherson strut, semi-trailing arm
Top speed:	125mph (201km/h)
0-60mph (96km/h):	8 seconds
Production:	156,076

LEFT: *The 240Z enjoyed a distinguished competition career on both road and track. This example, modified by Z car enthusiast, Spike Anderson, has had its engine bored out to 2.9 litres and develops 195bhp.*

PORSCHE 911 TURBO (1974 to date)

Despite the fact that the 911 Turbo was announced as long ago as in 1974, the current version is still one of the world's most desirable, accelerative and fastest sports cars, able to reach 60mph (96km/h) in under five seconds and capable of a top speed nudging the 170mph (273km/h) mark. The creation of the 911 Turbo was driven by the fact that Porsche needed to build 400 turbocharged cars, which was the number needed to be eligible for Group 4 racing, by 1976. In the first instance, it was thought that the formidable 911 Carrera RSR could be tamed to do double duty as a turbocharged road car but demand was, inevitably, limited and just 109 examples were built.

At this rate it seemed unlikely that four times that number could be sold by the required time, so Dr. Ernst Fuhrmann, Porsche's chief executive, decreed that the 911 Turbo should be a well equipped, luxuriously appointed model to challenge anything that Ferrari might produce. The outcome was a car that appeared at the 1974 Paris Motor Show; by 1983 output had exceeded the 10,000 figure.

Work on the project began in the 1974 season when a 2.1 litre version of the 911 flat six was fitted with a KKK turbocharger. It proceeded to develop no less than 520bhp. This powered a 911 with rear flared wings of truly alarming proportions; an example ran at Le Mans in 1974 where it was placed second. From this car sprang Porsche's all-important 935 and 936 Group 4 sports racers.

In the meantime, work was proceeding on the road car, designated the Type 930, and the 911 Turbo entered production early in 1975. Outwardly it resembled the Carrera with a front air dam and a large "tea tray" rear spoiler to help keep the 260bhp generated by the 3 litre engine in check. The flared wheel arches were distinctive and required for homologation purposes. Inside, the Turbo differed from the sparsely furnished mainstream 911 by having leather upholstery, air conditioning and electric windows. It was, accordingly, nearly twice the price of the 2.7 litre 911 at DM67,850 (£14,749).

The power developed by the turbocharged flat six proved to be too much for the standard five-speed Porsche gearbox, so the Turbo mounted its own purpose-designed, four-speed unit. But it was the model's phenomenal performance that could hardly fail to impress wealthy purchasers: top speed in excess of 150mph (241km/h) with 100mph (161km/h) reached in just 14 seconds. Yet the model was also extraordinarily flexible and handling and braking was the best yet.

Engine capacity was increased to 3.3 litres and output to 300bhp for 1978 which pushed the car's top speed to 160mph (257km/h). Unlike the mainstream 911, which became available in cabriolet form in 1982, the open body option was not extended to the Turbo until the 1988 season. A five-speed gearbox also belatedly made its appearance in 1989.

The 3.3 Turbo briefly came to the end of the road in July 1989, having become overshadowed by the normally aspirated, 3.6 litre, four-wheel-drive Carrera 4. So the 911 range was bereft of a turbocharged model for the first time since 1974. Not for long! After an eight month hiatus, the Turbo made a surprise reappearance at the 1990 Geneva Show with body and suspension courtesy of the flat fronted Carrera 2, and powered by a revised version of that seemingly everlasting flat six, now of 3.6 litres capacity and with 320bhp on tap.

BELOW: *The Porsche Turbo was initially powered by a 3 litre engine and the American cars, such as this, were detuned to 240bhp. Elsewhere the flat six developed 260bhp.*

Specifications: Porsche 911 Turbo

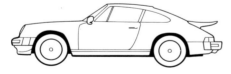

Length:	14ft (4267mm)
Width:	5ft 9in (1753mm)
Height:	4ft 3in (1295mm)
Wheelbase:	7ft 5in (2261mm)
Track:	front 4ft 8in (1422mm), rear 5ft 9in (1753mm)
Unladen weight:	2510lb (1140kg)

Engine: Rear-mounted, air-cooled flat six, single overhead camshafts, 95x70mm, 2994cc. Compression ratio, 6.5:1. Turbocharged. Fuel injection. Max power, 260bhp at 5500rpm. Max torque, 254lb/ft at 4000rpm.

Transmission:	Four-speed manual
Drive:	Rear
Suspension (front):	Independent, torsion bars, MacPherson struts
Suspension (rear):	Independent, torsion bars, trailing arms
Top speed:	152mph (245km/h)
0-60mph (96km/h):	6.3 seconds
Production to date:	30,000 (approx)

LEFT: *A 1987 Sport Equipment 911 Turbo with revised front end and engine boosted to 330bhp. It was available in Britain from late 1985.*

ABOVE: *A 1993 911 Turbo with 3.6 litre engine can be distinguished from the mainstream 911 by its wider wheels and famous rear spoiler.*

Porsche 911 Turbo

2 litre Porsche 911 1964

coupé

2.3 litre 911 1972

2.7 litre Carrera coupé 1972

2.7 litre 911 1974

3 litre Carrera RS 1974

3 litre 911 Turbo 1974

3.3 litre 911 Turbo 1978

911 cabriolet 1982

Carrera 4 1986

Turbo cabriolet 1988

Production ceases 1989

3.6 litre Turbo 1990

Carrera 2 1990

CHEVROLET CORVETTE (1983 to date)

The current Corvette appeared in 1983 and although now over 20 years old, it still retains the spirit, performance and vitality forever associated with America's well established and most famous sports car. Shorter, lower and faster than its long running predecessor, the new 'Vette was announced in February 1983 for the 1984 model year.

Glass-fibre bodywork was once again employed, indeed the front section of the body was said to be the largest moulded component in the industry. It was forward opening, while the car also incorporated a transparent hatchback and detachable roof panel. Quite deliberately, the body lacked decorative features to ensure a long production lifetime and the years have accordingly dealt lightly with the car's lines, which were the work of Chevrolet stylist, Jerry Palmer.

Overall responsibility for the project was vested in the Corvette's chief engineer, Dave McLellan, who began work on the car in 1978. The starting point reached even further back to a 1972 General Motors show car, the appropriately titled, Wankel-engined 4-Rotor, and the vehicle that sprang from it, following General Motors' decision to drop the rotary power unit, was the V8-powered Aerovette, an aerodynamically adventurous design with gullwing doors. This was eventually discarded but, in the course of this evolutionary phase, the arrival of the sixth generation Corvette was put back from 1980 to 1983.

This Corvette differed from all its predecessors in that a separate chassis was dispensed with and the body built up around a perimeter birdcage structure to which the panels were bonded. The power train of 350cid (5.7 litres) V8 was carried over but the transmission was new; a four-speed manual gearbox with a computer-controlled overdrive for the first three cogs. The engine/gearbox unit was separated from the differential and rear suspension by an aluminium C-section backbone chassis and the material was also used for the propeller and half shafts, as well as for some suspension components. The weight saving philosophy was also extended to the suspension medium, in which the established coil springs were replaced by transverse leaves made of glass-fibre instead of steel. This alone saved 250lb (113kg).

The downsizing of the Corvette's engine in the more fuel-conscious 1970's meant that the car's top speed of 125mph (201km/h) was about the same as that of its predecessor, although acceleration was noticeably better. This reflected the coupé's lighter weight and improved aerodynamics. In 1986 a convertible version appeared, so ending a 10 year absence of a roadster version of the Corvette.

Nineteen-eighty-nine witnessed the arrival of an exciting variant. The basic model was still powered by the venerable 350cid V8 but this was redesigned by Lotus in alloy for the new ZR-1, with 32 valve cylinder heads which pushed output up to 390bhp. These refinements made it the fastest Corvette yet, being capable of 180mph (290km/h) and all for a mere $50,000! A six-speed ZF gearbox was employed.

In 1991 came a new 350cid unit, developing 300bhp, which replaced the original that dated back to 1955. This put the 'Vette back in the fast lane; the car is now capable of 172mph (277km/h) and today, over 40 years young, is most certainly still a force to be reckoned with.

Specifications: Chevrolet Corvette

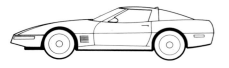

Length:	14ft 8in (4470mm)
Width:	5ft 11in (1803mm)
Height:	3ft 10in (1168mm)
Wheelbase:	8ft (2438mm)
Track:	front 4ft 11in (1499mm), rear 5ft (1524mm)
Unladen weight:	3192lb (1448kg)
Engine:	V8, overhead valve, 101x88mm, 350cid (5736cc). Compression ratio, 9:1. Fuel injection. Max power, 205bhp at 4200rpm. Max torque, 290lb/ft at 2800rpm.
Transmission:	Four-speed manual
Drive:	Rear
Suspension (front):	Independent, coil springs, wishbones
Suspension (rear):	Independent, coil springs, wishbones, transverse leaf spring
Top speed:	125mph (201km/h)
0-60mph (96km/h):	6.3 seconds
Production (to date):	294,475

LEFT: *A 1984 Corvette. Like all its predecessors, this sixth generation car features glass fibre bodywork but with a removable roof panel and hatchback. Accessibility of the 350cid (5.7 litres) V8 is excellent.*

Chevrolet Corvette

4-Rotor show car 1972
│
Aerovette 1978
│
    350cid Corvette 1982
│
└205bhp Corvette 1983
├───────────────┐
coupé   convertible 1986
│
390bhp 350cid
ZR-1 1989
│
300bhp 350cid Corvette 1991

RIGHT: *A 1994 Corvette ZR-1 with its engine today developing 405bhp. At $70,000, the car costs over $30,000 more than the standard coupé.*

BELOW: *A 1990 ZR-1 with its massive bonnet concealing a 32-valve alloy version, by in-house Lotus, of the long running 350cid (5.7 litres) V8.*

Toyota MR2 (1984-1990)

Toyota, which rivals the automotive giants of America in output, succeeded in making its Corolla saloon the world's best-selling car. With such a background, there was some surprise when in 1984 Toyota, which had hitherto almost exclusively produced saloons, unveiled a sports car in the shape of the mid-engined MR2 coupé. It was, however, an absolute winner, and set new standards which other car makers have since striven to emulate.

Like so many of its Japanese contemporaries, until the early 1980's Toyota concentrated on producing reliable, value-for-money cars which reflected a cautious approach to engineering. Then, however, the multinational decided on a more adventurous design philosophy, which was soon reflected in the 1983 fifth-generation Corollas that, belatedly, featured front- rather than the traditional rear-wheel drive.

An outward expression of this shift in design philosophy had come in 1981 when Toyota established connections with Lotus, and Toyota components were incorporated in the Excel model of 1982. Toyota had decided to produce a new generation of multi-valve, twin overhead camshaft engines and, by 1986, it led the world in this technology. Production of such units then exceeded the one million mark. With such potent, sophisticated engines in production, what better expression of this new approach could be made than for Toyota to produce a sports car? The outcome was the MR2, standing for Midship Runabout 2. Work on the project began in the early 1980's and prototypes were being tested in Europe by 1983, which was when a British motoring magazine incorrectly identified one as a new Lotus!

The Flying Wedge

When the MR2 was announced, there were obvious comparisons between it and Fiat's mid-engined X1/9 of eight years before. But the Toyota was far from being a copy of the Italian car, despite the echoes of it in the wedge-shaped styling, mid-engine location and all-independent strut suspension. The Japanese two-seater was larger and roomier, as well as being considerably faster, being capable of 120mph (193km/h) while returning an economical 29mpg (9.7 litres/100km). These figures were attainable with the larger 1.6 litre, fuel-injected, 112bhp, twin-overhead-camshaft, 16-valve engine, courtesy of the Corolla GTi. An alternative, lower capacity, 1.5 litre, single-overhead-camshaft version for the home market was also available.

It was, in particular, the MR2's ingenious packaging that impressed the international engineering community and, when combined with the model's formidable roadholding, it resulted in a truly outstanding sports car.

Further refinement came in 1986 when Toyota's engineers managed to squeeze a Roots-type supercharger into the crowded engine compartment. This increased output to 143bhp, although this option was only available in the American market.

For 1987 came a body variation with the arrival of a T-bar version. The roof of this model incorporated two detachable transparent panels which, when removed, revealed the distinctive, dividing, T-shaped spacer which joined the windscreen surround to the rollover hoop. The model remained available in these forms until 1990 when the original MR2 made way for its replacement, another car which perpetuated the by-then widely respected model name.

ABOVE: *Rear view of the soberly styled MR2 with little to betray the presence of a mid-mounted engine apart from the air intakes which are located behind the doors.*

BELOW: *The MR2 on the move. Coming from a company which had almost exclusively produced saloons, the MR2's performance and roadholding were all the more impressive.*

RIGHT: A first generation MR2 dating from 1984. It was built in this form until the 1987 season when it was joined by a T-bar version with detachable roof panels.

Specifications: Toyota MR2

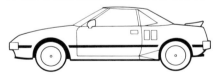

Length:	12ft 10in (3912mm)
Width:	5ft 5in (1651mm)
Height:	4ft 1in (1245mm)
Wheelbase:	7ft 7in (2311mm)
Track:	front and rear 4ft 8in (1442mm)
Unladen weight:	2028lb (920kg)

Engine: Mid-located, four cylinder, twin overhead camshaft, 81x77mm, 1587cc. Compression ratio, 9.4:1. Fuel injection. Max power, 135bhp at 6600rpm. Max torque, 110lb/ft at 5200rpm.

Transmission:	Five-speed manual
Drive:	Rear
Suspension (front):	Independent, MacPherson strut, lower transverse arms
Suspension (rear):	Independent, MacPherson strut, lower parallel transverse links
Top speed:	120mph (193km/h)
0-60mph (96km/h):	7.9 seconds
Production:	166,000 (approx)

BMW Z1 (1988-1991)

Despite having an impressive sporting tradition, BMW's formidable post-war reputation has been largely built on its fine range of high performance saloons. The arrival of a new BMW sports car is, therefore, a significant event and this certainly applied to the two-seater, plastic bodied Z1. Here, unusually, was an open performance car which eschewed the fashionable mid-engined approach of the 1980's and reverted to the traditional front engine/rear drive layout that was also employed by BMW's mainstream model range.

Work on the project began in 1985 when the Munich-based company set up BMW Technik, a corporate think tank under the direction of former Porsche engineer, Ultrich Bez. The division's wide-ranging briefs included examining the latest engine, suspension and electronic technology, together with a commission to revisit the processes required to design and develop new models, as well as the methods employed to build them. It was, therefore, decided to manufacture a production car to incorporate answers achieved in response to some of these questions.

The outcome was the Z1, an impressive blend of new and established thinking. Its engine was a six cylinder, 2.5 litre, 170bhp unit, courtesy of the BMW 325i, complete with its five-speed gearbox with drive conveyed by torque tube. These components were mounted in a strong monocoque chassis of galvanized steel and zinc with further rigidity contributed by a full-length, aerodynamically significant floor constructed from a corrosion-free, epoxy resin-and-foam sandwich. Suspension was all-independent using the familiar front struts while the rear layout incorporated what BMW called a Z axle. This would appear on its new generation of 3 Series saloons in 1990. The company described it as a "centrally guided, spherical double wishbone system", the principal virtues of which were low weight and absence of excessive complication.

Unconventional Looks

The most outwardly unusual aspect of the Z1 was its body. Most German high performance road cars are coupés, not roadsters, which benefit from the superior aerodynamics associated with a closed body. The Z1 flew in the face of this convention by showing that an open two-seater could be aero-dynamically efficient, while the easily detachable, non-load-bearing panels were made from a plastic material. The doors were of a particularly ingenious construction. To open them, the driver or passenger would simply touch a circular, chrome-plated button located just behind each door opening. The window glass would firstly descend, to be followed by the door itself, which disappeared into a space between the outer plastic panel and the steel sill until only projecting handles, used for emergencies, could be seen. In the normal course of events, the doors would be raised again by electric motors.

These ingenious features aside, the Z1 was also an impressive performer on the road. Top speed was 135mph (217km/h). BMW had only intended to build 5000 examples, but such was the demand for the car, its manufacture was extended to the summer of 1991, by which time 8000 cars had been produced by BMW.

Length:	12ft 10in (3912mm)
Width:	5ft 6in (1676mm)
Height:	4ft 2in (1270mm)
Wheelbase:	8ft (2438mm)
Track:	front 4ft 9in (1449mm), rear 4ft 10in (1473mm)
Unladen weight:	2756lb (1250kg)

Engine: Six cylinder, single overhead cam-shaft, 84x75mm, 2494cc. Compression ratio, 8.8:1. Max power, 170bhp at 5800rpm. Max torque, 164lb/ft at 4300rpm.

Transmission:	Five-speed manual
Drive:	Rear
Suspension (front):	Independent, MacPherson strut
Suspension (rear):	Independent, coil springs, wishbones, trailing arms
Top speed:	135mph (217km/h)
0-60mph (96km/h):	6.6 seconds
Production:	8000

LEFT: *A 1989 Z1 doing what it does best: at speed on a German autobahn. An uncompromising two-seater, the car's unusual doors are shown here in the lowered position.*

ABOVE: *A Z1 also with its driver's door lowered into the deep sill. The car can be so driven but the occupants often complain that such journeys are excessively windy!*

BELOW: *The Z1's boot was not vast and contained the hood, which could be erected in half a minute, along with the spare wheel. This car has its wind-up windows raised.*

MAZDA MX-5 MIATA (1989 to date)

In an era of such technological niceties as four-wheel drive, turbocharging and composite body structures, this American/Japanese design is an impressive restatement of the no-frills, front-engine/rear-drive theme of the open, two-seater, British sports cars of the 1960's. Mazda had for some years wanted to produce a model to slot in below its successful RX7 sports coupé and its engineers toyed with the options of a sophisticated mid-engined car, a front-wheel-drive model and an open version of its 323 saloon. But motoring journalist, Bob Hall, who in 1981 had joined Mazda North America's (MANA) product planning and research facility at Irvine, California, had other ideas.

Having grown up with British sports cars in his youth, he became an articulate advocate of the traditional but unfashionable front-engine/rear-drive configuration. Hall applied the well-proven KISS acronym to the project, standing for "Keep It Simple Stupid", and, fortunately, he had a firm ally in Tom Matano, head of the MANA team. After two years of deliberation, in 1986, Mazda agreed.

Having been given the corporate green light, Mazda went to the lengths of buying a second-hand Triumph Spitfire and Lotus Elan, which the engineers were encouraged to drive and then strip down to appreciate their simple but ingenious construction. The KISS car design process was overseen by Matano. A key player was Mark Jordan, son of Chuck Jordan, head of General Motors design, although the work proceeded with the closest consultation and input from Mazda at Hiroshima in Japan. The outcome was the widely acclaimed MX-5, announced early in 1989, eight months ahead of its rival, the outwardly similar but faster, more complicated and expensive Elan from the General Motors-owned Lotus company.

Mazda Power
The heart of the car was Mazda's 116bhp, four valve per cylinder, four-cylinder engine that had first appeared, transversely mounted, in a high performance version of Mazda's front-wheel-drive 323 saloon. But in the MX-5 it was located on the north/south axis with drive conveyed, through a five-speed gearbox, via a torque tube or what Mazda call the Power Plant Frame, to the differential. Suspension is by all-round coils and double wishbones with disc brakes on each wheel, which resemble British Minilites of the 1960's.

Great efforts have been made to keep the weight of this steel-bodied car to a minimum, and the MX-5 turns the scales at 2182lb (990kg). Construction features an aluminium bonnet, composite bumpers and boot lid, while the battery is a diminutive motor cycle cell. The result is a well-balanced, viceless car with predictable handling; top speed is around the 115mph (185km/h) mark. This is not much more than the original Lotus Elan, so the marketing emphasis is on enjoyment rather than flat-out motoring.

In mid-1993, the MX-5's 1.6 engine was replaced by an enlarged 128bhp, 1.8 litre unit, also used in the 323. It seems likely that the chunky lines of the MX-5 will continue to make friends around the world for many years to come.

Specifications: Mazda MX-5 Miata

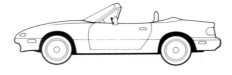

Length:	12ft 11in (3937mm)
Width:	5ft 5in (1651mm)
Height:	4ft (1219mm)
Wheelbase:	7ft 5in (2261mm)
Track:	front 4ft 7in (1397mm), rear 4ft 8in (1422mm)
Unladen weight:	2182lb (990kg)

Engine: Four cylinder, twin overhead camshaft, 78x83mm, 1597cc. Compression ratio, 9.4:1. Max power, 116bhp at 6500rpm. Max torque, 100lb/ft at 5500rpm.

Transmission:	Five-speed manual
Drive:	Rear
Suspension (front):	Independent, coil springs, wishbones
Suspension (rear):	Independent, coil springs, wishbones
Top speed:	115mph (185km/h)
0-60mph (96km/h):	9.2 seconds
Production (to date):	250,000 (approx)

LEFT: *With the 1.6 litre MX-5, Mazda reverted to the front-engined/rear-drive theme espoused by British sports cars of the 1960's. An enlarged 1.8 litre engine is due for 1994.*

RIGHT: *The MX-5's no nonsense interior which provides sufficient, but not an excessive amount of information for the driver and plenty of room for the long-legged. The gear lever has a particularly good change.*

BELOW: *A Le Mans Special Edition turbocharged MX-5, limited to 24 cars and created in 1991 to commemorate a Mazda winning that year's Le Mans 24-hour race. The distinctive livery was shared with the victorious 787B.*

LOTUS ELAN (1989-1994)

Any new Lotus attracts attention and the second generation Elan was no exception. The stubby, front-wheel-drive, open two-seater bristled with technical sophistication, from its turbocharged, twin-overhead-camshaft Isuzu engine to the backbone chassis and ingenious glass-fibre body structure. Alas, the Elan was destined for a manufacturing life of a little over two years when a combination of the world recession and production problems resulted in the car never attaining its sales targets, a state of affairs which forced Lotus to cease production.

When the original Elan, see page 38, was discontinued in 1974, Lotus moved upmarket with its new family of Elite, Eclat and Esprit models. So the arrival of the new Elan was, to some extent, a restatement of an original approach. Although Lotus's managing director, Mike Kimberley, had been a keen advocate of the concept since 1976, it would be a 10 years before the idea was finally approved. In the meantime, Lotus's chairman, Colin Chapman, had died in 1982 and the company was bought in 1986 by the American General Motors Corporation. GM wasted little time in sanctioning the project with its intended 3000 car a year output, and the model was launched, over three years later, at the 1989 London Motor Show.

Lotus's design team was led by Colin Spooner and the car's all important styling came from the accomplished Peter Stevens. The outcome of a £36 million investment was a distinctive, open two-seater body with an impressive drag coefficient. It was a glass-fibre structure consisting of 54 separate component pieces.

Engine For An Elan
The engine was a transversely mounted, 16-valve Isuzu unit with 165bhp on tap. There were corporate associations here because, in 1970, Lotus's GM parent had bought a share in the Japanese concern and Lotus engineering had played a role in the creation of the turbocharged, 1.6 litre, four-cylinder, twin-camshaft unit for its Gemini saloon. The five-speed gearbox was integral with the engine. The Elan's chassis was a modified version of Lotus's familiar backbone with all-round independent suspension — double wishbones at the front, and upperlinks and wide-based lower wishbones related to the Eclat at the rear. Disc brakes were fitted all round.

The intention was to build 1500 Elans in 1990, with that figure rising to the maximum of 3000 in 1992. The model was available in normally aspirated and turbocharged forms and its performance and handling was in keeping with the finest Lotus traditions. Despite the use of composites, the car weighed a little over a ton (2255lb, 1023kg). In turbocharged SE form, the Elan was capable of 135mph (217km/h). But impressive as performance was, road tests spoke of niggling faults in relation to the gear-change, and the fit of some of the body panels was not as good as might have been expected for a car costing £21,005.

Sadly, as the world economic recession began to bite, sales failed to reach the anticipated figure. American demand never materialized and the company had no choice but to shut the Hethel production line in the summer of 1992 after a mere 3857 Elans had been built. In 1993 General Motors sold Lotus to Bugatti. The line was restarted in June 1994 and a further, and final, 800 cars were completed.

Specifications: Lotus Elan SE

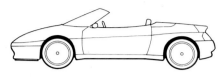

Length:	12ft 5in (3785mm)
Width:	5ft 8in (1727mm)
Height:	4ft (1219mm)
Wheelbase:	7ft 4in (2235mm)
Track:	front and rear, 4ft 10in (1473mm)
Unladen weight:	2255lb (1023kg)
Engine: Four cylinder, twin overhead cam-shaft, 80x79mm, 1588cc. Compression ratio, 8.2:1. Turbocharged, fuel injection. Max power, 165bhp at 6600rpm. Max torque, 148lb/ft at 4200rpm.	
Transmission:	Five-speed manual
Drive:	Front
Suspension (front):	Independent, coil springs, wishbones
Suspension (rear):	Independent, coil springs, upper link, lower wishbone
Top speed:	135mph (217km/h)
0-60mph (96km/h):	6.7 seconds
Production (total):	4657

ABOVE: *The Elan's transversely mounted, four-cylinder, turbocharged, twin-overhead-camshaft, 16-valve Izusu engine, in which Lotus had a hand, with aluminium 'head and cast iron block.*

LEFT: *Stubby and distinctive, the Elan's lines were the work of Peter Stevens. The hood was contained beneath the cover located just behind the seats.*

RIGHT: *A 1990 Elan SE. Front-wheel-drive is an unusual configuration for a sports car and was an important ingredient in the model's much praised roadholding and handling.*

DODGE VIPER (1992 to date)

The Viper is an unashamed, no-nonsense, open two-seater sports car which revives all the flamboyance and 1960's nostalgia of the legendary AC Cobra. Unusually for such a model, it was never intended as a production car, having begun life as a one-off show vehicle but the level of public response made Dodge's parent company Chrysler decide to put it into low volume production.

Finished in a dazzling shade of red, the Viper was not solely conceived as a head turner, but as a car with a more legitimate corporate message. By 1989 Chrysler had ceased production of rear-drive cars and switched exclusively to front-wheel-drive models. Having said that, for its next generation of large cars the Corporation was contemplating front-, rear- and four-wheel-drive options and, therefore, wished to remind the public of its long-standing commitment to the rear-drive theme. This is why Chrysler's president, dedicated old car enthusiast, Bob Lutz, sanctioned the Viper as an expression of this approach.

Back To Basics
In his quest to create such a vehicle, Lutz turned to Carroll Shelby, creator of the AC Cobra and this duo, coupled with the resources of the Chrysler Corporation, produced the Viper which, unexpectedly, became the star of the North American International Auto Show, staged in Detroit in January 1989. In the same way that Mazda's highly acclaimed MX-5 was a "back to basics" concept, so it was with this Dodge show car which, quite deliberately, lacked creature comforts and such mechanical niceties as four-wheel-drive, anti-lock brakes and the electronic wizardry of many of its contempories.

It was powered by a prototype cast-iron, 8 litre, V10 pushrod engine, intended for a new generation of Chrysler pickup trucks and sports utility vehicles. This was mounted in a tubular steel chassis with drive conveyed via a manual gearbox. Suspension was independent all round, with disc brakes employed front and rear. But it was the open two-seater body that was the most successful aspect of the design; created in steel with a glass-fibre nose and tail, it was a glorious cocktail of Ferrari, Jaguar, and Cobra themes.

The Viper was launched at the end of 1991 and the car entered, albeit limited, production in 1992. A number of changes have been made to the specification in the intervening three years with the production version still outwardly resembling the 1989 show car, although there are more substantial changes below the surface. The most significant applies to the V10 engine, which was refined by in-house Lamborghini and redesigned with an aluminium block. Power is now rated at 400bhp at 4600rpm, as opposed to the 300bhp of the original. A six-speed manual gearbox is employed.

Performance is, accordingly, sensational. Chrysler claim a top speed of 165mph (265km/h) and a 0-60mph (96km/h) figure of 4.5 seconds which is faster than a Ferrari F40. The design team went for the "minimum frills, maximum thrills" approach and the Viper is essentially an open car with no hood or windows. The optional soft top and side screens appear as afterthoughts. However, in 1993 the roadster was joined by a coupé version.

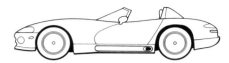

Specifications: Dodge Viper	
Length:	14ft 7in (4445mm)
Width:	6ft 4in (1930mm)
Height:	3ft 10in (1118mm)
Wheelbase:	8ft (2438mm)
Track:	front 4ft 11in (1514mm), rear 5ft 0½in (1538mm)
Unladen weight:	3300lb (1497kg)
Engine: V10, overhead valve, 101x98mm, 7997cc. Compression ratio, 9.1:1. Fuel injection. Max power, 400bhp at 4600rpm. Max torque, 480lb/ft at 3600rpm.	
Transmission:	Six-speed manual
Drive:	Rear
Suspension (front):	Independent, coil springs, wishbones
Suspension (rear):	Independent, coil springs, wishbones
Top speed:	165mph (265km/h)
0-60mph (96km/h):	4.5 seconds (claimed)
Production (to date):	1500

ABOVE: *Pictured here on home territory in America, the Viper has also been available in Britain since 1993, but it is only produced in left-hand-drive form.*

RIGHT: *Although the Viper was conceived as a roadster, in 1993 came a coupé version which retained the basic shape but with side-mounted exhausts rerouted to emerge at the car's rear. Note the huge back tyres.*

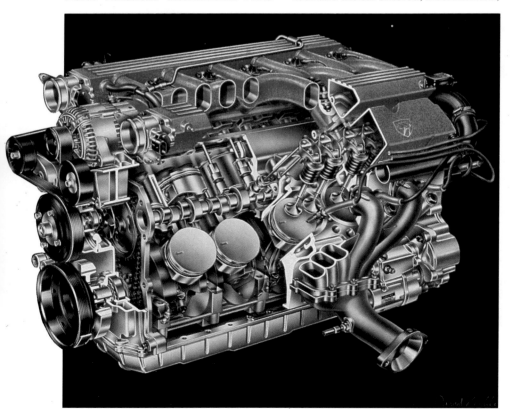

LEFT: *The Viper's aluminium 8 litre, pushrod V10 Chrysler engine began life as a diesel truck unit, and was developed by in-house Lamborghini for sports car use.*

RIGHT: *There is no room for rear passengers in a Viper, the two occupants no doubt being reassured by the presence of the rollover bar immediately behind them.*

When the 18 year old MGB ceased production in 1980, there were few who would have prophesied that the model would one day be revived but, 12 years on, precisely that happened. Announced at the 1992 Motor Show, the MGB's spiritual successor is the MG RV8 roadster which entered production in April 1993. Manufacture is scheduled to cease in 1995 after some 2000 cars have been built.

There would never have been an RV8 had it not been for the arrival, in 1988, of a revived MGB bodyshell. This was the brainchild of British Motor Heritage, a subsidiary of MG's parent, BL Car's, and, in particular, its executive director, David Bishop. The body was produced on tooling which, thankfully, had survived so that enthusiasts with badly rusted MGBs were able to rebuild them with an original replacement body – not a replica – and thus preserve the vehicle's integrity. This initiative has proved to be extremely successful and, to date, over 3000 shells have been completed.

It then occurred to Bishop that the next stage was to produce a complete car and, with the enthusiastic encouragement of BMH's managing director, Peter Mitchell, and the approval of its renamed Rover Group parent, in 1990 an experimental car was built. The MGB had originally been powered by a 1.8 litre, four-cylinder engine but Bishop was in no doubt that the only suitable power unit was the current version of the Rover V8 that had been used in the MGB GTV8 of 1973-76.

Marketing The MG

At this stage Bishop was still thinking of producing a V8-engined MGB roadster with some enhancement to its interior trim, but the concept was completely transformed when the project was, in 1991, handed over to Rover's newly formed Special Products division. Following customer research, RSP identified a potential market for the car, which would by its nature be expensive, among the prosperous clientele who already owned an executive saloon. The MG RV8 was created with them in mind.

The new MG was launched to an enthusiastic response at the 1992 Motor Show, chosen to celebrate the 30th anniversary of the MGB's arrival. Although based on the BMH-built body, the car's lines have been cleverly updated while still retaining the spirit of the original. Under the bonnet is the 188bhp, 3.9 litre Rover V8 engine

Specifications: MG RV8

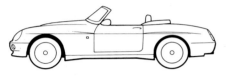

Length:	13ft 2in (4013mm)
Width:	6ft 7in (2007mm)
Height:	4ft 4in (1321mm)
Wheelbase:	7ft 8in (2337mm)
Track:	front 4ft 1in (1245mm), rear 4ft 4in (1321mm)
Unladen weight:	2430lb (1101kg)
Engine: V8, overhead valve, 94x71mm, 3946cc. Compression ratio, 9.35:1. Max power, 190bhp at 4750rpm. Max torque, 234lb/ft at 3200rpm.	
Transmission:	Five-speed manual
Drive:	Rear
Suspension (front):	Independent, coil springs, wishbones
Suspension (rear):	Live axle, half-elliptic springs
Top speed:	135mph (217km/h)
0-60mph (96km/h):	7 seconds
Production (projected):	2000

which endows the car with a top speed of 135mph (217km/h). Unlike the original B, the RV8's interior is particularly luxurious with a fine wood veneer dashboard and beautifully upholstered leather seats.

The model is produced on a purpose designed assembly line at the Rover Group's Cowley factory. The MG has been widely praised for the quality of its manufacture. However, this is not a new car and its 0-60mph (96km/h) acceleration time of around the 7 second mark cannot be considered sensationally rapid, while ride and handling inevitably reflect the model's 35 year old origins. But on a wider canvas, the RV8 represents the rebirth of the MG marque. Rover remain tight lipped about what will follow the model, but of one thing the public can be certain: the MG marque is back!

RIGHT: *Based on the MGB roadster substructure, the RV8 is powered by Rover's proven 3.9 litre V8 engine, which echoes the specification of the MGB GT V8 of 1973-76 vintage. RV8 production is limited to 2000 cars.*

MG RV8

1.8 litre MGB 1962

roadster   MGB GT 1965

to 1980   to 1980   MGB GTV8 1973-76

BMH bodyshell 1988

3.9 litre MG RV8 1992

3.5 litre V8 Buick
Special saloon 1962

3.5 litre Rover
3500 1968

Range Rover 1970

3.9 litre V8 engine
1990

- - - out of production

LEFT: *An impressive feature of the RV8 is its well appointed interior with veneered dashboard and beautifully upholstered seats.*

RIGHT: *The purposeful front end of a 1993 MG RV8. The famous brown and cream octagonal badge has been subtly redesigned for this model.*

TVR is one of the myriad of British sports car companies established in the 1950's that have survived to the present day. From the outset the philosophy has been to build a distinctive performance car, powered by a proprietary engine in a purpose-built tubular chassis, and cloaked in a distinctive glass-fibre body. Unquestionably, the best received TVR for many years is the Griffith, unveiled and acclaimed at the 1990 Motor Show, although it did not enter production, in refined form, until 1992.

TVR's origins date back to 1946 when 23 year old Trevor Wilkinson, opened a garage, Trevcar Motors, in Blackpool. Later he decided to enter the sports car business. From 1949 Ford-engined specials were produced and the cars were called TVR, derived from Tre-VoR's christian name. Complete cars were available from 1954 but, like many similar businesses, TVR experienced its fair share of financial upheaval. It did not achieve stability until 1965 when the father and son team of Arthur and Martin Lilley took the business over. Their stewardship endured for 17 years and in 1982 TVR was sold to Peter Wheeler, its present chairman.

Griffith Revived
The starting point for the Griffith was the Ford V6-powered S model of 1987, which slotted in below the 420, the company's Rover V8-engined flagship. For 1991 came the S3 version with longer doors and a stiffer shell and it was joined on TVR's 1990 Motor Show stand by the new Griffith. This also featured a Rover V8 engine but of 3.9 litres capacity. The name was a revival of a TVR model of 1963-5 vintage. The

backbone spaceframe chassis was based on that of the S3, and the Griffith's interior had the same origins. However, TVR was insistent that this was not simply a V8-engined S3 because the car had a brand new body and gearbox. The Blackpool company claimed a top speed of 148mph (238km/h) and a 0-60mph (96km/h) time of 4.9 seconds.

The beautiful black Griffith generated enormous interest at Birmingham National Exhibition Centre. This was a tribute to Peter Wheeler, who not only owns the company but also styles its products in conjunction with engineer John Ravenscroft. Recognizing that it had a winner on its hands, TVR decided to refine the concept while still retaining the spirit of the original. Detail modifications to the body included the introduction of concealed door hinges, air vents behind the wheel arches, a backlit number plate and integral rear lights. The S3-derived chassis was replaced by a suitably tailored version of a tubular backbone chassis and double wishbone suspension arrived from another TVR venture, the Tuscan racing car.

In February 1992 the Blackpool com-

Specifications: TVR Griffith 500

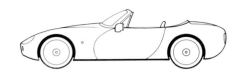

Length:	12ft 9in (3892mm)
Width:	6ft 4½in (1943mm)
Height:	3ft 11in (1205mm)
Wheelbase:	7ft 6in (2282mm)
Track:	front and rear 4ft 9in (1460mm)
Unladen weight:	2315lb (1050kg)

Engine: V8, overhead valve, 94x90mm, 4988cc. Compression ratio, 10:1. Fuel injection. Max power, 325bhp at 5500rpm. Max torque, 350lb/ft at 4000rpm.

Transmission:	Five-speed manual
Drive:	Rear
Suspension (front):	Independent, coil springs, wishbones
Suspension (rear):	Independent, coil springs, wishbones
Top speed:	155mph (249km/h)
0-60mph (96km/h):	4.1 seconds (claimed)
Production (to date):	700

pany announced that the first 24 cars had been dispatched, these being the first deliveries from a 350-strong order book. By this time there were two versions of the model: the 3.9 litre Rover V8-based engines had been joined by a TVR-modified 4.3 litre version. Production was restricted to the home market and exports began in the summer of 1993 with the Griffith 500 powered by a 5 litre V8, also of Rover origins.

Press reaction to this new generation of TVRs has been impressive with handling, performance and build quality receiving fulsome praise; the Griffith family looks set to take TVR successfully into the future.

LEFT: *The Griffith has been justly praised for the originality of its body lines. This is a 1992 car which was offered with a choice of 3.9 or 4.3 litre V8 engines.*

LEFT: *Like all TVRs, the Griffith has glass fibre bodywork. External decorative features are minimal, the car relies on its proportions to please.*

ABOVE: *The Griffith 500 of 1993 employs the ultimate version of the Rover V8 engine, the 5 litres capacity being attained by increasing the length of the stroke.*

TVR Griffith

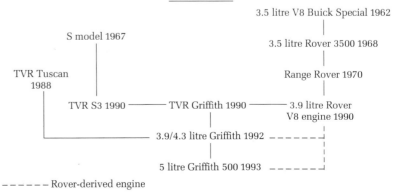

```
                                                        3.5 litre V8 Buick Special 1962
                                                                    |
                              S model 1967                  3.5 litre Rover 3500 1968
                                                                    |
        TVR Tuscan                                           Range Rover 1970
           1988
                    TVR S3 1990 ———— TVR Griffith 1990 ———— 3.9 litre Rover
                                                            V8 engine 1990
                         3.9/4.3 litre Griffith 1992 – – – –

                         5 litre Griffith 500 1993 – – – –
```

– – – – – Rover-derived engine

GRAND TOURERS

Unlike the traditional open two-seater sports car, the Grand Tourer is a relatively recent creation, having been born in Italy in the years immediately following the end of World War II. This was a car which triumphantly combined the comfort of a coupé with the performance of a sports car, and it soon overhauled the roadster in popularity.

The concept sprang from research, undertaken in Germany and Italy between the wars, which identified the fact that a closed car is aerodynamically more efficient, and therefore faster, than its open equivalent. No model more typifies the spirit of the GT, although the name was not then current, than the stunning Pinin Farina-bodied Cisitalia. Its engine capacity was just 1100cc but it was capable of close on 100mph (161km/h).

Cisitalia was a new make, as was Ferrari, but while the former firm only lasted until 1952, its great contemporary was soon producing the most famous Grand Tourers in the world. Enzo Ferrari built road cars to finance his racing activities, although his glorious V12-powered berlinettas were only built in relatively small numbers, and it was not until 1954 that production was placed on a more ordered footing. This came about after Ferrari had secured a body supply contract with Pinin Farina (which since 1960 has been known as Pininfarina) and this inspired alliance of visual and mechanical talents is, thankfully, maintained to this day.

The Turin-based styling house was also responsible for the Lancia Aurelia B20 coupé of 1951, a landmark car if ever there was one. Named the *Gran Turismo*, it bequeathed its name to the movement which, in Britain, was often rendered as Grand Tourer or, more usually, abbreviated to the universally recognized GT initials.

Britain had wasted little time in following Italy's example and the Elliot coupé from Healey, a new British make, was in its day the fastest closed car in the world, having attained over 104mph (167km/h) in 1947. That year's Bristol was another new make and the 400 was a finely engineered GT based on pre-war BMW designs. Since 1962, these cars were powered by a Chrysler V8 engine. The fitment of such a powerful,

understressed American unit had been popularized by the French Facel Vega in 1954 and also by Jensen with its 1962 CV8, and the same treatment was extended to the Interceptor of 1966. In its turn, this spawned a costly but impressive four-wheel-drive FF derivative.

Aston Martin was also V8-powered from 1969 but this engine was its own purpose-designed unit. The make's GT line had begun in 1950 with the six cylinder DB2 which in turn led to the DB4 of 1958 and this series survived, in DB6 guise, until 1970.

Up until 1964 the Grand Tourer could be regarded as a fast, expensive closed car for the fortunate few, but all this changed that year with the arrival of Ford's Mustang which, among other styles, was produced in GT form. Here was a Grand Tourer for Everyman and, such was its success, Ford transplanted the idea to its European arm with the Capri appearing in 1969. It remained in production for no less than 18 years.

The Italians, however, continued to be in the vanguard of the GT movement. Maserati followed Ferrari with its 3500GT in 1958 and, in 1963, a brand new marque appeared in the shape of the V12-powered Lamborghini, a Ferrari challenger created by tractor manufacturer Ferruccio Lamborghini. His first car, the 350GT, had a body by Touring but thereafter the company forged a fruitful association with the Bertone styling house.

The examples of Ferrari and Lamborghini were followed in Britain by Jaguar which offered a V12 engine that first appeared in the E-Type in 1971. It later powered the XJS, a car that is 19 years old in 1994 and still going strong.

Innovation has been the keynote of the Grand Tourer's evolution. In 1980 came the Audi Quattro from Germany which, for the first time, offered four-wheel-drive at an affordable price. The Wankel rotary engine was, in its day, similarly pioneering and was taken up by NSU, another German car maker. But it was Mazda, a Japanese company, which persevered with the invention and employed it, to great effect, in the RX7 of 1978. And the Far East still continues to set the technological pace with such offerings as the Nissan 300ZX, Toyota Supra and Honda NSX all challenging the Europeans who, it will be recalled, invented the GT in the first place . . .

HEALEY ELLIOT (1946-1950)

Healey was one of Britain's newest post-war marques when it introduced its Elliot saloon in 1946. Powered by the potent but heavy 2.4 litre Riley engine, on announcement it was the fastest closed car in the world, having recorded a top speed of over 130mph (166km/h).

Cornishman Donald Mitchell Healey began a distinguished rallying career in 1924, and it was crowned in 1931 with a victory in the Monte Carlo Rally. In the same year he got a job with Riley in Coventry, and this marked the start of a lifetime's involvement with the motor industry. In 1933 he moved to Triumph and subsequently became its technical director. However, the firm went into liquidation in 1939.

During World War II, Healey joined Humber and it was while there that he served in the Royal Air Force Volunteer Reserve where he met up again with salesman *par excellence* James Watt, whom he had known during his

Triumph days. Together they planned to buy the Triumph name, then owned by engineering company Thomas Ward, and restart production. But Ward refused to sell, so the concept was rethought and the resulting vehicle became the Healey. In the meantime Donald Healey and James Watt had discussed their plans with stylist Ben Bowden and engineer "Sammy" Sampietro, both of whom worked at Humber.

Healey was intent on producing a 100mph (161km/h) model in the spirit of the Invicta in which he had scored his famous "Monte" victory. A works was established in the town of War-

wick, conveniently close to the heart of the Midlands motor industry, and the Healey appeared early in 1946. The basis of the car was a light, box-section chassis fitted with costly hiduminium trailing arm front suspension. The Nuffield Organisation had made its 104bhp four-cylinder Riley engine available and Healey, aware of the aerodynamic advantage of a closed body over an open one, took the first car to Italy and proceeded to record 104.6mph (168.3km/h) over the flying quarter mile on the Milan to Cosmo autostrada.

Coachbuilding was bought from outside suppliers and the Elliot's body was built by a firm in Reading, Berkshire, Samuel Elliot and Sons, from which its name derived. The Healey was also produced in open Westland form, but the Elliot was by far the more popular of the two and proved to be a comfortable tourer in the Italian manner, even though its body lines dated faster than stylist Bowden would have wished.

Production ran at about five cars a week, so the model was, inevitably, expensive and initially listed at £1597. To promote sales, Donald Healey went to some lengths to publicize the Elliot's performance and in 1947 he achieved a speed of 110.8mph (178.3km/h) over the measured mile at Jabbeke in Belgium.

The car was originally built in A-type form but, after six months' production, it was replaced by the B-type with an adjustable steering column at a time when Elliot production was running at double that of the open Westland. It would not be until 1950 that the C-type frame, with improvements to its front suspension, was introduced. Just one chassis was completed as an Elliot, although the Healey saloon line continued until 1954 with the improved and more attractive Tickford sports saloon which was twice as popular as its predecessor, selling 224 examples compared with 101 Elliots.

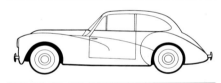

ABOVE: *An Elliot, second left, flanked to the left by an Abbott-bodied Healey with a Westland tourer to the right. The Elliot's Tickford-bodied successor is on the extreme right.*

LEFT: *A 1947 Elliot with body styled by Ben Bowden, which was built in Reading, Berkshire. This was an expensive car in its day; in 1947 the Elliot cost £1917.*

RIGHT: *This generation of Healeys was powered by Riley's potent 2.4 litre pushrod engine with high efficiency hemispherical combustion chambers.*

Specifications: Healey Elliot

Length:	14ft (4267mm)
Width:	5ft 5½in (1665mm)
Height:	4ft 10in (1473mm)
Wheelbase:	8ft 6in (2591mm)
Track:	front 4ft 6in (1372mm), rear 4ft 5in (1346mm)
Unladen weight:	2520lb (1143kg)
Engine: Four cylinder, overhead valve, 80x120mm, 2443cc. Compression ratio, 6.5:1. Max power, 104bhp at 4500rpm. Max torque, 132lb/ft at 3000rpm.	
Transmission:	Four-speed manual
Drive:	Rear
Suspension (front):	Independent, coil springs and trailing arms
Suspension (rear):	Live axle with torque tube, coil springs
Top speed:	102mph (164km/h)
0-60mph (96km/h):	12.3 seconds
Production:	101

Healey Elliot

```
                  ┌─ 2.4 litre Riley saloon 1937
                  ·
2.4 litre Healey 1946
      ┌───────────────────┐
  Elliot saloon        Westland tourer

Tickford saloon 1951   Abbott coupé 1951
```

CISITALIA 202 GRAN SPORT (1947-1952)

The car that can be seen as the progenitor of the Grand Touring movement, even though the name was not then current, was this stunning Cisitialia coupé. Though powered by a mere 1100cc engine, its low weight and aerodynamically inspired bodywork combined to ensure that it was capable of an impressive 99mph (159km/h).

Piero Dusio, founder of the Turin-based Cisitalia concern, had in 1946 marketed a Fiat-based 1100cc racing car, intended to be used as a curtain raiser for Formula 1 races, and he wished to produce a roadgoing version. Like the single seater, it was the work of the talented Fiat engineer, Dante Giacosa, who had that company's celebrated 500 model to his credit. He undertook the assignment on a freelance basis.

The racer had a pioneering tubular chassis, Giacosa having been inspired by the frame of the Beltram bicycle which Dusio also built; this was perpetuated in the road car along with the overhead valve, 1100cc Fiat engine. The independent front suspension was of the transverse leaf spring variety. The car's coupé body resembled that which Giacosa had produced for the Fiat 508C MM of pre-war days.

Savonuzzi Style

By the summer of 1945 Giacosa was giving Fiat his undivided attention, so the project was taken over by an engineering colleague, Giovanni Savonuzzi, who joined Cisitalia and designed a new aerodynamically efficient coupé body, the result of wind tunnel testing, which was dominated by two large tail fins. This car was capable of no less than 122mph (196km/h) but the body did not lend itself to quantity production. So Dusio told Savonuzzi that he wanted a car which was "wide like my Buick, low like a grand prix car, comfortable like a Rolls-Royce and light like our single seater." Faced with these apparently irreconcilable parameters, Savonuzzi set to work and produced a number of sketches for a projected design. Dusio chose one, and the lines of this were skilfully interpreted by Pinin Farina. The car first appeared on the evening of the Italian Grand Prix in September 1947, but made its international debut at the Paris Motor Show in the following month.

Production of the Cisitalia Gran Sport got under way in 1948. The bodies were built in aluminium so that the car weighed a mere 1713lb (777kg) and this, coupled with the "slippery"

properties of the coupé, ensured that the Cisitalia was a sparkling performer. When fitted with an optional 60bhp engine, it could exceed 105mph (169km/h). However, once 100 bodies had been completed, Pinin Farina ceased his involvement with the project and the contract was then shared between two other Turin coachbuilders, Stabilimenti Farina, established by Pinin's father, and Vignale. The resulting hulls were made of steel.

Alas, the Cisitalia was destined for a limited production life. Dusio became involved with a costly four-wheel-drive Grand Prix project and financial problems caused him to depart for the Argentine in 1948. Gran Sport production was maintained for a while, but the model was discontinued in 1952 after some 170 cars had been built.

Pinin Farina was luckier. In 1951 across the Atlantic in America, the New York Museum of Modern Art staged an Exhibition titled *Eight Great Automobiles* and the Cisitalia was displayed under the title of "Self Moving Sculpture". The international publicity that resulted was to serve the Turin styling house well, even though the car's lines were those of Giovanni Savonuzzi . . .

Specifications: Cisitalia 202 Gran Sport

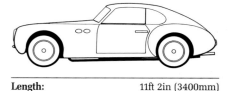

Length:	11ft 2in (3400mm)
Width:	4ft 9in (1450mm)
Height:	4ft 1in (1250mm)
Wheelbase:	7ft 10in (2400mm)
Track:	front, 4ft 1½in (1258mm), rear 4ft 1in (1247mm)
Unladen weight:	1713lb (777kg)
Engine: Four cylinder, overhead valve, 68x75mm, 1089cc. Max power, 55bhp at 5500rpm.	
Transmission:	Four-speed manual
Drive:	Rear
Suspension (front):	Transverse leaf spring and wishbones
Suspension (rear):	Live axle, half-elliptic springs
Top speed:	99mph (159km/h)
Production:	approx 170

Cisitalia 202 Gran Sport

1.1 litre Fiat 508C saloon 1937-39

Fiat 508C MM coupé

Fiat 1100 saloon 1939-48

Cisitalia single seater 1946

Cisitalia project 202 coupé 1946

Fiat 1100S coupé 1947-50

Cisitalia Savonuzzi coupé 1947

Cisitalia Gran Sport by Pinin Farina 1947

LEFT: *The Cisitalia was powered by Fiat's 1100cc overhead valve engine. Its twin-carburettors were, unusually, served by a scuttle-mounted, gravity-fed petrol tank.*

RIGHT: *The lines of the Pinin Farina Cisitalia coupé were enhanced by the absence of bumpers. Unlike mass-produced Italian cars of the day, this was a right-hand-drive car.*

BELOW: *Progenitor of the grand touring movement, this Cisitalia has been retained by Pininfarina for its museum. Note its badge at the bottom of the front wing.*

BRISTOL 400 FAMILY (1947-1961)

The Bristol, built to demanding aviation standards by the aircraft company of the same name, was, unquestionably, the best engineered British Grand Tourer of the early post-war years, even though the car's design originated with the German BMW company. The marque was the creation of the Bristol Aeroplane Company's George White and H.J. Aldington, who in pre-war days had built the Frazer Nash and, from 1934, imported BMWs into Britain.

Aldington's contribution was the BMW element in Bristol's pedigree. After the war he had brought the German company's personnel and its designs to Britain and through his brother, Donald, contact was established with Bristol, which was wanting to enter the car market. The resulting car was to have been called the Frazer Nash-Bristol, but in 1947 the deal was unscrambled and Aldington then went ahead with his own BMW-based Frazer Nash.

The first Bristol, the 400, appeared at the 1947 Geneva Motor Show and was an impressive cocktail of BMW themes, skilfully interpreted by Bristol's talented engineering team. The model combined what was, in effect, the chassis of the pre-war BMW 326, a 2 litre, six-cylinder engine which was courtesy of the famed 328 sports car, and a body that owed its inspiration to the 327 Autenrieth coupé.

Cars were hand-built at Filton, Bristol and, in a bid to maintain the highest possible engineering standards, the company manufactured as much as possible of the car itself. Not surprisingly, the Bristol was not cheap: the 400 sold for £2723, but performance and road-holding were impressive and the 90mph (145km/h) car remained in production until 1950, by when 700 examples had been completed.

It was joined by the 401 of 1949-53 which was, in essence, a rebodied 400 that had started life as a two-door saloon by Touring of Milan. It had then been carefully refined by Bristol engineers and the outcome was the aerodynamically efficient 100mph (161km/h) model with improved high speed acceleration. It was replaced in 1953 by the outwardly similar 403 with its engine boosted to 100bhp and improvements made to its gearbox, suspension and brakes.

For 1954 came the short chassis 404 which used, instead of a BMW-derived radiator grille, an intake which echoed the wing design of the Bristol Brabazon airliner. There were vestigial tail fins at the rear. It was pricey at £3542 and only 40 were built but its 110mph (177km/h) performance has forever dubbed it as "the businessman's express". Less happy was its four-door 405 derivative. The 406 of 1958-61 was more in the 404 tradition, although by this time the BMW-derived six, despite being enlarged to 2.2 litres for the 406, was becoming outdated.

Work had begun on a purpose-designed replacement engine but Bristol's aircraft division now began to tighten its financial belt and one casualty was this bespoke 2.9 litre, twin-overhead-camshaft six. As a result Bristol decided to adopt a proprietary engine and opted for the Chrysler 5.1 litre V8. Fitted to the 407 of 1962 which closely resembled the 406, it was the first of a new generation of Bristol cars.

Bristol 400 Family

BMW 326 1936-41 ——— 2 litre BMW 328 1936-40

BMW 327 1936-41

└— 2 litre Bristol 400 1947 ┘

Bristol 401 1949

Bristol 403 1953 ———

Bristol 404 1953

Bristol 405 1954

2.2 litre Bristol 406 1958

ABOVE: *First of the line, a BMW in all but name, a 1950 Bristol 400 with lines courtesy of the German car company's prewar Autenrieth coupé.*

ABOVE: *The short chassis Bristol 404 was built between 1953 and 1955. The spare wheel is located just behind the right front wheel arch on this left-hand-drive car.*

RIGHT: *A 1959 Bristol 406 on the move. Built until 1961, this was the last Bristol to be fitted with the BMW-derived six-cylinder engine. Thereafter a Chrysler V8 was employed.*

Specifications: Bristol 400

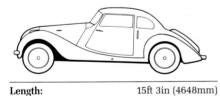

Length:	15ft 3in (4648mm)
Width:	5ft 5½in (1664mm)
Height:	4ft 11in (1499mm)
Wheelbase:	9ft 6in (2896mm)
Track:	front, 4ft 3¾in (1314mm), rear, 4ft 6in (1372mm)
Unladen weight:	2520lb (1143kg)
Engine: Six cylinder, overhead valve, 66x96mm, 1971cc. Compression ratio, 7.5:1. Max power, 80bhp at 4200rpm. Max torque, 96lb/ft at 3000rpm.	
Transmission:	Four-speed manual
Drive:	Rear
Suspension (front):	Independent, transverse leaf spring, wishbones
Suspension (rear):	Live axle, torsion bars, lateral link, A-bracket
Top speed:	90mph (145km/h)
0-60mph (96km/h):	19.1 seconds
Production (total six cylinder):	approx 2068

FERRARI 166 INTER (1948-1950)

The first true production Ferrari, the 166 was an unalloyed expression of its creator's famous dictum that he "built a good engine and then attached a chassis to it." The unit in question was a V12 of 1992cc and the 166 was graced with some of the finest examples of Italian coachwork of the day.

Enzo Ferrari built road cars to finance his racing activities and at the heart of both programmes lay the V12, essayed by the talented Gioacchino Colombo, who interpreted Ferrari's commitment to the configuration at a time when the motoring world had turned its back on such a power unit. But Ferrari had watched the V12-powered Mercedes-Benz and Auto Union Grand Prix cars triumph in the immediate pre-war years and was dedicated to the idea of a smooth running, understressed engine, despite his firm being small and its finances limited. His 1.5 litre V12 burst into life in 1947 and powered the first Ferrari which was the 125 Sport road car. It was followed in 1948 by the first Formula 1 racer.

The 125 was, in its turn, succeeded for 1948 by the 166 Sport. It was so called because each cylinder had a capacity of 166cc, hence 166 × 12

equals 1992cc. The specifications followed that of the 125, namely the V12 engine was mounted in an oval section, tubular cross braced chassis with transverse-leaf independent front suspension and half-elliptic springs at the rear. The soon-to-be legendary power unit was a 60 degree, alloy V12 with wet cylinder liners, the substantial seven bearing crankshaft was machined from a solid steel billet and the chain-driven, single overhead camshaft per bank actuated two valves per cylinder. This formidable power unit developed 90bhp which compared with 130bhp for the higher compression racing version. Adventurously, the 166's gearbox was a five-speed unit.

The model was soon to prove itself in sports racing events. In 1948 this Ferrari gave the marque no less than three sports racing successes, in the Targa Florio, Mille Miglia and Paris 12

Hours and in the following year a 166 provided Enzo Ferrari with his first victory in the Le Mans 24-hour race. Just three 166 Sports were built but enthusiasts wanted their own cars and its successor, the 166 Inter, an abbreviation of *Internazionale* (International), was unveiled at the 1948 Turin Show, which was the first occasion that the Maranello company had attended. A Touring-bodied 166 coupé displayed there was to pave the way for the *Gran Turismo* Ferraris of the 1950's.

Class Performance

The performance of these early cars is not in question, driven as they were by the powerful, smooth-running V12, even if the car's chassis was comparatively basic and the controls rather heavy. Capable of over 100mph (161km/h), the 166 Inter came into its own over long distances as a remarkably flexible, high-speed performer. Most 166s were magnificently bodied by Touring but Farina, Ghia and Vignale also made contributions.

The 166 was to endure until 1950 when it was replaced by the 195 Inter after some 36 examples had been built. Ferrari was on his way!

Ferrari 166 Inter

1.5 litre V12 engine 1947

Ferrari 125 Sport 1947

Ferrari 125 Grand Prix 1948

2 litre Ferrari 166 Sport 1948

Ferrari 166 Grand Prix 1948

Ferrari 166 Inter 1948

RIGHT: *Most 166s were bodied by Touring. This Inter, chassis 019S, was exhibited at the 1949 Paris Motor Show and the first owner, one J. Lodi, lived in the French capital.*

LEFT: *A few other coachbuilders bodied the 166. This 1950 car is one of four berlinettas produced by Stablimenti Farina of Turin and now bears an identifying number plate.*

Specifications: Ferrari 166 Inter

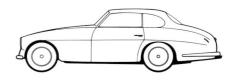

Length:	13ft (3962mm)
Wheelbase:	8ft 2½in to 8ft 7in (2500 to 2620mm)
Track:	front and rear, 4ft (1219mm)
Unladen weight:	1658lb (752kg)
Engine:	V12 cylinder, single overhead camshaft per bank, 60x58mm, 1992cc. Compression ratio, 7.5:1. Max power, 90bhp at 6000rpm.
Transmission:	Five-speed manual
Drive:	Rear
Suspension (front):	Independent, transverse leaf spring, wishbones
Suspension (rear):	Live axle, half-elliptic springs
Top speed:	100mph (161km/h)
Production:	approx 36

BELOW: *This 1949 car is fitted with an Aerlux Plexiglas roof. Note Superleggera badges on the bonnet sides which refer to the latticework of tubes concealed beneath the aluminium body panels.*

ASTON MARTIN DB2, DB2/4 (1950-1959)

The British car that came closest to the Italian concept of a potent, well-equipped and stylish Grand Tourer was the Aston Martin DB2 with its engine designed by the famous W.O. Bentley. This was in turn to lead in 1953 to the enlarged DB2/4 with an innovative opening tailgate which was to endure until 1959.

In 1947 David Brown of gear and tractor manufacturers, David Brown and Sons of Huddersfield, Yorkshire, bought the moribund Aston Martin company. Later in the same year he purchased Lagonda and established the revived concern at Feltham, Middlesex. Brown was attracted to the potential of Lagonda's Bentley-designed, 2.6 litre, twin-overhead-camshaft, six-cylinder engine because he was dissatisfied with the 2 litre, four-cylinder, pushrod unit which Aston Martin had produced and that powered the first model to be made under his ownership. This was the low production, touring Sports model of 1948, retrospectively titled the DB1, for David Brown.

Italian Influence

Brown decided that its successor would not be an open car in the spirit of the pre-war Aston Martins, but a closed model in the Italian manner. Three examples were completed in time for the 1949 Le Mans race although none performed well and it would not be until the spring of 1950 that the DB2 entered production.

Using the DB1 as a starting point, Aston Martin engineers retained its multi-tubular chassis and replaced the pushrod four with the Lagonda engine. The body was magnificently styled by Aston Martin's Frank Feeley, who had the lines of the Lagondas of the 1930's to his credit. Such was the competence of Feeley's work that many believed the body had been conceived in Italy.

The outcome was a fast, handsome car worthy of the Aston Martin name. In its original 105bhp form, the DB2 was capable of 110mph (177km/h) although, on the debit side, it suffered from a harsh ride and undue interior noise. In 1951 came the more potent 125bhp version which could be urged to 115mph (185km/h).

As originally conceived, the DB2 was strictly a two seater with space for luggage behind but for 1954 came the improved DB2/4 with two small back seats and a rear-opening hatch. This immediately widened the car's potential market so as to appeal to the family man and, consequently, many more examples of the 2/4 Mk I were sold than of its predecessor: 565, compared with 309 of the original DB2. The derivative was, however, heavier, so the Vantage engine was standardized.

LEFT: *Looking Italian but in fact styled by Aston Martin's own Frank Feeley, this is a DB2/4 of 1953 vintage. The opening tailgate was a popular and innovative feature.*

Aston Martin DB2 Family

Atom prototype saloon 1939

2.6 litre Lagonda saloon 1947

2 litre Aston Martin DB1 1948

2.6 litre DB2 1950

DB3 sports racer 1951

DB2/4 Mk I 1953

3 litre Lagonda engine 1954

DB2/4 Mk II 1955

DB Mk III 1957

ABOVE: *The Bentley designed twin-cam six used in every Aston Martin road car built between 1950 and 1959. This is the ultimate DBD series, 180bhp, triple-SU-carburettored unit.*

BELOW: *This DB Mark III is powered by the engine shown above and dates from 1959 which was the last year of DB2/4 production. The radiator grille is related to the DB3S sports racer.*

LEFT: *The DB2 in its original form was essentially a two-seater and was powered by the Lagonda engine in its basic 2.6 litre version. This 1952 car is chassis LML/50/202.*

In 1954 the capacity of the twin cam six was increased to 3 litres. It produced a healthy 165bhp in optional Vantage form.

The 2/4 was produced in an outwardly similar Mark II state for 1956 with coachwork by Tickford which David Brown had bought in late 1954 and whose factory at Newport Pagnell, Buckinghamshire would, from 1958, be Aston Martin's new home.

The ultimate version of the line, the DB Mark III, the 2/4 designation having been dropped, appeared in 1957 with a revised radiator grille and front disc brakes. The standard version of the 3 litre twin cam developed 162bhp and from 1958 there was a triple carburettored 192bhp variant. But, in truth, the line was beginning to show its years and the model was discontinued in 1959, by which time its illustrious DB4 successor had made its triumphant appearance.

Specifications: Aston Martin DB2

Length:	13ft 6in (4115mm)
Width:	5ft 5in (1651mm)
Wheelbase:	8ft 9in (2667mm)
Height:	4ft 5in (1346mm)
Track:	front and rear, 4ft 6in (1372mm)
Unladen weight:	2662lb (1207kg)
Engine: Six cylinder, twin overhead camshaft, 78x90mm, 2580cc. Compression ratio, 6.5:1. Max power, 105bhp at 5000rpm. Max torque, 125lb/ft at 3100rpm.	
Transmission:	Four-speed manual
Drive:	Rear
Suspension (front): Independent, trailing arms, coil springs	
Suspension (rear):	Live axle, coil springs
Top speed:	110mph (177km/h)
0-60mph (96km/h):	11.2 seconds
Production (total DB2, 2/4, Mark III):	1726

PEGASO Z102 (1951-1958)

Spain does not have any great tradition for indigenous car production, the legendary Hispano-Suiza of the pre-war years excepted, so there was some surprise when in 1951 the government-owned National Lorry Company unveiled its sensational and fearsomely complex Pegaso Z102 grand tourer. Built in limited numbers over the next seven years, this glorious anachronism was produced in numerous and bewildering permutations made possible by the fact that its makers looked upon the car as a publicity exercise for its commercial vehicles. This was just as well because the Pegaso was an undisputed loss maker.

The driving force of the project was Wilfredo Ricart, a Barcelona-born engineer who in 1936 had left Spain for Alfa Romeo and, four years later, became its technical director. He spent the duration of the war in Milan but in 1945 left Italy and returned to his native Spain.

There he joined the Barcelona-based *Empresa Nacional de Autocamiones SA*, better known by its ENASA acronym, which had been created in 1946 by the Spanish government. It absorbed Hispano-Suiza which had ceased car production in 1940. The lorries it built were called Pegaso which is the Spanish name for Pegasus, the flying horse of Greek mythology.

Then in 1951 came the Pegaso car powered by a high compression, alloy, 2.5 litre V8 with twin overhead camshafts per bank. The gearbox was located at the car's rear and was a five-speed, non-synchromesh unit. The suspension medium was torsion bars in conjunction with wishbones at the front and a de Dion rear axle, complete with inboard drums. The steering gear was said to have been one of the most complicated ever seen on a motor car. Apart from the Bosch electrics, practically everything else was made at ENASA's Barcelona factory. As if this was not enough, the cars were not even bodied locally but hundreds of miles away by Touring in Italy and by the Parisian Saoutchik concern although, later, Spanish styling was adopted.

Fast But Noisy

The Pegaso cost £3000 in Britain and was mostly built in closed form, which exacerbated the fact that the engine was impossibly noisy, Ricart having specified efficient but raucous camshaft gears rather than the more conventional chains. The specification of the engine did not remain constant for long; a supercharger was added and capacity then upped, in unblown form,

to 2.8 litres. By 1954 there was a 3.2 litre version and a top line model with *two* superchargers. Most Pegasos were good for over 125mph (201km/h) and could manage 100mph (161km/h) in fourth gear.

After approximately 100 examples of the Z102 had been built, it was succeeded in 1955 by the Z103 in which the engine's overhead camshafts were replaced by less audible and efficient pushrods. Even then, the model was offered in three capacities of 4, 4.5 and 4.7 litres. However, very few cars were built and production ceased in 1958. Ricart left to become president of the French Lockheed brake concern and Pegaso concentrated on its commercial vehicles, an activity that continues to this day.

RIGHT: *A 1955 Pegaso Z102B with the customary Touring coachwork. Power was provided by a V8 engine which was offered with a wide choice of capacities and states of tune.*

LEFT: *A 1951 Z102, a pre-production prototype with coachwork by Pegaso. The world's oldest Z102, it was used as a demonstration car at the 1951 Paris Motor Show.*

ABOVE: *This is probably the most original surviving Pegaso, having always been in the same family. Gears are a mirror image of the norm. First cog is on the right of the gate . . .*

Pegaso Z102

2.5 litre Pegaso Z102 1951
|
2.8 litre Z102 1953
(unsupercharged or supercharged)
|
3.2 litre Z102 1954
(unsupercharged or twin supercharged)
|
4, 4.5, 4.7 litre Z103 1955

Specifications: Pegaso Z102

Length:	13ft 5in (4090mm)
Width:	5ft 4½in (1580mm)
Wheelbase:	7ft 8in (2337mm)
Height:	4ft 3in (1295mm)
Track:	front, 4ft 4in (1321mm), rear, 4ft 2in (1270mm)
Unladen weight:	2160lb (980kg)

Engine: V8, twin overhead camshafts per bank, 75x70mm, 2472cc. Compression ratio, 8:1. Max power, 165bhp at 6500rpm. Max torque, 138lb/ft at 3900rpm

Transmission:	Five-speed manual
Drive:	Rear
Suspension (front):	Independent, torsion bars, wishbones
Suspension (rear):	De Dion rear axle, torsion bars
Top speed:	125mph (201km/h)
0-60mph (96km/h):	10.3 seconds
Production (total Z102/103):	approx 96

B-88959

B-81702

LANCIA AURELIA B20, 2500GT (1951-1958)

The Grand Touring movement can be seen to have reached maturity at the 1951 Turin Motor Show when Lancia unveiled its Aurelia B20 Pinin Farina *Gran Turismo* coupé in which the comfort of a saloon was triumphantly united with the performance of a sports car. The GT had come of age.

The Turin-based Lancia company had a long-standing tradition of offering coachbuilt alternatives to its factory coachwork and Pinin Farina was the company's favoured *carrozzeria*. So when in 1950 Lancia introduced its Aurelia saloon, it was inevitable that a coupé version would be in the offing. However, the rather anonymous four-door saloon concealed a technological

tour de force, overseen by the masterly Vittorio Jano, who had joined Lancia from Alfa Romeo in 1938.

It had been during the war that Franceso de Virgillio, a young Lancia engineer, had come up with the idea of extending the concept of Lancia's long-running V4 power unit, and creating what was to be the world's first production V6 engine. Used in the Aurelia

in 1.8 litre pushrod form, drive was conveyed by a two-piece propeller shaft to a four-speed gearbox mounted integrally with the differential. The independent rear suspension by semi-trailing arms was also a world first. At the front Lancia's familiar sliding pillar suspension, introduced in 1922, was retained. Although roadholding was up to the usual Lancia standards, Aurelia sales were relatively modest and accounted for a mere 30,000 or so examples by the time production ceased in 1955.

Far more exciting was the Aurelia B20 coupé of 1951. Mounted on a shortened Aurelia underframe, the Pinin Farina body was a masterpiece of line

and proportion and is today recognized as the design classic it is. In its original form, the Aurelia saloon had proved to be underpowered and, in 1951, it and the B20 employed an enlarged 2 litre engine. Fitted in the coupé in 74bhp, high compression, twin carburettored form, this – combined with a higher rear axle ratio – ensured that the *Gran Turismo* Lancia could attain 95mph (153km/h), making it the fastest Lancia of its day.

In 1952 the Second Series B20s had their engines boosted to 80bhp and from 1953 the V6's capacity was once again increased, this time to 2.5 litres. These Third Series coupés were accordingly renamed the 2500 GT. As

a result, the GT broke the 100mph (161km/h) barrier and was capable of speeds exceeding 110mph (177km/h). The model also lived up to its looks; in 1952 a B20 won the Targa Florio road race, and in 1954 a 2500 GT gave Lancia its first Monte Carlo Rally victory.

In the meantime the model was continuing to evolve. The Fourth Series coupés of 1954 had a simplified rear end with the semi-trailing arms being replaced by the Aurelia saloon's new de Dion rear axle. By the time that production ceased in June 1958, only 3614 coupés had been built but it did not take the rest of the world's car makers long to copy the Grand Touring concept of this landmark Lancia.

Lancia Aurelia B20

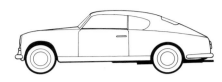

1.8 litre B21 Aurelia saloon 1950

2 litre B22 saloon 1951 —— B20 *Gran Turismo* coupé 1951

Second Series 80bhp 1952

Third Series 2.5 litre 1953

2.3 litre B12 de Dion rear axle 1954   Fourth Series, de Dion rear axle 1954

LEFT: *A 1953 B20 Third Series Aurelia known as the 2500 GT and built until 1954. This car was not originally available in Britain but, in common with other Lancias of the day, it is a right-hand-drive model.*

Specifications: Lancia Aurelia B20

Length:	14ft 1in (4293mm)
Width:	5ft 1in (1549mm)
Wheelbase:	8ft 8¾in (2661mm)
Height:	4ft 5in (1346mm)
Track:	front, 4ft 2½in (1283mm), rear, 4ft 3in (1295mm)
Unladen weight:	2344lb (1063kg)
Engine: V6, overhead valve, 72x81mm, 1991cc. Compression ratio, 8.8:1. Max power, 80bhp at 4700rpm. Max torque, 138lb/ft at 3900rpm	
Transmission:	Four-speed manual
Drive:	Rear
Suspension (front):	Independent, sliding pillar
Suspension (rear):	Independent, semi-trailing arms, coil springs
Top speed:	95mph (153km/h)
0-60mph (96km/h):	15.1 seconds
Production (total Aurelia Gran Turismo): 3614	

RIGHT: *The B20's 2.5 litre V6 engine was a world first. The component on the left of the bulkhead is the oil reservoir to lubricate the sliding pillar independent front suspension.*

ABOVE: *The elegant lines of the Pinin Farina coupé looking remarkably up to date even though designed for 1951. The twin exhaust pipes indicate the presence of a V6 power unit.*

FERRARI 340, 342, 375 AMERICA (1951-1954)

As will have already become apparent, Ferrari's road cars were, in the earliest days, closely allied to the requirements of racing. This certainly applied to the 166 Inter of 1948 and when, in 1950, Ferrari switched from a supercharged 1.5 litre V12 engine to an unblown 4.5 litre unit, it could only be a matter of time before a road-going version followed. The result was the 340 America, so called because it was targetted at the all-important transatlantic market.

In 1949 Ferrari's chief engineer, Gioacchino Colombo, had been replaced by young Aurelio Lampredi and it was he who advocated dispensing with the traditional supercharger and redesigning the V12 so that its capacity was extended from 1.5 to a maximum of 4.5 litres, as permitted by the racing formula. Such an increase could not be achieved within the original block and the result was the so called "long" engine, the length of which was 5.1in (130mm) greater than previously. This increased its overall dimensions from 37in (940mm) to 42in (1067mm). Yet another difference was that the cylinder heads were no longer detachable which permitted the use of higher compression ratios than hitherto and more potent racing fuels.

This engine first ran, in 3.3 litre sports racing form, in April 1950. Capacity was upped to 4.1 litres in the 340 Formula 1 Ferrari in July and finally to 4.5 litres in September. The 4.1 litre, 220bhp, sports racing 340 America appeared at the following month's Paris Motor Show. But the first road-going America proper, a fine Touring coupé, was displayed on the Ferrari stand at the 1951 Turin show.

The mechanical specification was otherwise similar to that of the 212 Inter, apart from the larger capacity engine which made the America the fastest roadgoing car of its day. It was capable of 150mph (241km/h), even if braking left something to be desired.

As befitted Ferrari's activities at this time, the 340 was made in small numbers with each example differing slightly from its neighbour. Grand Touring versions were also produced by Ghia and Vignale and, despite 22 Americas being built, only eight were tamed for street use. One of the more celebrated customers was Juan Peron, president of Argentina.

New Americas

The 340 was built until 1952 when it was replaced by the similar capacity 342, in which the engine's output was reduced to 200bhp. It was, therefore, more flexible than hitherto and a new synchromesh gearbox replaced the original non-synchro, five-speed unit. Only six examples were built; five of these were bodied by Pinin Farina with the remaining car allotted to Vignale. Production only ran for four months, from October 1952 to January 1953, and it was then replaced by the 4.5 litre 375 America, introduced later in the year at the Paris Motor Show. This featured a redesigned chassis. Once again, production was limited and accounted for a mere 12 cars although the model remained available until 1955. But, more significantly, these powerful, V12-engined models would establish a large-car Ferrari line.

ABOVE: *A 1954 375 America, chassis 0329/AL, with a coupé body by Pinin Farina. Exported new to America, this car has since returned to Europe.*

Ferrari 340, 342, 375 America

1.5 litre V12 "Colombo" engine 1947
|
3.3 litre V12 "Lampredi" engine 1950

4.1 litre 340 Grand Prix car 1950   4.1 litre 340 America sports racer 1950
|
4.5 litre 375 Grand Prix car 1950

4.1 litre 340 America road car 1951

4.1 litre 342 America road car 1952

4.5 litre 375 America road car 1953

LEFT: *A 340 America Touring berlinetta, one of two built, of 1951. There were, by contrast, rather more Touring barchettas (open bodies) in this albeit limited series.*

Specifications: Ferrari 340 America

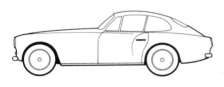

Wheelbase:	7ft 11in (2420mm)
Track:	front 4ft 2in (1278mm), rear 4ft 1in (1250mm)
Unladen weight:	2400lb (1088kg)
Engine: V12, single overhead camshaft per bank, 80x68mm, 4101cc. Compression ratio, 8:1. Max power, 220bhp at 6500rpm.	
Transmission:	Five-speed manual
Drive:	Rear
Suspension (front):	Independent, transverse leaf and wishbones
Suspension (rear):	Live axle, half-elliptic springs
Top speed:	150mph (241km/h)
0-60mph (96km/h):	9.5 seconds
Production (total 340, 342, 375):	approx 26 (roadgoing examples)

Note: Figures are not included for Length, Width and Height because all bodies built were different. Only the chassis dimensions remained constant

RIGHT: *Perhaps the best known 375, a 1954 car owned by Prince Leopold of Belgium. It has a 4.9 litre 375 Plus engine and a Pinin Farina cabriolet body on a shorter than usual chassis.*

FACEL VEGA (1954-1964)

The idea of combining a large, powerful but unde-manding American engine with a European chassis and coachwork is not new but the concept was successfully revived in the 1950's with the arrival of the Facel Vega. Fast, comfortable and highly individual, it was the only significant French Grand Tourer of the decade.

Facel is an acronym for *Forges et Ate-liers de Construction d'Eure et Loire*, a Paris-based firm which originally undertook work for the aviation indus-try and, after World War II, diversified into producing bodywork for such French car makers as Panhard and Simca and Ford's French subsidiary. When the company lost its Panhard contract, Facel's head, Jean Daninos, decided to use the spare capacity to build his own car.

Gallic Flair
The result, in the form of the Vega, was introduced at the 1954 Paris Motor Show. Stylist Brasseur designed a large and aggressive looking two-plus-two coupé with distinctive, vertically mounted twin headlamps. At the rear,

radio aerials sprouted from each wing. As Facel has no established automo-bile engineering tradition, under the car's bonnet was a 180bhp, 4.5 litre Chrysler Firedome V8 and a choice of Facel's own four-speed, all-synchro-mesh manual gearbox or automatic transmission. The car's interior was also significant for having an instru-ment layout resembling that of a small private aircraft and its central console was to be widely imitated in the 1960's. Luxurious, so-called roly poly seats were fitted and electric windows were a notable refinement.

In this form the Vega was capable of an effortless 120mph (193km/h). Capa-city subsequently rose to 4.8, 5.4 and ultimately 5.9 litres, by which time the model had been renamed the FVS and

power steering had become an option-al extra. The FVS endured until 1959, by which time a total of 357 cars had been built. There was also a four-door derivative named the Excellence, pro-duced between 1957 and 1964.

Ups And Downs
The FVS was uprated in 1959 as the HK500 with the capacity of the gas-guzzling V8 maintained at 5.9 litres but there was an optional 360bhp version. Demand was still strong and the 500 was replaced for 1962 by Facel II which retained the same chassis but was fit-ted with a new body with revised, lowered lines and an enlarged 6.3 litre Chrysler engine. Borrani lightweight wheels were used. A top line 390bhp version was capable of speeds

approaching the 140mph (225km/h). The last of 184 examples was built in 1964 which was when the company ceased car manufacture.

Facel's demise was on account of the firm having decided to produce a small car named the Facellia which re-sembled a scaled-down HK500. Unlike the existing Facels, it was powered by the firm's own purpose-designed 1.6 litre, twin-overhead-camshaft engine but was plagued by reliability prob-lems which devastated sales. Only 1258 examples were built and its failure doomed the company. In retro-spect, it is quite clear that Daninos should have stuck to his big cars with their ultra-reliable power units origi-nating from the American motor city of Detroit.

LEFT: *A left-hand-drive Facel Vega HK500 with its unmistakable front end and vertically located twin headlights. This example has been in England since 1970 and was the subject of an extensive restoration.*

BELOW: *A 1959 Facel Vega Excellence, this time with right-hand-drive. It was originally ordered by Tommy Sopwith who ran the Equipe Endeavour motor racing team.*

ABOVE: *The lines of the HK500 shown to good effect. Note that the twin exhaust pipes from the V8 engine neatly emerge from the extremities of the rear bumper.*

Facel Vega

4.5 litre Vega 1954
|
4.8 litre version 1955
|
5.4 litre version 1956
|
4.9 litre FVS version 1957 ——— 4.9 litre Excellence saloon 1957
|
5.9 litre version 1958 ——— 5.9 litre Excellence 1958
5.9 litre KH500 1959
|
6.3 litre HK500 1960 ——— 6.3 litre Excellence 1960
6.3 litre Facel II 1962

Specifications: Facel Vega FVS (1958)

Length:	15ft (4572mm)
Width:	5ft 10in (1778mm)
Wheelbase:	8ft 9in (2667mm)
Height:	4ft 5in (1346mm)
Track:	front 4ft 8in (1422mm), rear 4ft 9in (1448mm)
Unladen weight:	4033lb (1829kg)
Engine: V8, overhead valve, 100x92mm, 5801cc. Compression ratio, 9.25:1. Max power, 325bhp at 4600rpm. Max torque, 430lb/ft at 2800rpm.	
Transmission:	Four-speed manual
Drive:	Rear
Suspension (front):	Independent, coil springs and wishbones
Suspension (rear):	Live axle, half-elliptic springs
Top speed:	134mph (216km/h)
0-60mph (96km/h):	9.8 seconds
Production (total V8):	1271

FERRARI 250 GT (1954-1964)

Prior to the arrival of the 250 GT in 1954, Ferrari had produced its cars piecemeal and with no two alike. Not only did this change to a great extent with the 250's appearance, this was the first Ferrari to be built in anything like reasonable quantities, an event made possible by an historic agreement between Enzo Ferrari and Battista Pinin Farina. As a result, the respected Turin coachbuilding concern undertook to produce bodies for Ferrari on a regular basis and it has been doing precisely that ever since.

Ferrari 250 GT

```
2 litre 166 Inter 1948
    │
2.3 litre 195 Inter 1950
    │                              4.1 litre
    │                           340 America 1951
    │                                  │
2.6 litre 212 Inter 1952              4.1 litre
    │                           342 America 1952
    │                                  │
    │                               4.5 litre
    │                           375 America 1953
    │                                  │
    │                                3 litre
    │                           250 Europa 1953
    │                                  │
3 litre 250 GT Europa 1954 ───────────┘
    │
250 GT Boano 1956
    │
250 GT Pininfarina 1958 ──────┐
    │                         │
              250 GTE 2 + 2 1960
```

With its source of bodies assured, Ferrari was able to increase production. To give this initiative perspective, in the years between 1948 and 1954 the firm built some 35 road cars per annum, but in 1964, which was the year 250 GT production ended, this had risen to around the 670 figure.

The 250 Europa GT, to give this two-seater model its (brief) full title, was introduced at the 1954 Paris Motor Show. Outwardly the Pinin Farina body resembled that of its 250 Europa predecessor, although there were some subtle changes made beneath the bodywork. The oval section tubular chassis was reduced by 7.9in (200mm) to improve roadholding, the rear members now swept over the back axle rather than passed beneath it, and the established transverse leaf front suspension was replaced by more conventional coils and wishbones. The 2.9 litre V12 engine was a reaffirmation of Colombo's design, which had been supplanted by a second V12 created by his successor Lampredi, and had, therefore, not powered a Ferrari road car since 1952.

Speed and Looks
But the magic was soon apparent. The 250 looked good, the superbly tractable race-breed engine was like no other and ensured that this Ferrari could comfortably exceed 125mph (201km/h). Handling was impressive, although steering and ride still left something to be desired.

In 1956 the range developed with the arrival of the 250 GT Boano coupé. This was essentially similar to its predecessor and was so called because the body, although designed by Pinin Farina, was built by Boano, as Farina was in the throws of reorganization. The last cars carried the Ellena name, the *carrozzeria* having been so retitled after Boano left in 1957 to join Fiat.

The new 250 GT of 1958-60 was a restatement of the original Pinin Farina theme but, more significantly, it was

the best-selling Ferrari of its day with an unprecedented 350 examples built.

These 250s were uncompromising two-seaters but, in 1960, Ferrari unveiled the first car he had marketed with two-plus-two accommodation. Developed in more than rigorous secrecy, the 250 GTE 2 + 2 was first seen at the 1960 Le Mans race, where it was used as the course car. From the outset, the intention was that the introduction of two small rear seats would not sully the magnificent lines of the Pinin Farina berlinetta body. So the 250's 8ft 6in (2600mm) chassis remained inviolate but more interior space was created by moving the 3 litre V12 engine 8in (203mm) forward in the frame. In 1963, the final year of manu-

facture, the car was fitted with a 4 litre engine. Sales eventually reached the 950 mark, which ensured that a two-plus-two would remain a feature of the Ferrari range from there on.

It should not be assumed that Ferrari had ignored its traditional two-seater line and this was most memorably perpetuated in the breathtakingly elegant 250 GT Berlinetta Lusso of 1962 which is described on pages 106-7.

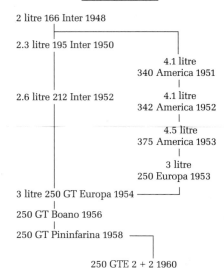

ABOVE: *The 250 GT was produced in short wheelbase form between 1959 and 1962. This right-hand-drive example of 1960 was the first Ferrari to be sold by British distributors, Maranello Concessionaires.*

LEFT: *The first version of the 250 GT was called the Europa and 35 examples were built in 1954 and 1955. As with the vast majority of 250s, the body is by Pinin Farina.*

LEFT: *The Pinin Farina-styled 250 Boano GT of 1956-58 was completed from 1957 by Ellena, and these later cars are identifiable by a higher roof line than hitherto. This is one of 50 examples built.*

Specifications: Ferrari 250 GT

Length:	15ft 5in (4699mm)
Width:	5ft 6in (1676mm)
Wheelbase:	8ft 6in (2600mm)
Height:	4ft 2in (1270mm)
Track:	front, 4ft 5⅓in (1354mm), rear, 4ft 5in (1349mm)
Unladen weight:	2816lb (1277kg)

Engine: V12, single overhead camshaft per bank, 73x58mm, 2953cc. Compression ratio, 8.5:1. Max power, 220bhp at 7000rpm. Max torque, 198lb/ft at 5500rpm.

Transmission:	Four-speed manual
Drive:	Rear
Suspension (front):	Independent, coil springs and wishbones
Suspension (rear):	Live axle, half-elliptic springs
Top speed:	125mph (201km/h)
0-60mph (96km/h):	9.1 seconds
Production (total 250 GT):	approx 2500

In 1955 Alfa Romeo introduced its popular but visually undistinguished 1.3 litre Giulietta saloon although it was preceded in 1954 by its handsome Bertone-styled Sprint derivative! This in turn led to the Giulietta Sprint Speciale of 1957, also by Bertone, and universally acclaimed as being one of the best looking and memorable Alfa Romeos of the post-war years.

The creation of the Giulietta SS is closely entwined with Alfa Romeo's relationship, formed in 1953, with Bertone. The Milan car company was seeking a coachbuilder to give practical expression to its researches into the relationship between automobile styling, speed and aerodynamics. The outcome, later in the year, was the visually extravagant Berlina Aerodinamica Tecnica, better known as BAT-5, the earlier four examples having proved to be unsuitable for one reason or another. Three further variations, BAT-7, 8 and 9 were produced, the latter in 1955. These exercises brought both parties much publicity, but in the meantime the firm had launched the Bertone-styled and Alfa Romeo-completed Giulietta Sprint, which was a highly competent exercise in inspired though conventional styling built on the saloon's underframe.

Inspired By A BAT

However, the Giulietta SS, introduced at the 1957 Turin Motor Show, was a far more adventurous rendering in which the wind-cheating BAT influences were readily apparent. Unlike the Sprint, the complete car was built by Bertone, first at its Turin factory and from 1959 at a new and larger premises at Grugliasco outside the city.

The Sprint was an impressive performer, capable of a spirited 110mph (177km/h) but the idea of the Sprint Speciale was to create a lighter, more aerodynamically efficient and therefore faster version. As it happened, the weight of both cars would ultimately be about the same, apart from the first 153 examples of the SS which were bodied in aluminium. When Bertone moved to its new factory, however, the construction material was changed to steel. There was also a characteristically distinctive Zagato version, designated the SZ, which accounted for 200 units. A similar Giulia TZ1/2 appeared during the 1963-1967 era.

The two-seater Sprint Speciale was built on a shortened Giulietta underframe, with a 7ft 5in (2260mm) wheelbase, which was 4in (102mm) less than

RIGHT: *In addition to the Bertone-bodied Giulietta SS, Zagato also produced its own very distinctive version, which was created for use in Grand Touring competition,*

that of the Sprint. But unlike that car, which used an 80bhp version of the Giulietta's 1.3 litre, twin-overhead-camshaft engine, the SS was powered by a 100bhp derivative with a higher compression ratio and a pair of twin choke Weber carburettors. A five-speed gearbox was specified. These ministrations meant that it was capable of speeds approaching 120mph (193km/h). The SS remained in production throughout the Giulietta's life, although output was relatively modest and accounted for a mere 1366 cars built by 1962.

In that year the Giulietta saloon made way for the 1.6 litre Giulia but those lovely SS lines had not begun to date and in 1963 came the outwardly similar 112bhp Giulia version. Top speed was not affected but acceleration was improved. It was also more popular than its predecessor, although demand remained limited and the last of 1400 examples of this stylish, small Alfa Romeo left Bertone's works in 1965.

Alfa Romeo Giulietta and Giulia Sprint Speciale

1.9 litre experimental BAT 1953

1.3 litre Giulietta Sprint 1954

1.3 litre Giulietta saloon 1955

1.3 litre Giulietta Sprint Speciale 1957

1.6 litre Giulia saloon 1962

1.6 litre Giulia Sprint Speciale 1963

Specifications: Alfa Romeo Giulietta SS

Length:	13ft 11in (4242mm)
Width:	5ft 5in (1651mm)
Wheelbase:	7ft 4in (2235mm)
Height:	4ft 1in (1245mm)
Track:	front, 4ft 2¾in (1290mm), rear, 4ft 2in (1270mm)
Unladen weight:	1896lb (860kg)
Engine: Four cylinder, twin overhead camshaft, 74×75mm, 1290cc. Compression ratio, 9.7:1. Max power, 100bhp at 6500rpm.	
Transmission:	Five-speed manual
Drive:	Rear
Suspension (front):	Independent, coil springs and wishbones
Suspension (rear):	Live axle, coil springs
Top speed:	120mph (193km/h)
0-60mph (96km/h):	12.4 seconds
Production (total Giulietta/ Giulia Bertone SS):	2766

DLA 755T

ABOVE: *The sensational lines of the Bertone-bodied Giulietta Sprint Speciale. Although this is a British domiciled car, the model was only produced in left-hand-drive form.*

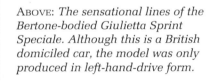

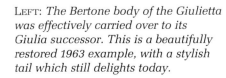

JGC 276C

LEFT: *The Bertone body of the Giulietta was effectively carried over to its Giulia successor. This is a beautifully restored 1963 example, with a stylish tail which still delights today.*

Maserati 3500 GT (1957-1964)

During the 1950's Ferrari enjoyed an almost unrivalled supremacy on the motoring circuits of the world. The eventual challenge to this dominance came from another Italian marque in the shape of Maserati. In 1957 its all-conquering 250F provided Juan Fangio with his fifth world championship title. But grand prix competition is an expensive business and the Orsi family, which owned Maserati, was forced to withdraw from racing at the end of that triumphant season. In addition, it recognized the urgent need to generate funds by following Ferrari's example and producing a line of road cars. The outcome, in 1957, was the 3500 GT.

This was by no means the first such model. Road cars had been produced since the company's inception in 1926, but they had always played second fiddle to the racers and output had been limited and the programme uncoordinated. All this changed with the arrival of the 1957 grand tourer.

Introduced at that year's Geneva Motor Show, the new model was powered by a detuned 226bhp version of the 3.5 litre, twin-overhead-camshaft, six-cylinder engine from the firm's 350S sports racer. It was mounted in a tubular chassis with coil and wishbones independent front suspension and a cart sprung rear. Like Ferrari, the Modena-based firm possessed no bodyshop, so coachwork was bought out, in this instance from Touring of Milan, which produced an agreeable two-plus-two coupé.

By the 1957 Turin Motor Show, Maserati's chief engineer, Giulio Alfieri, dissatisfied with the lubrication system of the engine, redesigned it and modifications were made to the camshafts and porting which produced a further 4bhp. Production of the 3500 GT began late in 1957 and got properly into its stride in 1958.

Not surprisingly the new Maserati was a formidable performer. Capable of 130mph (209km/h), it looked and sounded sensational but road-holding and cornering, particularly in the wet, left something to be desired.

In 1959 Alfieri redesigned the car's engine with a view to making it a smoother and more flexible unit and power output rose to 260bhp. Maserati also swiftly responded to other limitations as soon as they became apparent. The original four-speed gearbox had proved unsatisfactory and the car's drum brakes, although servo-assisted, were not really up to the job. Optional front discs arrived late in 1959 and were standardized in 1960, while a five-speed gearbox followed in 1961. The engine was fitted with fuel injection in 1962 and disc brakes were extended to the rear wheels. From 1959 there was also a short chassis version although this was mostly produced in Vignale Spider form.

Touring was responsible for bodying practically all 3500s although Allemano, Bertone and Frua all made contributions. Sales were encouraging and 3500 GT production stood at 1972 examples by the time that it made way for its Sebring successor in 1964.

Maserati 3500 GT

3.5 litre 350S sports racer 1956

3.5 litre 3500 GT 1957

Touring coupé   Vignale spider 1959

Sebring Vignale coupé 1962

3.5 litre Mistral 1964

Frua coupé | Frua spider

3.7 litre Mistral 1965   3.7 litre 1965

4 litre 1966   4 litre 1966

LEFT: *The 3500 GT was Maserati's first essay into series production. Like most examples of this car, this is a Touring-bodied coupé.*

ABOVE: *Virtually all the open 3500s featured Vignale coachwork but this was a 1959 attempt by Frua to produce a 3500 Spider. Only this example was built, although Frua later bodied the Maserati Mistral.*

RIGHT: *Head-on view of the Frua-bodied 3500. Maserati's trident badge is prominently featured and was inspired by the statue of Neptune in Bologna where the marque was born.*

Specifications: Maserati 3500 GT

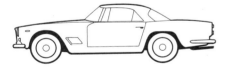

Length:	15ft 8in (4775mm)
Width:	5ft 9in (1753mm)
Wheelbase:	8ft 6in (2591mm)
Height:	4ft 3in (1295mm)
Track:	front, 4ft 7in (1397mm), rear, 4ft 6in (1372mm)
Unladen weight:	2866lb (1300kg)
Engine: Six cylinder, twin overhead camshaft, 86x100mm, 3485cc. Compression ratio, 8.5:1. Max power, 220bhp at 5500rpm. Max torque, 259lb/ft at 4000rpm.	
Transmission:	Four-speed manual
Drive:	Rear
Suspension (front):	Independent, coil springs and wishbones
Suspension (rear):	Live axle, half-elliptic springs
Top speed:	130mph (209km/h)
0-60mph (96km/h):	8.1 seconds
Production:	1972

LOTUS ELITE (1957-1963)

Although Britain is the true home of the open two-seater sports car, in the 1950's increasing numbers of its car companies began to turn to the Grand Touring concept. Unquestionably the most impressive, both from a stylistic and mechanical standpoint, was Lotus's Elite which also had the distinction of being the world's first glass-fibre monocoque car.

In 1956 the North London-based Lotus Cars produced the open, sports-racing Lotus Eleven. Colin Chapman, the company's dynamic founder engineer, wished to produce a new closed car but felt that the Eleven was unsuitable for such an exercise, so in 1955 work began on a completely new design titled the Mark 14. It was provisionally named Lynx and in 1957 became the two-seater Elite.

A key player in the model's creation was chartered accountant Peter Kirwan-Taylor, who already owned a Mark 6 Lotus and possessed a formidable flair for styling. It was he who was responsible for the Elite's timeless lines which, quite deliberately, possessed the minimum of external decoration. As work proceeded, there was some further input from aerodynamicist Frank Costin and Ford stylist John Frayling.

The Lynx became the Elite at the 1957 London Motor Show where *The Autocar* described it as "the most significant single exhibit". It thus attracted considerable attention, both for its looks and adventurous mechanicals. Power came from a 75bhp, 1.2 litre Coventry Climax engine, canted to permit a low bonnet line. Suspension was all independent, with coils and wishbones at the front and Chapman struts at the rear. Disc brakes were fitted all round and were inboard at the rear.

A Revolutionary Body

However, it was the monocoque glass-fibre body which bristled with flair and ingenuity. In its original form it consisted of no less than 60 separate components although, for production purposes, this was reduced to just three. An unusual feature was the curved windows which did not wind down; they could only be removed entirely and stored behind the seats.

As the Elite turned the scales at the mere 1484lb (673kg), it proved to be a sensational performer, being able to attain 115mph (185km/h) and the impressive roadholding reflected Lotus's racing experience. The car was also economical and could average 34mpg (8.3 litres/100km).

It would be 14 months before the first customer, band leader Chris Barber, took delivery of the first Elite in December 1958. In the meantime, Lotus had moved in mid-1959 from its cramped Tottenham premises to a new, larger factory in Cheshunt, Hertfordshire. Once again, production began in earnest. The car cost £1951 and, from late 1961, the Elite was also offered in kit form for £1299. Early examples did suffer from quality shortcomings, although the Series 2 cars for 1961, with a revised rear suspension, were an improvement. A new Special Equipment version was also offered with twin rather than a single carburettor, 83bhp engine and close-ratio ZF gearbox. In 1961 came the Super 95 (which reflected the power developed by its engine) for those enthusiasts who wished to race their Elites. This was, in turn, followed by the Super 100 and 105.

Ironically, it was the Elite's fixed roof that proved to be unpopular with many enthusiasts as the monocoque hull tended to amplify mechanical noises. When the Elite was replaced by the Elan in 1962, Colin Chapman ensured that it was an open model. He also calculated that he was losing £100 on every Elite Lotus built . . .

BELOW: *The Elite's 1.2 litre, single-overhead-camshaft Coventry Climax FWE engine was canted to permit the low bonnet line. The twin SU carburettors arrived for 1962.*

RIGHT: *The Elite was the world's first glass fibre monocoque. It was a closed car so that reinforcement could be provided by the roof. This is a 1962 example.*

LEFT: The Elite ran with some success at Le Mans between 1960 and 1964 as private and works entries. This car, complete with British Racing Drivers Club badge, is one of the latter.

BELOW: The lack of any external decoration makes the rear of the Elite still look surprisingly modern. Stylist Peter Kirwan-Taylor did not want the car to date.

Specifications: Lotus Elite

Length:	12ft 6in (3810mm)
Width:	4ft 10in (1473mm)
Wheelbase:	8ft 5in (2565mm)
Height:	3ft 10in (1168mm)
Track:	front, 3ft 11in (1194mm), rear, 4ft 4in (1321mm)
Unladen weight:	1484lb (673kg)
Engine: Four cylinder, single overhead camshaft, 76x66mm, 1216cc. Compression ratio, 10:1. Max power, 75bhp at 6700rpm. Max torque, 76lb/ft at 3500rpm.	
Transmission:	Four-speed manual
Drive:	Rear
Suspension (front):	Independent, coil springs and wishbones
Suspension (rear):	Independent, Chapman strut, coil springs
Top speed:	115mph (185km/h)
0-60mph (96km/h):	13.4 seconds
Production:	approx 988

The most celebrated Aston Martins of the post-war years were the new series of Grand Tourers, of which the first was the DB4. This evolved into the greatly refined DB5, forever remembered as James Bond's lovely but lethal transport in the 1964 film *Goldfinger*. The series was completed by the longer wheelbase DB6 with its distinctive spoilered tail.

When the DB4 was unveiled at the 1958 London Motor Show at £3976, it was the most expensive Aston Martin in the company's history. Unusually, the car was completely new with no carryover parts from previous models. The magnificent, close coupled coupé, two-plus-two body was styled by Touring of Milan and made at Aston Martin's Newport Pagnell factory under the Italian company's *Superleggera* principles whereby a network of load-bearing steel tubes were built up, to which light aluminium body panels were then attached.

Teething Troubles

Under the bonnet was a 3.7 litre, twin-overhead-camshaft, aluminium, six-cylinder engine developing 240bhp. All-round disc brakes were fitted to arrest the model's 0-60mph (96km/h) time of around nine seconds and a flat-out speed of 140mph (225km/h). In truth, the model's development had not been fully completed by the time that it entered production and early DB4s suffered from engine and gearbox reliability problems, although these were largely resolved by the time its manufacture ceased in 1963. As followed Aston Martin precedent, for 1962 there was a more powerful and popular 260bhp Vantage version.

For sports racing there was also an outwardly similar, lightweight, short chassis, 300bhp DB4 GT of 1959-63, of which 81 were built. Some examples were bodied by Zagato and this rare and desirable variant is described on page 176.

The Impressive DB5

In 1964 the mainstream model was replaced by the greatly improved DB5, with an enlarged 4 litre engine, which outwardly resembled the last of the DB4s. Soon after the DB5 entered production, its troublesome gearbox, built by David Brown, was replaced by a five-speed ZF unit and no more problems were experienced from that quarter. The model was offered with a 282bhp engine as standard, but for 1965 a 314bhp Vantage option was offered. By the time that the DB5

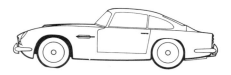

Specifications: Aston Martin DB4

Length:	14ft 8in (4470mm)
Width:	5ft 6in (1676mm)
Wheelbase:	8ft 2in (2489mm)
Height:	4ft 3in (1295mm)
Track:	front, 4ft 6in (1372mm), rear, 4ft 5in (1346mm)
Unladen weight:	2884lb (1308kg)
Engine: Six cylinder, twin overhead camshaft, 92x92mm, 3670cc. Compression ratio, 8.2:1. Max power, 240bhp at 5500rpm. Max torque, 240lb/ft at 5500rpm.	
Transmission:	Four-speed manual
Drive:	Rear
Suspension (front):	Independent, coil springs and wishbones
Suspension (rear):	Live axle, coil springs
Top speed:	140mph (225km/h)
0-60mph (96km/h):	9.3 seconds
Production (total DB4, DB5, DB6):	3876

ceased production in 1965, 1023 examples had been built which compared with a total of 1100 DB4s. It made way for the DB6 which remained in production for six years.

Despite the fact that the DB4 and 5 had small back seats, the reality was that they could only be comfortably used by children. In a bid to broaden the new model's appeal by improving the rear leg room, the DB6's wheelbase was 3¾in (95mm) greater than that of the DB5. The car also differed by having an aerodynamically efficient Kamm tail with a distinctive spoiler.

The 4 litre engine was essentially carried over from the DB5 and there was once again the option of a Vantage engine, of 325bhp, and from 1967, power steering. Because the model remained in production for longer than any of its predecessors, the DB6 was the best-selling Aston Martin of the range and found 1753 buyers. A Mk II version appeared for 1970. From 1967 it was produced alongside the new DBS, which was powered by the DB6's engine until 1969, when it received Aston Martin's long awaited V8. A new chapter was beginning.

ABOVE: *A Mark II DB6 Vantage, identifiable by its flared wheel arches. Introduced for 1970, it was only built in that year.*

RIGHT: *The scarce and delectable short wheelbase DB4GT. Outwardly similar to the DB4, this example, DB4GT/0111/R, is identifiable by its lightweight Borrani wheels.*

Aston Martin DB4, DB5, DB6

3.7 litre DB4 1958

— DB 4 sports racer 1959

— DB4 GT Zagato 1960

4 litre DB5 1964

4 litre DB6 1965 —

4 litre DBS 1967

5.3 litre V8 DBS 1969

RIGHT: *The DB5 which appeared in 1964 was made famous by James Bond. This is a 1965 example with a personalized number plate which Ian Fleming's hero might not have appreciated!*

VOLVO P1800, 1800S, 1800E (1961-1972)

Like Spain with its Pegaso, Sweden could never be considered to have a Grand Touring tradition. Nevertheless, in 1961 the Volvo company introduced the P1800, a distinctive model which was destined for a respectable 11 year manufacturing life. Until 1963 it was built in Britain by Jensen, although thereafter its manufacture reverted to Sweden.

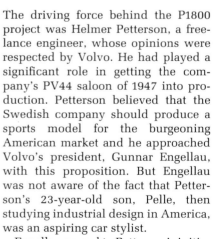

ABOVE: *The P1800, P stood for personwagen, with distinctive cows' horn front bumpers. They were replaced for 1965 by more conventional straight ones.*

BELOW: *A very presentable P1800S, so named because from 1963 the cars were Swedish built. The twin exhaust pipes were a notable feature and arrived for the 1966 season.*

Volvo P1800

1.6 litre 120 series saloon 1956

1.8 litre P1800 1961

Swedish-built P1800S 1963

2 litre P1800E 1969

P1800ES estate 1971

The driving force behind the P1800 project was Helmer Petterson, a free-lance engineer, whose opinions were respected by Volvo. He had played a significant role in getting the company's PV44 saloon of 1947 into production. Petterson believed that the Swedish company should produce a sports model for the burgeoning American market and he approached Volvo's president, Gunnar Engellau, with this proposition. But Engellau was not aware of the fact that Petterson's 23-year-old son, Pelle, then studying industrial design in America, was an aspiring car stylist.

Engellau agreed to Petterson's initiative and the latter then went to Italy on Volvo's behalf to engage in dialogue with the Ghia and Frua styling houses. The outcome was no less than five paper proposals, but the design chosen was Pelle Petterson's, whose involve-

ment in the project was still not known to the Volvo president.

Nevertheless, this was fortuitous because the P1800, with its well executed lines and by-then unfashionable tail fins, looked like no other car. It was to become well-known to a worldwide audience because this sleek Volvo coupé provided transport for Simon Templar, *The Saint* of the television series of the same name.

Made In England

Originally the P1800's body was to have been built by Karmann in Germany. When this proved impossible, the company approached Pressed Steel in Britain and it produced P1800 hulls at Linwood, Scotland. They were then delivered to the West Bromwich factory of Jensen Motors for final completion in left- and right-hand-drive forms as appropriate.

Mechanicals were mostly courtesy of Volvo's P120/Amazon saloon range with the 1.8 litre four coaxed to produce 100bhp. The specifications were otherwise conventional with coils and wishbones at the front and rear half-elliptics.

The car was strictly a two-seater although there was some room in the back for children. Well received by the motoring press, the P1800 could attain a top speed of 105mph (169km/h) and was a pleasing, seemingly viceless, well-equipped car, and good value in Britain where it was priced at £1850.

But Volvo soon became concerned at the quality of Jensen's work. In 1963 final assembly was transferred from West Bromwich to Volvo's factory at Lundby, although Pressed Steel continued to produce the bodies. The model was accordingly renamed the 1800S, for Sweden.

ABOVE: *The P1800ES estate car which appeared in 1971 and was built until 1973, a year after the coupé in the background had ceased production. The ES was fitted with a distinctive glass hatchback.*

Engine capacity was increased to 2 litres for 1969 and the car became known as the 1800E, E standing for *Einspritzung*, which is German for fuel injection, the component in question being a Bosch system.

From 1970 the cars were completely Swedish built, the body tooling having been transported there from Scotland. Production ceased in 1972 but then was extended for a further year because of the arrival, in 1971, of the 1800ES estate car. However, only 8078 examples of the estate were built before the entire series came to the end of the line in 1973.

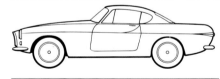

Specifications: Volvo P1800	
Length:	14ft 5in (4394mm)
Width:	5ft 6in (1676mm)
Wheelbase:	8ft (2438mm)
Height:	4ft 2in (1270mm)
Track:	front and rear, 4ft 3in (1295mm)
Unladen weight:	2403lb (1090kg)

Engine: Four cylinder, overhead valve, 84x80mm, 1778cc. Compression ratio, 9.5:1. Max power, 100bhp at 5500rpm. Max torque, 110lb/ft at 3800rpm.

Transmission:	Four-speed manual
Drive:	Rear
Suspension (front):	Independent, coil springs and wishbones
Suspension (rear):	Live axle, coil springs
Top speed:	105mph (169km/h)
0-60mph (96km/h):	13.5 seconds
Production (total P1800, 1800S, 1800E):	41,406

Ferrari 250 GT Berlinetta Lusso (1962-1964)

Since 1954 the development of Ferrari cars has been inexorably linked with the respected Turin styling house of Pininfarina. While its coachwork has invariably been impressive, a handful of renderings stand out for being veritable milestones in the history of car design. One such is the berlinetta (closed two-door) body which graced Ferrari's 250 GT chassis produced between 1962 and 1964.

In 1960 Ferrari introduced its first two-plus-two in the form of the 250 GTE 2+2 (see pages 94-5), but the two-seater line was perpetuated in the 250 GT Lusso (for luxury) berlinetta of the same year which, perversely, was strictly a competition machine and, as such, unsuitable for street use. Only about 80 examples were built until the end of 1962, but by this time Ferrari and Pininfarina had come up with a new road car which, confusingly, shared the same name. It was one in which comfort and refinement were the keynotes.

Pininfarina's Favourite

One of the prototypes was unveiled at the 1962 Paris Motor Show in October, where it was personally presented by Battista Pininfarina who was to run a Lusso as his own chosen transport. The coupé body was a triumph with echoes at the front of the 1960-62 250 GT berlinetta, while at the back was a sharply truncated Kamm tail. This had been first used by Ferrari in 1961 and was a notable feature of the legendary sports-racing GTO announced earlier in 1962. Although designed by Pininfarina, the bodies were built in Modena by Scaglietti.

As far as the chassis was concerned, the short 7ft 10½in (2400mm) wheelbase was retained but the GTO-derived frame was redesigned to permit the engine to be moved forward to allow more interior room; there was even space for a certain amount of luggage behind the bucket seats.

The triple-carburettored, 3 litre V12 engine, with a single overhead camshaft per cylinder bank, developed 250bhp. Its block was shared with its 250 GT contemporaries while the internals were courtesy of the Lusso of the 1960-62 era. The gearbox was a four-speed, all-synchromesh unit. Suspension followed previous practice with the customary coil springs and wishbones at the front, while the half-elliptic-sprung live rear axle was retained at the rear.

A further Lusso prototype, which

Specifications: Ferrari 250 GT Berlinetta Lusso

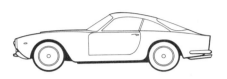

Length:	14ft 5in (4394mm)
Width:	5ft 8in (1727mm)
Wheelbase:	7ft 10½in (2400mm)
Height:	4ft 2in (1270mm)
Track:	front, 4ft 7in (1394mm), rear, 4ft 6½in (1387mm)
Unladen weight:	2337lb (1060kg)
Engine:	V12, single overhead camshaft per bank, 73x58mm, 2953cc. Compression ratio, 9.2:1. Max power, 250bhp at 7000rpm. Max torque, 206lb/ft at 5500rpm.
Transmission:	Four-speed manual
Drive:	Rear
Suspension (front):	Independent, coil springs and wishbones
Suspension (rear):	Live axle, half-elliptic springs
Top speed:	140mph (225km/h)
0-60mph (96km/h):	7.4 seconds
Production:	approx 350

barely differed from its predecessor, appeared at the 1962 Turin Motor Show in November and the first deliveries were made at the end of the year. Like the 2+2 GTE, the car was also available in right-hand-drive form for some export markets.

Speed And Style

The model performed as well as it looked. Top speed was in excess of 140mph (225km/h) with its standard rear axle ratio, and over 150mph (241km/h) with the optional higher one. On the debit side, the stock ratio tended to be on the low side so that the engine ran at a higher speed than necessary, which contributed to interior noise. The only other notable limitation was the absence of a five-speed gearbox.

The final Berlinetta Lusso was built late in 1964, by which time 350 cars had been completed. This was the last of the 250 GT series; in the course of ten years, approximately 2550 cars had been produced.

ABOVE: *Breathtaking elegance; this Pininfarina-bodied Berlinetta Lusso with its distinctive Kamm tail dates from 1963. Ferrari had first used the feature on the GTO sports racer.*

RIGHT: *Ferrari's prancing horse badge adorns the radiator grille of this Lusso. The fog lamps, recessed into the body, were standardized shortly after the model entered production.*

Ferrari 250 GT Berlinetta Lusso

3 litre 250 GT Europa 1954
|
250 GT Boano 1956
|
250 GT pininfarina 1958
|
3 litre
250 GT Lusso
short wheelbase
sports racer 1960

3 litre 250 GT————————3 litre
Berlinetta Lusso 1962   250 GTO 1962

– – – – out of production

RIGHT: *Head-on view of this legendary roadgoing Ferrari, complete with identifying registration number. Although this is a left-hand-drive Berlinetta Lusso, there were some right-hand-drive examples.*

STUDEBAKER AVANTI (1962-1963)

The Avanti coupé, a glass-fibre-bodied American sports car with a distinctly European appearance, was produced in the final years of the foundering Studebaker company. Although it made little impact on the firm's tottering finances, so advanced were its specifications that the car does not look out of place today.

Studebaker, which had been building cars at South Bend, Indiana since 1904, was in deep financial trouble when in 1961 it acquired a new president named Sherwood H. Egbert. He wasted little time in commissioning the Avanti which was to be one of the company's most famous cars. From 1936 until 1955 Studebaker had retained the services of leading American industrial designer, the French-born Raymond Loewy, to style its products and Egbert was quick to reactivate the association. The outcome, announced at the 1962 New York Auto Show, was the strikingly unconventional Avanti (which significantly is the Italian word for "forward").

The car was based on a shortened version of the company's Lark convertible chassis and its engine was Studebaker's 289cid (4.7 litres) V8 which developed 240bhp in its basic R1 form. There was also a Paxton supercharged R2 option in which the engine was enlarged to 304cid (5 litres) and was available in three phases of tune. Mechanical innovation did not stop there as the car, along with some of its Lark and Hawk contemporaries, was fitted with Dunlop front disc brakes made under licence by Bendix, the first occasion that they had been specified for an American production car.

Radical Style

The most striking feature of the glass-fibre body was the apparent absence of a radiator grille. Instead, like Citroën's revolutionary DS of 1955, in the interests of good aerodynamics the air intake was located beneath the front bumper. There was no external decoration; the car featured a sharp wing line, a so-called "Coke bottle" shape and large rear window. The Avanti's interior was similarly distinctive and possessed an aviation flavour: the white on black instruments were bathed in a soft red light for night driving and many of the controls were placed, aircraft style, in the roof.

The choice of glass-fibre for the Avanti's body was dictated by the fact that it would have taken 15 months and $20 million to tool up in steel, whereas the respective figures were six months and $1 million to do the job in glass-fibre. Unfortunately, this choice proved to contribute to the project's undoing because the Moulded Glass Fiber Works of Astrabula, Ohio, which was to build the bodies, ran into production difficulties and Studebaker took over the work itself. Although a prototype was ready in time for the New York Auto Show in April 1962, and the first of the 125mph (201km/h) Avantis was delivered in June, the cars were continually in short supply and many potential customers turned to another glass-fibre-bodied sports car in the shape of Chevrolet's Corvette Sting Ray, sensationally restyled by William Mitchell.

Only 3834 Avantis were built in

1963 and, in November, Egbert retired from the Studebaker presidency suffering from cancer. A further 809 examples were manufactured in 1964 but, in December, it was decided to transfer Studebaker production to the company's factory at Hamilton, Canada and cars continued to be built there until 1966.

This did not include the Avanti, however, because in 1965 two South Bend Studebaker dealers, Leo Newman and Nathan D. Altman, bought the model's jigs and tooling. Later in the same year came Avanti II, externally similar to the original car but powered by a 327cid (5358cc) Chevrolet Corvette V8 engine. It was built at South Bend until 1987, no less than 25 years after the Avanti first appeared.

RIGHT: *The Avanti coupé had an unorthodox front end in which the air intake was located below the bumper, so anticipating current trends. Note the stylized S for Studebaker on the bonnet of this 1963 example.*

ABOVE: *As with the front of the Avanti, there was the minimum of decoration at the rear, unlike many of its contemporaries. This is one of the post-Studebaker cars.*

LEFT: *A 1977 Avanti highlights the timeless quality of the Raymond Loewy design. Little wonder that this example still looks good 14 years after Studebaker ceased production.*

Specifications: Studebaker Avanti

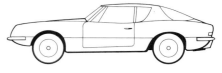

Length:	16ft (4877mm)
Width:	5ft 10in (1778mm)
Wheelbase:	9ft 1in (2769mm)
Height:	4ft 5in (1346mm)
Track:	front 4ft 9in (1448mm), rear 4ft 8in (1422mm)
Unladen weight:	3310lb (1501kg)
Engine: V8, overhead valve, 90x91mm, 289cid (4725cc). Compression ratio, 8.5:1. Max power, 210bhp at 4500rpm. Max torque, 300lb/ft at 2800rpm.	
Transmission:	Three-speed manual
Drive:	Rear
Suspension (front):	Independent, coil springs and wishbones
Suspension (rear):	Live axle, half-elliptic springs
Top speed:	125mph (201km/h)
0-60mph (96km/h):	8.2 seconds
Production:	4643

BUICK RIVIERA (1962-1965)

What was regarded in its day as the best looking car in America was not a roadster but the Buick Riviera sports coupé. It was visually impressive, and it handled considerably better than the vast majority of its transatlantic contemporaries. But what made the Riviera so memorable was the magnificent, crisply styled body by General Motors' design supremo, William Mitchell, in which European design influences were ingeniously united with those of the New World.

This was a car which did not start life as a Buick but as a Cadillac. Mitchell had wanted to revive La Salle, which was a sort of poor man's Cadillac built between 1927 and 1940, and the La Salle II convertible was displayed at the 1955 General Motors' Motorama, where new ideas and concepts were publicly aired. Its lines were the work of Buick stylist Ned Nickles but the car never entered production. Although the concept was, stylistically, a dead end, its creation did encourage the corporation to pursue the "personal luxury" theme to compete with Ford's four-seater Thunderbird introduced in 1958. At this time Buick sales were in the doldrums and so the division took over the project and gave it the Riviera name that had been used by the marque since 1949.

Unquestionably, the most impressive aspect of the Riviera was its body, masterminded by the talented Mitchell, which represented a careful blend of American and European themes. The latter contribution emerged as a result of a visit by Mitchell to London where he stayed at the exclusive Claridge's hotel. While there, he was greatly impressed by the lines of a Rolls-Royce saloon which he saw parked outside and, on his return to America, informed his stylist, Chuck Jordan, that he wanted a change of direction – a car that was a "Ferrari-Rolls-Royce". The first styling clay was completed early in 1961 and a projected run of 40,000 cars was specified. The Riviera was to be launched in 1962 for the 1963 season.

The Riviera was only produced in hardtop coupé body form and its fine and delicately proportioned roof contours, low lines and distinctive frameless side windows were widely applauded. Power was provided by Buick's top line 325bhp, 401cid (6.5 litres) V8 engine but it was only available with automatic transmission. Selling for $4333, this put the car at the top of the Buick range; for $50 extra, a 425cid (7 litres), 340bhp version was on offer.

The big V8 engine ensured that the Riviera was a formidable performer, being capable of close on 125mph (201km/h) but, unlike many American cars of the day, it was not simply a rapid straight liner but could corner without excessive pitch and body roll.

Sales Success

Just as predicted, Buick built 40,000 Rivieras in the initial 1963 model year and it helped the division to rise from sixth in the American sales league in 1962 to fifth position in 1964 and 1965. The model was destined for a three year manufacturing life in its original form and when it was visually updated in 1966, its replacement had much stylistically in common with the in-house Oldsmobile Toronado. From there on sales of the model remained buoyant until 1970, when the third generation Riviera arrived with a boat-tailed type body which was as ungainly as the original had been elegant.

Specifications: Buick Riviera

Length:	17ft 4in (5283mm)
Width:	6ft 2in (1880mm)
Wheelbase:	9ft 9in (2972mm)
Height:	4ft 5in (1346mm)
Track:	front 5ft (1524mm), rear, 4ft 11in (1499mm)
Unladen weight:	4188lb (1900kg)
Engine: V8, overhead valve, 106x92mm, 401cid (6555cc). Compression ratio, 10.25:1. Max power, 325bhp at 4400rpm. Max torque, 445lb/ft at 2800rpm.	
Transmission:	Two-speed automatic
Drive:	Rear
Suspension (front):	Independent, coil springs and wishbones
Suspension (rear):	Live axle, coil springs
Top speed:	125mph (201km/h)
0-60mph (96km/h):	6.9 seconds
Production:	112,244

LEFT: *One of the best looking American cars of the 1960's, the Buick Riviera successfully integrated British and American styling themes.*

BELOW: *The Riviera's hardtop coupé body was essayed by General Motors' William Mitchell. A 401cid (6.5 litres) V8 was the standard fitment in this 1963 example.*

MERCEDES-BENZ 230, 250, 280SL (1963-1971)

Crisply and conservatively styled, the 2.3 litre 230SL incorporated all the engineering refinement for which Mercedes-Benz is justifiably famous and, such was the competence of the design, it remained outwardly unchanged throughout its production life. It is the model's convex, so-called "pagoda roof" which is perhaps its most memorable feature. But the car did benefit from two engine capacity increases, first to 2.5 litres in 1966 and, ultimately, to 2.8 litres in 1967.

The 230SL, introduced at the 1963 Geneva Motor Show, was powered by an overhead-camshaft six-cylinder engine. It replaced the 190SL which was a four. Although it was a two-seater roadster, when its distinctive and substantial hardtop was in place, it was transformed into a handsome Grand Tourer. Later in 1963 these lines were incorporated in a coupé version of the design. The 2281cc fuel-injected engine was a bigger bored version of the unit used in the 220SE saloon of 1959 and endowed the model with a top speed of 124mph (200km/h). A four-speed manual gearbox was fitted but Daimler-Benz's own automatic unit was available at extra cost.

Good Roadholding

The all-independent suspension also came from the saloon, and featured coils and wishbones at the front, while Mercedes-Benz's traditional low pivot swing axle was employed at the rear. The use of these components ensured that the model was relatively wide in relation to its length, and this contributed to the car's excellent roadholding. Disc brakes were fitted at the front, while power steering was an optional and popular extra.

In 1966 the model was uprated with a 150bhp, 2496cc, longer stroked engine and a more robust seven-bearing crankshaft, a four-bearing unit having previously been deemed sufficient. Disc brakes were now extended to the rear wheels. Top speed remained about the same although the car was rather faster through the gears than its predecessor.

The 250SL was only destined for a limited production life. In 1967, the overhead camshaft six was once again enlarged by a further increase in bore size, this time to 2778cc. Power went up to 170bhp, although top speed was not much greater because the model had also put on extra weight.

The 280SL remained in production until 1971 and, significantly, demand for the entire series did not peak until

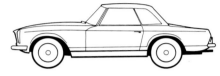

Specifications: Mercedes-Benz 230SL

Length:	14ft 1in (4293mm)
Width:	5ft 9in (1753mm)
Height:	4ft 3in (1295mm)
Wheelbase:	7ft 10in (2388mm)
Track:	front and rear 4ft 10in (1473mm)
Unladen weight:	2668lb (1210kg)
Engine:	Six cylinder, single overhead camshaft, 82x72mm, 2281cc. Compression ratio, 9.3:1. Max power, 170bhp at 5600rpm. Max torque, 159lb/ft at 4500rpm.
Transmission:	Four-speed manual
Drive:	Rear
Suspension (front):	Independent, coil springs and wishbones
Suspension (rear):	Independent, low pivot swing axle with coil springs
Top speed:	124mph (200km/h)
0-60mph (96km/h):	10.3 seconds
Production (total 230, 250, 280SL):	48,912

1969, when 8047 units were delivered. It was also by far and away the most popular model with 23,885 built, compared with a mere 5196 250SLs produced and 19,831 examples of the original 230 manufactured.

Pros And Cons

In their day, these Mercedes-Benz were praised for the quality of their construction and, above all, roadholding. Features such as the power steering and automatic transmission were up to the expected standards and, on the 230SL, 60mph (96km/h) came up in just over 10 seconds. But the model sold for £3414 on its 1963 introduction in Britain and for that price it would have been possible to have bought no less than four home-produced MGBs!

ABOVE: *That distinctive pagoda roof in close-up on a right-hand-drive 1966 230SL. The horn ring is D-shaped so as not to obscure the speedometer and rev counter.*

RIGHT: *The 230 SL of 1963-67 vintage. This is a 1966 car, a total of 4945 being built in that year. The model was available with either manual or automatic transmission. Power came from a 2.3 litre single cam six.*

Mercedes-Benz 230SL, 250SL, 280SL

2.2 litre 220SE saloon 1959

2.3 litre 230SL 1963

roadster   coupé

2.5 litre 250SL 1966

roadster   coupé

2.8 litre 280SL 1967

roadster   coupé

RIGHT: *An American registered 280SL coupé of 1969 vintage. This is the last of the series and the model remained available until 1971.*

Lamborghini 350GT and 400GT (1963-1967)

The 350GT, the first car of the Lamborghini line, was a deliberate attempt by its maker to challenge Ferrari's pre-eminent position as the world's leading manufacturer of Grand Tourers. The model had a purpose-designed 3.5 litre, V12 engine, all-independent suspension and a body by Touring. It made way in 1966 for the 400GT with enlarged 4 litre power unit and two-plus-two seating.

Ferruccio Lamborghini was a successful Italian tractor manufacturer with a passion for fast cars who, in the early 1960's, decided to found his own marque. He established a purpose-built factory to the north of Milan at Sant' Agata Bolognese and recruited a talented young team which consisted mostly of former Ferrari engineers. The glorious V12 engine with twin overhead camshafts per cylinder bank was the work of 35-year-old Giotto Bizzarrini and was based on a 1.5 litre V12 that he had designed during his time working with Ferrari.

Bizzarrini was also responsible for the Lamborghini's chassis and he was able to incorporate all-independent suspension which was a refinement which Ferrari did not enjoy. However, in mid-1963, Bizzarrini left Lamborghini to pursue other assignments and his

place was taken by the equally talented Giampaolo Dallara, then only 24.

The first car was unveiled, in 360bhp 350GTV form, at the 1963 Turin Show. But while its mechanicals were undoubtedly impressive, the two seater coupé body by Franco Scaglione was an uneasy amalgam of styles. More positively, for his marque badge Lamborghini chose a charging bull to reflect the fact that he was born under the sign of Taurus. The model names of subsequent cars were also to have associations with bulls or bullfighting.

Improving The Line

Understandably, Ferruccio Lamborghini was disappointed by the appearance of his new car and immediately entered a dialogue with Touring of Milan to refine Scaglione's design. The outcome, unveiled at the 1964 Geneva Show, was a considerable improvement on what had gone before. It was lower and sleeker than its predecessor with its wheelbase extended by 4in (102mm) although the V12 engine was detuned to 270bhp.

The 350 did not enter production until the end of 1964, by which time a mere 13 cars had been delivered. Manufacture got properly into its stride in 1965. The car was praised for its impressive performance and 145mph (233km/h) top speed but, on the debit side, Lamborghini was dissatisfied with the excessive noises generated by the ZF gearbox and Salisbury final drive.

A limitation of the original design was that the car was a two-seater and this shortcoming was resolved at the 1966 Geneva Motor Show with the arrival of the 400GT, distinguished by its quadruple headlamps. As the model number indicated, the capacity of the engine was enlarged to 3.9 litres, and it also benefitted from a five-speed, all synchromesh gearbox produced at Sant' Agata, in which the facility was even applied to the reverse cog, and a Lamborghini-created final drive. The 400 proved to be more popular than its predecessor and it remained in production until 1968. But for all Ferruccio Lamborghini's ambitions, these first cars never quite achieved his high hopes. These were to be realized with the arrival, in 1966, of the stunning mid-engined Miura.

RIGHT: *The 400GT with body by Touring – note badge on the side of the upper front wing. It was outwardly similar to the 350GT, apart from its quadruple headlamps.*

BELOW: *Driving compartment of a 1966 Lamborghini 400GT. The car was only produced in left-hand-drive form and, unlike the 350GT, a Lamborghini-built five-speed gearbox was fitted.*

Specifications: Lamborghini 350GT

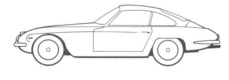

Length:	15ft 2in (4623mm)
Width:	5ft 8in (1727mm)
Height:	4ft (1219mm)
Wheelbase:	8ft 4in (2540mm)
Track:	front and rear 4ft 6in (1372mm)
Unladen weight:	2860lb (1297kg)

Engine: V12 with twin overhead camshafts per cylinder bank, 77x62mm, 3464cc. Compression ratio, 9:1. Max power, 270bhp at 6500rpm. Max torque, 241lb/ft at 4500rpm.

Transmission:	Five-speed manual
Drive:	Rear
Suspension (front):	Independent, coil springs and wishbones
Suspension (rear):	Independent, coil springs and wishbones
Top speed:	145mph (233km/h)
0-60mph (96km/h):	6.5 seconds
Production (total 350, 400GT):	391

BELOW: *A 1965 350GT. This example, chassis 0229, was originally owned by that great British enthusiast Peter Hampton, who covered thousands of miles of reliable motoring in it.*

FORD MUSTANG (1964-1967)

Until the early 1960's, the Grand Tourer could be defined as a fast, low production, expensive car with closed bodywork. All this changed in 1964 when Ford in America introduced its Mustang which was destined to become one of the fastest selling cars in the history of the US motor industry. An amazing 1.7 million examples were produced within four years. Across the Atlantic in Britain it also spawned the Ford Capri which extended the concept to the European market.

The executive responsible for the Mustang was Ford division chairman, Lee Iacocca, who recognized that the post-war "baby boom" was set to reach adulthood in the early 1960's, and corporate market research indicated that individuals tended to remain loyal to the make of car that they first bought. As youth and fast motoring are synonymous, Ford, which had hitherto lacked a sporting profile, adopted what it called a "total performance" image. The Mustang was the car to break new ground: it was the first manifestation of this new philosophy.

The key to the success of the concept was the right type of bodywork and the first design, completed in 1962, revealed a mid-engined, wedge-shaped, open two-seater. But despite a good public response, Mustang I, as it was called, did not lend itself to quantity production.

Ash's Mustang
Four corporate styling divisions were duly asked to submit rival designs of the proposed car. The winning creation, titled Mustang II and the work of Ford stylist David Ash, was a racy looking hardtop coupé; there was also a convertible version. The lines were finalized in September 1963 and the car launched a mere eight months later, in April 1964. The shell was created to accommodate Ford's six cylinder and V8 engines and there were numerous trim and accessory packs available so purchasers could "personalize" their cars.

During its initial planning stages, it was envisaged that 100,000 Mustangs might be built in a year but, as interest in the concept accelerated, Iacocca upped the projected figure to 240,000. It was fortunate that he did. The 100,000 ceiling was breached within four months of the model's introduction and the latter figure in seven. By the end of 1965 a record 680,992 cars had been produced, and the millionth Mustang was built in March 1966.

Engine options ranged from the Ford Falcon's 170cid (2.8 litres) six but this only lasted until September when it was replaced by a 200cid (3.3 litres) unit. At the other extreme was the 289cid (4.7 litres) V8 in two stages of tune. For 1967, the top line engine had grown to a 390cid (6.4 litres) V8. This meant that at best the Mustang, a small car by American standards, was capable of speeds approaching 125mph (201km/h).

As befitted Ford's design philosophy, mechanicals were predictably orthodox with coils and wishbones at the front and a half-elliptic sprung rear axle. The model was initially offered with two body styles: a hardtop coupé and a convertible. Five months after the model's launch, in September 1964, came what Ford called its GT which was a 2+2 fastback coupé with front disc brakes and five dial instrument panel.

Shelby's GT-350
The most potent version of the Mustang came from former racing driver, Carroll Shelby, creator of the AC Cobra. His car, built by Shelby American, was called the GT-350 and based on the GT finished in white with an optional Le Mans blue stripe and black interior trim. Power came from a 306bhp version of the 289 V8. The intention was to challenge the rival Chevrolet Corvette in Sports Car Club of America's B-Production racing class. It succeeded, with the GT-350 acclaimed as class champion between 1965 and 1967.

Ford built an impressive 1.7 million Mustangs between 1964 and 1967 when the model was revised and the car has remained part of the Ford model line right up to the present day, a total endorsement of Iacocca's inspired decision if ever there was one.

Ford Mustang

Mid-engined Mustang I roadster 1962

Mustang II hardtop coupé 1963

170cid 6/390cid V8 Mustang 1964

hardtop coupé   convertible   GT coupé

Shelby 289cid V8
GT-350 1965

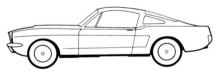

LEFT: *The popular Mustang hardtop. This 1965 car is powered by a 260cid (4.3 litres) V8, as indicated by the badge on the front wing, which cost an extra $108.*

ABOVE: *The absence of radiator grille, the white and blue colour scheme and twin racing stripes identify this 1965 example of the sought-after Shelby Mustang. Only 562 were built in '65.*

BELOW: *The Shelby Mustang's 289cid (4.7 litres) V8 engine which developed 306bhp. Note the "Cobra Powered by Ford" name cast into the rocker box cover. Compression was raised to 10:1.*

Specifications: Ford Mustang

Length:	15ft 1in (4597mm)
Width:	5ft 8in (1727mm)
Height:	4ft 3in (1295mm)
Wheelbase:	9ft (2743mm)
Track:	front 4ft 6in (1372mm), rear 4ft 8in (1422mm)
Unladen weight:	2755lb (1250kg)
Engine: V8, overhead valve, 101x72mm, 289cid (4735cc). Compression ratio, 9.2:1. Max power, 225bhp at 4800rpm. Max torque, 305lb/ft at 3200rpm.	
Transmission:	Three/four-speed manual/ three-speed automatic
Drive:	Rear
Suspension (front):	Independent, coil springs and wishbones
Suspension (rear):	Live axle, half-elliptic springs
Top speed:	118mph (190km/h)
0-60mph (96km/h):	9 seconds
Production (total 1964-67):	1,760,678

AC 428 (1965-1973)

This handsome British-assembled Grand Tourer had a truly international pedigree as it was the result of a marriage between the American-designed Mark III Cobra 427 chassis and a stylish body from the Italian Frua concern. The result was a potent 140mph (225km/h) machine which would have probably been built in greater numbers had AC not experienced body supply difficulties. The model was therefore discontinued in 1973, its potential unrealized.

The original Cobra of 1962 was based on AC's all-independent transverse-leaf-sprung Ace but, in 1965, came the Ford-developed Mark III frame with all-round coil spring and wishbones suspension. AC's chairman, Derek Hurlock, recognized that this chassis could form the basis of a luxurious road car which would be complemented by the fitment of Italian coachwork. He therefore travelled to Turin and first went to Bertone and then Carrozzeria Frua. This firm responded positively to his requirement and, as a result, a lengthened Cobra chassis was dispatched to Italy at the beginning of 1965. The completed car returned to AC's Thames Ditton factory in the summer. This first example was a convertible, although it was intended to produce the model in both open and closed forms. After some further refinement by AC engineers, the 428 was displayed at the 1965 London Motor Show priced at £4250.

Under the bonnet was the same Ford 428cid (7 litres) V8 that was being used in the Mark III Cobra. Initially, it had a four-speed manual gearbox. This looked like the start of a successful exercise for AC and the intention was to produce 150 examples with Frua bodies while Hurlock sought a suitable firm to manufacture them in Britain. This was because of the elaborate nature of the car's manufacturing process. The AC-built chassis, less engines and gearboxes, were shipped to Italy where they were bodied by Frua and then returned to Britain for their power units and trains to be fitted, the cars then being painted, trimmed and, finally, road tested.

A Closed Version

The first of the closed 428s appeared at the Frua stand at the 1966 Geneva Motor Show. Unlike the three convertibles already completed, this was fitted with Ford automatic transmission which was thereafter standardized.

Like its Cobra forebear, the 428 was an impressive performer, able to reach 60mph (96km/h) in under six seconds. Roadholding was similarly good although ride never quite reached the same standard and the big V8 did suffer from unresolved overheating problems.

Despite the high hopes that had greeted the 428's arrival, AC was experiencing severe manufacturing difficulties and, by March of 1969, a mere 50 examples had been built. This was because Frua was unable to deliver bodies on time and of sufficiently good quality, itself a reflection of the labour problems that were then besetting the Italian motor industry.

In addition, AC was forced to raise the car's price as Cobra sales dwindled – in 1968 it went up to £5573 making the 428 over twice the price of the E-Type Jaguar. Even then the car was losing money and, with great reluctance, the firm decided to discontinue production in 1973, by which time 51 convertibles and 29 coupés had been completed.

LEFT: The "office" of a 1973 AC 428 with its comprehensive suite of instrumentation which replaced the original in 1970. Note the U-shaped automatic transmission selector.

RIGHT: The lines of the Frua body of a 1973 428 shown to good effect. This example has chromed wire wheels which were available at £50 extra, otherwise a silver finish sufficed.

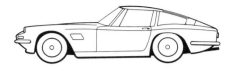

Specifications: AC 428	
Length:	14ft 8in (4470mm)
Width:	5ft 8in (1727mm)
Height:	4ft 1in (1245mm)
Wheelbase:	7ft 11in (2413mm)
Track:	front 4ft 5in (1346mm), rear 4ft 6in (1372mm)
Unladen weight:	3155lb (1431kg)
Engine: V8, overhead valve, 104x101mm, 428cid (7014cc). Compression ratio, 10.5:1. Max power, 345bhp at 4600rpm. Max torque, 462lb/ft at 2800rpm.	
Transmission:	Three-speed automatic
Drive:	Rear
Suspension (front):	Independent, coil springs and wishbones
Suspension (rear):	Independent, coil springs and wishbones
Top speed:	140mph (225km/h)
0-60mph (96km/h):	5.9 seconds
Production (coupé):	29

KJB 318L

AC 428

2 litre 6 cylinder AC Ace 1954
|
4.2 litre V8 Cobra 1962
|
7 litre V8 Cobra MkIII 1965
|
7 litre AC 428 1965

roadster   coupé 1966

LEFT: *Looking very Italian, the 428's long rear quarter lights ensured the minimum of blind spots. This 1973 car dates from the final year of production.*

FERRARI 330 GTC AND 365 GTC (1966-1970)

The best selling two-seater, grand touring, Maranello-built car of the 1960's, the 330 GTC has been rightly acclaimed for being the "best all-round Ferrari". A combination of a 4 litre, 300bhp V12 and a short chassis with independent rear suspension resulted in a model which revealed a degree of refinement that had been absent from many of Ferrari's earlier GTs. In 1967 the model was updated with an enlarged 4.4 litre power unit, and the outwardly similar 365 GTC lasted – in open and closed versions – until 1969.

The 330 was an intoxicating cocktail of Ferrari ingredients. It consisted of the customary tubular 7ft 10in (2400mm) chassis, courtesy of the 275 GTB of 1964-66, and the single cam V12 engine which resembled that used in the 1965 Ferrari 330 2+2. Despite the engine's similarity to this earlier model, the block was redesigned for the GTC because it differed by having its five-speed, all-synchromesh gearbox incorporated, for better balance and refinement, in a rear-mounted transaxle. Suspension was all-independent, Ferrari having no doubt responded to the challenge in that regard presented by the Lamborghini 350GT of 1964.

Pininfarina Style

All these elements were brought together by the fitment of a beautifully proportioned though understated coupé body, designed and built by Pininfarina, in which frontal elements of the 500 Superfast and a tail inspired by the 275 GTS were brought together into a harmonious whole.

In the 1950's Ferrari's road cars had been closely related to its sports racers, but in the following decade the divide became greater. The 330 GTC was a world away from its noisy and sometimes harshly sprung predecessors. Fast and comfortable, particularly when the optional air conditioning and electric windows were fitted, this was a quiet and civilized 150mph (241km/h) car. Contemporary road tests spoke of the 330's engine being commendably free of vibration and the car's handling was on a par with that of a racing car.

Introduced at the 1966 Geneva Motor Show, by the time that production ceased in 1968, no less than 600 examples had been produced, which was tantamount to mass production for a V12-engined Ferrari. It was replaced by the outwardly similar 365 GTC, the only visual difference between the two being the transference of the cooling vents from the front wings to the bonnet, a change that had been applied to the last of the 330s.

The principal mechanical difference was that the 320bhp engine was enlarged to 4.4 litres. This bigger-bored unit had first been seen in the 365 GT 2+2 which appeared at the 1967 Paris Show. Despite the increase in capacity and output, the car's top speed remained about the same, although acceleration times were marginally improved. As it happened, this model was only destined for a relatively brief production life; 150 cars were produced between 1968 and 1970.

Both models were available in convertible forms, the 330 GTS followed the coupé later in 1966 and, like the closed car, this was duly designated the 365 GTS in 1969.

Specifications: Ferrari 330 GTC

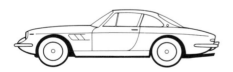

Length:	14ft 7in (4445mm)
Width:	5ft 5in (1651mm)
Height:	4ft 3in (1295mm)
Wheelbase:	7ft 10in (2400mm)
Track:	front 4ft 7in (1401mm), rear 4ft 8in (1417mm)
Unladen weight:	3060lb (1388kg)
Engine: V12 with single overhead camshaft per cylinder bank, 77x71mm, 3967cc. Compression ratio, 8.8:1. Max power, 300bhp at 7000rpm. Max torque, 241lb/ft at 5000rpm.	
Transmission:	Five-speed manual
Drive:	Rear
Suspension (front):	Independent, coil springs and wishbones
Suspension (rear):	Independent, coil springs and wishbones
Top speed:	150mph (241km/h)
0-60mph (96km/h):	6.7 seconds
Production (total 330, 365 GTC):	750

Ferrari 330 GTC, 365 GTC

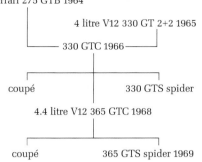

Ferrari 275 GTB 1964

4 litre V12 330 GT 2+2 1965

330 GTC 1966

coupé   330 GTS spider

4.4 litre V12 365 GTC 1968

coupé   365 GTS spider 1969

LEFT: *A right-hand-drive 1967 330 GTC, one of 21 imported for the British market. The Pininfarina-designed and built body is one of the finest both in terms of style and quality.*

BELOW: *The magnificent lines of the Pininfarina two-seater 330. A luxurious and well equipped car, air conditioning was available as an optional extra.*

ABOVE: *Rear view of the 365 GTC which was successor to the 330. Outwardly similar, this is a 1969 car and the model is identifiable by the absence of front wing louvres.*

JENSEN INTERCEPTOR AND FF (1966-1976)

The Interceptor was numerically the most successful car in Jensen's history; a fast, well equipped, V8-powered GT with fine body lines and a distinctive opening tailgate. It was also available in supplementary four-wheel-drive FF form, and as such was the first series production road car to feature the system, appearing 14 years before the Audi Quattro brought the configuration to a wider public.

The Interceptor has its origins in the four-cylinder, 4 litre, glass-fibre-bodied 514 of 1954, which was revised in 1962 as the CV8, with a 5.9 litre Chrysler V8 engine and new controversial body designed by Jensen.

When Kevin Beattie, Jensen's chief engineer since 1965, was planning a replacement for this slow selling model, he was determined that the company should look to Italy for the lines of its new car and that its body should be made of steel instead of glass fibre. In the face of much internal opposition, Beattie won the day and, during the winter of 1965-66, he travelled to Turin

where he visited Ghia, Vignale and Touring. It was the design which Touring produced that impressed Beattie most but, sadly, the respected *carrozzeria* was on the point of closure. In these circumstances Jensen bought the Touring design outright. Vignale then took the job over, building the first Interceptor bodies and producing the all important tooling for Jensen ultimately to manufacture the hulls at its West Bromwich factory.

Once this contract had been agreed, in February 1966, a CV8 was dispatched to Turin and its body removed. By June, Jensen engineers were

road testing the car on the Continent and October saw Jensen begin to receive two or three ready trimmed and painted hulls a week.

First Public Appearance

The Interceptor was unveiled at the 1966 London Motor Show. Selling for £3742, which was the same price as the CV8 that it replaced, the model was acclaimed for its appearance which more than justified Beattie's determination to go to Italy for its styling. Mechanicals were essentially a carryover from the CV8 with a Chrysler 6.3 litre V8 engine and automatic transmission. In this form the Interceptor was capable of a comfortable, effortless 130mph (209km/h) but could only return 14mpg (20 litres/100km). The V8 was enlarged to 7.2 litres from 1971 for the more expensive SP version in which air conditioning and a stereo radio were standard equipment and, in 1972, this larger engine was standardized for all versions which from 1974

included a convertible version.

Until 1971 the FF (for Ferguson Formula) four-wheel-drive Interceptor was produced alongside the mainstream model. Initially listed but not produced in CV8 form, at a price of £5340 in 1966 it cost £1598 more than the Interceptor and was identifiable by twin rather than single cooling grilles in the front wings. Dunlop Maxaret anti-lock brakes complemented the model's legendary roadholding qualities. Despite such innovation, only 320 examples of this expensive, thirsty car were built.

The Interceptor itself continued to sell although sales were badly hit by the international oil price rise of late 1973. The firm eventually went into liquidation in 1976. The business survived as a parts and service organization and, in 1983, the Interceptor was revived. However, production was limited to 12 cars a year and even this ceased in 1990, the model once again being a victim of economic recession.

Jensen Interceptor

4 litre 541 coupé 1954
|
5.9 litre V8 CV8 coupé 1962
|
6.3 litre CV8 1964 ————
| |
| Prototype
| four-wheel-drive
| CV8 1965
|
6.3 litre Interceptor 1966 — FF version
|
7.2 litre Interceptor SP 1971
|
7.2 litre Interceptor 1972
|
coupé   convertible 1974

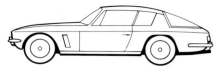

Specifications: Jensen Interceptor

Length:	15ft 8in (4775mm)
Width:	5ft 9in (1753mm)
Height:	4ft 5in (1346mm)
Wheelbase:	9ft 9in (2972mm)
Track:	front 4ft 7in (1397mm), rear 4ft 9in (1448mm)
Unladen weight:	3500lb (1587kg)
Engine: V8, overhead valve, 108x86mm, 6276cc. Compression ratio, 10:1. Max power, 325bhp at 4600rpm. Max torque, 225lb/ft at 2800rpm.	
Transmission:	Three-speed automatic
Drive:	Rear
Suspension (front):	Independent, coil spring and wishbones
Suspension (rear):	Live axle, half-elliptic springs
Top speed:	130mph (209km/h)
0-60mph (96km/h):	7.4 seconds
Production (total Interceptor and FF):	5897

BELOW: *A 1969 Jensen Interceptor, a Mark I car, which can be identified by the low mounted front bumper with side lights located above it. Later cars had a higher bumper line.*

BELOW: *Head-on view of a Mark III Jensen Interceptor of 1974 with its revised bumper line which looks tidier than the Mark I version. A 7.2 litre V8 was employed.*

ABOVE: *The Interceptor's distinctive and functional tailgate. This is the FF four-wheel-drive version. Note the identifying twin cooling outlets just discernible in the front wing.*

(FERRARI) DINO 206 GT AND 246 GT (1967-1974)

Just as the 250 GT of 1954 was the first Ferrari to be produced in quantity, so the Dino represented a further manufacturing milestone for the Maranello company. It was the cheapest and best selling Ferrari of its day and, by the time that production ceased, over 4000 examples had been built.

The model was named after Enzo Ferrari's son, Dino, who had died in 1956 at the early age of 24. When the firm's V6-engined Formula 2 car appeared in 1957, it was so named in his memory. This was a front-engined design but in 1960 Ferrari's Grand Prix cars adopted a central location for the engine, and its sports racers followed suit.

It was one of the latter category, in this instance the 2 litre V6-engined Dino 206S, that formed the basis of the road cars of the same name. One of these, cloaked in a curvaceous Pininfarina body, was displayed at the 1965 Paris Motor Show where it was described as the Dino 206 GT Speciale. As this car was based on an existing chassis, the V6 power unit was longitudinally located and so it was also in a further prototype that was visually closer to the finished product, which appeared at the 1966 Turin Show.

Engines From Fiat

At that same event there appeared another car which would make this small Ferrari a practical reality. This was a *Fiat* Dino, a front-engined sports model which shared the same 2 litre V6 engine. It existed because Ferrari wished to use the power unit in Formula 2 events but it would not be eligible until 500 examples had been produced, a figure which was beyond the manufacturer's capabilities. So Fiat agreed to undertake the V6's production, hence the arrival of its Dino.

This Fiat appeared in 1967, well ahead of the definitive Ferrari – another prototype was displayed at that year's Turin Show. Unlike the earlier examples, on this car the V6 aluminium engine was mounted transversely behind the driver while the chassis was a ladder tubular frame with all-independent suspension.

The Ferrari Dino 206 GT did not enter production until 18 months later, in the spring of 1969, with Scaglietti in Modena producing the body to Pininfarina's design. Interestingly, this Ferrari was not badged as such but simply named Dino as there were thoughts about developing it as a separate marque name.

The model's performance was as impressive as its good looks. The engine was a 180bhp, 2 litre, aluminium V6 unit with twin overhead camshafts per cylinder bank and its mid location endowed the Dino with excellent road holding, it being capable of speeds in excess of 140mph (225km/h). The cheapest Ferrari of its day, the 206 sold in Britain for £6243.

The Faster 246

One hundred and fifty examples were built by the end of 1969 when the 206 was replaced by the 246 GT. This was powered by a larger capacity 2.4 litre V6 which differed from its predecessor by having an iron rather than alloy block, as did its Fiat counterpart which continued to be built until 1972. In addition, the Ferrari's wheelbase was extended by 3.9in (100mm) while weight went up 400lb (181kg) to 2700lb (1225kg) as the metal construction of the body was also changed – it was now made of steel rather than aluminium. Nevertheless, performance was improved; the extra power made the 246 Dino a 150mph (241km/h) car.

In 1972 the coupé was joined by a spider (open) version of the design, designated the 246 GTS, of which 1274 examples were built. This was discontinued in 1974, the same year as its coupé equivalent which accounted for 2609 units. The Dino's V6 engine, however, continued in production and it powered the rally-winning, in-house Lancia Stratos of 1973-75.

ABOVE: *Rear view of a 246 Dino GTS with its Targa-style roof panel detached. There is a Ferrari prancing horse motif on the tail even though the car was not badged as such.*

BELOW: *A Dino 246 in profile showing the lines of the Pininfarina-styled and Scaglietti-built coupé to perfection. The mid-located engine permitted a low bonnet line.*

Dino 206 GT and 246 GT

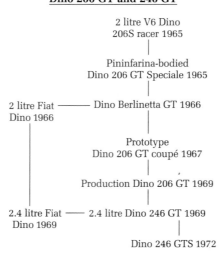

```
                  2 litre V6 Dino
                  206S racer 1965
                         |
                  Pininfarina-bodied
                  Dino 206 GT Speciale 1965
                         |
2 litre Fiat ——— Dino Berlinetta GT 1966
Dino 1966                |
                  Prototype
                  Dino 206 GT coupé 1967
                         |
                  Production Dino 206 GT 1969
                         |
2.4 litre Fiat ——— 2.4 litre Dino 246 GT 1969
Dino 1969                |
                  Dino 246 GTS 1972
```

Specifications: (Ferrari) Dino 206 GT

Length:	13ft 7in (4140mm)
Width:	5ft 7in (1702mm)
Height:	3ft 6in (1067mm)
Wheelbase:	7ft 6in (2286mm)
Track:	front 4ft 8in (1422mm), rear 4ft 7in (1397mm)
Unladen weight:	2300lb (1043kg)
Engine: Mid-located V6 with twin overhead camshafts per cylinder bank, 85x57mm, 1987cc. Compression ratio, 9:1. Max power, 180bhp at 8000rpm. Max torque, 138lb/ft at 6500rpm.	
Transmission:	Five-speed manual
Drive:	Rear
Suspension (front):	Independent, coil springs and wishbones
Suspension (rear):	Independent, coil springs and wishbones
Top speed:	140mph (225km/h)
0-60mph (96km/h):	7.5 seconds
Production (total 206 and 246 GT/GTS):	4033

RIGHT: *A right-hand-drive 246 GT which was one of the 488 coupés built for the British market. On this example the Dino badge has been replaced by a Ferrari one.*

ASTON MARTIN V8 (1969-1989)

Britain's fastest car of its day, the V8 was capable, in its most potent form, of a top speed of 170mph (274km/h). Magnificently hand built at Aston Martin's Newport Pagnell factory, the model helped the firm to weather switchback years of recession and growth and the (by then) ageing design was not replaced until 1989, a full 20 years since it had been introduced.

The starting point of the V8 model was the DB6 of 1965. Work began in 1966 on the car which was based on the 6's platform chassis suitably modified to incorporate a de Dion rear axle, although the front suspension remained essentially unchanged. William Towns, who had originally been recruited by Aston Martin to re-design the DB6's interior, came up with a fine two-plus-two coupé which was a worthy successor to the Touring-styled DB4, 5 and 6. It was, however, 6in (152mm) wider to accommodate a new V8 engine then under develop-ment. The car was completed in time for announcement at the 1967 Paris and London Motor Shows. However, work on the new power unit was not yet completed, so what was named the DBS was fitted with the DB6's 4 litre, six cylinder engine and it endured in this form until 1973.

BELOW: *Aston Martin's potent V8 Vantage. This Series 1 car dates from the introductory year of 1977 with its distinctive blanked off radiator, bonnet scoop and air dam.*

It was not until 1969 that the fuel-injection, 5.3 litre V8, with twin over-head camshafts per cylinder bank, was ready and, although power was undis-closed, it was in the region of 300bhp. The car was accordingly named the DBS V8 and there was the option of a five-speed ZF gearbox or Chrysler automatic transmission. Not surpris-ingly, the V8 was a spirited performer, being capable of over 160mph (257km/h) and 60mph (96km/h) came up in an electrifying six seconds. The car was built in this form until 1972 when Sir David Brown sold Aston Martin to Company Developments, a property company. They dropped the DBS prefix and the car became the plain V8. The original four headlamp design was discontinued at this time and replaced by a tidier twin 'lamp layout. The mechanicals were other-wise unchanged, apart from the intro-duction of four carburettors which re-placed the Bosch fuel injection system in 1973, although this reappeared in Weber form in 1986.

A more powerful Vantage option had been a feature of Aston Martin cars

since the 1950's and a Vantage version of the V8 was introduced in 1977 with the engine boosted to 370bhp and a top speed in excess of 170mph (273km/h). It was only available in manual gear-box form. In 1978 came an open V8, called, like its predecessors, Volante.

At the end of 1974, Company De-velopments had filed for bankruptcy and Aston Martin was refinanced in 1975. A number of reconstructions fol-lowed until 1987 when the firm was bought by Ford.

Until 1986 the V8 was only available with its impressive factory coachwork but, in that year, Aston Martin intro-duced the Vantage Zagato coupé, in memory of the legendary DB4 Zagato of 1960 vintage. The latter day version was limited to 52 cars built on a short-ened floor pan and cloaked in Italy with chunky Zagato coachwork. The V8 was boosted to 432bhp and the car was capable of 187mph (300km/h) . . . It was also produced in convertible form.

Finally, after a 20 year manufactur-ing life, the V8 bowed out in 1989 to make way for its long awaited replace-ment, the Virage, which is intended to take Aston Martin into the 21st century.

RIGHT: *A Series 4 V8 introduced for 1979 and built until late 1985. This generation is identifiable by its lack of bonnet air intake. There was also a new built-in rear spoiler.*

Specifications: Aston Martin V8

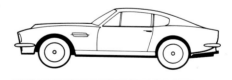

Length:	15ft (4572mm)
Width:	6ft (1829mm)
Height:	4ft 4in (1321mm)
Wheelbase:	8ft 6in (2591mm)
Track:	front and rear 4ft 11in (1499mm)
Unladen weight:	3800lb (1724kg)
Engine: V8 with twin overhead camshafts per cylinder bank, 100x85mm, 5340cc. Compression ratio, 9:1. Fuel injection. Max power, undisclosed. Max torque, 400lb/ft at 4500rpm.	
Transmission:	Five-speed manual/ three-speed automatic
Drive:	Rear
Suspension (front):	Independent, coil springs and wishbones
Suspension (rear):	Coil springs and De Dion rear axle
Top speed:	160mph (257km/h)
0-60mph (96km/h):	6 seconds
Production (including Volante and Zagato):	3308

Aston Martin V8

3.7 litre 6 cylinder DB4 1958

4 litre DB5 1964

4 litre DB6 1965

4 litre DBS 1967

5.3 litre V8 DBS V8 1969

Renamed V8 1972

Volante 1978

370bhp Vantage 1977

Vantage Zagato 1986

BELOW: *The DBS V8 was produced between 1969 and 1972 and was in production when Sir David Brown sold the company. The twin headlamps were then replaced by single units.*

FORD CAPRI (1969-1987)

"The Car You Always Promised Yourself" declared Ford when it introduced the Capri, which was the European equivalent of the Mustang that had proved such a runaway success in America. This was a Grand Tourer for Everyman. The Capri was remarkably enduring being built by Ford's British and German plants (from 1976 only in Germany), and when production ceased in 1987, no less than 1.8 million had been manufactured.

Work on the car began in 1964 when the concept was allotted the Colt coding. The corporate requirement was that it should be able to accommodate the British range of Ford engines while a programme of varying trim options followed the Mustang approach.

After styling concepts for a two-door fastback coupé had been considered from America and from Ford's still separate German arm, the project was given the corporate green light in June 1966. It was originally intended to build the Capri only at Ford's Halewood plant in Britain but the creation, in 1967, of Ford of Europe, which integrated the company's British and German branches, meant that production would also take place in Cologne. As a result the design was modified to accommodate Ford Germany's V4.

The model was launched, appropriately bearing in mind its European manufacturing and sales base, at the 1969 Brussels Motor Show. It was destined for an 18 year production life, which was longer than any other Ford model. Mechanically uncomplicated, with MacPherson strut suspension at the front and a leaf spring rear axle, the Capri's smallest capacity engine was 1.3 litre four, courtesy of the Ford Escort saloon, which could be coaxed to 85mph (137km/h). Then there was a 90mph (145km/h) 1300GT with cross flow cylinder head, a 1600 and 1600GT which was a 100mph (161km/h) car, while the 105mph (169km/h) 2000GT was powered by Ford Germany's 2 litre V4 unit. The top line 3 litre V6 did not arrive until the 1970 model year and in GXL form it could reach 60mph

(96km/h) in a little over eight seconds and exceed 120mph (193km/h). There was also a rare RS3100 version for racing with an enlarged 3.1 litre V6 developing 148bhp.

The Capri proved to be remarkably enduring. The body lines were face-lifted in 1974; Capri II was longer, wider and higher than the first generation of cars and a useful tailgate was introduced. The engines varied quite considerably over the years. From 1973 the pushrod 1600 was replaced by Ford's single-overhead-camshaft Pinto engine and, with the arrival of the revised body style, a 2 litre version took over from the V4.

From 1976 the model was only built in Germany but was still sold in Britain. In 1978 Capri III with quadruple headlamps arrived. Eventually as sales fell away, the range began to contract; the 1300 disappeared in 1982, the same year that the 3 litre V6 was dropped, to be replaced by a 2.8 litre fuel injection version. This and the 1.6 and 2 litre cars survived to the very end. The last of the 2.8s were produced in "limited edition" form with Brooklands Green livery, all leather trim and limited slip differential.

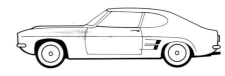
BELOW: *A 1986 Capri Laser with 1.6 litre, four cylinder, overhead-camshaft engine. Introduced in 1984, this special edition model had a body coloured grille and tinted windows.*

ABOVE: *A Capri in its original 1969 form. Thankfully the rear located imitation cooling grilles were dispensed with on the arrival of the Mark II Capri in 1974.*

RIGHT: *A Capri RS3100. Made in 1973-74 and intended for track rather than road, it was powered by a 3.1 litre V6 engine and was also lower than the standard product.*

Ford Capri

Capri I 1969

| 1.3 litre pushrod 4 | 1.6 litre pushrod 4 | 2 litre pushrod V4 | 3 litre pushrod V6 |

1.6 litre Pinto overhead camshaft 4 1973

Capri II 1974

| 1.3 litre pushrod | 1.6 litre Pinto | 2 litre Pinto | 3 litre V6 |

Capri III 1978

| 1.3 litre pushrod | 1.6 litre Pinto | 2 litre Pinto | 3 litre V6 |

2.8 litre V6 1982

CITROËN SM (1970-1975)

The fearsomely complex Maserati-engined SM has the distinction of being the world's first front-wheel-drive Grand Tourer. It was also a factor in Citroën purchasing Maserati but the model was not a sales success and the SM's production span coincided with the Michelin-owned company being itself taken over by the rival French manufacturer, Peugeot.

When in the late 1960's Citroën was planning to extend its range to include a prestigious GT, it was restricted by not having a suitably powerful engine in its existing model line-up. It therefore turned its attention to smaller car makers, the requirements of the SM being one of the reasons for the firm buying Maserati, in which it took a majority shareholding in 1968, with the deal being completed in 1971.

The engine on which the Maserati range relied was a V8, with twin overhead camshafts per bank, then produced in 4.1 and 4.7 litre forms. Even the smallest capacity V8 was too large for Citroën's requirements, so Maserati's chief engineer, Giulio Alfieri, was ordered to lop off two cylinders, produce a V6 and have the engine running within six months. It was, in fact, completed in a mere three weeks but the resulting 3.1 litres capacity was still too great and, eventually, the size was reduced to 2.7 litres in deference to France's 15CV tax ceiling, a measure which financially penalized cars of over 2.8 litres capacity.

Since 1934 Citroën had led the world in the production of front-wheel-drive cars and the SM would be no exception. However, it meant that the engine had to be mounted back to front and this required that the ancillaries be relocated. The 170bhp V6 drove the wheels via a purpose-designed five-speed gearbox.

A Smoother Ride

The SM's aerodynamically efficient body and mechanicals were based on Citroën's long running DS saloon and, accordingly, benefitted from that model's sophisticated hydropneumatic self-levelling suspension. In addition the VariPower steering, requiring a mere two turns from lock to lock, incorporated an artificial feel system which was something of a limitation to such a facility. As if this was not enough, the SM had no less than six Cibie quartz halogen headlights, located behind a perspex cover, the inner pair turning with the steering.

When announced in March 1970, the SM was the most expensive Citroën

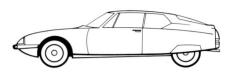

Citroën SM

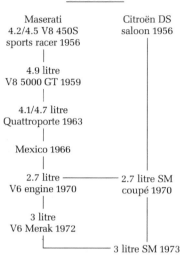

```
Maserati                Citroën DS
4.2/4.5 V8 450S         saloon 1956
sports racer 1956
     |
4.9 litre
V8 5000 GT 1959
     |
4.1/4.7 litre
Quattroporte 1963
     |
Mexico 1966
     |
2.7 litre ─────────── 2.7 litre SM
V6 engine 1970         coupé 1970
     |                     |
3 litre
V6 Merak 1972
     |
     └─────────────── 3 litre SM 1973
```

ever, selling for 46,000 francs, and when marketed in Britain from 1972, the price was £5342, even though the model was only built in left-hand-drive form.

The SM was capable of 135mph (217km/h) but drivers took time to get used to the idiosyncrasies of the steering and rear passengers complained of cramped seating. Despite these limitations, the model got off to an encouraging start with 4988 cars produced in 1971, and 4036 in the following year. However, output slumped to 2619 in 1973. Modifications included fuel injecting the V6 in 1972 and a supplementary 3 litre version with automatic transmission followed in mid-1973.

These developments did little to slow the model's decline and the knock-out blow was provided by the oil crisis of late 1973. In the following year production was transferred from Paris to a small Ligier factory at Abrest, near Vichy, but manufacture ceased in 1975 after 12,920 SMs had been produced. By this time the over-extended Citroën company had also changed hands, having been bought, in December 1974, by the rival Peugeot concern.

RIGHT: *A 1975 SM with its six Cibie headlamps, the inners turning with the steering. This is a British registered car but the SM was only available in left-hand-drive form.*

Specifications: Citroën SM

Length:	16ft (4877mm)
Width:	6ft (1829mm)
Height:	4ft 4in (1321mm)
Wheelbase:	9ft 8in (2946mm)
Track:	front 5ft (1524mm), rear 4ft 4in (1321mm)
Unladen weight:	3197lb (1450kg)

Engine: V6 with twin overhead camshafts per cylinder bank, 87x75mm, 2670cc. Compression ratio, 9:1. Max power, 180bhp at 6250rpm. Max torque, 172lb/ft at 4000rpm.

Transmission:	Five-speed manual
Drive:	Front
Suspension (front):	Independent, twin transverse arms with trailing mountings, hydropneumatic spring damper units interconnected with rear
Suspension (rear):	Independent, trailing arms, hydropneumatic spring damper units interconnected with front
Top speed:	135mph (217km/h)
0-60mph (96km/h):	8.4 seconds
Production (total):	12,920

LEFT: *The SM's packed engine compartment was a jumble of V6 Maserati engine and the plumbing associated with hydropneumatics of the all-independent suspension.*

RIGHT: *The distinctive rear profile of a 1974 SM. By this time the model was powered by a 3 litre engine and, as indicated, fuel injection which was adopted from 1972.*

BMW 3.0 CS, CSL, CSi (1971-1975)

Sleek, fast and well built, the CS family of 3 litre BMW coupés more than lived up to their good looks and were able to convey their occupants in considerable comfort at speeds of over 130mph (209km/h). These were road cars but they also spawned the sensational racing lightweight CSL which dominated the European Touring Car Championship for much of the 1970's.

The origins of these handsome cars are rooted in BMW's four cylinder 2 litre 2000C coupé of 1965. Built by Karmann, it is perhaps best remembered for its controversial front end styling. In 1968 it was replaced by the six cylinder 2.8 litre 2800C, which was concurrent with a new generation of similarly powered saloons. On the 2800 coupé the substructure from the windscreen backwards was shared with its predecessor, but the fitment of the six cylinder engine meant that the front end was reworked and the wheelbase extended by 3in (76mm) to 8ft 7in (2616mm). Suspension was all-independent, with front MacPherson struts, rear semi-trailing arms and all-round coil springs, a system also shared by its saloon stablemates. Karmann was once again responsible for its construction and 9399 examples were produced before the model was discontinued in 1971, to be replaced by the 3.0 CS.

Introduced in April 1971, it retained the 2800's Karmann-built body and much of its mechanicals, with the exception of the overhead camshaft six that was enlarged to 3 litres and developed 180bhp. This pushed the car's top speed up to 132mph (213km/h);

braking was provided by new all-round ventilated discs.

In the same year of 1971 two derivatives appeared. The first, announced in May, was the 3.0 CSL, which similarly developed 180bhp but had lightened bodywork and wider wheels. Later, in September, came the fuel-injected CSi, which was outwardly similar to the CS but, as its model name indicated, was powered by a 200bhp D jetronic fuel-injected six.

The CSi was to remain essentially unchanged throughout its lifespan, but the CSL evolved dramatically into a successful racing coupé. In late 1972 its engine was enlarged to 3003cc, by increasing the bore size from 89 to 89.25mm. The fuel-injected unit now developed 200bhp.

In the same year of 1972, BMW's competition department was revitalized by the arrival from Ford of Jochen Neerpasch and it was he, along with Martin Braungart whose forte was for

aerodynamic refinement, who transformed the CSL into the "Batmobile", so named because of its front and highly distinctive rear spoilers. The six was once again enlarged, this time to 3153cc by increasing the engine's stroke from 80 to 84mm. In standard form this CSL developed 206bhp but factory cars eventually produced in excess of 470bhp. The coupé proved unbeatable in European Touring Car Championship events. It was victorious in 1973 and for five successive seasons between 1975 and 1979.

By this time the 3 litre coupés were no more – they had been discontinued in 1975 and replaced by the 6 Series cars. The 3.0 CS accounted for 11,063 units, while the CSi found 8199 buyers. By contrast, the potent CSL was produced in relatively small numbers – only 1039 were built – but they did wonders for BMW's image as a producer of a series of road cars with distinct racing potential.

LEFT: *A 1973 BMW 3.0 CSL with its lightened bodywork and wider wheels but otherwise outwardly similar to the basic 3.0 CS and its 2800 CS predecessor.*

RIGHT: *The aerodynamically refined BMW 3.0 CSL "Batmobile" with its memorable rear spoiler. This is a 1974 car and, by this time, the fuel-injected six had grown to 3.1 litres.*

Specifications: BMW 3.0 CS

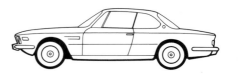

Length:	15ft 3in (4648mm)
Width:	5ft 6in (1676mm)
Height:	4ft 6in (1372mm)
Wheelbase:	8ft 7in (2616mm)
Track:	front 4ft 9in (1448mm), rear 4ft 7in (1397mm)
Unladen weight:	3085lb (1402kg)
Engine: Six cylinder, single overhead camshaft, 89x80mm, 2985cc. Compression ratio, 9:1. Max power, 180bhp at 6000rpm. Max torque, 188lb/ft at 4300rpm.	
Transmission:	Four-speed manual/three-speed automatic
Drive:	Rear
Suspension (front):	Independent, MacPherson struts, coil springs
Suspension (rear):	Independent, semi-trailing arms, coil springs
Top speed:	132mph (212km/h)
0-60mph (96km/h):	14.2 seconds
Production (3.0 CS, CSL, CSi):	20,301

BMW 3.0 CS, CSL, CSi

1.5 litre four cylinder 1500 saloon 1962

1.8 litre four cylinder 1800 saloon 1963

2 litre engine

2000C coupé 1965   2000 saloon 1966

2.5 litre six cylinder 2500 saloon 1968

2.8 litre 2800 saloon 1968 — 2.8 litre 2800 CS coupé 1968

3.0 saloon 1971

3 litre 3.0 CS coupé 1971

3.0 CSL   3.0 CSi

3003cc 1972   3153cc 1973

RIGHT: *A 3.0 CSL coupé, foreground, on the move in company with a 3.0 CSL "Batmobile", complete with obligatory front air dam, roof-mounted aerofoil and rear wing.*

The E-Type was Jaguar's last sports car and its final manifestation was the V12-powered Series III. From 1948 Ferrari was the sole exponent of this engine configuration. It was joined in 1964 by Lamborghini, although both engines were low production units. By contrast, Jaguar's was the first European V12 designed for quantity manufacture. It was used in Jaguar's most famous sports car and, later, in the XJ12 saloon and the more exclusive XJS.

RIGHT: *A 1971 V12-powered E-Type. Unlike its six cylinder predecessors, the Series III has a radiator grille and flared wheel arches. Optional wire spoked wheels are fitted.*

The E-Type dated back to 1961 when it was launched in 3.8 litre form. The capacity of the six cylinder XK engine was extended to 4.2 litres in 1966. In that year the roadster and coupé were joined by the longer wheelbase 2+2 model which was only available in closed form. Like its predecessors, the majority of E-Types were exported to America with around 80 per cent of production being so designated and when that country introduced its emissions and safety regulations, Jaguar had little choice but to abide by them. The detoxing equipment fitted to the 4.2 litre six drastically reduced its performance but this was rectified in 1971 by the fitment of the 5.3 litre V12 which improved the car's acceleration, although its top speed remained at around 140mph (225km/h).

The Roadgoing V12

Jaguar's long anticipated V12 engine had been waiting in the wings since the 1950's. It had initially appeared in 5 litre form with twin overhead camshafts per cylinder bank, effectively two XK engines on a common crankcase, in the 1966 XJ13 sports racer built for Le Mans but never raced there. However, the roadgoing versions of the V12 employed single overhead camshaft heads which were more suitable. The unit was first used in the E-Type although its ultimate destination was under the bonnet of the XJ12 saloon that appeared in 1973, two years after the Series III E-Type.

This was produced in both roadster and coupé forms and was built on the longer 8ft 9in (2667mm) two-plus-two wheelbase. It visually differed from its six cylinder predecessors by the frontal air intake being fitted with a chromed grille and new, wider pressed steel wheels with both front and rear arches flared to accommodate them.

The 272bhp engine employed four Zenith Stromberg carburettors and the smooth, turbine-like unit was able to propel the Series III to 100mph (161km/h) in around 15 seconds. But

while the six cylinder E-Type was an out and out sports car, the V12 transformed it into a more refined Grand Tourer able to eat up the miles in speed and silence. Indeed many examples were fitted with optional automatic transmission.

Unfortunately American demand for the model virtually ceased in 1973 for two reasons. Firstly, its ageing specifications and lack of air conditioning told against it. Secondly, the devastating oil price rise of that year savaged sales of thirsty, large-engined cars. Production of the Series III coupé therefore ceased in that year. The roadster soldiered on although an arctic economic climate resulted in sluggish sales. The last car was built in September 1974 although the news of its discontinuation was not made public until February 1975 because there were still plenty in dealer showrooms. The final fifty examples were finished in distinctive black paintwork and the last car was bought by that great British Jaguar enthusiast, Robert Danny, who specified dark green paint.

Of the 72,233 E-Types built, just over 20 per cent were V12s, with production split almost evenly between 7975 roadsters and 7008 coupés.

Jaguar E-Type Series III

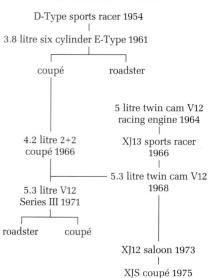

D-Type sports racer 1954
|
3.8 litre six cylinder E-Type 1961
|
coupé   roadster

5 litre twin cam V12 racing engine 1964
|
4.2 litre 2+2   XJ13 sports racer
coupé 1966   1966
|
                    5.3 litre twin cam V12
                            1968
5.3 litre V12
Series III 1971
|
roadster   coupé

XJ12 saloon 1973
|
XJS coupé 1975

Specifications: Jaguar E-Type Series III

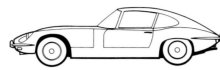

Length:	15ft 4in (4674mm)
Width:	5ft 6in (1676mm)
Height:	4ft (1219mm)
Wheelbase:	8ft 9in (2667mm)
Track:	front 4ft 6in (1372mm), rear 4ft 5in (1346mm)
Unladen weight:	3316lb (1505kg)
Engine: V12 with single overhead camshafts per cylinder bank, 90x70mm, 5343cc. Compression ratio, 9:1. Max power, 266bhp at 5750rpm. Max torque, 304lb/ft at 3500rpm.	
Transmission:	Four-speed manual
Drive:	Rear
Suspension (front):	Independent, torsion bars, wishbones
Suspension (rear):	Independent, coil springs, lower wishbones/drive shaft
Top speed:	142mph (228km/h)
0-60mph (96km/h):	7.3 seconds
Production (total V12):	14,983

BELOW: *A 1971 E-Type with its standard disc wheels. The V12-powered model was only produced in two-plus-two form although there was also a roadster version.*

ABOVE: *There isn't much room under a Series III's bonnet. The 5.3 litre V12 engine was used in carburettored form and this was its first application in a roadgoing Jaguar.*

FERRARI 365 GT4 2+2, 400, 412 (1972-1989)

The last of the front V12-engined Ferraris was also the firm's longest running model. It started life in 1972 as the 365 GT4 2+2 and its finely proportioned Pininfarina body was endowed with a timeless quality which ensured that it enjoyed a long production life without any major external modifications. During this time, the engine had benefitted from two increases in capacity.

Ferrari's first car with rear accommodation for children was the 250 GTE of 1960 and this design theme was continuously maintained throughout the decade. However, when the 365 GTC/4 of 1968 ceased production in 1971 there was a year's hiatus before its replacement arrived.

It had been worth the wait. The 365 GT4 2+2 was introduced at the 1972 Paris Show but, unlike its predecessor which had a production life of a mere four years, this was destined to endure for 17 seasons. Mechanically, it had more in common with the 365 GTC/4 two seater of 1971-72 rather than the two-plus-two it was replacing. This was because that model had a 4.4 litre V12 engine with single overhead camshafts per bank while the new car had twin cam heads, *à la* GTC/4, which had been introduced by Ferrari in 1966. Otherwise the engine's origins were rooted in Colombo's 1948 creation. Developing an undisclosed 320bhp, the unit aspirated through no less than six side-draught Weber carburettors which permitted a low bonnet line.

Drive was taken, via a five-speed gearbox and torque tube, to the differential which was chassis mounted, the latter being a tubular steel design. Independent suspension by coil springs and wishbones had been a feature of the marque since 1964 and self-levelling oleopneumatic struts were fitted at the rear.

Impressive as these mechanicals were, it was the extraordinarily assured body, designed and built by Pininfarina, that was the truly impressive aspect of the car. Longer, lower and wider than the 365 GT 2+2, well proportioned and with virtually no external decoration, the car's 8ft 10in (2700mm) wheelbase was longer than its predecessor but it was 2in (51mm) shorter overall. Consequently it was roomier than previously, both for the passengers – it had separate seats at the rear – and in terms of luggage accommodation. Refinements included air conditioning and power steering.

Performance was, inevitably, impressive with the big V12 providing the car with an effortless top speed of 150mph (241km/h), even though fuel consumption was undeniably heavy, coming in at around the 11mpg (25.6 litres/100km) mark.

The model endured in this form until 1976, by which time 524 had been built, when it was renamed the 400GT on account of the introduction of a longer stroked 4.8 litre engine. The simultaneously announced 400A was fitted with General Motors automatic transmission, which was the first time that Ferrari had done this.

The V12 continued to employ a battery of carburettors until 1979 when the Webers were replaced by a Bosch fuel injection system. The model was accordingly redesignated the 400i. In 1985 came yet another engine enlargement, this time to 4.9 litres, and automatic transmission was standardized on what was now called the 412, though a manual gearbox remained available as an option. By then it was the only Ferrari in which the V12 engine was front positioned; all other cars had mid-located power units. The 412 continued to be produced in this form until 1989.

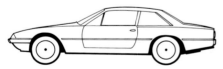

Specifications: Ferrari 365 GT4

Length:	15ft 9in (4801mm)
Width:	5ft 10in (1778mm)
Height:	4ft 4in (1321mm)
Wheelbase:	8ft 10in (2692mm)
Track:	front and rear, 4ft 9in (1448mm)
Unladen weight:	4250lb (1928kg)

Engine: V12 with twin overhead camshafts per cylinder bank, 81x71mm, 4390cc. Compression ratio, 8.8:1. Max power, 340bhp at 7000rpm. Max torque, 312lb/ft at 4600rpm.

Transmission:	Five-speed manual
Drive:	Rear
Suspension (front):	Independent, coil springs and wishbones
Suspension (rear):	Independent, coil springs and wishbones
Top speed:	150mph (241km/h)
0-60mph (96km/h):	7.2 seconds
Production (total 365, 400, 412):	2405

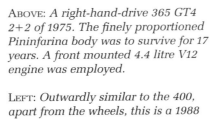

ABOVE: *A right-hand-drive 365 GT4 2+2 of 1975. The finely proportioned Pininfarina body was to survive for 17 years. A front mounted 4.4 litre V12 engine was employed.*

LEFT: *Outwardly similar to the 400, apart from the wheels, this is a 1988 412 with engine enlarged to 4.9 litres. A further refinement was self-levelling rear suspension.*

Ferrari 365 GT4, 400 and 412

4.4 litre V12 Ferrari 365 GTC/4 1971

365 GT4 2+2 coupé 1972

4.8 litre 400 1976

4.9 litre 412 1985

RIGHT: *The magnificent Ferrari 4.8 litre V12 engine, with twin overhead camshafts per cylinder bank, of a 400i of 1979 vintage. The i suffix indicates the fitment of Bosch K-Jetronic fuel injection, as evidenced by the pump in the centre foreground. This impressive looking power unit developed 310bhp at 6400 rpm.*

JAGUAR XJS (1975 to date)

It is difficult to think of a more inopportune time to launch a thirsty, V12-powered GT than September of 1975 when the world was still reeling from the effects of the oil price rise. But this is when Jaguar introduced the XJS, at that time its most expensive car ever, selling at £8900. Despite this unfavourable economic climate and the fact that the model got off to an uncertain start, it remains in production to this day, nearly 20 years after its introduction to the market.

One thing that the XJS was not, was a successor to the E-Type which had been discontinued earlier in 1975. The thinking behind the new model was that Jaguar decided to sidestep sports cars, a feature of the marque since 1935, and move upmarket into the more expensive Grand Tourer sector where sales volumes were lower but profit margins higher.

Despite being styled by Malcolm Sayer, who had the lines of the legendary D and E-Types to his credit, the consensus was that the XJS two-plus-two coupé lacked the visual impact of its predecessors. It was, initially, only available in closed form. It proved itself able to eat up the miles in silence and passenger comfort (air conditioning was a standard fitment) thanks to the 5.3 litre V12 engine, fuel injected in the XJS, which had first appeared in the 1971 Series III E-Type. Despite the car being offered with a choice of manual or automatic transmission, the latter option was almost exclusively employed. Based on the shortened floor pan of Jaguar's highly acclaimed XJ6 saloon, the running gear was also courtesy of that car and featured all independent suspension with coils and wishbones at the front, and fixed length drive shafts and lower wishbones at the rear.

Fast But Thirsty

Top speed was an effortless 150mph (241km/h) plus, but this was achieved at the expense of a fuel consumption of 14mpg (20.1 litres/100km). This was the principal factor why, at the end of the 1970's, XJS production had, to all intents and purposes, ceased. However, in 1981, the V12 was fitted with new cylinder heads, developed by Michael May, which improved fuel consumption to an average of 16mpg (17.6 litres/100km). At the same time the interior was impressively uprated with extensive use of leather and walnut veneer which, curiously, were absent from the original version.

Later, for 1984, came the supplementary XJS 3.6, so called because it was

Specifications: Jaguar XJS

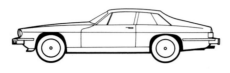

Length:	15ft 11in (4851mm)
Width:	4ft 1in (1245mm)
Height:	5ft 10in (1778mm)
Wheelbase:	8ft 6in (2591mm)
Track:	front 4ft 10in (1473mm), rear 4ft 10½in (1488mm)
Unladen weight:	3710lb (1683kg)

Engine: V12 with single overhead camshafts per cylinder bank, 90x70mm, 5343cc. Compression ratio, 9:1. Fuel injection. Max power, 285bhp at 5500rpm. Max torque, 294lb/ft at 3500rpm.

Transmission:	Three-speed automatic
Drive:	Rear
Suspension (front):	Independent, coil springs and wishbones
Suspension (rear):	Independent, coil springs, modified wishbones, drive shafts and lower links
Top speed:	152mph (245km/h)
0-60mph (96km/h):	7 seconds
Production (total to date):	102,587

the first recipient of Jaguar's new 3.6 litre, twin-overhead-camshaft, 24 valve, six cylinder engine which also replaced Jaguar's long-running XK unit in the XJ6 saloons from 1987. The XJS's fuel consumption figures rose to around 17mpg (16.6 litres/100km), aided by the standardization of a five-speed manual gearbox. However, this was achieved at the expense of top speed, which dropped to about the 140mph (225km/h) mark. A cabriolet (open) option also appeared in 1984 and an automatic version of the six followed in 1987.

The mainstream V12 continued to be impressively refined over the years and, in mid-1989, JaguarSport's XJR-S coupé appeared, with enlarged 6 litre V12 engine. Later in 1991 the six's capacity was increased to 4 litres, and the V12 went to 6 litres in 1993. Today, after a chequered history, the XJS has established itself as one of the world's finest V12-powered Grand Tourers.

LEFT: *A 1991 XJ-S cabriolet. Introduced in 1984, it was available in 3.6 litre six and 5.3 litre V12-engined forms which were enlarged to 4 and 6 litres in 1992 and 1993 respectively.*

FAR LEFT: *The PPB Special, essentially a styling exercise, that brought some of the E-Type's curves into the XJ-S, on which it was based. This single car was built in Bristol in 1991.*

Jaguar XJS

5 litre four cam V12 racing engine 1964

XJ13 sports racer 1966

4.2 litre six cylinder XJ6 saloon 1968

5.3 litre twin cam V12 1968

E-Type Series III 1971

5.3 litre XJ12 saloon 1973

V12 —— XJS coupé 1975

3.6 litres 1984

6 litre XJR-S 1989

4 litres 1991

6 litre XJS 1993

BELOW: *The XJ-S received the 6 litre engine from the XJ12 saloon in May 1993. It also benefitted from new moulded bumpers and five-spoked alloy wheels.*

LOTUS ESPRIT (1975 to date)

Britain's sole series production, mid-engined road car is the exclusive Lotus Esprit, introduced in 1975 and followed in 1980 by a potent turbocharged version. Today these Esprits remain as the company's only models in production and are the sole survivors of three models of glass-fibre-bodied car introduced by the Norfolk company in 1974 and 1975.

All were powered by Lotus' new 2 litre, twin-overhead-camshaft, four cylinder engine which first appeared in the front-engined Elite of 1974. This was followed in 1975 by the cheaper Eclat hatchback that shared its mechanicals. Unlike its stablemates, the Esprit, the flagship of the range, was not styled in-house but essayed by the respected Turin-based Ital Design concern. The first thoughts of cooperation between the two firms occurred when Lotus's Colin Chapman and Ital's Giorgetto Giugiaro met by chance at the 1971 Geneva Motor Show. It was decided that the new car was to follow the mid-engined theme of the Lotus Europa of 1966-75.

The Esprit was built up around the make's familiar backbone chassis, with the 160bhp engine located longitudinally and driving through a five-speed gearbox, which was courtesy of the recently discontinued Citroën SM. As ever, suspension was all-independent with coil springs and wishbones at the front and coils and semi-trailing arms at the rear. The model also featured all-round disc brakes – the first Lotus model to feature them front and rear.

Announced at the 1975 London Motor Show, the new car cost £5844, although the price had soared to £7883 by the time that deliveries began in mid-1976. Its critics were the first to point out that it was the most expensive four-cylinder-engined car in the world . . .

Brilliant Cornering
Like any Lotus, the Esprit cornered as if on rails but a claimed top speed of 138mph (222km/h) regrettably did not materialize, although the car was capable of a still rapid 124mph (200km/h). The anticipated figures would have to wait for the improved S2 Esprit of 1978. In 1980 the engine's capacity was increased to 2.2 litres.

Performance was the theme of the

RIGHT: *Transport for 007 James Bond, who used this Esprit Turbo, complete with skis, in the film* For Your Eyes Only. *It was released in 1981, the year following the Turbo's arrival.*

exciting Esprit Turbo which appeared in 1980 and which was a great improvement on the original, with output of the enlarged four boosted to 210bhp. This was mounted in a redesigned chassis intended for a V8 version of the unit which, alas, never materialized. Changes were also made to the rear suspension and the body lines sharpened. The model's top speed leapt to close on 150mph (241km/h) and the 60mph (96km/h) threshold was breached in a shade over 6 seconds. The Turbo got valuable international publicity when it provided

transport for 007 James Bond in the 1981 film *For Your Eyes Only*.

Both Esprits continued as steady sellers but these were difficult years for any car company, let alone a small one like Lotus. In 1986 the firm was taken over by the American General Motors Corporation. For 1988 the Esprit was restyled both inside and out, the body update being undertaken by Lotus itself with a softening of the contours and the introduction of a removable roof panel. The car also benefitted significantly from the introduction of a new five-speed gearbox.

The General Motors association was destined to last until 1993 when Lotus was bought by the revived Bugatti company. But by this time all the Esprit's contemporaries had been discontinued. The last Elite was built in 1982 while the Excel, which was the successor to the Eclat, remained in production until 1992.

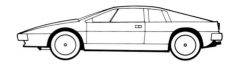

ABOVE: *The Esprit was updated in 1993, the S4 had a more rounded nose and new tail while power steering, wider wheels and revised suspension were introduced.*

Lotus Esprit

2 litre four cylinder engine

Front-engined Elite 1974

Front-engined Eclat 1975   Mid-engined Esprit 1975

2.2 litre engine 1980 — Esprit Turbo

To 1982

Excel 1985

To 1992

S4 restyle 1993

To date

PORSCHE 928 (1977 to date)

Between 1948 and 1976, the Porsche company exclusively produced rear-engined, air-cooled road cars, an engineering creed that was exemplified by the apparently irrepressible 911. However, in the early 1970's the firm decided to turn its back on what it considered to be an outdated concept and consequently it introduced a new generation of front-engined, liquid-cooled models. The first of these appeared in 1976 in the form of the popular 924 coupé and it was followed in 1977 by the prestigious 928, which was powered by the firm's first V8 engine.

Porsche 928

First 928 prototypes 1975
|
4.5 litre single cam V8 928 coupé 1977
|
4.7 litre engine 1979
|
5 litre twin cam V8 1985
|
928S-4 version 1987
|
330bhp GT version 1989

As nothing was to be carried over from previous models, the 928's gestation spanned no less than six years, having began in 1971, perversely before that of the 924. With emissions regulations in Porsche's all-important American market becoming increasingly demanding, the company opted for a V8 unit which could, unlike the 911, also be adapted for use with automatic transmission which was a further transatlantic requirement. A need for increasing levels of comfort and refinement was yet another consideration and, as a result, the front-located engine was balanced with a rear-mounted transaxle.

Input From Weissach
The 4.5 litre V8 engine, with a single overhead camshaft per bank, developed 240bhp and was separated from its five-speed gearbox by a tubular backbone which, unusually, contained a flexible drive shaft running in no less than five bearings. The all-independent suspension featured coil springs and wishbones at the front while the coil-sprung rear trailing arms incorporated what Porsche called its Weissach axle, named after the firm's research and development facility. The intention was to prevent the car spinning if the 928 driver had the misfortune to take his foot of the accelerator while taking a corner.

These mechanicals were cloaked in a distinctive two-plus-two coupé body with a large opening tailgate. Much of the shell (namely the front wings, door and bonnet) was made of aluminium with the remainder of the body built in steel. A further innovation concerned the model's apparent lack of bumpers. In fact, they were present under front and rear panels made of a deformable plastic material which was the same colour as the rest of the body. If the car was involved in an accident, they would return to their predetermined contours after the impact.

The ingenious technological package was unveiled at the 1977 Geneva Motor Show. It was greeted with many plaudits, of which the most prestigious was the 1978 Car of the Year award.

The 928 was a 140mph (225km/h) car. However, the 0 to 60mph (96km/h) figure of a little over 8 seconds was inferior to that of the well established 911, and this underlined the perception that the new car lacked the sparkle of its legendary rear-engined contemporary. These criticisms were met, to some extent, by the arrival in mid-1979 of the 928S with a bigger bored 4.7 litre engine. The car could now exceed 145mph (233km/h). In 1985 928s for the U.S. market were fitted with an enlarged 5 litre V8, employing twin cam, four valve cylinder heads, which developed 288bhp. For 1987 this power unit, boosted to 320bhp, was extended to the 928S-4 distinguished by an aerodynamically improved nose.

A 330bhp GT version, with stiffened suspension and wider tyres, followed in 1989; a claimed top speed of 170mph (274km/h) made it the fastest series production Porsche. It was only available in manual gearbox form. Paradoxically, changes in corporate thought mean that today it is not a car of the 928 type, but of the 911 theme on which Porsche is now staking its future. However, this beautifully engineered car does remain in production at the time of writing as one of Europe's finest Grand Tourers.

BELOW: *A 1982 928 with 4.4 litre V8 engine which benefitted from higher compression ratio and revised camshafts. It was, however, overshadowed by the 928S.*

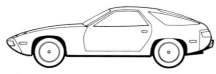

Specifications: Porsche 928

Length:	14ft 7in (4445mm)
Width:	6ft (1829mm)
Height:	4ft 4in (1321mm)
Wheelbase:	8ft 4in (2540mm)
Track:	front 5ft 4in (1626mm), rear 5ft 1in (1549mm)
Unladen weight:	3200lb (1450kg)
Engine: V8 with single overhead camshaft per cylinder bank, 95x78mm, 4474cc. Compression ratio, 8.5:1. Fuel injection. Max power, 240bhp at 5250rpm. Max torque, 267lb/ft at 3600rpm.	
Transmission:	Five-speed manual/ three-speed automatic
Drive:	Rear
Suspension (front):	Independent, coil springs and wishbones
Suspension (rear):	Independent, coil springs, trailing arms
Top speed:	142mph (228km/h)
0-60mph (96km/h):	8.1 seconds
Production (total to date):	65,000

ABOVE: *A 928S of 1989 with its headlamps in the raised position. By then the 928's V8 engine had been enlarged to 4.9 litres. The S was replaced in 1989 by the 928 GT.*

BELOW: *Other driver's view of a 1988 928S, complete with tail-gate-mounted rear spoiler. It was introduced, along with other aerodynamic aids on Series 4 cars, in 1986.*

MAZDA RX-7 (1978-1985)

The world's most successful Wankel-engined performance car, the RX-7, was the first of Mazda's RX series to combine the turbine-like efficiency of rotary power with the handling of a European Grand Tourer. As a consequence the car proved to be a great success for Mazda, particularly in America, and over half a million examples were built.

In the 1960's, the appeal of the Wankel rotary engine with its smooth performance and relative lack of moving parts was considerable when compared with a conventional, reciprocating engine. But, on the debit side, there were heavier fuel and oil consumption, poor emissions and problems with the rotor's vital apex seals which seemingly took aeons to resolve. The German NSU concern owned the Wankel licence and, in 1961, it was taken up in Japan by the Toyo Kogyo group's Mazda company, which persevered with rotary power long after NSU had ceased to. Today it is the world's sole maker of Wankel-engined cars.

Early Ideas
The first fruits of this research appeared in 1967 with the arrival of the 110S coupé, which was not only Mazda's first rotary powered car but was also the first in the world to be powered by a twin rotor unit. It was a few weeks ahead of NSU's sensational and similarly driven Ro80 saloon. The following year came Mazda's rather characterless Wankel-engined R100 saloon. Some similarly lacklustre RX series cars followed but all this changed with the arrival, in 1978, of the RX-7, a sleek coupé which purred to an effortless 125mph (201km/h).

Aimed foursquare at the Datsun 280Z and Porsche 924 markets, the RX-7 was a sleek hatchback coupé with an impressive 0.32 drag coefficient, which made it the most aerodynamically efficient car of its day. Under its low bonnet line nestled a twin rotary engine with a nominal 2.3 litres capacity. Designated Type 12A, it was an evolutionary version of the units found in other cars in the Mazda range. In the RX-7's engine the all-important apex seals were made of a long wearing iron alloy, rather than carbon which had been used previously. A single four barrel downdraught carburettor was fitted and the unit developed 100bhp at 6000 revolutions per minute. Transmission to the live coil-sprung rear axle was via a five-speed manual gearbox; automatic transmission was available as an option. Front suspension was by MacPherson struts and disc brakes were fitted at the front.

Originally only available in Japan and America, the model reached Britain late in 1979. The RX-7 received universal praise for its performance with 60mph (96km/h) coming up in around 9 seconds. Handling was equally impressive. Fears of problems with the unconventional engine had been largely dispelled with units shown to be capable of over 100,000 miles (161,000km) with little more than routine maintenance. Drivers found that the twin rotor unit sounded smoother as the revs increased and, so deceptive were the revolutions, the RX-7 was fitted with a warning buzzer which was activated at 6000rpm. Less desirable were complaints of heavy steering and high fuel consumption.

No major changes occurred in 1981 when the car's front end was redesigned and a spoiler introduced at the rear. At the same time disc brakes were extended to the rear wheels and electric windows introduced. In 1984 came a 160bhp turbocharged version for the American market. The model was discontinued in 1985 when it was replaced by a new and larger RX-7.

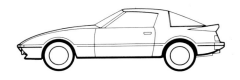

Length:	14ft 1in (4293mm)
Width:	5ft 5in (1651mm)
Height:	4ft 1in (1245mm)
Wheelbase:	7ft 11in (2413mm)
Track:	front 4ft 8in (1422mm), rear 4ft 7in (1397mm)
Unladen weight:	2350lb (1066kg)
Engine: Twin rotor Wankel, 2x573mm, 2292cc. Compression ratio, 9.4:1. Max power, 100bhp at 6000rpm. Max torque, 105lb/ft at 4000rpm.	
Transmission:	Five-speed manual/ four-speed automatic
Drive:	Rear
Suspension (front):	Independent, MacPherson strut
Suspension (rear):	Live axle, coil springs
Top speed:	125mph (201km/h)
0-60mph (96km/h):	8.9 seconds
Production:	570,500

ABOVE: *A 1982 Mazda RX-7 Elford Turbo. All British registered RX-7s were also equipped with sun roof, driver's door mirror and a rear window wash/wipe facility.*

LEFT: *The Elford RX-7 with Garrett turbocharger was distinguished by extra spoilers and wide alloy wheels. Faster than the basic car, it could reach 135mph (217km/h).*

RIGHT: *Head-on view of the Elford Turbo RX-7 with the front air dam and twin spotlamps, which were only fitted to this variant, readily apparent. Pirelli P6 tyres were supplied.*

Mazda RX-7

2 litre twin rotor Wankel engine

|

Mazda 110S coupé 1967

|

R100 coupé/saloon 1968

|

2.3 litre RX-2 coupé/saloon 1970

|

2.3 litre RX-3 coupé/saloon 1971

|

2.3, 2.6 litre RX-4 coupé/saloon 1972

|

2.3, 2.6 litre Cosmo (RX-5) coupé/saloon 1975

|

2.3 litre RX-7 coupé 1978

AUDI QUATTRO (1980-1991)

Until the arrival of the Quattro, the concept of a four-wheel-drive road car had been confined to the big, costly Jensen Interceptor of 1966-71 vintage. All this changed with the appearance of this revolutionary Audi which introduced the system to a wider public. The car was soon dominating the rallying scene and, inevitably, the world's motor manufacturers have since followed in its sure-footed wheel tracks.

From 1965 Audi has been owned by Volkswagen and the Quattro's origins are to be found in the four-wheel-drive VW Iltris cross-country vehicle, conceived and built by Audi since 1978. During the winter of 1976/7, a pre-production example was tested by Jörg Bensinger, Audi's chief chassis engineer. He had conceived the notion of the vehicle's compact, permanently engaged drive system being applied to a road car. Most significantly, it dispensed with the weighty and expensive transfer box which had been a feature of the Jensen FF.

Audi's head of research and development, Ferdinand Piech, gave the idea his blessing and prototypes were running by the spring of 1978 with the car making a memorable debut at the 1980 Geneva Motor Show. The Quattro was based on the floorpan of the 80 model while the two-door body was that of the as yet unannounced Audi GT, which appeared in the following year. The engine was the firm's 2.1 litre, turbocharged, fuel-injected, five cylinder, overhead-camshaft unit, which had been so enhanced for the top-of-the range Audi 200 saloon also announced in 1980.

Four-Wheel Wizardry
The ingenuity of the system lay in the car's gearbox, located behind the in-line engine, which contained no less than two differentials. Drive from the power unit was conveyed via an upper gear train to a hollow lower transfer shaft and a small grapefruit-sized central differential. From there it went to the back wheels through the customary propeller shaft and rear-mounted diff. But the master stroke of the design was that drive was simultaneously conveyed to the front wheels, through a second shaft which ran inside the lower transfer cluster, to their own differential in the usual manner. Suspension was by all-round struts and disc brakes were fitted throughout.

Ironically, Bensinger had not been thinking of a competition element when he proposed the Quattro's creation, but the configuration, with its leech-like roadholding and tenacious grip of appalling road surfaces, made it a natural machine for rallying. For three years, it dominated international competition. In 1981 Audi was placed fifth in the World Championship of Makes but it won the title in 1982, and was second in 1983 when it was successfully challenged by Lancia. It was triumphant again in 1984. In 1983 came the rally-proven Quattro Sport road car, limited to 200 units, with shorter 7ft 3in (2204mm) wheelbase and 20 valve (as opposed to the usual 10) engine of a slightly smaller 2135cc capacity.

These engines developed in excess of 300bhp but the mainstream roadgoing Quattro produced a slightly more docile 200. This was a 115mph (185km/h) machine, capable of reaching 100mph (161km/h) in under 20 seconds. But it was on narrow, twisting roads that the car really came into its own, being about 20mph (32km/h) faster in such conditions than its more conventionally driven contemporaries. In fact, such was the success of the concept, by 1985 the four-wheel-drive system had been extended as an option to the entire Audi range.

The original model remained in production until 1991 by which time a host of other manufacturers had joined the once exclusive four-wheel-drive club, thanks to Audi's pioneering Quattro.

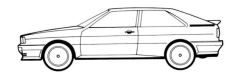

Specifications: Audi Quattro

Length:	14ft 5in (4394mm)
Width:	5ft 7in (1702mm)
Height:	4ft 4in (1321mm)
Wheelbase:	8ft 3in (2515mm)
Track:	front 4ft 7in (1397mm), rear 4ft 9in (1448mm)
Unladen weight:	2844lb (1290kg)
Engine: Five cylinder, single overhead camshaft, 79x86mm, 2144cc. Compression ratio, 7:1. Turbocharged. Max power, 220bhp at 5500rpm. Max torque, 210lb/ft at 3500rpm.	
Transmission:	Five-speed manual
Drive:	Four wheel
Suspension (front):	Independent, MacPherson strut
Suspension (rear):	Independent, MacPherson strut
Top speed:	115mph (185km/h)
0-60mph (96km/h):	7.4 seconds
Production:	11,425

RIGHT: *A 1983 example of the sensational four-wheel-drive Quattro. This is a version produced by Audi's former competition manager, Walter Treser, who left the firm in 1981.*

LEFT: *The short wheelbase Audi Sport road car, with its enlarged wheel arches, was based on the running gear of the production Quattro. Seating was a limited two-plus-two!*

Audi Quattro

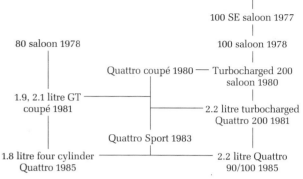

2.1 litre five cylinder engine
|
100 SE saloon 1977
|
80 saloon 1978   100 saloon 1978

Quattro coupé 1980 — Turbocharged 200 saloon 1980

1.9, 2.1 litre GT coupé 1981

2.2 litre turbocharged Quattro 200 1981

Quattro Sport 1983

1.8 litre four cylinder Quattro 1985   2.2 litre Quattro 90/100 1985

BELOW: *The Audi Sport's smaller capacity, 2.1 litre, five cylinder, turbocharged engine with 20 valve head, four per cylinder, which developed 300bhp at 6500 rpm. This is a 1985 example.*

PORSCHE 944 (1981-1992)

The third member of Porsche's water-cooled, front-engined family, the 944 contained elements of the earlier 924 and 928 models and was positioned, from a marketing standpoint, between them. In 1985 came a turbocharged version and although the range was discontinued in 1992, the cars were replaced by the closely related and current 968.

The 944 has its origins in the Audi-engined 924 of 1976 which Porsche had originally designed for Volkswagen but bought back when VW lacked the funds to put it into production. The 924, with its front-mounted, water-cooled engine and rear-located transaxle, reflected the mechanical theme of the yet unannounced 928 and was to be the best selling Porsche of its day with, eventually, over 122,000 built. The next car to appear in the family line was the prestigious and costly 928 of 1977, while the 944 arrived four years later in 1981.

Work on the project began in 1977 and the 944's two-plus-two coupé body bore a close resemblance to that of the 924, although it was 2in (50.8mm) wider to accommodate larger wheels. But where the 944 most radically differed from the 924 was in its 163bhp, 2.5 litre, four cylinder, single-overhead-camshaft engine which was, in effect, one bank of the 928's V8 unit. Its bore size was upped to 100mm but the 78mm stroke was retained. Large capacity fours have a reputation for rough running and Porsche sought to reduce this disturbance by introducing a pair of contra-rotating balance shafts to counteract the secondary forces that were generated in the engine.

The Genuine Article

As with the 924 and 928, the five-speed gearbox was located at the car's rear, while the all-independent suspension was an uprated version of that used in the 924, comprising front MacPherson struts and semi-trailing arms with Porsche-patented torsion bars at the rear. However, unlike the 924, this was a car which could be sold as exhibiting genuine Porsche pedigree.

The 944's top speed was in excess of 135mph (217km/h) and the model was much praised for the smoothness and flexibility of its engine, which countered valid criticism of the 924's unit. Commentators were less happy about the quality of the ride though.

Four years into the model's production, in 1985, a 220bhp turbocharged

Specifications: Porsche 944

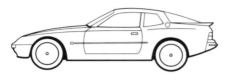

Length:	13ft 9in (4191mm)
Width:	5ft 8in (1727mm)
Height:	4ft 2in (1270mm)
Wheelbase:	7ft 10in (2388mm)
Track:	front 4ft 10in (1473mm), rear 4ft 9in (1448mm)
Unladen weight:	2602lb (1180kg)
Engine:	Four cylinder, single overhead camshaft, 100x78mm, 2479cc. Compression ratio, 10.6:1. Fuel injection. Max power, 163bhp at 5800rpm. Max torque, 151lb/ft at 3000rpm.
Transmission:	Five-speed manual
Drive:	Rear
Suspension (front):	Independent, MacPherson strut
Suspension (rear):	Independent, semi-trailing arms, torsion bars
Top speed:	135mph (217km/h)
0-60mph (96km/h):	7.5 seconds
Production:	163,249

version of the 944 was introduced. This involved some reworking of the car's nose to improve aerodynamics. The original instrument panel that derived from the 924 was replaced by one similar to that fitted in the 928. The Turbo could exceed 150mph (241km/h). This was followed for 1987 by the 190bhp 944S, which benefitted from a new 16 valve, twin-overhead-camshaft cylinder head similar to that fitted to the 928. In terms of performance, the S slotted in between the basic 944 and the Turbo and was capable of about 140mph (225km/h).

In August 1988 came a further enlargement to 3 litres, as well as an upgraded chassis and revisions to the body. A cabriolet version also appeared at the same time. The model remained in production until 1992, when it was replaced by the 944-based 968. This was powered, in essence, by the existing 3 litre four, while the front of the body echoes that of the 928, revealing itself as yet another permutation conceived by Porsche on the front engine/transaxle design.

ABOVE: *The 944's four cylinder, 16 valve engine was, in essence, half that of the 928's V8 unit. This is an S2 version of 1990, which by then had been enlarged to 3 litres.*

BELOW: *A 1987 944 Turbo. Introduced in 1985, it had an aerodynamically refined front, flush fitting windscreen and rear spoiler. These reduced the drag coefficient to 0.33.*

Porsche 944

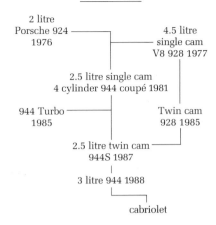

2 litre
Porsche 924
1976

4.5 litre
single cam
V8 928 1977

2.5 litre single cam
4 cylinder 944 coupé 1981

944 Turbo
1985

Twin cam
928 1985

2.5 litre twin cam
944S 1987

3 litre 944 1988

cabriolet

RIGHT: *The 944S, introduced for 1987, was powered by a 2.5 litre 16 valve 190bhp engine and featured revised gearbox ratios. ABS braking was also standardized.*

When Nissan introduced its new, sleek 300ZX in 1989, the company immodestly described it as "the best sports car in the world" and it was, in truth, light years away from its chubby, overweight, identically titled predecessor. This was a part of a coupé line which began in 1969 with the top selling Datsun 240Z (until 1983 Nissans were marketed abroad under the Datsun name), that evolved into the 280Z and led in turn to the 300ZX of 1984. Like all Z cars, its replacement was targetted at the American market, but the new 300ZX was virtually a new car. Unusually, it was built in two versions: one was a two-plus-two while the other was an uncompromising two-seater.

Announced at the 1989 Chicago Motor Show, the most striking element of the 300ZX, for which Nissan claimed a formidable drag coefficient of 0.31, was the body. Both versions were hatchback coupés, with removable transparent roof panels, both wider than, and the two-plus-two also longer than, the previous model with reduced overhang at either end. The driving position was moved forward more in the manner of a mid-engined car. The longer of the two body styles had a 8ft 5in (2565mm) wheelbase and the shorter was 5in (127mm) less.

The only resemblance between the car's front-mounted 3 litre V6 unit and the old 300 was the cylinder configuration and its 87x83mm bore and stroke. This retained an iron block strengthened to cope with no less than 7000rpm, but the alloy heads now incorporated twin overhead camshafts with four valves per cylinder, rather than less efficient pushrods. The inlet and exhaust systems were similarly redesigned. This fuel-injected unit ran at the unusually high compression ratio of 10.5:1, while the Nissan distributorless ignition system meant that each

plug had its own coil. The engine was normally aspirated and developed a healthy 222bhp at 6400rpm, while there was also an alternative 300bhp twin turbocharged version.

Transmissions were similarly advanced, there being an electroni-

BELOW: Although the appearance of the 300ZX suggests a mid-engined location, the 3 litre six is, in fact, front mounted. Note the 60 degree projector beam headlamps which contribute to the car's impressive 0.31 drag coefficient.

cally controlled four-speed automatic unit that communicated with the engine courtesy of a computer. There was also a more conventional five-speed manual 'box. The steering was similarly computer-controlled and was a vehicle-speed-sensitive rack and pinion unit which was high-geared but light in action at low speeds. But as the revs soared, it provided the driver with all-important "feel".

The ZX's multilink suspension was a development of that used in Nissan's stillborn mid-engined MID4 concept car, which had also been extended to

the American 240SX/Silvia range. The front was new for a production Nissan and, like the rear, had multiple upper links, lower A arms, coil springs and an anti-roll bar.

Vented disc brakes were fitted front and rear and arrested by twin aluminium calipers. Distinctive five-spoked, cast aluminium wheels were designed to show off the handsome brake mechanism.

The Turbo version could be specified with Nissan's sophisticated four-wheel steering, in which the rear wheels briefly steered in the opposite

direction to the front ones and then switched to the same plane. This is said to improve stability and tyre grip.

Priced in Britain at a competitive £34,600, the turbocharged version of the 300ZX was capable of 155mph (250km/h) with 60mph (96km) coming up in a little under six seconds. While the car was applauded for its looks and performance, some commentators complained of excessive road noise. Although handling was above average, the car was less happy in the wet. Nevertheless, this latest model is unquestionably the best Z car for years.

BELOW: The model's interior resembles that of the in-house Silvia with its doors, instrument panel and centre console all combining to produce an harmonious whole.

ABOVE: The 300ZX looks as good from the rear as its does from the front. The spoiler helps to keep those rear-driven wheels in check. Brakes are all-round twin caliper discs.

Specifications: Nissan 300ZX Two-plus-Two Turbo

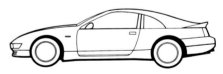

Length:	14ft 10in (4521mm)
Width:	5ft 10in (1778mm)
Height:	4ft 2in (1270mm)
Wheelbase:	8ft 5in (2565mm)
Track:	front 4ft 10in (1473mm), rear 5ft (1524mm)
Unladen weight:	3313lb (1503kg)
Engine: V6 with twin overhead camshafts per bank, 87x83mm, 2960cc. Compression ratio, 10.5:1. Twin turbocharged. Fuel injection. Max power, 222bhp at 6400rpm. Max torque, 198lb/ft at 4800rpm.	
Transmission:	Five-speed manual/ four-speed automatic
Drive:	Rear
Suspension (front):	Independent, multilink, coil springs, lower wishbones
Suspension (rear):	Independent, multilink, coil springs, lower wishbones
Top speed:	155mph (250km/h)
0-60mph (96km/h):	5.7 seconds
Production:	124,114 (to end 1992)

Mercedes-Benz SL300, SL500, SL600 (1989 to date)

Such is the allure of the new SL, it has become required transport for the rich and famous, be they film stars, royalty or grand prix drivers. With its arrival Mercedes-Benz certainly re-established itself as the manufacturer of some of the world's finest cars. Originally offered with a three engine range of 3 and 5 litres capacity, in 1992 the top line V12 version – the SL600 – arrived. This is the most expensive and luxurious variant that conveys the car and its occupants at an effortless 155mph (250km/h).

This sleek, complex, ultra-sophisticated model is longer, wider and heavier than the previous generation SL. It is, in fact, a convertible but, once its substantial hardtop is fitted, it becomes very much of a Grand Tourer, like the model it replaced. The SL also performs better in closed form; it possesses a drag coefficient of 0.32 with the roof on, but this increases by 30 per cent when driven as an open car.

À La Carte Suspension

Built on a purpose-designed floor pan, the SL's suspension is carried over, with detail refinements, from the 190 and 200/300 models. Employing coil springs all round, it uses them in conjunction with struts at the front and a five-link system at the rear. Both layouts are available with what Mercedes-Benz calls its Adaptive Damping System in which five sensors convey instructions to an electronic control unit that automatically adjusts the suspension setting in accordance with road conditions.

On its announcement, the model was offered with a choice of three engines, of which the most basic version is the SL300, powered by a 3 litre, two valve straight six as fitted to the 300E and SE saloons. Next is the 300-24 engine based on the 3 litre, two valve unit but fitted with the new four valve cylinder head. Similarly, the top line SL500 uses Mercedes-Benz's established 5 litre V8 but with new twin-overhead-camshaft 'heads, also with four valves per cylinder. This version remained the top range SL while a new V12 waited in the wings. The revised V8's first application was in the SL. In fact, the car is fitted with a restricter which prevents drivers from exceeding 155mph (250km/h); without it the SL500's top speed would be over 170mph (274km/h).

The provision of this limiter was all part of a bid by Mercedes-Benz to make the SL the world's safest car. In its most remarkable manifestation, if sensors

on the car detect conditions that indicate an accident is imminent, a roll-over arch automatically springs up from behind the seats to protect the occupants in the event of the car overturning. Their well-being is also considered when they are driving with the roof or hardtop in place, because the elaborate ventilation system excludes not only dust and pollen but also smoke and harmful bacteria.

In 1992 the 300s and 500s were joined by the top line SL600 powered by a new V12 6 litre engine with four valves per cylinder. This is a tuned version of the unit fitted in the S class saloons. The price in Britain was £92,000. As ever there were the usual refinements with the 600 employing "intelligent" anti-lock brakes, adaptive damping and air conditioning as standard. As on the V8, top speed is similarly restricted but Mercedes-Benz claims a 0 to 62mph (100km/h) rate of just 6.1 seconds.

Specifications: Mercedes-Benz SL500

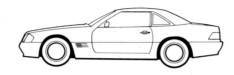

Length:	14ft 7in (4445mm)
Width:	5ft 11in (1803mm)
Height:	4ft 3in (1295mm)
Wheelbase:	8ft 3in (2515mm)
Track:	front 5ft (1524mm), rear 4ft 11in (1499mm)
Unladen weight:	3903lb (1770kg)
Engine: V8 with twin overhead camshafts per bank, 96x85mm, 4973cc. Compression ratio, 10:1. Fuel injection. Max power, 326bhp at 5500rpm. Max torque, 332lb/ft at 450Nm	
Transmission:	Five-speed manual/ four-speed automatic
Drive:	Rear
Suspension (front):	Independent, struts, coil springs
Suspension (rear):	Independent, five link, coil springs
Top speed:	155mph (250km/h)
0-60mph (96km/h):	6 seconds
Production (total 300, 500, 600 to date): 94,041	

LEFT: *The SL500's sumptuous interior. The wood-veneered console is favoured by the American market. The leather upholstered seats are activated by no less than five electric motors.*

RIGHT: *A right-hand-drive 1990 SL300 convertible. The range has a drag coefficient of just 0.32 but this is increased by 30 per cent with the hood lowered.*

BELOW: *A 1989 SL500 with its alloy hardtop in position. The model looks good whether the fitment is in place or not. The range is wider, longer and heavier than its predecessor but is visually superior to it, and has sold well.*

Honda NSX (1990 to date)

Although announced within days of the new Nissan 300ZX (see page 150), Honda's mid-engined 160mph (258km/h) NSX is intended for a different market sector, being considerably faster than the Nissan. It is also more expensive. Despite the model's 1989 unveiling, the car then revealed was, in truth, a prototype and the NSX proper did not enter production until 1990.

Of all the major Japanese car makers, Honda is the most recent recruit to the business, having progressed from being the world's largest producer of motor cycles to join the ranks of the motor manufacturers in 1962. Work on the NSX project began in 1984 and experimental cars were running in that year in the form of a mid-engined version of Honda's diminutive front-wheel-drive City saloon. This was followed by a CRX that was powered by a 2 litre 180bhp Accord engine tucked under its rear seat. In addition, the firm used HP-X, a Pininfarina design study, which was powered by a V6 engine from a Formula 2 Honda racer, to contribute to development.

These trials were followed by the construction of 15 experimental cars, some of which were fitted with 3 litre V6 engines with single overhead cam-shafts per cylinder bank. Other variations included twin turbochargers, which were also applied to the V8 version of the design.

Once the concept was finalized, prototypes were built and one of these featured in the model's American launch, staged at a Chicago hotel in 1989. There it was stressed that the NS-X would enter production in 1990. It did so with some subtle restyling of its bodywork and the wheelbase extended by 1½in (41mm) to 8ft 3½in (2530mm) to increase stability and the dimensions of the engine bay. In addition the model also lost the hyphen in its title and became the plain NSX!

The transversely located power unit is a 3 litre alloy V6 with four valves per cylinder and twin overhead camshafts per bank. Robust titanium connecting rods are fitted which permit the engine to rev to 8300rpm. Drive is taken to the rear wheels via a five-speed manual gearbox and limited slip differential. There is also the option of an electronically controlled four-speed automatic transmission.

The all-independent double wishbone suspension uses coil springs and nitrogen-gas-filled struts. Brakes are all-round ventilated discs.

Weight Watching

It was originally intended to build the NSX's body in steel, but Honda instead chose aluminium which saved 390lb (177kg) and contributed to the car's overall weight of 2821lb (1280kg). Aluminium is also used for the lovely forged suspension wishbones and, as already noted, the engine.

BELOW: *The mid-engined NSX, this being a 1992 example. Visibility is particularly good because of the large windows and the car's short nose. This only contains the spare wheel and luggage space is limited.*

Such is the seriousness with which Honda views the production of what, at £52,000, is by far and away its most expensive car, the NSX is built in a special factory at Tochigi by 200 selected employees turning out a maximum of 25 examples a day.

On the road the NSX's V6 engine emerged as a magnificent power unit which is mounted in an outstanding chassis that set new standards in handling for a mid-engined sports car in a field that had hitherto been almost exclusively reserved for European Grand Tourers. Maybe the slabsided styling lacks the elegance of a Pininfarina but the NSX is a reminder to the likes of Porsche and Ferrari, if it were needed, of the levels of expertise and technical excellence that Japanese automobile engineering has reached.

RIGHT: *Aluminium features extensively in the NSX and the roof panels are made of thin 1mm gauge aluminium panels. The flush-fitting glass contributes to the model's impressive windcheating qualities.*

Specifications: Honda NSX

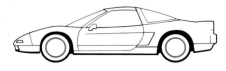

Length:	14ft 5in (4394mm)
Width:	5ft 11in (1803mm)
Height:	3ft 10in (1168mm)
Wheelbase:	8ft 3½in (2530mm)
Track:	front 4ft 11in (1499mm), rear 5ft (1524mm)
Unladen weight:	2821lb (1280kg)
Engine: Mid-located V6 with twin overhead camshafts per cylinder bank, 90x78mm, 2977cc. Compression ratio, 10.2:1. Fuel injection. Max power, 274bhp at 7300rpm. Max torque, 209lb/ft at 5400rpm.	
Transmission:	Five-speed manual/ four-speed automatic
Drive:	Rear
Suspension (front):	Independent, coil springs and wishbones
Suspension (rear):	Independent, coil springs and wishbones
Top speed:	160mph (258km/h)
0-60mph (96km/h):	5.9 seconds
Production (total to date):	13,000

BELOW: *The NSX's engine is a transversely mounted 3 litre, alloy, fuel-injected, twin-cam V6 unit which was specifically developed for this prestigious Honda.*

FERRARI 456GT (1992 to date)

With the 456 Ferrari has reverted to the front V12-engined theme which dominated its design philosophy until the 1960's, which was when the mid-located power unit began to hold sway. The 456 is not simply a reaffirmation of an earlier approach, but is a visual restatement of Ferrari's legendary Daytona (see page 188) of the 1968-73 era. The result is a distinctive and gloriously elegant two-plus-two coupé with 186mph (299km/h) performance and a vitality and allure which is not shared by any other make in the world.

The car has had an unusually long gestation, work on the project having begun in 1987. As originally conceived, the 456 is said to have resembled an elongated version of the Testarossa developed to accommodate an engine in the front. At this stage the gearbox was mated directly to the engine, but Enzo Ferrari expressed his disapproval of this arrangement not long before his death, at the age of 90, in 1988 and the Maranello engineers went back to their drawing boards. As a result Pininfarina rethought the bodywork, while the six-speed gearbox was relegated to the rear of the car to create a transaxle. The outcome was the first Ferrari two-plus-two since the demise of the 412i model in 1989.

Body Beautiful

Announced at the 1992 Brussels Motor Show, the most striking element of the 456 is, inevitably, its two-door, Pininfarina-designed coupé body with its deep swage lines which begin at the hot air engine outlets in the front wings and are continued into the doors and beyond. The shell is built up around a steel framework which is specially treated to prevent corrosive electrolytic action between it and the aluminium body panels. The bodies are built for Ferrari by its long time supplier, Scaglietti in Modena, and the complete body-in-white (unpainted) hulls are then transported to Pininfarina in Turin where they are sprayed and trimmed throughout in the finest Connolly hides. Back at Ferrari's Maranello factory, the mechanicals are fitted and the Kevlar composite bonnet added.

The alloy, four valve V12 with twin overhead camshafts per bank develops 442bhp. With the 456, Ferrari has revived its practice of naming the car after the cubic capacity of a single cylinder. Drive is then conveyed to the rear transaxle while the all-independent suspension is by coil springs and wishbones. There is a three position adaptive damping system which is computer controlled and there are no less than 25 such units contained within the car. Another operates an adjustable aerofoil contained within the rear bumper.

With a £150,000 price tag, demand for the 456 will be clearly limited and the company intends to build a maximum of just 200 examples in the first year with production building up to ten a week or a limit of 500 cars a year in 1994.

The 456 has been rightly praised for its beautifully appointed interior. A distinctive feature is the way in which the gearlever moves in its traditionally exposed gate. Ferrari claim that 60mph (96km/h) comes up in an electrifying 5.2 seconds and the car is capable of 186mph (299km/h) even when fully loaded with people and luggage. This performance is complemented by magnificent brakes, not always a Ferrari strong point. The 456 is probably the most refined and comfortable Ferrari yet and does everything that is expected of it. At a time when Europe's Grand Tourers are under continual threat from the products of the Far East, it is reassuring to state that, in this market sector, Italy, and Ferrari in particular, still leads the world.

BELOW: *A sight worth getting used to: the rear view of the 456GT in which Ferrari, surprisingly, has reverted to a front-engined theme. As ever, the body is by Pininfarina.*

ABOVE: *The spirit of the Daytona lives! This 1993 456GT is the pre-production right-hand-drive prototype. The bonnet and headlamp covers are made of Kevlar composite.*

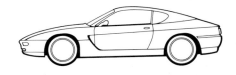

RIGHT: *Connolly hides are used to good effect in the 456. Note the gearlever, with its polished aluminium knob, which moves in a six-speed exposed gate.*

Specifications: Ferrari 456GT

Length:	15ft 6in (4724mm)
Width:	6ft 3in (1905mm)
Height:	4ft 3in (1295mm)
Wheelbase:	8ft 6in (2591mm)
Track:	front 5ft 2in (1575mm), rear 5ft 3in (1600mm)
Unladen weight:	3726lb (1690kg)
Engine: V12 with twin overhead camshafts per cylinder bank, 88x75mm, 5474cc. Compression ratio, 10.6:1. Fuel injection. Max power, 442bhp at 6250rpm. Max torque, 405lb/ft at 4500rpm.	
Transmission:	Six-speed manual
Drive:	Rear
Suspension (front):	Independent, coil springs and wishbones
Suspension (rear):	Independent, coil springs and wishbones
Top speed:	186mph (299km/h)
0-60mph (96km/h):	5.2 seconds
Production (projected in 1994):	500

Aston Martin has looked to its six-cylinder-powered DB4, 5 and 6 series of the 1960's as the visual inspiration for the DB7, which has the distinction of being the most impressive British Grand Tourer of recent years. With a top speed of 165mph (266km/h) and costing £80,000, this is also the first model in the marque's history to be powered by a Jaguar engine.

There would never have been such a car, however, were it not for the fact that Ford, which bought Jaguar in 1989, was also the owner, since 1987, of Aston Martin. This is because the DB7 is essentially a Jaguar design.

In 1988 Aston Martin introduced its Virage model, developed prior to the Ford takeover. Today selling in its most basic form for £133,574, it is, inevitably, a low production model and is now being built at the rate of about 60 vehicles a year. When Walter Hayes took over as Aston Martin's chairman in 1991, he recognized that the firm required a new cheaper line to sell in greater volumes than the Virage.

Reviving The Name
Hayes decided to reactivate the famous DB initials, standing for David Brown who owned Aston Martin between 1947 and 1972, which had been in abeyance since then. When it came to the design, Hayes was fortunate that, soon after Ford took over Jaguar, it commissioned what was titled project XX, which was a rethink of a projected F-Type sports car. Although Jaguar did not proceed with the concept, this is the origin of the DB7.

However, there was no room at Aston Martin's cramped factory in Newport Pagnell, Buckinghamshire to build it, so Aston Martin Oxford was created as a joint venture with Tom Walkinshaw's TWR Group. The DB7 will, therefore, be produced at its Bloxham, Oxfordshire factory which is where Jaguar's XJ220 supercars were manufactured.

In view of its ancestry, the DB7 does not contain any components common with the current Virage. Indeed its 8ft 6in (2591mm) wheelbase is shared with the Jaguar XJS as the new car uses a modified version of that model's floorpan. The intention was to recreate the spirit of the DB4, 5 and 6 of the 1958-71 era and this was the brief given to stylist Ian Callum. The result is a two-plus-two coupé which clearly echoes its illustrious forebears. While the structure is essentially a metal one, such components as the front wings, sills and boot lid are moulded from a composite material. The DB7's drag coefficient is an impressive 0.31.

The engine is a 335bhp turbocharged version of Jaguar's 3.2 litre, twin-overhead-camshaft, AJ6 six cylinder unit and there is a choice of five-speed manual gearbox or an automatic unit. Suspension is all-independent with double wishbones all round, coil springs at the front and longitudinal control arms are incorporated at the rear. The interior reflects the traditional leather and walnut veneer so beloved of British coachbuilders.

The DB7 was introduced at the 1993 Geneva Motor Show and displayed at the same year's London Motor Show with production scheduled to begin in April 1994. Top speed is a claimed 165mph (266km/h) with 60mph (96km/h) said to arrive after a mere 5.5 seconds and 100mph (161km/h) possible in only 13 seconds. An impressive performer, the DB7 looks set to provide Aston Martin with just the sales boost it requires.

Specifications: Aston Martin DB7

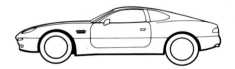

Length:	15ft 2¼in (4629mm)
Width:	5ft 11½in (1820mm)
Height:	4ft 2in (1270mm)
Wheelbase:	8ft 6in (2591mm)
Track:	front 5ft (1524mm), rear 5ft 0¼in (1530mm)
Unladen weight:	3638lb (1650kg)

Engine: Six cylinder, twin overhead camshaft, 91x83mm, 3228cc. Compression ratio, 8.3:1. Fuel injection. Turbocharged. Max power, 335bhp at 5500rpm. Max torque, 360lb/ft at 3000rpm.

Transmission:	Five-speed manual/ four-speed automatic
Drive:	Rear
Suspension (front):	Independent, coil springs and wishbones
Suspension (rear):	Independent, coil springs and wishbones incorporating longitudinal control arms
Top speed:	165mph (266km/h)*
0-60mph (96km/h):	5.5 seconds*
Production (projected in 1994):	300

*Manufacturer's claim

LEFT: *The DB7's lovely interior is unmistakably British in origin with Connolly "natural look" leather seats, discreet use of walnut veneers and carpeting by Wilton.*

RIGHT: *The DB7 is one of those cars which look right from any angle. The boot lid is made of a composite material. This is a 1993 pre-production car.*

BELOW: *The magnificently styled DB7, by TWR's Ian Callum, which retains the spirit of the DB4, 5 and 6 of the 1950's and 60's while still being thoroughly modern in appearance.*

TOYOTA SUPRA (1993 to date)

The front engined/rear drive Supra is a state-of-the-art 155mph (250km/h) Grand Tourer which took a lengthy eight years to evolve and is the latest and by far and away the most impressive manifestation of a line which began in 1981. Toyota started work on the project in 1984 and, from the outset, its objective was to produce a car with a power of a Chevrolet Corvette and the refinement of an NSX, which was being developed by the rival Honda company at the same time.

Another key parameter was that weight should be kept to an absolute minimum, so there was no question of the Supra employing four wheel steering. For the same reason, it features only a single exhaust pipe, an aluminium bonnet and plastic fuel tank, while the four upper wishbones are made from aluminium and the front suspension members and front engine mountings employ the same material. Even the carpet fibres are hollow! The car turns the scales at 3450lb (1566kg) which is 57lb (26kg) less than its predecessor, yet the new Supra is a third more powerful than the car it replaces.

For the same weight-saving reason, a 3 litre, twin-overhead-camshaft, six cylinder engine, rather than a V8, was chosen, coupled with its ability to contain compactly the optional twin turbochargers. Power from this engine is a healthy 326bhp; the non-turbo engine is shared with Toyota's Lexus SC300 coupé and GS300 saloon. A manual gearbox containing no less than six speeds is fitted. Suspension is by double wishbones, coil springs and struts all round. The body is, inevitably, a two-plus-two coupé. The distinctive rear spoiler wing is an optional extra which, ironically, pushes the drag coefficient up to a figure of 0.33.

Compared with the Supra's flamboyant body lines, the car's interior is rather low key, and although the seats are upholstered in leather, the rear ones are of limited value. However, air conditioning is a standard fitment.

Competitively priced in Britain, the twin turbocharged Supra cost £37,500 on its announcement, which is substantially cheaper than the Honda NSX, but more expensive that the Nissan 300ZX. Top speed is restricted to 155mph (249km/h), otherwise 180mph (290km/h) would be possible. This limitation is shared by the Nissan, but even so these Japanese GTs are some of the fastest front engine/rear drive cars of their day. The Toyota possesses a sparkling 0-60mph (96km/h) figure of 5.1 seconds. So performance is one of the model's prime virtues, even if road testers found that throttle response at the lower end of the rev range was not as crisp as it might have been. On the road, handling and ride were particularly impressive, even though the use of a single exhaust pipe ensures that the engine, despite its efficiency, sounds unimpressive. Also the power-assisted steering is said to lack feel but, on the plus side, the Supra's massive ventilated disc brakes are outstanding, interior noise agreeably muted and the car's build quality excellent.

As the world's largest car maker, Toyota has shown that it can not only successfully create family saloons for the mass market, but also come up with an excellent Grand Tourer which, by its very nature, is built in much smaller numbers. The Supra will be a hard act to follow!

ABOVE: *Looking good; the rear spoiler is an optional fitment on the Supra Turbo but it makes a positive contribution to this rear-drive car's appearance. The boot is rather shallow but this is a two-plus-two.*

LEFT: *The front-mounted inline 3 litre six has twin overhead camshafts and four valves per cylinder. It is enhanced by twin turbochargers.*

ABOVE: *The sensational front-engined Supra. Note the cooling ducts for the all-round ventilated discs in the front spoiler and ahead of the back wheel.*

Specifications: Toyota Supra

Length:	14ft 10in (4521mm)
Width:	5ft 11in (1803mm)
Height:	4ft 2in (1270mm)
Wheelbase:	8ft 4in (2540mm)
Track:	front 4ft 11in (1499mm), rear 5ft (1524mm)
Unladen weight:	3450lb (1566kg)
Engine: Six cylinder, twin overhead camshafts, 86x86mm, 2997cc. Compression ratio, 10:1. Fuel injection. Twin turbochargers. Max power, 320bhp at 5600rpm. Max torque, 315lb/ft at 4000rpm.	
Transmission:	Six-speed manual
Drive:	Rear
Suspension (front):	Independent, coil springs and wishbones
Suspension (rear):	Independent, coil springs and wishbones
Top speed:	155mph (250km/h)
0-60mph (96km/h):	5.1 seconds
Production (total to date):	approx. 24,000

SUPERCARS

When motor cars appeared in the last years of the 19th century, each was hand built and their resulting high price ensured that they were only available to the rich and well-to-do. Since then the development of mass production, with the price reductions that followed in its wake, have brought the automobile within reach of the man in the street.

Despite this, there have always been individuals who wanted the best and most exclusive cars of the day and, since the World War II, their needs have been met by the supercar. This rare breed is usually built in small numbers, as in days of yore, with cost playing second fiddle to panache and performance.

Since its creation in 1904, Rolls-Royce has been accommodating such a clientele. However, few of their cars would qualify for such status because, before the war, they were only manufactured in chassis form and it was the buyer who chose the all-important coachwork. In 1931 Rolls-Royce bought the Bentley marque and the costly and exclusive Continental coupé of 1952 was the firm's first true supercar with a purpose-designed fastback body. In its day, it was the fastest four-seater in the world. The Pininfarina-styled, two-door Rolls-Royce Camargue coupé of 1975 was of the same breed, while a resurgence of the Bentley name resulted in the Continental R coupé in 1992, which is a car that is very much in the spirit of its illustrious predecessor.

Of all the new makes to have emerged after World War II, Ferrari has probably produced more cars to qualify for supercar status than any other manufacturer. Of these, perhaps the finest was the formidable Daytona of 1968 with Pininfarina, as ever, matching mechanical excellence by producing a body of unsurpassed beauty. The mid-engined Testarossa of 1984 was similarly memorable and was immediately at home among the palms of the French Riviera which is the playground of the supercar set.

Since 1963 Ferrari has been faced with a direct rival in the shape of Lamborghini. Admittedly its first car, the 350GT, exuded competence without persona, but the appearance in 1966 of the mid-engined Miura saw the marque attain overnight maturity. A key ingredient in this success was its body, brilliantly essayed by Bertone, and this talent was similarly applied to the Miura's Countach successor of 1971. Here was the quintessential supercar with sensational looks, stunning performance, along with the apparently essential requirement of wild impracticality. And it was also, of course, very expensive.

All of these supercars hailed from the Old World but, in addition to European sales, their makers have always looked across the Atlantic to rich Americans to buy their cars. This, thankfully, they have done in abundance although the New World, the home of mass production, has manufactured comparatively few supercars of its own. A notable exception was Cadillac's exclusive Eldorado Brougham which appeared in the booming 1950's yet, curiously, this costly and bechromed car found relatively few buyers.

Rather more successful, in a competitive sense, was the Ford GT40, an Anglo-American confection created to win the Le Mans 24 Hour race. The regulations required that a number of road cars be built; they were, in limited quantities, and are today front runners in the supercar league.

Another manufacturer which, like Ford, ran triumphantly at Le Mans was Aston Martin. In addition to its road cars, this company also produced sports racers of which the most impressive was the DB4GT Zagato of the 1960's. It was a concept that was successfully revived in 1987 for its V8-powered successor. There was also the related Lagonda saloon, a futuristic model for the fortunate few which, after a long gestation, appeared in 1978.

A milestone in the evolution of the supercar undoubtedly came in 1983 when Porsche unveiled its formidably complex, four-wheel-drive, 911-based 959. Production did not begin until 1987 at some cost to Porsche itself, but Ferrari responded with its 40th anniversary F40, so heralding the establishment of the exclusive 200mph (322km/h) plus club. Subsequent members of this elite band included the Jaguar XJ220, Lamborghini Diablo and the EB110 from the revived Bugatti concern.

But the most outstanding supercar of its day is the McLaren F1 of 1994 which is capable of speeds approaching 240mph (386km/h), and has a price tag of over £500,000. It is as memorable in its way as that greatest of all supercars, the race-bred two-seater Mercedes 300SL coupé of the 1950's. And those gullwing doors have never dated . . .

BENTLEY CONTINENTAL (1952-1959)

Bentley's glorious sporting tradition was revived in 1952 with the arrival of the fastback Continental which, with a top speed of over 115mph (185km/h), made it the fastest four-seater car in the world. It remained in production until 1955 when it was succeeded by the outwardly similar S-type Continental which endured until 1959. The name was then transferred to the V8-powered S2 Series chassis and survived in diluted coachbuilt form until 1965.

The origins of the Continental can be traced to the 1948 Paris Motor Show where the Bentley stand featured a Mark VI chassis which was fitted with a magnificent two-door fastback body by Pinin Farina. It had been commissioned by Jean Daninos, head of Facel Metallon, who would later produce the Facel Vega Grand Tourer. The chassis had been obtained by Walter Sleator, of Franco Brittanic Autos, Rolls-Royce and Bentley's Paris agent, and was dispatched to Turin a mere two months before the Motor Show. Pinin Farina followed this offering with a further fastback body built in 1950 which was the year that Rolls-Royce became officially involved with a view to putting such a Bentley into production.

The task was allocated to the company's chief project engineer, Ivan Evernden, with the car's lines being the responsibility of chief stylist, John Blatchley. For internal purposes the car was allotted the title of Corniche II as it was the spiritual successor of an experimental Grand Touring Bentley named the Corniche, the production of which was halted by the outbreak of World War II.

Upping The Specification
Inevitably the running gear was that of the current Bentley R-Type with its 4.6 litre overhead inlet/side exhaust engine. The compression ratio was upped from 6.4 to 7.3:1 and the power unit fitted with a new exhaust system which absorbed 25bhp less than the usual arrangement although, as ever, total power output was not disclosed. A higher 3.77:1 rear-axle ratio was the only further significant departure from the standard specification.

Blatchley's two-door fastback coupé body was essentially similar to Pinin Farina's renderings and suggested both flair and speed. Significantly, once a quarter-scale model had been completed, it was wind-tunnel-tested for aerodynamic efficiency by the Flight Test Establishment based at Hucknall, Nottinghamshire. However,

Specifications: Bentley R-Type Continental

Length:	17ft 2in (5232mm)
Width:	5ft 11in (1803mm)
Height:	5ft 3in (1600mm)
Wheelbase:	10ft (3048mm)
Track:	front 4ft 8in (1422mm), rear 4ft 10in (1473mm)
Unladen weight:	3696lb (1676kg)

Engine: Six cylinder, overhead valve, 92×114mm, 4566cc. Compression ratio, 7:1. Max power, not disclosed. Max torque, not disclosed.

Transmission:	Four-speed manual
Drive:	Rear
Suspension (front):	Independent, coil springs and wishbones
Suspension (rear):	Live axle, half-elliptic springs
Top speed:	115mph (185km/h)
0-60mph (96km/h):	13.8 seconds
Production (total R and S-Type Mulliner coupés):	411

the model's windcheating properties were somewhat compromised as Evernden had to retain the marque's very upright radiator because his masters had decreed that the car should be "recognizably a Bentley". Interestingly, Pinin Farina had not been so constrained and produced a truncated version of the radiator design which made the front of its car considerably lower than that of the production Continental.

London-based coachbuilder H. J. Mulliner expressed an interest in the project and was commissioned to build the prototype's body. The resulting car was completed in 1951. Registered OLG 490, it has thereafter been affectionately known as "Olga". Taken to the Montlhéry circuit near Paris, it proceeded to complete five laps at 118.75mph (191.1km/h). By contrast, the contemporary R-Type saloon was capable of around 100mph (161km/h).

LEFT: *Bentleys have been fitted with the flying B mascot since the 1930's while the badge has featured since the marque's inception in 1919. This is on a 1957 S1 Continental.*

LEFT: *The prototype R-Type Continental of 1951 which, happily, still survives. It differed from the production cars in having a divided windscreen and no radiator cap or mascot. It is also 1in (25mm) lower than standard.*

BELOW: *This R-Type Continental, chassis BC5B, was delivered, in May 1953, to its first owner, one W. Zietz. The years have dealt lightly with the H.J. Mulliner body.*

ABOVE: *Those magnificent fastback lines shown to advantage. Some cars were fitted with rear spats although this one does not have them.*

BENTLEY CONTINENTAL

Mulliner secured the contract to build the aluminium coupé body. The model was called Continental which revived a pre-war Rolls-Royce rather than a Bentley name. Announced in February 1952, the car's top speed, at around 115mph (185km/h), was slightly less than the prototype's. The India company produced special tyres for it to cope with the demands of sustained high-speed touring. At £6929, which was £2106 more than the standard R-Type, the Continental was the most expensive production car in the world.

Here was a model in the spirit of the pre-war Grand Tourer, able effortlessly to cruise at speeds of up to 100mph (161km/h) for hours on end, making it ideal for trans-continental journeys. It was equally at home on arrow-straight French roads, German autobahns or quiet country lanes.

The R-Type Continental was produced until 1955 by which time 208 examples had been completed. The overwhelming majority, no less than 193, were Mulliner-built coupés with the remaining 15 cars being variously bodied by in-house Park Ward, as well as Franay in France, the Swiss Graber company and also Pinin Farina.

A few changes were made to the specification during these four years. The car was originally built with a manual gearbox but automatic transmission became available from the spring of 1954, and this version was the first recipient of an enlarged 4.9 litre engine which was to power the Bentley S-Type/Rolls-Royce Silver Cloud saloon of 1955.

The S-Type chassis and mechanicals were extended to the Continental, the body of which was perpetuated, although it was slightly longer on account of a new frame with a 10ft (3048mm) wheelbase which was 3in (76mm) greater than its predecessor. Unlike the R Continental, the S Continental was offered with a choice of three body styles; the established coupé was joined by a two-door Park Ward saloon and convertible which were similar to those that had been available on the last of the sixes.

Mechanically, the 4.9 litre engine was the same as that fitted to the saloons though with an upped 7.25:1 compression ratio and a higher 2.923:1 final drive. A delightful manual gearbox was still listed, although the vast majority of cars used automatic transmission and in 1957 the manual option was withdrawn.

In the same year of 1957, the existing body styles were joined by the four-door Flying Spur line which, in addition to being built by Mulliner, was also offered by coachbuilders Park Ward and James Young. The Continental remained in production until 1959, by which time a total of 411 coupés had been built. This marked the end of the stylish Mulliner fastback.

End Of The Continental

Its demise came about because in that year Rolls-Royce introduced the Silver Cloud II and Bentley S2 saloons powered by a new 6.2 litre V8 engine, and there would have been little difference between the performances of the Continental and its standard-bodied counterparts. The name was, however, perpetuated and the resulting car was only available with bespoke coachwork and it had a slightly higher rear-axle ratio. It was similarly extended to the S3/Cloud III of 1962 but with the 1965 demise of the series, the Continental finally came to the end of the road. Over 30 years on, the theme was then triumphantly revived in 1991 in the form of the Continental R, which is the true successor of the famous Mulliner coupé of the 1950's.

BELOW: *One of the last R-Type Continentals to be built. This car, chassis BC4E, was delivered in April 1955, to H.C. Farnsworth.*

ABOVE: *In-house Park Ward bodied 185 S1 Continentals, some of which were handsome drophead coupés like this. This car dates from 1956.*

Bentley Continental

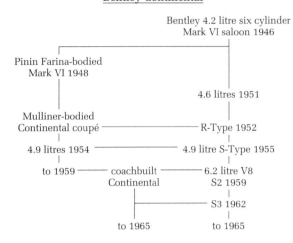

```
                                            Bentley 4.2 litre six cylinder
                                                Mark VI saloon 1946

          Pinin Farina-bodied
            Mark VI 1948                              4.6 litres 1951

          Mulliner-bodied
        Continental coupé ————————————————— R-Type 1952

          4.9 litres 1954                      4.9 litre S-Type 1955

             to 1959 ———— coachbuilt ————— 6.2 litre V8
                          Continental             S2 1959

                                                  S3 1962

                to 1965                            to 1965
```

ABOVE: *Frontal view of an R-Type Continental, dispatched in March 1954. Note that this example has a painted radiator, as opposed to the usual chromed one.*

RIGHT: *The Continental was also built in S-Type form between 1955 and 1959. This example dates from the latter year which was the last for the H.J. Mulliner fastback coupé, and marked the end of Rolls-Royce's six cylinder engine.*

ABOVE RIGHT: *The unmistakable luxury of a Continental's driving compartment with beautifully appointed walnut veneer instrument panel and leather upholstered seats. This is a 1957 S1; note the fitment, on the extreme right, of a revolution counter.*

Mercedes-Benz 300SL (1954-1957)

Perhaps the most legendary and charismatic car of the early post-1945 era, the 300SL coupé is forever remembered for its distinctive gullwing doors. Significantly, they were no stylistic whim but played a very real functional role, because at the heart of the car was a light but complex tubular space-frame structure. To provide the necessary rigidity, it had to intrude into part of the space usually occupied by conventionally hung doors so the car's designers decided, ingeniously, to hinge them from the roof.

The origins of this memorable model are rooted in Mercedes-Benz's decision, taken in 1952, to return to sports car racing. That year the famous Le Mans 24-Hours Race was won by a C-Type Jaguar and the German company was particularly impressed that its 3.4 litre XK engine was borrowed from the Mark VII saloon. Mercedes-Benz decided to do the same by producing a competition car powered by a 3 litre, six cylinder, single-overhead-camshaft engine, courtesy of its 300S (for super) model of 1951. The same car also contributed its transmission and suspension, which incorporated front coils and wishbones and the traditional swing axle at the rear.

As these components had been created for a road car they were, inevitably, much heavier than if they had been designed with racing in mind. The response to this limitation was to produce a light, rigid space-frame in place of the usual chassis. The team responsible, under the overall direction of Rudolph Uhlenhaut, was headed by Franz Roller and its key members were Ludwig Kraus and Manfred Lorscheidt. The outcome was a load-bearing latticework of tubes, which had to be as deep as possible along the cockpit sides. This made the fitment of a conventional door impossible. To allow the driver into the coupé, the Daimler-Benz engineers created the concept of the famous gullwing door which, instead of hingeing on the body sides, did so along the centre line of the roof.

Racing Certainty

Titled 300SL, on account of its being a 3 litre super light car, it first appeared at the 1952 Mille Miglia competition in May, won the sports race at the Swiss Grand Prix later in the month and went on to take first and second places at Le Mans. Later, in November, the 300SLs were similarly successful across the Atlantic in the Mexico City Road Race. There was also a roadster version of the

design and, at a sports car meeting at the Nürburgring, it scored an impressive one, two, three victory.

After such a triumphant start, in 1953 the design was mildly improved, the wheelbase slightly reduced and the triple Weber carburettors first replaced the original Solexes and, then, the single-cam six was fuel injected, which contributed to its power output rising from its 1952 figure of 172bhp to 208. The body lines were refined with the front of the car being reworked and grilles introduced into the front wings to allow hot air to escape from the engine compartment. Despite these modifications, the cars were not used competitively in 1953 because the company decided instead to commit its engineering resources to develop a grand prix car for the 1954 season. In consequence the lovely silver-finished 300SL coupés were set aside.

Specifications: Mercedes-Benz 300SL

Length:	14ft 10in (4521mm)
Width:	5ft 10in (1778mm)
Height:	4ft 3in (1295mm)
Wheelbase:	7ft 10in (2388mm)
Track:	front 4ft 6in (1372mm), rear 4ft 8in (1422mm)
Unladen weight:	2552lb (1157kg)

Engine: Six cylinder, single overhead camshaft, 85×88mm, 2996cc. Compression ratio, 8.5:1. Max power, 190bhp at 6000rpm. Max torque, 207lb/ft at 5000rpm.

Transmission:	Four-speed manual
Drive:	Rear
Suspension (front):	Independent, coil springs and wishbones
Suspension (rear):	Independent, coil springs and swing axle
Top speed:	154mph (248km/h)
0-60mph (96km/h):	8.3 seconds
Production (including lightweight):	1400

ABOVE: *A magnificent example of a 300SL, the road car that evolved from a highly successful sports racer. This is a 1956 car but the chromed wheels are a later addition.*

LEFT: *The 300SL was strictly a two-seater. Although the boot looks commodious, there is not much room for luggage and it mostly contains the spare wheel!*

RIGHT: *Those memorable gullwing doors shown to advantage. They were obligatory because of the model's space-frame substructure which prevented the use of conventionally hung doors.*

Mercedes-Benz 300SL

300SL 3 litre six cylinder
sports racer 1952
|
1953 version
|
300SL coupé 1954
|
to 1957 ——————— 300SL roadster
|
to 1963

It was at this point that the New York-based Max Hoffman, who imported a number of European makes, including Mercedes-Benz, into America, proposed that the company should market the 300SL as a road car. If the Stuttgart firm agreed, he would place an order for 1000 cars. Daimler-Benz responded positively and the model duly entered production in 1954. It was, appropriately, launched at that year's New York Motor Show in February.

The roadgoing coupé closely resembled the 1953 version of the coupé body with the notable exception of the air outlet grilles, which were enlarged, while stylish flutes were introduced above the wheel arches. Under the bonnet the engine was canted 45 degrees to the left, as had been the case from 1952, to permit the fitment of an aerodynamically efficient low bonnet line. Still retaining the race-proven fuel injection system, the 190bhp six was the first road car in the world to be so equipped. A dry sump lubrication system was a further inheritance from the model's racing days. The power unit drove the low pivot rear-swing axle, another '53 modification, via a four-speed, all synchromesh gearbox. Such was the flexibility of the engine, the company claimed that the 300SL would accelerate from 15.5mph (25km/h) to flat out in top gear. The space-frame was essentially the same as was fitted to the competition cars, although some modifications were made which increased the weight of the complete car by 181lb (82kg), to 2552lb (1157kg). Servo-assisted brakes, with heavily finned drums, were used all round.

As befitted its origins, the cockpit provided accommodation for two people and, to permit ease of access, the steering wheel hinged forwards to be repositioned when the driver was seated. There was space for luggage on a platform behind the seats, as available room in the boot was mostly taken up by the spare wheel.

Fast As A Ferrari

Despite the car only being built in left-hand-drive form, it sold in Britain where it retailed for £4932. Performance was, not unnaturally, formidable and a top speed of around 155mph (50km/h) meant that the 300SL was one of the fastest cars on the road with only Ferrari offering any challenge. Despite this impressive performance, the car's handling could be unpredict-

ABOVE: *A British-registered 300SL. The model was only produced in left-hand-drive form. This is a 1955 car, expensive in its day, costing a substantial £4932.*

BELOW: *The 300SL roadster that replaced the coupé in 1957 but which, by the nature of its body, could not feature those memorable doors, although it did use a space-frame.*

able and a further disadvantage was that if a 300SL was involved in an accident, the complex frame was difficult and expensive to repair.

The model was destined for a four-year manufacturing life and was discontinued in 1957 after 1371 examples had been completed. There was also a more potent lightweight version which accounted for a further 29 cars. Both were replaced in 1957 by the simpler 300SL roadster which, by the nature of its body, could not feature those memorable gullwing doors. This remained in production until 1963 by which time 1858 had been built.

There was one further version of the gullwing door coupé but this, alas, never reached the public. Mercedes-Benz's 1954 sports racer the 300SLR, was powered by a 3 litre, straight eight engine. Stirling Moss drove to a memorable victory in the 1955 Mille Miglia in an example which helped Mercedes-Benz to win that year's Sports Car Championship. This was an open car but the factory built two 300SLR coupés which outwardly resembled the gullwing 300SL although they could be easily identified by twin exhaust pipes that wickedly sprouted from the body side, just ahead of the passenger's door. Development engineer Rudi Uhlenhaut delighted in driving one which was capable of around 180mph (290km). It did not, alas, reach production and could thus never overshadow the 300SL's legendary position as one of the truly great cars of motoring history.

LEFT: *The roadster's 3 litre six cylinder engine was essentially the same as that used in the coupé version of the car, apart from the standardization of a sports camshaft.*

RIGHT: *While the 300SL roadster does not possess gullwing doors, it is rather easier to enter on account of its conventional sills.*

BELOW RIGHT: *The 300's fuel-injected engine is dominated by the inlet manifold with three double pipes feeding into the cylinder head.*

BELOW: *The 300SL roadster was, in fact, more popular than the gullwing coupé and survived until 1963. This example dates from that year. Road-holding was improved by the fitment of a low-pivot swing axle.*

CADILLAC ELDORADO BROUGHAM (1956-1958)

If the 1950's was a golden era for the American motor industry, it was also the decade in which Cadillac emerged as the country's most prestigious marque. To underline this pole position, and no doubt spurred by its Lincoln rival having revived the costly Continental, Cadillac unveiled its most expensive car ever, the Eldorado Brougham, which sold for a cool $13,074.

The Brougham's origins can be traced back to 1953 and that year's General Motors Motorama. This was an annual event staged by the Corporation where some of its more extravagant and adventurous visual initiatives could be displayed to gauge the public's reaction to them. GM styling supremo, Harley Earl, would then incorporate some of the less outlandish ideas in the following year's models. At the '53 event Earl did not fail to notice the response engendered by a four-door hardtop coupé named the Orleans. This was American's first car without door pillars, the feature having first gained popularity in Europe, in particular in designs created by Lancia. Earl had seen an example on a recent visit that he had paid to Italy.

At the following year's 1954 Motorama, Earl displayed another experimental car named Park Avenue which stylistically anticipated the Brougham. However, unlike the Orleans, this four-door saloon reverted to the customary door pillars. The show opened in January 1954, and there was an immediate positive public response to the design. Even before the Motorama had closed its doors, Earl sought out Cadillac's manager, Don Ahrens. He obtained his approval to build a further show car in 1955; what would be called the Cadillac Eldorado Brougham would enter production in 1956.

Using the body of the Park Avenue as a starting point, the Cadillac studio, under the direction of Ed Glowacke, began work in May 1954. The principal difference between it and the '54 show car was that the door pillars were eliminated in the manner of the Orleans. In November 1954 the studio took delivery of the car's special chassis and work proceeded at a frantic pace to have it completed in time for the 1955 Motorama which opened in New York on 17th January. There was a last minute hitch when the Brougham fell off its jacks on the night before the opening day and some frantic tin bashing then ensued to repair a damaged wing and bumper. The public, blissfully unaware of such tribulations, clearly liked what it saw and a production version of the Brougham was announced, a little belatedly, in December 1956. The finished product did indeed look sensational and confirmed the rumours that were circulating in Detroit that it would make the Lincoln's new $9695 Continental look like a haywagon.

Cadillac had introduced its Eldorado model in 1953 and the name remains part of the marque's model line to the present day. At $13,074 the Brougham was about twice the price of the other '57 Eldorados. With a wheelbase of 10ft 9in (3277mm) it was also the shortest of that year's Cadillacs and was a mere 4ft 7in (1397mm) high. A four-door pillarless saloon with a distinctive brushed stainless steel roof and quadruple headlamps, below the surface the Brougham was similarly innovative and was the first production car in the world to employ air suspension. Standard fitments included power steering and power-assisted brakes along with automatic starting for the car's 365cid (6 litres), 325bhp V8 engine.

Take Your Seats

Inevitably the car was packed with refinements and accessories to justify its high price. On entering the Brougham, there could be little doubt that here was something rather special. When the doors were opened, the bench-type front seat automatically moved back to permit the driver to get behind the wheel and, when they were closed, it would return to its original position. The seats were also electrically adjustable to suit their respective occupants and were upholstered in leather and brocade. Air conditioning was also a

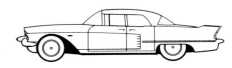

Length:	17ft 6in (5334mm)
Width:	6ft 8in (2032mm)
Height:	4ft 7in (1397mm)
Wheelbase:	10ft 9in (3277mm)
Track:	front and rear, 5ft 1in (1549mm)
Unladen weight:	5315lb (2410kg)
Engine:	V8, overhead valve, 101×92mm, 365cid (6 litres). Compression ratio, 10:1. Max power, 325bhp at 4800rpm. Max torque, 399lb/ft at 2800rpm
Transmission:	Four-speed automatic
Drive:	Rear
Suspension (front):	Independent, air springs and wishbones
Suspension (rear):	Live axle, air springs and trailing arms
Top speed:	115mph (185km/h)
0-60mph (96km/h):	Not disclosed
Production:	704

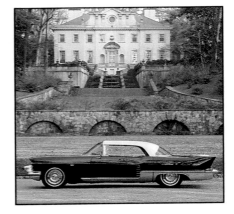

ABOVE: *The Brougham's rather intimidating front end. The rubber tipped protrusions were nicknamed Dagmars after a curvaceous TV star!*

LEFT: *Cadillac's Eldorado Brougham in all its glory. Interestingly, this was not a particularly large car by the prevailing standards of the day.*

BELOW: *As a hardtop, there were no central pillars. The front seat moved back when the doors were opened.*

ABOVE: *An Eldorado Brougham in an appropriate setting. It retailed for an astronomical $13,074.*

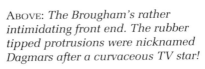

CADILLAC ELDORADO BROUGHAM

LEFT: *The Brougham's engine compartment is dominated by a large air filter with the 365bhp (6 litres) V8 breathing through either a Carter or Rochester carburettor.*

RIGHT: *Despite its impressive specifications, the Brougham was not a great sales success for Cadillac. Yet this 1957 example still looks a lot better than its contemporaries.*

BOTTOM: *The Eldorado's Brougham's novel quadruple headlamps were illegal in many American states in 1957, but were subsequently to attain great popularity the world over.*

BELOW: *The car's steering wheel and instruments with air conditioning unit on the lower right. Note the massive brake pedal. A distortion-free wraparound 'screen featured.*

standard fitment and occupants had available to them five magnetized gold coffee cups which fitted in a compartment let into the back of the front seat. Ladies were provided with a complimentary vanity compact, tissue dispenser, perfume and lipstick. Electrically-operated windows were fitted and the radio aerial was similarly activated. These features were the icing on a rather over-rich cake.

Unconventional Suspension

Cadillac did break new ground with the Brougham's innovative suspension, but the system employed was not an unqualified success. The claimed advantages were that it permitted the car to ride at a constant height, and took no account of the load carried, with the air springs charged from a compressor driven by its own electric motor. These took the form of a dome air chamber at each wheel together with a rubber diaphragm and piston. In reality, the domes developed a tendency to leak, a failing which smacked of under-development. Some owners found it cheaper to have the system completely removed and replaced with more conventional coil springs. It was an unforgivable shortcoming on such an expensive car.

When the Brougham, which was hand-built at Cadillac's Detroit factory, went on sale in 1957, the division rather curiously underplayed the model. It was only merited the briefest of mentions in sales literature and those affluent potential customers who did hanker to own one were referred to

dealers for further information. At such a price, sales were, inevitably, limited. Too much so for Cadillac's liking. Just 400 examples were produced in the introductory year of 1957 and fewer still, 304, in 1958. In other words the Brougham, with a total of 704 cars built, was a monumental flop.

So the model was discontinued in 1958 but the name survived for a further two years. The 1959 cars were revised with a new Pinin Farina body, which was also Italian built. The Cadillac's substructures were therefore made in America, shipped to Italy where they were bodied and then returned home for completion. This elaborate manufacturing process reaped no dividends for Cadillac. Even less were sold, 99 in 1959 and 101 in 1960 and that really was the end of the story. The Eldorado Brougham was a car that would probably have never been built had it not been for Lincoln's Mark II Continental. In the event, that sold only 1769 examples in 1956 and 1957...

Cadillac Eldorado Brougham

Cadillac Eldorado 1953	Orleans four-door hardtop 1953 Motorama
	Park Avenue saloon 1954 Motorama
	Eldorado Brougham 1955 Motorama
365cid (6 litres) V8 1956	Production Eldorado Brougham 1956
1957	1957
1958	to 1958

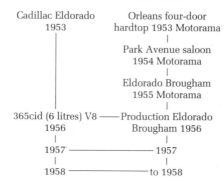

ABOVE: *The Brougham's elegant rear fin with exhaust emerging from an outlet incorporated in the bumper.*

RIGHT: *Like many 1950's cars, the Brougham used a bench-type front seat to accommodate three people.*

The most charismatic Aston Martin of the post-war years, the Zagato was a special bodied version of the short chassis DB4GT. Intended for sports car racing and selling for £5469, demand was inevitably limited and only 19 cars were produced. But this was not quite the end of the story because 28 years after the last example had been completed, in 1991, the final and hitherto unused batch of chassis numbers was applied to four further cars, so making a grand total of 23 Zagatos built.

The origins of the DB4 Zagato are to be found in the production 3.7 litre DB4 announced in the autumn of 1958. It was fitted with a magnificent two-door coupé body styled by the Italian Touring concern and built under licence by Aston Martin at its Newport Pagnell factory. A year later, in October 1959, came a sports racing derivative, the outwardly similar, lightened DB4GT with a wheelbase 5in (127mm) shorter than that of the standard car. The six cylinder, twin-overhead-camshaft engine also differed by having a 9:1 compression ratio, twin-sparking-plug cylinder head and triple Weber DCO E4 twin choke carburettors. It developed 267bhp, which compared with the 240bhp of the standard car. A close ratio gearbox was employed, while the boot was mostly occupied by a 30 gallon (137 litres) fuel tank. Production lasted until 1963 by which time 75 cars had been built. In 1960 came a new, more powerful version of the DB4GT in the shape of the Zagato-bodied car, which was unveiled at that year's London Motor Show.

Anglo-Italian Creation

Unlike the DB4 and DB4GT, which were built entirely in Britain, these cars were shipped in chassis form to Italy and bodied at Zagato's Milan factory. Afterwards the majority were returned to Aston Martin for trimming. They were, inevitably, expensive and at £5469 apiece cost around £1000 more than the Touring-styled DB4GT.

The Zagato business was founded in Milan in 1919 and still survives there. It soon established a close association with nearby Alfa Romeo and the *carrozzeria*'s most famous body was the open two-seater which appeared in 1929 on that company's 1750 chassis. Zagato continued its association with Alfa Romeo in the post-war years. In 1960, 23-year-old Ercole Spada joined what was still a family business. It was he who was responsible for the lines of the DB4GT Zagato, as well as stylish designs for Lancia and Alfa Romeo.

The Zagatos fell within the DB4GT allocation and the first example was chassis number 0200R. This was used to suggest that the necessary 100 cars had been completed for Appendix J Group 2 competition. In fact only 19 were built and a further chassis was bodied by Bertone. Otherwise production was almost evenly divided between right- and left-hand-drive versions which accounted for ten and nine cars respectively.

The Zagato was impressively chunky in appearance and was even

Specifications: Aston Martin DB4GT Zagato	
Length:	14ft (4267mm)
Width:	5ft 5in (1651mm)
Height:	4ft 2in (1270mm)
Wheelbase:	7ft 9in (2362mm)
Track:	front, 4ft 6in (1372mm), rear 4ft 5½in (1359mm)
Unladen weight:	2765lb (1254kg)
Engine: Six cylinder, twin overhead camshaft, 92×92mm, 3670cc. Compression ratio, 9.7:1. Max power, 285bhp at 6000rpm. Max torque, 278lb/ft at 5400rpm,	
Transmission:	Four-speed manual
Drive:	Rear
Suspension (front):	Independent, coil springs and wishbones
Suspension (rear):	Live axle, coil springs and trailing arms
Top speed:	151mph (243km/h)
0-60mph (96km/h):	6.3 seconds
Production (including Sanction II):	23

ABOVE: *The Z badge adjoining the air outlet indicates that the bodywork of this DB4GT was designed and built by Zagato in Milan.*

BELOW: *This 1962 right-hand-drive Zagato 0176/R was one of the last built and is a low-mileage, original condition example.*

RIGHT: *Another right-hand-drive Zagato, this time 0193/R. Built for French racing driver, Jean Kerguen, it ran at Le Mans in 1962 and 1963 but did not finish. The design of the air outlet on the front wing is a notable feature.*

ABOVE: *The Zagato's 3.7 litre, DB4 GT's, six cylinder, twin-overhead-camshaft engine with twin 10mm sparking plug head fired from two distributors driven off the ends of the camshafts. The triple 45 DCOE4 Weber carburettors were peculiar to the GT series.*

RIGHT: *One of the most famous Zagatos, 0182/R, memorably registered 1 VEV and campaigned by David Ogier's Essex Racing Stable. Now beautifully restored, it is pictured at the 1993 Goodwood Festival of Speed.*

faster than the GT on account of its higher compression ratio engine being boosted to 285bhp. Turning the scales at 2765lb (1254kg), the cars were slightly lighter than the standard DB4GT. The lovely coupé bodies were made of aluminium panels secured to a tubular frame. To save weight the side and rear windows were made of perspex and as the boot mostly consisted of the large petrol tank and spare wheel, room for luggage was created on a shelf behind the front seats where the rear squabs would normally have been.

Road-Runners

Although principally conceived for sports car racing, the vast majority of Zagatos were registered for the road, no doubt to the considerable alarm of other drivers! This was on account of the fact that the cars were capable of over 150mph (241km/h) and could reach 60mph (96km/h) in a little over 6 seconds. They had a suitably impressive exhaust note to match!

The cars were run competitively in Britain and Europe in the year's between 1961 and 1963. They performed with consistency and invariably finished races, but were usually outclassed by Ferrari. Perhaps the best known exponent of the Zagatos was John Ogier's Essex Racing Stable that campaigned two cars which were memorably registered 1 VEV and 2 VEV. Aston Martin had withdrawn from the competitive fray in 1959 but lent Ogier some works support.

By the mid 1960's the Zagatos were no longer competitive on the track and they went into dignified retirement. By the late 1980's they had begun to soar in value and in 1990 the former Ogier car 1 VEV, with a well documented racing record, fetched an amazing £1.5 million at auction.

Then, to the surprise and delight of many enthusiasts, in 1991 Aston Martin unveiled a further four Zagatos that were given the Sanction II designation. When the cars were new, four of the allotted chassis numbers were unused and DB4GT/0192, 0196, 0197 and 0198 never built. In 1987 Aston Martin's joint chairmen, Victor Gauntlett and Peter Livanos, decided to produce a further quartet of cars that would be built to follow the original specifications as closely as possible.

Aston Martin specialist Richard Williams constructed four platform chassis to DB4GT specifications and they were then dispatched to Zagato's Milan premises to be bodied there, just

like their predecessors of 30 years before. Williams' own Zagato had the same destination and was dismantled so that the workforce could reacquaint itself with its construction. Then work began on bodying the chassis and, once completed, the cars, along with the Williams' now rebuilt Zagato, were returned to his premises at Cobham, Surrey. There they were trimmed and completed.

Outwardly these Sanction II cars are almost identical to their predecessors although they have 4.2 rather than 3.7 litre engines. In addition, minor changes have been made to the suspension and slightly smaller and wider wheels are fitted. These glorious sports racing Aston Martins represent a happy union of the best of British automobile engineering and the finest tradition of Italian styling, a truly unbeatable combination.

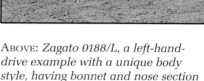

Aston Martin DB4GT Zagato

3.7 litre DB4 1958
|
Short wheelbase DB4GT 1959
|
DB4GT Zagato 1960
:
:
4.2 litre Sanction II
DB4GT Zagato 1991

- - - - - out of production

ABOVE: *Zagato 0188/L, a left-hand-drive example with a unique body style, having bonnet and nose section related to the standard DB4.*

BELOW: *The Zagato's boot mostly consists of fuel tank and spare wheel. This belongs to one of the 1991 Sanction II cars, chassis 0196.*

ABOVE: *The "office" of left-hand-drive Zagato 0188. It is essentially similar to the Touring-styled DB4GT. Note bottom-hinged pedals. This car has occasional rear seats.*

LEFT: *Virtually indistinguishable from the original series of the 1960's, this is one of the four Sanction II cars, chassis 0196, which were built in 1991. The wheels are, however, smaller than the originals.*

FORD GT40 (1966-1968)

In the early 1960's, the Detroit-based Ford company shook off its entrenched, staid approach to car design and embraced a new policy under the Total Performance banner. As part of this strategy, the company decided that it must win the Le Mans 24 Hours race. The outcome was the Lola-derived, Anglo-American GT40 which gave Ford four victories in a row at the Sarthe circuit between 1966 and 1969. For a handful of lucky owners this successful sports racer was available in roadgoing form and, between 1966 and 1968, a tantalizingly small number of cars were produced.

From its inception in 1903, the Ford Motor Company had concentrated on producing no-nonsense, value-for-money cars for the populace. This philosophy reigned until the early 1960's when market research told Ford that customers tended to remain loyal to the make of car they first bought. The post-war baby boom was about to reach car-buying age so Ford brought out, in 1964, the best-selling sporty Mustang. The company decided that it would further enhance its corporate profile by winning the world's most famous race: the Le Mans 24 Hours event. To these ends, it made strenuous efforts to buy the Ferrari company and talks had reached an advanced stage when, in May 1963, the Italians suddenly withdrew. Soon afterwards Fiat took a controlling interest in Ferrari, and Ford was left to develop its own car.

While attending the 1963 Le Mans race, the company's executives, apart from witnessing yet another Ferrari victory, were impressed by the appearance of the new Lola GT. Despite being forced to withdraw in the fourteenth hour, it was an advanced concept. Its 4.3 litre Ford V8 engine followed Grand Prix practice in being mounted longitudinally behind the driver.

Co-operation With Lola
It was realized that the Lola could form the basis of a Ford sports racer so an approach was made to Eric Broadley, the car's creator, and, as a consequence of this, Lola Cars transferred its activities from Bromley, Kent to Slough, Berkshire where Ford Advanced Vehicles was established under the direction of John Wyer, former general manager of Aston Martin.

Creating such a facility from scratch proved to be no easy task but a three-strong team of GT 40s was completed in time for the 1964 Le Mans event. Inevitably, the car's overall layout fol-

Specifications: Ford GT40 Mark III

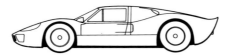

Length:	14ft 1in (4293mm)
Width:	5ft 10in (1778mm)
Height:	3ft 5in (1041mm)*
Wheelbase:	7ft 11in (2413mm)
Track:	front 4ft 7in (1397mm), rear 4ft 5½in (1359mm)
Unladen weight:	2200lb (998kg)

Engine: Mid-located V8, overhead valve, 101×72mm, 4736cc. Compression ratio, 10.5:1. Max power, 306bhp at 6000rpm. Max torque, 329lb/ft at 4200rpm.

Transmission:	Four-speed manual
Drive:	Rear
Suspension (front):	Independent, coil springs and wishbones
Suspension (rear):	Independent, trailing links, coil springs and lower wishbones
Top speed:	160mph (258km/h)
0-60mph (96km/h):	5.5 seconds
Production:	31

*This was one inch higher than the original GT40 but the name stuck!

lowed that of the mid-engined Lola, although it differed from it in detail. The power unit was a light alloy version of Ford's 4.2 litre V8 which developed 350bhp. The body had been put through wind tunnel testing in America. A scale model had been dispatched there for refinement by the University of Maryland and the outcome was the low, wickedly purposeful GT40 coupé with its body made of glass fibre panels. The car was so called because on the road it was a mere 40in (1016mm) high.

RIGHT: *The car that Ford built to win Le Mans, a Mark I GT40 of 1965. It was to pass through a number of evolutionary phases and this example displays the definitive GT40 front end.*

LEFT: *A 1965 GT40 with a short nose which was a feature of the Mark I and some Mark II cars. By this time, the wire wheels had been replaced by steel ones. This example has been registered for the road.*

ABOVE: *The Mark I was powered by a 4.2 litre V8 engine. Below, cockpit with the GT40's ventilated seats. The interior could get very hot!*

Ford GT40

At the '64 race none of the GT40s, alas, finished. Although spectacularly fast – one example was timed at 187mph (301km/h) down the Mulsanne Straight – two of the cars succumbed to gearbox problems, after one had set a new lap record. The third car had developed a fuel leak and, as a result, caught fire.

After this inauspicious start, at the end of 1964 Ford Advanced Vehicles was reorganized. It remained responsible for production, but Broadley

departed, successfully to resume his activities with Lola Cars. The innovative torch passed to America and the business of Kar Kraft which Ford had bought with the GT40 in mind. There, working under the direction of Carroll Shelby, creator of the AC Cobra, the Mark II GT40 took shape. This was intended to rectify the faults of the original. The principal difference between the two versions was that the alloy V8 was replaced by an iron 7 litre "Cobra" unit developing no less than 485bhp and ministrations were made to the fragile Colotti gearbox. At Le Mans in 1965 the cars fared little better. A total of six works and semi-official GT40s were entered but, once again, all cars failed for a variety of reasons. Gearbox troubles once again were to the fore. So Ford had to think again.

The Mark II was further revised and no less than eight cars appeared at Le Mans in 1966 where, at long last, there was a clean sweep with Ford taking the

ABOVE: *A 1966 car converted for the road. This is chassis number GT40/ 1035, one of several cars destined for Shelby-American but returned to Ford Advanced Vehicles because of documentation troubles.*

RIGHT: *Rear view of a 1969 GT40 equipped for road use. The Ford V8 engine was longitudinally mounted and this type of tail appeared on all but the first cars.*

first three places. It was the company's first every victory at the circuit. The cost of the entire programme, since 1964, was estimated at $9 million (£2.1 million).

Meanwhile Ford Advanced Vehicles was undertaking the manufacture of a roadgoing version of the GT40 which

was designated the Mark III. Announced in December 1965, it sold for £6647. These cars were powered by a 4.7 litre V8 engine and outwardly differed from the racers by having a modified front end with four headlamps behind perspex covers, while the tail was enlarged to incorporate a somewhat basic, and warm, luggage container. Inside, trim was improved while additional sound deadening was introduced to the cockpit.

Mark III Performance

The engine was, inevitably, detuned to around 306bhp but even so the Mark III was capable of around 160mph (258km/h) and was able to reach 100mph (161km/h) in under 12 seconds. Production endured until 1968 by which time just 31 examples had been built. Since 1967 the cars had been produced by JW Automotive Engineering, founded by John Wyer and his associate John Willment, which took over the premises and activities of Ford Advanced Vehicles.

Across the Atlantic, work was underway on a Mark IV version of the design, which appeared in April 1967.

This differed radically from its predecessors in having a chassis cum body made of aluminium honeycomb sandwich material that possessed the stiffness of steel but was claimed to be 88 per cent lighter. Four Mark IVs were among no less than seven Fords entered for Le Mans in 1967, and one took first place with another coming in fourth. At this high point the company decided to withdraw from racing, but that was not the end of the story.

John Wyer was convinced that the GT40 in its original form still had plenty of potential. Racing under the colours and sponsorship of Gulf Oil, 4.9 litre cars, prepared and refined by J W Automotive, ran at Le Mans in 1968 and 1969 and were victorious on both occasions, so giving Ford a creditable four Le Mans triumphs.

Nineteen-sixty-nine really marked the end of the GT40's competitive career. A total of 211 cars were produced and they survive today in remarkable numbers. Even by the early 1980's there were more GT40s in existence, some having been built up from spares and crashed cars, than had ever been produced at Slough. . .

Ford GT40

4.3 litre V8
Lola GT 1963
|
4.2 litre GT40 1964 ─────────────
                    | |
              7 litre Mark II   4.7 litre Mark III
                  1965   1965
                    |
              Mark IV 1967

BELOW: *One of the last GT40s, this is a 1969 example and shows how the coupé's appearance had altered since the car's inception. It dates from after Ford's withdrawal from racing but the GT40 went on winning!*

LAMBORGHINI MIURA (1966-1972)

W hen in 1963 Ferruccio Lamborghini created the marque that bore his name, its first product was the 350GT. While this was an impressive car, it did lack that elusive quality of charisma that appeared to be the almost exclusive preserve of Ferrari in the Grand Touring sector. All this changed in 1966 when Lamborghini unleashed the Miura with its sensational Bertone-styled bodywork. It also had the distinction of being the world's first mid-engined road car.

Production of the 350GT ceased in 1967 but work on what was to become the Miura had begun late in 1964. It was then that technical supremo Giampaolo Dallara, his assistant Paolo Stanzani and road tester Bob Wallace began thinking of a car which they hoped would form the basis of a GT that could do double duty as a sports racer. Dallara, in particular, had been greatly influenced by the mid-engined Ford GT40, which had first run at Le Mans earlier in 1964, powered by a squat, longitudinally mounted V8 engine. He envisaged a Lamborghini with a similar layout. However, if the firm's V12 unit had been so positioned, the resulting car would have been excessively long.

Dallara resolved the problem by following Alec Issigonis's philosophy. The Mini was a front-wheel-drive car but, to save space, its engine was transversely mounted. The Lamborghini engineer did precisely the same thing with his proposed car and positioned the V12 behind the passenger compartment. Had the five-speed gearbox been attached in the usual way, it would have resulted in an unacceptably wide unit. So Dallara again followed the Issigonis approach and the 'box was located underneath it, à la Mini, in the engine's sump.

He submitted the design to Ferruccio Lamborghini, who vetoed the concept of a sports racer but liked the idea of a mid-engined road car. It was a revolutionary concept for the day – while the configuration was by then the norm for racing and competition machinery, it had never been applied to a production car. Certainly the roadholding advantages of the layout were readily apparent, but excessive engine noise would undoubtedly present a problem to the designer.

Dallara wasted little time in proceeding with the concept, which was designated P400, P standing for *posteriore* (rear) and 400 designating the capacity of the V12 engine. While the 350GT had started life, as its name in-dicated, as a 3.5 litre car, an enlarged 3.9 litre version was in the offing for its 400GT derivative which appeared in 1966. However, as the engine of the P400 would also have to incorporate the gearbox, a new design for the cylinder block was required.

Bertone Style

Work on the project was underway by mid-1965 and the finished chassis was displayed, alongside a 350GT, at the 1965 Turin Motor Show. But Lamborghini had not yet decided on a coachbuilder to design a body to cloak these revolutionary mechanicals. Virtually all the *carrozzerias* were closely involved with other car makers and Touring, which had created the bodywork for the 350GT, was on the verge of bankruptcy. Fortunately Lamborghini was able to forge an association with the Turin-based Bertone concern and, in particular, Marcello Gandini, its 26-year-old chief stylist. Almost as soon as the Turin show had closed its doors, he began work on the body of

Specifications: Lamborghini Miura P400

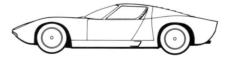

Length:	14ft 2in (4318mm)
Width:	5ft 9in (1753mm)
Height:	3ft 5in (1041mm)
Wheelbase:	8ft 2in (2489mm)
Track:	front and rear, 4ft 7⅜in (1412mm)
Unladen weight:	2160lb (980kg)
Engine: Mid-located V12 with twin overhead camshafts per bank, 82×62mm, 3929cc. Compression ratio, 9.5:1. Max power, 350bhp at 7000rpm. Max torque, 271lb/ft at 5100rpm.	
Transmission:	Five-speed manual
Drive:	Rear
Suspension (front):	Independent, coil springs and wishbones
Suspension (rear):	Independent, coil springs and wishbones
Top speed:	170mph (274km/h)
0-60mph (96km/h):	6.3 seconds
Production (including S and SV):	765

ABOVE: *A 1969 Lamborghini Miura SV, identifiable by its lack of headlamp "eyelashes". The two bonnet grilles act as exit routes after air has flowed through the radiator. One is raised to gain access to the petrol tank. Inset, the magnificent profile of the Bertone-styled Miura.*

LEFT: *The Miura's pioneering mid-located, transversely mounted 4 litre V12 engine. Its gearbox is mounted in the sump in a manner reminiscent of the British Mini.*

RIGHT: *Rear visibility was not the Miura's strong point, always a problem on a mid-engined car. This so-called "venetian blind" was an ingenious compromise.*

the mid-engined chassis, the dimensions of which had been slightly extended by this time. The intention was to have the first car completed in time for Lamborghini to display it at the 1966 Geneva Motor Show in March. Thankfully the car, completed in startling orange paint, was finished in time, placed on a lorry and dispatched over the Alps to the Swiss city.

Taurean Associations

It was at Geneva that the P400 project became the Miura. It was named after Don Eduardo Miura, a well known breeder of fighting bulls. Lamborghini's marque badge was a bull, chosen because Ferruccio's Lamborghini was born on 28th April 1916 under the zodiac sign of Taurus. The car sold for

LAMBORGHINI MIURA

7,700,000 lire (£4425), which was around £1000 more than the newly introduced 400GT that was also on display at the show.

The new Lamborghini was the star of the event. Just 3ft 5in (1041mm) high, it looked sensational from any angle. A particularly noteworthy feature was the headlamps which were flush with the body contours and which, when necessary, could be raised by electric motors. The lights were surrounded by what looked remarkably like "eyelashes" which concealed air ducts to cool the front disc brakes.

The mechanical specifications were equally impressive. The transversely mounted 3.9 litre V12, with twin overhead camshafts per cylinder bank, developed 350bhp. Suspension, as in the 350 and 400GT cars, was by all-round wishbones and coil springs.

It would be another year, before the first production Miura, also finished in a dazzling orange hue, was delivered to its first owner in March 1967. It looked outwardly similar to the Geneva car, but the Lamborghini team had worked hard to eliminate the twin shortcomings of noise and heat generated by the omnipresent power unit. To these ends the original Plexiglass rear window was replaced by what many likened to a venetian blind which permitted rear visibility for the driver and also helped to keep the engine cool.

The Miura was capable of a genuine 170mph (274km/h) with roadholding greatly benefitting from the central engine location. Acceleration was positively frightening and 60mph (96km/h) came up in around six seconds. On the debit side were a rather cramped cockpit, limited luggage space and, above all, excessive noise, which was almost inevitable with the V12 engine located where the rear passengers would have sat in a two-plus-two. No matter! The Miura possessed charisma in abundance for here, at last, was a car to appeal to the millionaire clientele who had previously bought Ferraris.

Miura S And SV

Lamborghini continued to refine the model and at the 1968 Turin Show unveiled the Miura S which entered production in January of 1969. It outwardly resembled the original with the exception of its wider section tyres. Engine output was boosted to 370bhp. This continued to be the definitive Miura until 1971 when, at that year's Geneva show, the firm unveiled the

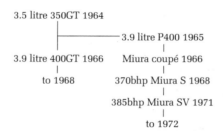

ABOVE: *There was only one Miura built in convertible form and this is it, created for the International Lead-Zinc Research Organization.*

Lamborghini Miura

```
3.5 litre 350GT 1964
        |
        |————————————3.9 litre P400 1965
        |                        |
3.9 litre 400GT 1966      Miura coupé 1966
        |                        |
      to 1968           370bhp Miura S 1968
                                 |
                         385bhp Miura SV 1971
                                 |
                              to 1972
```

ultimate version of the model. The SV, V standing for *veloce* (fast), dispenses with the distinctive eyelashes while engine output was boosted to 385bhp. The rear track was widened by just over 5in (127mm) and the attendant suspension redesigned as a quadrilateral layout. The chassis was also strengthened to make it more rigid than its predecessors.

The SV did not enter production until the autumn of 1971 but, in 1972, Lamborghini took the ill-fated decision to discontinue Miura production just at the time when most of its shortcomings had been resolved. So production ceased in 1972. Although its equally sensational Countach successor had appeared alongside the Miura SV at the 1971 Geneva Show, there was a hiatus of well over three years before that car finally entered production. During this time many more examples of this memorable mid-engined Grand Tourer could, undoubtedly, have been sold.

ABOVE: *The Miura in its original form. Note the engine air intakes behind and below the door.*

BELOW: *The Miura Spider which, for publicity, had as many parts as possible made from zinc. This applied to the engine compartment and, externally, such features as the radiator grille and door handles.*

LEFT: *A right-hand-drive Miura S with those distinctive eyelashes in place. They concealed ducts that fed cooling air to the front brakes. Note the Bertone badge on the side panel. This is a 1970 car.*

Last of the great, front-engined, V12 Ferrari berlinettas, the Daytona was also the fastest and most expensive Maranello-built car of its day. Cloaked in one of the finest of all Pininfarina bodies, the model sold in respectable numbers and nearly 1300 were produced. The Daytona also differed from its predecessors in that it was raced with success by some of its more enthusiastic owners, rather than them opting for purpose-designed sports racers as had previously been the case.

The Daytona evolved over a two year period. The appearance, in 1964, of Lamborghini's 350GT powered by a V12 engine, with costly and more efficient twin overhead camshafts per cylinder bank, stung Ferrari into a response. The marque had hitherto used single camshafts but matters were put to rights in 1966 with the arrival of the front-engined 3.3 litre 275 GTB/4, which was the first roadgoing Ferrari with twin cam heads. It was destined to endure until 1968.

Work was soon underway on an even more powerful development of the theme. This was a project that began in 1967 and, by the end of the year, a Daytona prototype was in existence clothed in a two-door coupé body which pointed the way to the finished product. Its engine was a 4 litre V12 with twin cam heads and, unusually, three valves per cylinder. In the event, this unit was not proceeded with and was replaced by a more conventional V12 with a 4.4 litre capacity. It was a dry sump unit which aspirated through no less than six Weber carburettors and developed 352bhp at 7500rpm. Front mounted, the engine was balanced by a rear-located, five-speed, all-synchromesh transaxle.

Chassis And Suspension
The car's chassis followed the usual Ferrari practice of welded oval section tubes, while all-round independent suspension was by wishbones and coil springs, the rear refinement (also Lamborghini-prompted) having first appeared on Ferrari's 275 GTB of 1964.

These mechanicals were cloaked with a two-seater Pininfarina body of outstanding beauty and refinement. Unlike the 275 GTB/4, its most memorable feature was a chisel-shaped nose in which four headlights were contained, for aerodynamic considerations, behind Plexiglass covers. The two-door body was completed by a handsome truncated tail although, unlike other potent Ferraris of the day, it bore no spoiler.

The first Pininfarina-designed and -built body was fitted to the prototype which was finished in a rather startling shade of strawberry mousse and exhibited at the 1968 Paris Motor Show. It was presented as the 365 GTB/4 but elements of the press named it Daytona following Ferrari's win in the American 24-hour race of the same name in the previous year.

Ferrari was criticized for not having produced a mid-engined car, for Lamborghini's innovative Miura had appeared two years before. But the public clearly loved what was now universally known as the Daytona. Numerous orders were received for the car but deliveries did not begin until the middle of 1969. Unlike the prototype, the bodies were built by Scaglietti and made of steel with the exception of the doors, bonnet and boot lid, which were of aluminium.

The Daytona was an extremely fast car. The factory claimed a top speed of 174mph (280km/h) which was en-

ABOVE: *The breathtaking elegance of a 1971 Daytona, one of 158 produced in right-hand-drive form.*

RIGHT: *This Daytona Spider has its headlamps concealed behind flaps which were applied to the later cars.*

Specifications: Ferrari Daytona

Length:	14ft 4in (4369mm)
Width:	5ft 9in (1753mm)
Height:	4ft 1in (1245mm)
Wheelbase:	7ft 10½in (2400mm)
Track:	front 4ft 8⅜in (1440mm), rear 4ft 8in (1425mm)
Unladen weight:	3151lb (1429kg)
Engine: V12 with twin overhead camshafts per bank, 81×71mm, 4390cc. Compression ratio, 9.3:1. Max power, 352bhp at 7500rpm. Max torque, 318lb/ft at 5500rpm.	
Transmission:	Five-speed manual
Drive:	Rear
Suspension (front):	Independent, coil springs and wishbones
Suspension (rear):	Independent, coil springs and wishbones
Top speed:	174mph (280km/h)
0-60mph (96km/h):	5.4 seconds
Production (including spider):	1406

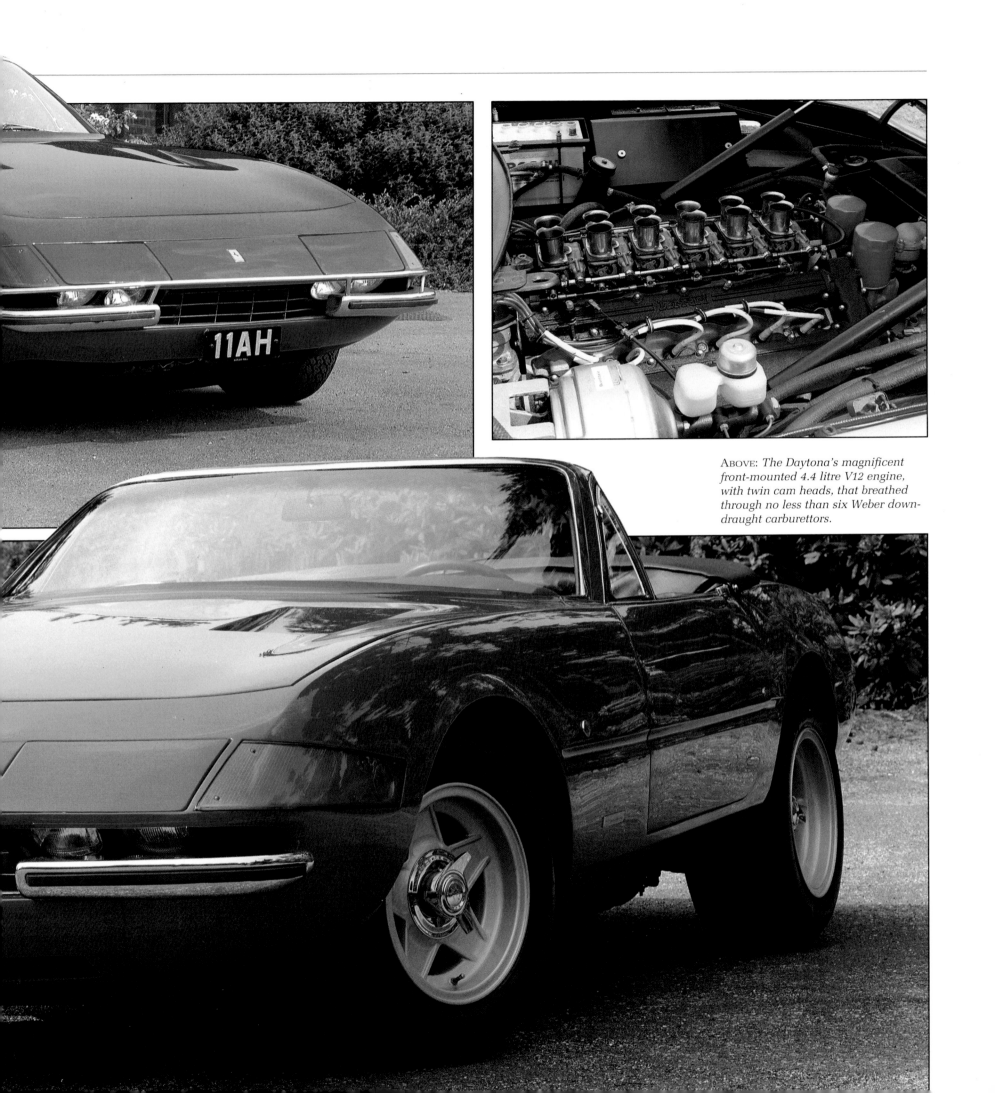

ABOVE: *The Daytona's magnificent front-mounted 4.4 litre V12 engine, with twin cam heads, that breathed through no less than six Weber down-draught carburettors.*

FERRARI GTB/4 DAYTONA

dorsed by road tests undertaken by motoring magazines. It also possessed extraordinarily rapid acceleration; Ferrari said that the car could reach 59mph (95km/h) in first gear and 60mph (96km/h) came up in just 5.4 seconds.

The Frankfurt Motor Show of 1969 saw the arrival of an open version, which was designated the 365 GTS/4, S being for spider. The body lent itself admirably to this treatment and the only other obvious difference between the versions was the replacement of the Cromadora five-spoked alloy wheels by Borrani wire ones.

The Daytona was designed as a road car and the factory had no intention of racing it. However, in August 1971, the 500 car production barrier was broken which, inadvertently, meant that it could be homologated for Group 4 special Grand Touring racing. At this time, Ferrari's philosophy was that it should produce purpose-designed cars for sports racing, and it was not inclined to put the process into reverse. However, privately entered cars had already appeared at Le Mans, firstly and unsuccessfully in 1969, and again in 1971 when an example achieved a creditable fifth place.

As a result of this pressure, in 1971 Ferrari produced what it called a Competition Daytona, but even then these cars were not prepared in the racing shops at Maranello, but at another Customer Assistance facility in Modena. Three examples, of an eventual total of five cars, were prepared with the accent on weight saving, each having wholly aluminium bodywork and glass fibre doors, bonnet and boot lid. Plexiglass windows were fitted to the first batch. Two cars ran in that year's Tour de France race and achieved fourth and ninth placings.

Success On The Track

A further five competition cars were prepared in 1972 with steel bodywork and wider wheels. The ultra-reliable V12 engine required little attention, other than careful assembly and tuning. At Le Mans in 1972 no less than nine Daytonas were entered and examples of these works-converted cars occupied fifth to ninth places overall and took the first four positions in the special Grand Touring class. Similar class wins occurred at Watkins Glen in America and at Kyalami in South Africa.

These successes spurred on Ferrari to even greater efforts and for 1973 it

RIGHT: *This Daytona, chassis 15681, was the last car to be entered by British importers, Maranello Concessionaires, which had run a racing team since 1961. It ran at Le Mans in 1972, driven by Westbury and Hine, but retired in the eighth hour with piston failure.*

produced a further five special cars with their engines boosted to 450bhp. A privately prepared example was, appropriately, second in the Daytona 24-hour race of 1973, and the special Grand Touring class at Le Mans once again fell to Daytonas with the victorious car then being driven on the road back to Paris.

The Daytona finally bowed out in 1973. Of the 1274 examples built, 158 were produced in right-hand-drive form for the British market. It was one of Ferrari's best-selling road cars and remarkably few modifications had been made during its four-year production life. The most notable related to the headlamps. The Plexiglass headlamp covers did not feature on those cars specified for the all important American market. They were replaced by retractable units and by 1971 all Daytonas had followed this pattern.

One of the truly legendary Ferraris, today the model is avidly sought by collectors, having proved its worth on the road and also on the track.

ABOVE: *The Daytona Spider arrived in 1969 and is a particularly sought-after version. Only 122 Spiders were built, although some coupés have subsequently been converted*

Ferrari Daytona

3.3 litre V12 275 GTB
1964

275 GTB/4 1966

to 1968

365 GTB/4 Daytona
1968

to 1973

365 GTS/4 Spider
1969

to 1973

LEFT: *A 1973 Daytona, which was the last year of production. This Pininfarina body still looks refreshingly modern, despite being over 20 years old.*

LAMBORGHINI COUNTACH (1971-1990)

If Lamborghini came of age as a marque with the pioneering mid-engined Miura, its Countach successor was, if anything, even more sensational. Low, angular and capable of speeds approaching 180mph (290km/h), this was the quintessential supercar which even over-shadowed its Ferrari contemporaries. Announced in 1971 but not in production until 1974 and destined for a 16 year production life, the Countach also has the distinction of being the best-ever-selling Lamborghini with some 2000 examples built.

RIGHT: *Those extraordinary lines shown to full advantage. The duct is for engine cooling.*

Just as the Miura had its driving force in Giampaolo Dallara, so it was Paolo Stanzani, his assistant, who conceived the essentials of the Countach, having taken over as Lamborghini's chief engineer in 1968. He began work on what was coded Project 112 after the Miura SV of 1971 had been completed. Stanzani had decided that the new car would perpetuate the Miura's centrally positioned V12 engine but not the engine's transverse orientation.

The design also differed from the Miura, which had a tendency for nose lightness, in having its gearbox in the centre of the car rather than at its rear along with the differential, as was normally the case with an in-line, mid-located engine. By placing these components at opposite ends of the power unit, Stanzani was then faced with the problem of conveying the drive between the two and he came up with the ingenious solution of taking it, via a sealed tube, through the engine's sump. With the five-speed gearbox positioned alongside the driver, a further virtue of this arrangement was an excellent gear change, which was a characteristic that many mid-engined cars did not possess.

On Display
The V12's 3.9 litre capacity was enlarged to 4971cc by increasing both the bore and stroke. It was intended to display the car at the 1971 Geneva Motor Show. As so much time had been expended on the engine, it was mounted, for display purposes, in a simple chassis of square section tubes. By this time the design had become known as the LP500, for *Longitudinale Posteriore 5 litri*, a description of the engine.

These ingenious mechanicals required an equally audacious body and Bertone's Marcello Gandini magnificently rose to the occasion by creating a design that was even more remarkable than the Miura's. The starting point of the creation was his Alfa Romeo-based Bertone Carabo (Scarab

Specifications: Lamborghini Countach LP400

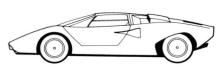

Length:	13ft 7in (4140mm)
Width:	6ft 2in (1880mm)
Height:	3ft 6in (1067mm)
Wheelbase:	7ft 11½in (2426mm)
Track:	front 4ft 11in (1499mm), rear 4ft 11¾in (1519mm)
Unladen weight:	2348lb (1065kg)
Engine: Mid-located V12 with twin overhead camshafts per bank, 82×62mm, 3929cc. Compression ratio, 10.5:1. Max power, 375bhp at 8000rpm. Max torque, 267lb/ft at 5500rpm.	
Transmission:	Five-speed manual
Drive:	Rear
Suspension (front):	Independent, coil springs and wishbones
Suspension (rear):	Independent, coil springs and wishbones
Top speed:	180mph (290km/h)
0-60mph (96km/h):	6.9 seconds
Production (including LP400S, 5000, QV, Anniversary):	1979

Beetle), which had appeared at the 1968 Paris Motor Show. It was so called because the doors of the wedge-shaped coupé opened upwards, just as a beetle extended its wings. Using this theme as his starting point, Gandini created a daring two-seater, only 40in (1016mm) high. As the Turin workers were racing to complete the car, one suddenly exclaimed "Countach!" which is a local slang word of praise or expressing astonishment. The very appropriate name stuck and the Countach was the first Lamborghini, the formative 350 and 400 GT family excepted, not to have a name with bull or bullfighting associations.

The car was completed on the very eve of the Geneva event and the lemon yellow coupé was then loaded into a lorry which was driven, in the small hours, over the Alps to the show. There it was displayed in the coachwork sec-

tion as the Bertone Countach. The sensation that it caused at the show was sufficient to convince the Lamborghini company that it had found the Miura's successor.

Time For Modification
There was still much development work to be undertaken and it was a further three years before the car reached the public with the first production Countach exhibited at the 1974 Geneva Show. By this time some crucial body and mechanical modifications had been effected. These principally concerned cooling the centrally mounted in-line engine: the twin radiators, instead of being side-mounted, were now positioned at right angles to the V12. But this necessitated

BELOW RIGHT: *A 1974 Countach pictured, unusually, with its twin headlamps and spotlights ablaze.*

RIGHT: *A 1974 Countach. The large windscreen is an integral part of the model's wedge shape.*

BELOW: *It could not be anything else! Rear view of a Countach. The protusions on top of the wings are air intakes for the radiators.*

the introduction of two large intakes on the top of the rear wings and the side air ducts were also increased in size. It was also decided to revert to the original 3.9 litre 375bhp engine after the original car's unique 5 litre version exploded. The car was accordingly re-designated the LP400. Its chassis also evolved into a massive tubular space-frame, while the all-independent sus-pension was of Lamborghini's usual coil spring and wishbone variety.

Despite the reduction in engine capacity, the car had a top speed in excess of 180mph (290km/h) and 60mph (90km/h) came up in under six seconds. While the extraordinary body was guaranteed to turn the heads of

fellow drivers and pedestrians alike, it did contribute some impracticalities, such as the driver and passenger experiencing difficulty in getting into and out of the low slung coupé. More positively, the Countach showed itself as very much a driver's car with phenomenal acceleration and hard, unyielding suspension.

Arrivederci Lamborghini

The model's formative phase coincided with Ferruccio Lamborghini severing his connections with the firm that bore his name. He had disposed of a minority shareholding in 1972 and sold out completely in 1974. There followed an era of financial instability which was only truly resolved in 1987 when the business was purchased by America's Chrysler Corporation.

In the meantime the Countach was continuing to evolve. A mere 23 examples left the Lamborghini factory at Sant' Agata Bolognese in 1974 and the effects of the world recession began to bite. Nevertheless, the manufacturing figure rose to 60 cars in 1975, but plunged again to a mere 16 in 1978, which was when the Italian government stepped in to prevent the business from collapsing. That year saw the first significant development of the design. After 150 examples of the LP400 had been completed, it was replaced by the Countach S, easily identifiable by its flared arches to accommodate the Campagnolo alloy wheels, with "telephone dial" apertures, which were shod with wider, low profile, Pirelli P7 high performance tyres. Their fitment was accompanied by modifications to the rear suspension. A rear wing became an optional but popular extra.

The S continued until 1982 and, after the completion of 466 cars, it was succeeded at that year's Geneva Show, by the LP500S which represented the first engine capacity increase since 1966. This was necessary because of increasingly stringent emissions regulations demanded by the important American market which were taking the edge off the car's performance. Chief engineer Giulio Alfieri, formerly of Maserati who had replaced Stanzani in 1978, oversaw this work. The V12's bore and stroke were increased to produce 4.7 litres and it developed 375bhp, the same as its predecessor. The model was sometimes designated the 5000S.

This endured until 1985 when there were further engine revisions. The V12, with its twin-cam cylinder heads, had employed two valves per cylinder; the 5000QV (for *Quattrovalvolve*) used four. Capacity was once again increased, this time to 5.2 litres. Power rose appreciably, to 455bhp, although the car's top speed remained at around 180mph (290km/h).

The QV was the most popular version of the design with 610 cars built. It was replaced for 1989 by the Anniversary Countach, created to celebrate Lamborghini's 25 years as a car maker. Mechanically, it was essentially the same as its predecessor, although there were some body modifications which were executed, not by Gandini, but Lamborghini itself.

An era ended in July 1990 when the last Countach was built – its extraordinary, futuristic lines essentially intact. By contrast, its Diablo replacement was destined for a more controversial gestation and manufacturing life. . .

ABOVE: *A Countach 5000S with its pop-up headlamps activated. The flared wheel arches are designed to accommodate the wider alloy wheels. This is a 1981 example.*

BELOW: *What the birds see. The sculptural quality of the Countach's Bertone body, the lines of which reflect the longitudinal location of the V12 engine, is here very apparent.*

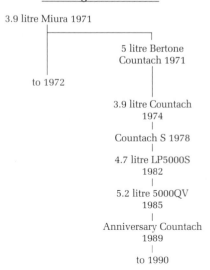

Lamborghini Countach

3.9 litre Miura 1971
|
|—— 5 litre Bertone Countach 1971
|
to 1972
|
3.9 litre Countach 1974
|
Countach S 1978
|
4.7 litre LP5000S 1982
|
5.2 litre 5000QV 1985
|
Anniversary Countach 1989
|
to 1990

ABOVE: *A 1982 Countach fitted with its optional aerofoil. It looks impressive but is said to make only a marginal contribution to the car's formidable performance.*

ABOVE: *Worm's eye view of a Countach underlining the aerodynamic element to its bodywork. This is a 5000S of 1982, complete with aerofoil and memorable number plate!*

BELOW: *Open wide! An Anniversary Countach – note badge on rear panel. This is a 1989 car also revealing those distinctive upward opening doors, a feature of the model from the outset.*

The world's first purpose-designed rally car, the highly successful Stratos ironically had very little of Lancia about it. The stubby dartlike lines were conceived by Bertone while the power unit was courtesy of Ferrari. But the Stratos did exactly what was required of it and provided Lancia with the accolade of the World Rally Championship for Makes consecutively in 1974, 1975 and 1976. Although only a handful of cars were used in the Lancia team, homologation rules required that the coupé enter (albeit) limited production and, in all, 492 examples were built.

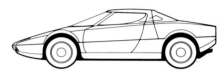

Specifications: Lancia Stratos	
Length:	13ft 10in (4216mm)
Width:	5ft 9in (1753mm)
Height:	3ft 7in (1092mm)
Wheelbase:	7ft 2in (2184mm)
Track:	front 4ft 8in (1422mm), rear 4ft 9in (1448mm)
Unladen weight:	1918lb (870kg)
Engine: Mid-located V6 with twin overhead camshafts per bank, 92×60mm, 2418cc. Compression ratio, 9:1. Max power, 190bhp at 7000rpm. Max torque, 159lb/ft at 7600rpm.	
Transmission:	Five-speed manual
Drive:	Rear
Suspension (front):	Independent, coil springs and wishbones
Suspension (rear):	Independent, coil springs and struts
Top speed:	140mph (225km/h)
0-60mph (96km/h):	5.9seconds
Production:	492

The Stratos story really begins at the 1970 Turin Motor Show where the Bertone coachbuilding concern unveiled its show stopper, the Stratos. This futuristic two-seater was created by Marcello Gandini who was also responsible for styling the Lamborghinis Miura and Countach. The Stratos, the name has echoes of stratosphere, had no doors in the accepted sense; access was by a single hinged flap at the front of the vehicle. Significantly, in the light of future events, it was built up around the much modified floorpan of a Lancia 1.6 HF coupé. Because of the steeply sloping front, this was a mid-engined car and the 1.6 litre V4 engine was mounted transversely behind the passenger compartment. This sensational creation did not escape the attention of Lancia's racing manager, Cesare Fiorio, who immediately visualized that this advanced concept car could form the basis of a world-beating rally machine. Pivotally, it was mid-engined just like a racing car.

Lancia's ownership had changed in 1969 when it was taken over by Fiat which, in the same year, also took a controlling interest in Ferrari. Lancia's recent history had been one of falling output and mounting debts, although in the 1960's the make, under Fiorio's steady direction, had triumphed in rallying. In these competitions, the HF Fulvia coupés had been extraordinarily successful and, in 1972, Lancia had won, for the first time, rallying's International Championship accolade which, in the following year, became known as the World Rally Championship for Makes.

Finding The Right Engine

Despite these triumphs, Fiorio was determined that the Stratos would not be powered by the Fulvia's V4 engine which was coming to the end of its life. He looked around within the group for a suitable power unit and settled on the transversely mounted, Fiat-built, 2.4 litre V6 engine and five-speed transmission of the Ferrari Dino 246, which was due to cease production in 1974.

Fiorio was supported in this choice by Lancia's technical director, Piero Gobbato, formerly of Ferrari, who was well acquainted with the Dino and had been at Maranello when it had been introduced. The corporate green light was given and work on the model, which would perpetuate the Stratos name, involved Lancia engineer, Gianni Tonti, with further input from former Lamborghini designer, Giampaolo Dallara, best known for essaying the innovative mid-engined Miura. As creator of the original Stratos, Bertone was also involved and its prize was to manufacture the car's body. This would be built at its Grugliasco plant on the outskirts of Turin, with the coupés then being finished off at the nearby Lancia factory.

The first prototype was completed in great haste for the 1971 Turin Show. The stubby car had a wheelbase of a mere 7ft 2in (2184mm). Although greatly refined and with two conventional doors, it retained much of the vitality of the previous year's design exercise. Finished in matt Dayglo red paint, Lancia clearly meant business. The Stratos was built up around a strong steel monocoque, although the body panels were made of glass fibre. In addition to the Ferrari engine and gearbox, suspension was all independent by coil springs and wishbones.

There was still some internal corporate wrangling about the choice of power unit. For marketing reasons, the

LEFT: *A Stratos in action in the 1974 RAC Rally. Driven by Munari and Sodano, it was the only Stratos competing and finished in a creditable third place.*

LEFT: *The stubby lines of the mid-engined Stratos are unlike those of any other car.*

ABOVE: *The Stratos looked equally distinctive from the back with a rear "venetian blind" similar to that of the Lamborghini Miura, also with a body by Bertone.*

RIGHT: *The Stratos name hailed from Bertone, not Lancia, and was carried over from its one-off 1970 Turin Show styling exercise.*

LEFT: *As the wedge-shaped Stratos is mid-engined, beneath the forward hingeing louvred glass fibre bonnet is the brake servo and radiator, cooled by twin electric fans.*

LANCIA STRATOS

TOP: *The Stratos's transversely mounted 2.4 litre V6 engine is courtesy of the in-house Ferrari Dino 246. An inspired choice, this proven engine gave the Stratos the reliability and genuine staying power that is required by a rally car.*

ABOVE: *The Stratos was only produced in left-hand-drive form. The dashboard was neatly laid out with the revolution counter positioned directly in front of the driver. Note the speedometer, which reads to 250km/h (155mph), on the right.*

Lancia Stratos

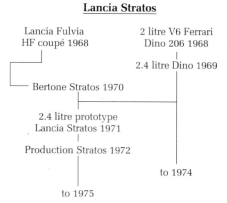

Lancia Fulvia HF coupé 1968
2 litre V6 Ferrari Dino 206 1968
2.4 litre Dino 1969
Bertone Stratos 1970
2.4 litre prototype Lancia Stratos 1971
Production Stratos 1972
to 1974
to 1975

company would have much preferred the Stratos to have been powered by the Fiat-derived, 2 litre, twin-cam four used in the Lancia Beta. Despite it being tested in 150bhp form, thankfully Fiorio's wish held sway and the definitive Ferrari-engined Stratos appeared at the 1972 Turin Show. The only major modification to have been effected by this time was that, at the rear, suspension struts replaced the wishbones originally specified.

The car was unleashed for the first time, in the autumn of 1972, in the Turin de Corse event when a Stratos was entered as a non-homologated prototype. Unfortunately, it retired with rear suspension failure. The Lancia's first victory came in the Spanish Firestone rally of April 1973 and the car showed its mettle by winning the Tour de France later in the year.

However, production proper did not begin until early in 1974, after the Dino

had ceased manufacture and; until homologation was achieved later in the year, the Lancias ran in the prototype class. Then, on 1st October, it was announced that the 500 cars required to conform with homologation regulations had been built. It is now known that total production amounted to 492 examples, despite Bertone having assembled 502 body shells. This did not prevent Lancia from winning the 1974 Championship and, from then on, the car appeared to be practically invincible, with many of the world's major rallies falling to the stubby projectile with its distinctive, rasping exhaust note. The celebrated Monte Carlo Rally, for instance, was conquered on three successive occasions between 1975 and 1977.

Lancia won the Championship for Makes again in 1975 and repeated the feat in 1976. However, the last Stratos had been built in 1975 and although

there were successes in 1977, in that year the Lancia and Fiat teams merged. The Fiat 131 Abarth moved to the fore and it subsequently gave Fiat the World Championship laurels in 1978.

Mid-Engined Marvel

Driving a Stratos took some getting used to because of its short wheelbase but, once mastered, this small mid-engine coupé's roadholding had an almost leechlike quality. Despite having been built solely with competition in mind, the Stratos was perfectly tractable as a road car. It was comfortable and while the V6 produced its characteristic bark, the car suffered no significant vibration, despite top speed being in the region of 140mph (225km/h). A practical note was struck by the provision of storage bins in the doors, which were deep enough to take a crash helmet (luggage room is always a problem in a mid-engined car).

Inevitably, the Stratos's appeal went into sharp decline from 1979 when works participation officially ceased, but today's examples of what is seen as an utterly distinctive and successful rally car are keenly sought after.

BELOW: *The futuristic lines of the Stratos, which was built specifically for competition and dominated rallying in its day, providing Lancia with successive Championships in 1974, 1975 and 1976.*

ABOVE: *Like the Stratos's bonnet, the engine cover was also made of a plastic material. The aerodynamic wings on the roof and tail were intended to keep that ferocious engine output on the road.*

ROLLS-ROYCE CAMARGUE (1975-1985)

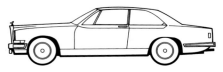

The top of the range two-door Camargue saloon by Pininfarina was the first Rolls-Royce to have a body designed by an outside stylist. A magnificently appointed car, it was also notable for being the first recipient of the company's advanced split-level air-conditioning system. Destined for a ten-year production life, the Camargue was duly listed until 1985, but perhaps its full potential went unrealized.

The Camargue was a long time coming, having been conceived in the late 1960's under the Delta coding. Rolls-Royce's original intention was to produce a coachbuilt version of the unitary construction Silver Shadow model, but the last mainstream British exponent of the coachbuilder's craft, James Young, had closed its doors in 1967. The Crewe-based car company therefore decided to look overseas, and specifically to the Turin studios of Pininfarina, with whom it had some past associations. The intention was to produce an exclusive two-door car for the owner-driver, the ultimate in personal transport. Having said that, the firm already had the two-door Silver Shadow on its books, and this was revised as the Corniche in 1971. Unlike the Shadow, there would be no Bentley equivalent; the model would be solely offered with a Rolls-Royce radiator, this being one of the inviolable design criteria presented to Pininfarina. Mechanically, it was closely related to the Shadow and shared its running gear, floorpan and thus its wheelbase.

This prestigious styling assignment was personally undertaken by Sergio Pininfarina, son of the company's founder. While work was underway on the Rolls-Royce commission, the styling house was also in the final stages of completing the lines of the much admired Fiat 130 coupé which appeared in 1971. When the Camargue followed four years later, parallels were immediately drawn between the appearances of the two otherwise unrelated models. In addition to the car's exterior, Pininfarina was also responsible for the dashboard which was to incorporate a new air-conditioning system, work having been underway on that project since 1968. Once the design was finalized, the construction of the Delta prototype began in 1971 at Rolls-Royce's north London-based Mulliner Park Ward subsidiary.

This car was completed in mid-1972 and with the mechanicals already resolved, the model could have been in production by 1973. However, a number of unforeseen diversions conspired to delay its introduction. The most significant of these was the bankruptcy, in 1971, of the Rolls-Royce company which was followed by its nationalization and the 1973 public flotation of the car division. That year was also overshadowed by a damaging strike at Mulliner and this, together with the need to perfect the sophisticated air-conditioning meant that it was not until early in 1975 that the Camargue was finally unveiled. But by then the world was reeling from a depression triggered by a rise in the price of oil . . .

The French Connection
Named, like the Corniche, after an area in the south of France which was a playground for the rich who were its potential buyers, the Camargue was the most expensive Rolls-Royce of its day: at £29,250 it was nearly £6500 more than the Corniche. The Pininfarina-styled, two-door saloon body got mixed reviews. It was a massive affair with a brutally angular front which retained the famous Rolls-Royce radiator daringly tilted 10 degrees forward. By contrast, the tail was refreshingly uncluttered by embellishments and was supremely elegant. Weighing 5175lb (2347kg), it tipped the scales at 4991lb (226kg) more than the Corniche.

Rolls-Royce wanted the model to have a performance edge on the saloons so, after 60 cars had been completed, the 6.7 litre V8 was fitted with a German Solex four choke carburettor in place of the usual twin SUs. Transmission, like the Shadow, was a three-speed automatic unit and the all-independent suspension and self-levelling systems were similarly sourced.

Where the car really differed from its four-door stablemate was inside. The dashboard, although apparently wood, was in fact a thin layer of veneer over an aluminium base, and incorporated the controls of a new split-level air-conditioning unit which set new standards for such a system. It was extended to the Shadow II of 1977 and

Specifications: Rolls-Royce Camargue

Length:	16ft 11in (5156mm)
Width:	6ft 3in (1905mm)
Height:	4ft 10in (1473mm)
Wheelbase:	10ft (3048mm)
Track:	front 5ft (1524mm), rear 4ft 11in (1499mm)
Unladen weight:	5175lb (2347kg)

Engine: V8, overhead valve, 104×99mm, 6750cc. Compression ratio, 8:1. Max power, not disclosed. Max torque, not disclosed.

Transmission:	Three-speed automatic
Drive:	Rear
Suspension (front):	Independent, coil springs and wishbones
Suspension (rear):	Independent, coil springs and semi-trailing arms
Top speed:	120mph (193km/h)
0-60mph (96km/h):	Not quoted
Production:	531

has since been used on all subsequent Rolls-Royce and Bentley models. Otherwise the Camargue proclaimed the established message of discreetly

RIGHT: *A 1978 Camargue which that year sold for £50,450, around £6000 more than its Silver Shadow contemporary. Built on the Shadow's floorpan, it thus shared the same wheelbase. The Pininfarina-styled body, produced at this stage by Mulliner Park Ward, was mostly of steel but the doors, bonnet and boot lid were made of aluminium.*

LEFT: *The Camargue's two doors were internally reinforced to protect the occupants against accidents. Note the chromium-plated marker at the top of each wing to help the driver judge the car's width.*

RIGHT: *Head-on view of a Camargue. The famous Rolls-Royce radiator was tilted 10 degrees forward. The twin headlamps were shared with the Rolls-Royce Silver Shadow.*

orchestrated comfort, the finest leather upholstery and walnut veneers, all of which contributed to the occupants being enveloped in an air of well being. The car had a claimed top speed approaching 120mph (193km/h) although, unlike its other models, Rolls-Royce never offered an example for testing and road evaluation by a motoring magazine.

Building the Camargue was initially a lengthy and unwieldy business. It was produced at the rate of one a week and each example took no less than six months to finish. Like the Shadow, the hull began life at Pressed Steel at Cowley and was then delivered to Mulliner Park Ward at Willesden for completion, whereupon it was dispatched to Crewe for rustproofing and fitment of the mechanicals. Then it was returned to London, where the craftsmen at Hythe Road trimmed the interior and completed each car, which was then subjected to a road test.

Manufacturing Modifications

Camargue production continued at this careful rate. In 1977, some engineering changes, notably the introduction of rack-and-pinion steering, were made coincidentally with the arrival of Shadow II. The Camargue also acquired a front air dam. Then, from late in 1978, the manufacturing process was simplified as the Cowley-sourced floorpans, instead of being sent to London, were delivered instead to Motor Panels in Coventry where the bodies were assembled and dispatched to Crewe. There they were rust proofed and completed in a new, specially created department.

Outwardly the cars changed little over the years. However, below the surface, in 1979, the rear suspension was revised and extended for the 1980

Silver Spirit and from 1981 Bosch fuel injection was fitted to those cars destined for overseas market. This was standardized in 1987. Output remained relatively modest and numbers built annually declined as time went on. Just 19 Camargues were built in 1983 and only 22 in 1984. At such a rate, production could hardly have been economic and Rolls-Royce ceased to list the car from the beginning of 1986. In March of that year, it was announced that the car would be discontinued in 1987. Since 1975 just 531 Camargues had been made.

Rolls-Royce Camargue

```
6.2 litre V8
Silver Shadow 1965
       |
6.7 litre V8
   1970
       |                Delta prototype 1972
       |                        |
Silver Shadow II 1975 ——— Camargue 1975
                                |
                           Revised rear
                           suspension 1979
                                |
Silver Spirit 1980 ————
       |                        |
       |                     to 1987
   to date
```

RIGHT: *The Camargue's lines remained virtually unchanged throughout its life, However, this late left-hand-drive car is fitted with wheels similar to those used on the in-house Bentley Turbo R.*

BELOW: *Detail of the Camargue's twin headlights. The wash and wipe facility shown here appeared in 1979 with more efficient brushes, rather than wiper blades, employed.*

RIGHT: *Although not outwardly apparent, the Camargue bristled with refinements by having monitors to check such factors as brake servo pressure, as well as coolant levels and external icing conditions.*

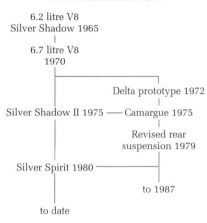

RIGHT: *The luxurious interior of the Camargue. Here, rear seats, with television and vanity case. Below, the driving compartment; air conditioning was fitted from the outset.*

Sylistically audacious in concept and featuring space age instrumentation, the Aston Martin Lagonda saloon was born from the ashes of a company restructured after bankruptcy and it attracted much attention on its unveiling at the 1976 London Motor Show. A prediction that the car would be ready for sale by the spring of 1977 proved to be wildly over-optimistic, and because of unforeseen problems with its revolutionary electronics, it was well over two years before deliveries began in earnest. Once in production, the car was destined for a 11-year manufacturing life and provided the company with valuable funding at a time when it needed it most.

Industrialist David Brown bought Aston Martin in 1947, and later in the same year he also purchased Lagonda, principally for its twin-overhead-camshaft, six cylinder engine which powered every Aston Martin road car between 1950 and 1959. In addition, a small number of Lagonda cars were produced, but the marque effectively ceased to exist in 1964 with the demise of the DB4-based Rapide saloon.

However, when the new Aston Martin DBS coupé appeared in 1967, William Towns, its stylist, also prepared a long wheelbase four-door version which was badged a Lagonda and a prototype was built in 1969 for the use of Sir David Brown (knighted 1968). In 1972 Brown sold Aston Martin to Company Developments and, in 1974, this concern decided to put the car into production, although it was now badged an Aston Martin Lagonda with the former marque name relegated to a model designation. Just seven examples were built over a two year period, the last in July 1976, but by this time Aston Martin had changed hands once again.

Company Developments filed for bankruptcy late in 1974 and it was not until June 1975 that the business was restructured. Although the original Aston Martin Lagonda had proved to be a costly failure, the management believed that its chassis and mechanicals could form the basis of a new model. Not only would this provide a vital second car line for the factory but also proclaim to the world that the company's new owners were totally committed to its long term future.

Towns At The Double
The talented William Towns was once again recruited to produce a new body style. He came up with a low, futuristic-looking, four-door saloon with crisply angular body lines. Although it

shared the same wheelbase as the earlier Aston Martin Lagonda, an overall length of 17ft 4in (5283mm) meant that it was 14in (356mm) longer. Starting on 1st February 1976 and working a 12-hour day, Towns completed the design in a single month, finishing his task on 1st March. Meanwhile, at the factory, Mike Loasby was responsible for engineering the Lagonda's mechanicals. Nine months after Towns had started work, in October 1976, the car was ready for display at the London Motor Show.

Apart from its dramatic appearance, it was the Lagonda's electronic equipment that aroused enormous interest. The driver was faced with what appeared to be a blank sheet of glass but when the ignition was switched on, the read-outs lit up as if on an electronic calculator. They graphically and digitally proclaimed such information as average speed and fuel consumption

ABOVE: *A pre-production Lagonda of 1977; deliveries proper did not begin until early in 1979. Note that this car is fitted with a radiator motif which did not feature on the production models. William Town's sensational body lines remained intact, however.*

Specifications: Aston Martin Lagonda

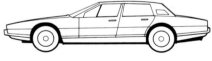

Length:	17ft 4in (5283mm)
Width:	5ft 10in (1778mm)
Height:	4ft 3in (1295mm)
Wheelbase:	9ft 7in (2921mm)
Track:	front and rear 4ft 11in (1499mm)
Unladen weight:	4459lb (2022kg)

Engine: V8 with twin overhead camshafts per bank, 100×85mm, 5340cc. Compression ratio, 9.5:1. Max power, not disclosed. Max torque, not disclosed.

Transmission:	Three-speed automatic
Drive:	Rear
Suspension (front):	Independent, coil springs and wishbones
Suspension (rear):	De Dion and coil springs
Top speed:	141mph (227km/h)
0-60mph (96km/h):	9.1 seconds
Production:	639

LEFT: *Another Lagonda prototype, built in 1978 but getting closer to the finished product. It bears Aston Martin's familiar AML 1 number plate which was switched from car to car. Note the absence of the radiator mascot, which featured on the car pictured above.*

ABOVE: *The engines of the production cars certainly looked rather tidier than this! It is the bay of an experimental Lagonda. The engine was essentially the same 5.3 litre V8 used in the Aston Martin coupé.*

LEFT: *The space-age instrumentation which, in its earliest stages, presented Aston Martin with so many problems. Note the touch switches and distinctive single-spoke steering wheel. This is a 1981 car.*

LEFT: *AML 1 featured on yet another Lagonda. This is a 1980 car photographed at Woburn Abbey, home of the Marquis of Tavistock, a dedicated Aston Martin enthusiast.*

during a particular journey while, at the flick of a switch, the speedometer would convert from miles to kilometres per hour. Everything else was operated by touch switches and there were microchips to store information about seat, pedal and steering positions. Air conditioning was standard and, in view of this, the windows of the rear doors were fixed.

The price was around the £20,000 mark and, such was its impact, Aston Martin took orders for over 100 cars. Then came the difficult bit: getting such a revolutionary concept into production. The main problem was centred around the electronic elements of the design, for the company was unable to find a British manufacturer with the resources to develop the devices. Costs quadrupled, and consequently the entire project began to threaten the firm's future.

It was not until April 1978 that the first Lagonda was handed over to its owners, Lord and Lady Tavistock, at their Woburn Abbey home. By then the original price had risen by half as much again, to £30,000, but unfortunately the car was undrivable because its electronics had failed.

These were once again redesigned to incorporate a self-contained American system but by 1979 the car's price had soared to £40,000. This was double the 1976 figure and, at the end of the year, a further £10,000 was added. By this time the car had been in production for about a year. Manufacture had begun, late in 1978, at the rate of about one car a week, with deliveries proper starting early in 1979.

Aston Martin Lagonda

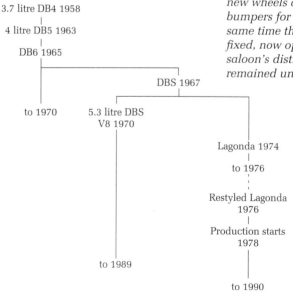

3.7 litre DB4 1958
|
4 litre DB5 1963
|
DB6 1965
|
├──────────────┐
| DBS 1967
| |
to 1970   5.3 litre DBS
           V8 1970
              |
        Lagonda 1974
              |
            to 1976
              ┊
        Restyled Lagonda
            1976
              |
        Production starts
            1978
              |
to 1989 |
            to 1990

Drivers found that once they had accustomed themselves to the instruments, the Lagonda carried them in considerable comfort to a top speed in excess of 140mph (225km/h). The 5.3 litre engine was essentially the same as that used in the Aston Martin V8 coupé, apart from being fitted with larger valves, the timing of which was modified to enhance its flexibility. Three-speed automatic transmission was employed.

Revising The Design

Despite the lengthy gestation, demand for the car was strong and in 1982 it was cleared for sale in America. Up until the 1984 season, the Lagonda's lines remained essentially unsullied but that year came American safety bumpers and spoilers, new seats and rear windows that opened. At the 1983 London Motor Show Aston Martin introduced a version by in-house Aston Martin Tickford which sold for £85,000, and which included colour televisions in both back *and* front. Around five were sold. A further variation on the theme came in 1984 in the form of a long wheelbase Tickford limousine, retailing for £110,000, which found three customers.

Curiously, between the end of 1981 and 1983 this unusual saloon dropped the Aston Martin prefix and became a plain Lagonda. Thereafter it reverted to its original name. For 1985 the controls were further developed with messages displayed on three 5in (127mm) cathode ray tubes, information being conveyed in English, French, German or Arabic, as required.

ABOVE RIGHT: *The Lagonda received new wheels and American-type safety bumpers for the 1984 season. At the same time the rear windows, hitherto fixed, now opened. Otherwise the saloon's distinctive angular outline remained unsullied.*

RIGHT: *Rear view of a 1982 car with its stylish tail. While boot space was generous, there were complaints that there could have been more leg room for rear passengers. There was certainly no shortage of lights at the back of the Lagonda. A total of 11, including reversing ones, were built into the boot lid.*

Refinements continued and the 1986 cars saw the arrival of fuel injection. William Towns had, in the meantime, been smoothing out those sharp body lines and, at the 1987 Geneva Motor Show, the Lagonda appeared in revised form with softer contours and no less than six headlights in place of the original four.

The car remained in production for a further three years, and manufacture ceased in 1990 by which time Aston Martin's future looked considerably more secure, as it had been absorbed in 1987 into the ownership of the Ford Motor Company.

ABOVE: *This is a Series 4 car of 1987 with more rounded body lines, and pop-up headlamps replaced by these six fixed units. Inside push buttons replaced the touch switches.*

BELOW: *The driving compartment of a 1987 Lagonda, the interior of which differed somewhat from the earlier cars. The single spoke steering wheel has been dispensed with.*

There can be little doubt that in the supercar stakes of the 1980's, the pace was being set by Lamborghini's potent and visually stunning Countach which made Ferrari's top line Boxer look unspectacular. The Maranello-based company redressed the balance at the 1984 Paris Motor Show when it unveiled the Testarossa with a sensational Pininfarina coupé body dominated by heavily finned engine air intakes which were adventurously extended into the door panels. Such was the competence of the design that the model remains in production at the time of writing having, in 1992, been revised in 512TR form.

The Testarossa's origins are rooted in Ferrari's mid-engined 365 GT4 BB two-seater Pininfarina coupé of 1973, better known as the Boxer. It was so called because that is the name applied by European engineers to describe a horizontally opposed engine in which the pistons move towards and away from each other. The model was the first Ferrari road car to be so equipped, despite the firm having first used such a unit for sports racing in 1964. The compact 12 cylinder 344bhp carburettored engine created for the 365 had a capacity of 4.4 litres. There were two valves per cylinder and each bank employed belt-driven twin overhead camshafts. This car was replaced in 1976 by the outwardly similar BB 512 in which the flat 12 was enlarged to 4.9 litres and converted to dry sump operation. The model endured until 1984 having, since 1981, been fuel injected and known as the 512i.

Its replacement, the Testarossa, was named in memory of a successful Ferrari sports racer of the 1950's. It means, in Italian, "red head" and the road car's cam boxes were, accordingly, stove enamelled red. While it mechanically perpetuated the theme of the earlier cars, it was visual *tour de force* – the Pininfarina-designed and built coupé bore no relationship to its Boxer predecessors.

The dramatic change in the model's appearance came as the direct result of a modification to its mechanical specification. On all previous Boxers the radiator for the mid-located engine was mounted at the front of the car and the cooling water thereafter made a tortuously piped journey midway down the vehicle. On the Testarossa the flat 12 engine was cooled by two radiators

RIGHT: A real head turner! The 5 litre flat 12 engine of a 1985 Testarossa, complete with its red painted cam box covers, as the name implies.

Specifications: Ferrari 512TR

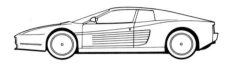

Length:	14ft 8in (4470mm)
Width:	6ft 6in (1981mm)
Height:	3ft 8in (1118mm)
Wheelbase:	8ft 4in (2540mm)
Track:	front 5ft (1524mm), rear 5ft 5in (1651mm)
Unladen weight:	3321lb (1506kg)
Engine: Mid-located V12 with twin overhead camshafts per bank, 82×78mm, 4942cc. Compression ratio, 9.2:1. Max power, 390bhp at 6300rpm. Max torque, 365lb/ft at 4500rpm.	
Transmission:	Five-speed manual
Drive:	Rear
Suspension (front):	Independent, coil springs and wishbones
Suspension (rear):	Independent, coil springs and wishbones
Top speed:	175mph (282km/h)
0-60mph (96km/h):	5.6seconds
Production (Testarossa):	7183

RIGHT: A 1984 Testarossa looking sensational. Such was the competence of Pininfarina's styling, the car remained unchanged until 1992 when it was replaced by the 512TR.

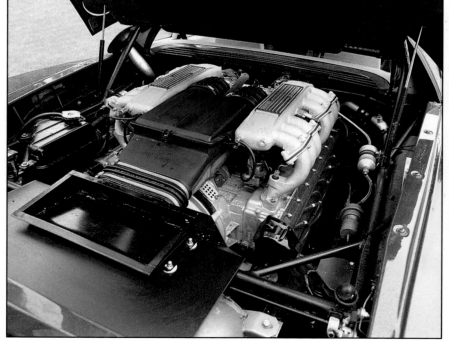

ABOVE: *One of the all-important engine air intakes, which were dramatically extended into the doors, and so stylistically enhanced the Testarossa's body.*

BELOW: *Like many performance cars with wind-tunnel-tested bodies, the Testarossa's headlamps were, for aerodynamic requirements, usually concealed when not in use.*

LEFT: *A right-hand-drive 1985 Testarossa, not in red for once. Inevitably, it was an expensive car and this uncompromising two-seater sold in Britain for £62,666.*

BELOW: *A familiar view, for many drivers, as a Testarossa passes them. The use of a compact, flat 12 engine allowed for some rear visibility, not always a strong point in mid-engined cars such as this.*

mounted either side of it, which meant that the air intakes emerged just ahead of each rear wheel arch. This modification meant that the car was over 5in (127mm) wider than the 512.

Pininfarina transformed this functional requirement into a styling feature which first appeared, in embryo form, on Ferrari's mid-V8-engined Mondial of 1980. On the larger car, the cooling fins were dramatically extended into the doors, a feature which made an extraordinarily impressive visual contribution to the coupé body. It was generally constructed of aluminium, apart from the steel doors and cockpit area while some of the smaller panels were made of a composite material. Weighing 3320lb (1506kg), the Testarossa was fractionally lighter than the Boxer. It was also 3½in (86mm) longer, while the track was also greater to improve roadholding.

Keep It Cool

Despite the engine being cooled by side-mounted radiators, there was still an intake grille at the front of the car which was where air entered to cool the front brakes and to feed the air conditioning system which was a standard fitment.

Although the dry sump engine retained the same 82×78mm dimensions and the 4942cc capacity of the 512, it developed 390bhp instead of the 340bhp of its predecessor. This was because the unit followed the 308 and Mondial in having four, rather than two, valves per cylinder which had the effect of improving power, torque and fuel consumption. A five-speed, all-synchromesh gearbox was employed. The chassis followed the traditional Ferrari practice of employing a trellis of tubes and all-independent suspension with wishbones and coil springs front and rear.

Inside, the Testarossa's two seats were beautifully upholstered in leather while the gear lever moved in the customary Ferrari open gate. Behind the seats there was sufficient space for a weekend suitcase, and there was more (albeit limited) room under the bonnet. For the Ferrari owner who lacked nothing these spaces could be filled with a six-piece leather luggage set by Schedoni, specifically tailored for the Testarossa, which alone cost around £2000. The car itself retailed, on its introduction in Britain, for £62,666, but, as with most Ferrari's, there was no shortage of customers.

RIGHT: *A Testarossa of 1990 vintage finished, unusually, in white. Little changed since its 1984 introduction, its price had by then risen to £115,500. Around 70 examples of this memorable Ferrari were sold in Britain each year.*

It went as well as it looked. As the fastest Ferrari road car, top speed was a little over 170mph (274km/h) which took it within reach of the larger capacity Lamborghini Countach. Despite this performance, the Testarossa was not particularly thirsty and returned on average, around 16mpg (17.6 litres/100km).

Demand for the model was soon exceeding Ferrari's expectations and, by 1986, production was running at the rate of 17 cars a week. Red was by far and away the most popular colour choice with black coming a very poor second. Around half of production was destined for America and, to meet this demand, Pininfarina increased its body production by 50 percent.

The car was built in essentially unchanged form until 1992 when it was replaced by the similar looking 512TR. By this time the price had soared to within a whisker of £130,000. The car's designation reflected its 5 litre, 12 cylinder engine, while the TR initials echoed its Testarossa parentage.

More Power On Tap

At a cursory glance, the 512 appeared outwardly similar to its predecessor, the most obvious change was the nose that was redesigned in the manner of the smaller 348 model. Ferrari succeeded in extracting yet more power from the flat 12 engine which received new camshafts and inlet porting. These changes, with other refinements, raised its output from 390 to 428bhp. This endowed the car with a top speed of 175mph (282km/h), although this still could not match the Countach's Diablo successor which could travel in excess of 200mph (322km/h). Nevertheless, acceleration was sparkling, the 512 reaching 60mph (96km/h) in around 5 seconds. Performance, handling and ride were impeccable and the car was surprisingly easy to drive although the effectiveness of the all-round disc brakes came in for some criticism by commentators.

Now 10 years old, this magnificently styled coupé remains one of the world's fastest cars. It can still turn heads and looks like doing so for many years to come.

Ferrari Testarossa

4.4 litre flat 12
365 GT4 BB 1973
|
4.9 litre BB 512
1976
|
Testarossa 1984
|
512TR 1992
|
to date

RIGHT: *Discreet luxury, the driving compartment of a right-hand-drive 512TR with the familiar exposed gear gate and the famous badge.*

RIGHT: *The 512TR which arrived in 1992 outwardly resembled the Testarossa, although its nose was redesigned in the manner of the 348 model. Changes were, however, made to the flat 12 engine.*

ABOVE: *The 512TR's 428bhp engine
still carries the Testarossa name. More
powerful than its predecessor, it
retains a 5 litre capacity.*

PORSCHE 959 (1983-1988)

Conceived as the world's fastest production car, the 197mph (317km/h) 959 was a state-of-the-art, four-wheel-drive road model based on the long running 911. When Porsche revealed this costly, complex creation at the 1983 Frankfurt Motor Show, it anticipated having it in production by 1985, but delays meant that it was 1987 before the first example was delivered.

The 959 was the fastest and most expensive car in the history of the Porsche company. It was eventually priced at DM 420,000 (£109,660). Above all, it was a public reaffirmation of the 911 concept which, a decade earlier, had appeared doomed. Since its introduction in 1963, the rear-engined, air-cooled 911 had been Porsche's potent mainstay but, in 1972, Dr Ernst Fuhrmann took over as chief executive. He decreed that the Stuttgart-based company should turn its back on its sports car roots and initiated a new generation of front-engined, water-cooled cars. The outcome was the 924, 944 and, in particular, the big, expensive 928 flagship. It was a policy that brought him into conflict with Ferry Porsche who had no regrets when Fuhrmann retired at the end of 1980. His replacement was Peter W. Schultz, a German-born American and, above all, a great car enthusiast.

One of Schultz's first actions was to reverse Fuhrmann's diktat and reprieve the 911, which had also been starved of much needed investment.

The outcome of the company's renewed confidence in the model was the appearance, at the 1981 Frankfurt Motor Show, of a long awaited cabriolet version of the 911, which also incorporated four-wheel drive. As a result the convertible was offered to the public in 1982 and the four-wheel-drive car, which presaged the definitive 959, appeared at the 1983 Frankfurt Show.

Group B Regulations

This took the form of what Porsche called its *Gruppe B*. Although clearly related to the 911, as the title suggested, the car had been created with a view to its participating in Group B competition. As such, production would be limited to only 200 cars and, in addition, there were a further 20 "evolution" sports racers.

The silver metallic coupé's spoilered tail concealed a 2.8 litre twin-turbocharged engine. But the revolutionary concept of the car was an extraordinarily sophisticated four-wheel-drive system, yet to be fully developed. This

Specifications: Porsche 959

Length:	13ft 11in (4242mm)
Width:	6ft 4in (1930mm)
Height:	4ft 2in (1270mm)
Wheelbase:	7ft 5in (2261mm)
Track:	front 4ft 11in (1499mm), rear 5ft 1in (1549mm)
Unladen weight:	3197lb (1450kg)
Engine:	Rear-mounted, horizontally opposed, air-cooled six cylinder, with twin overhead camshafts per bank, 95×67mm, 2849cc. Compression ratio, 8.3:1. Fuel injection. Twin turbochargers. Max power, 450bhp at 6500 rpm. Max torque, 369lb/ft at 5500rpm
Transmission:	Six-speed manual, computer-controlled torque split
Drive:	Four-wheel
Suspension (front):	Independent, coil springs and wishbones
Suspension (rear):	Independent, coil springs and wishbones
Top speed:	197mph (317km/h)
0-60mph (96km/h):	3.6 seconds
Production:	250

was the first occasion that Porsche offered such a drive configuration on a production model.

The company's intention was to have all cars sold and completed by the middle of 1985. There was no lack of demand but, in the event, it was not until April 1987 that a 959 was handed over to its first, patient customer.

RIGHT: *The 959's relationship to the 911 is immediately apparent. Its arrival triggered fierce competition among its rivals in the supercar league.*

BELOW RIGHT: *The 959's wind-cheating profile. The massive disc brakes, designed to arrest speeds approaching 200mph (322km/h), are visible.*

LEFT: *Rigorous baptism. The 959 proved its worth in the atrocious conditions of the highly demanding Paris to Dakar Rally. A version in its formative stage won in 1984 and the definitive 959 triumphed in 1986.*

Despite there being a three-and-a-half year hiatus between appearance and production, the concept of a four-wheel-drive 911 had initially proved its worth in the demanding Paris to Dakar Rally of 1984. Three such cars were entered and, to the delight of Porsche, one car won and a second was sixth. In the 1985 event the three cars came much closer to the 959 concept, but none survived competing over the devastating terrain. However, there would be no such mistakes in the 1986 competition and a 959 won while another car took second place.

An event of equal significance, as far as the 959's evolution was concerned, occurred in 1986 when Group B, which was one of the principal reasons for the

PORSCHE 959

car having been created, was banned following a spate of fatalities on the rally field.

Ironically, Porsche had not looked upon the 959 as a rally car but believed that its true potential would be seen on the race track. Its 961 sports racing derivative made a debut at Le Mans in 1986. It was entered in the GTX class, which it won, and was placed seventh overall. A single 1987 entry was forced to retire with gearbox trouble but, by then, the 959 was, at long last, in production.

So what made the 959 so special? Above all, it bristled with an unparalleled level of mechanical and electronic refinement which was masterminded by Porsche's famous Weissach research centre. While it shared the 911's 7ft 5in (2261mm) wheelbase, the coupé's 6ft 4in (1930mm) width meant that it was a substantial 10in (254mm) more than the 911. The wings were beautifully flared to accommodate the wider wheels and the aerodynamically honed body possessed an impressive 0.31 drag factor.

The mainstream 911 coupé was an all-metal structure and the 959 retained its hot galvanized metal underframe. However, much of the bodywork was made of a variety of plastic materials more associated with the aircraft than the motor industry. This applied to most of the shell, with the exception of the doors, bonnet and front boot lid which were aluminium.

Turbo Charger

When it came to the engine, rated at 450bhp, the 2.8 litre flat six, with twin overhead camshafts per bank and four valves per cylinder, had the distinction of being the most powerful turbocharged unit ever to be offered in a road car. Its origins were rooted in the 911-derived 956/962 sports racers of the 1982-84 period, and the main difference between them and the 959's engine was that the noisy but efficient camshaft gears were replaced by a quieter double chain. As befitted its origins, this was an air-cooled unit with the exception of the cylinder heads which were water-cooled. When it came to the twin turbochargers, Porsche's engineers went to great lengths to ensure that the car possessed the maximum of tractability and minimum of turbo lag.

Drive passed first to a six-speed gearbox and thereafter it went in two directions: back to a transaxle and also forward to a computer-controlled

Porsche 959

911 coupé 1963

Four-wheel-drive 911 1981

956/962 sports racers 1982

Group B cars 1983

Paris to Dakar cars 1984

961 sports racer 1986

Production 959 1987

Porsche Control Clutch. This apportioned the required amount of torque between the front and rear wheels.

These specifications meant that the 959 possessed all the roadholding advantages of front-wheel drive and it was also phenomenally fast. Porsche cautiously claimed that it was capable of speeds over 193mph (310km/h) but, in truth, it could attain 197mph (317km/h). However, these figures were only possible when the 959's body was a mere 4.9in (124mm) from the ground. On uneven surfaces ride height could be altered to a more practical 5.9in (150mm) or even 7in (178mm) by computer control.

Inside, the 959 was well equipped but not lavishly so. The interior resembled that of the 911 Turbo, although air conditioning was fitted, this being made possible by the use of the engine's water-cooled 'heads, a luxury that the 911 did not enjoy.

The 959 was pipped at the post for the accolade of being the world's fastest road car by the 1987 arrival of the Ferrari F40 which was starker, lighter and quicker than the four-wheel-drive Porsche by some 4mph (6km/h).

By the time that the 959 ceased production in 1988, a total of 250 had been built — an extra 50 were produced because of demand. However, Peter Schultz, the architect of its creation, had left the company. Porsche undoubtedly gained much technical knowledge and prestige from the development of the 959 but it must have been costly in terms of time and resources for a business which was subsequently financially stretched. Nevertheless, Porsche is today looking towards the rear-engined, air-cooled concept for its future products so, in that respect, the 959 is the greatest 911 of them all.

RIGHT: Only produced in left-hand-drive form, the 959 built in 1987 and 1988 was the fastest roadgoing Porsche. This is a 1988 car.

BELOW: The 959's fixed rear spoiler, intended to help keep that 450bhp in check, with the hot air outlets below. They are not only functional, but also make a visual contribution to the car's rear profile.

ABOVE: *Detail of one of the 959's air intakes in the aerodynamic body.*

BELOW: *One of the 959's virtues is that it is very easy to drive.*

ABOVE: *All that can be seen of the 959's formidable turbocharged 2.8 litre horizontally opposed six cylinder engine. The all-important fan for this air-cooled unit can be clearly seen.*

LEFT: *The body's lines were conceived so that the 959 had no lift characteristics and maintained the same downforce, regardless of the car's speed. The sophisticated drive system can be changed, at the touch of a button, to cope with the demands of wet or dry roads.*

BELOW: *The driving compartment of this costly Porsche is well but not sumptuously equipped and is not dissimilar to that of the 911 Turbo. It is, however, fitted with air conditioning.*

ASTON MARTIN V8 VANTAGE ZAGATO (1986-1990)

The DB4 Zagato was one of the legendary Aston Martins of the post-war years and in 1986 the concept was revived in V8 form. This stubby two seater was to be limited to just 50 examples and the outcome was one of the fastest production cars of its day, capable of speeds approaching 187mph (300km/h). It was followed in 1987 by an open Volante version and this V8 convertible remained in production until 1990.

At the time of the appearance of the Zagato coupé, Aston Martin's V8 model had been in production for a sometimes turbulent 16 years. Following the firm's 1975 reconstruction there came another change of ownership in 1981 with the majority of the company's capital shared equally between Victor Gauntlett's Pace Petroleum and CH Industrials. In 1983 the Pace holding was effectively taken over by the American-based Automotive Investments Inc., owned by the Greek shipping interests of the Papanicolaou and Livanos families, which in 1984 became a majority shareholder, with the balance held by Gauntlett.

The last new model that Aston Martin had introduced was the Lagonda saloon which, after a protracted gestation and birth, entered production in 1978. While a replacement for the long-running V8 would be under way by 1986, the company clearly required something new and Gauntlett came up with the idea of rekindling the concept of the Aston Martin Zagato. At the 1984 Geneva Motor Show he and his co-chairman, Peter Livanos, raised the idea with the Zagato brothers, Elio and Gianni, who responded positively to the proposal. Like the original, this car would have to be faster than the Vantage V8; Aston Martin was looking for a top speed of 187mph (300km/h) and a 0-60mph (96km/h) figure of under five seconds.

Not only did this initiative make sense to Aston Martin, it also appealed to Zagato which, at the time, was working on a contract for armouring cars, mostly Alfa Romeo Alfettas, and it relished the opportunity that this presented to revert to its mainstream coachbuilding activity.

A year later, at the 1985 Geneva Show, the V8 Zagato was announced.

It was the first two-seater Aston Martin since the 1963 demise of the DB4GT. An alluring sketch of the proposed car was displayed at the Show where it was stated that the batch would be limited to 50 coupés which would sell for around £70,000 apiece. A deposit of £15,000 was required to secure an order and, by August of 1985, all of the project output had been allocated.

First Off The Line
The first example was on show at the 1986 Geneva event although by then the price had risen quite considerably to £87,000. Deliveries were scheduled to begin in May 1986 and would continue over the following 18 months. In fact it was July before the first car was handed over to its owner, long-time Aston Martin enthusiast, Brian Taylor, who already had seven examples of the make to his credit.

RIGHT: *The chunky lines of the potent V8 Vantage Zagato which was 10 per cent lighter than the standard model. This is a 1987 car, chassis 20032.*

Specifications: Aston Martin V8 Vantage Zagato

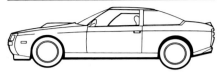

Length:	14ft 5in (4394mm)
Width:	6ft 2in (1880mm)
Height:	4ft 3in (1295mm)
Wheelbase:	8ft 6¾in (2610mm)
Track:	front and rear 4ft 11in (1499mm)
Unladen weight:	3638lb (1650kg)

Engine: V8 with twin overhead camshafts per bank, 85×110mm, 5340cc. Compression ratio, 9.5:1. Fuel injection. Max power, 432bhp at 6000rpm. Max torque, 395lb/ft at 5100rpm.

Transmission:	Five-speed manual
Drive:	Rear
Suspension (front):	Independent, coil springs and wishbones
Suspension (rear):	De Dion axle, coil springs
Top speed:	186mph (299km/h)
0-60mph (96km/h):	4.8 seconds
Production (including Volante):	87

ABOVE RIGHT: *The Zagato's all round visibility and flush fitting windows shown to good effect. The rear spoiler contributed to stability and the 0.29 drag factor.*

RIGHT: *The Zagato had far less rear overhang than the standard Vantage.*

ABOVE: *The car's double ZZ badge, identifying this second generation Zagato, fitted to the boot lid.*

BELOW: *The Vantage Zagato's driving compartment is beautifully finished with leather upholstered seats.*

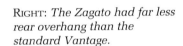

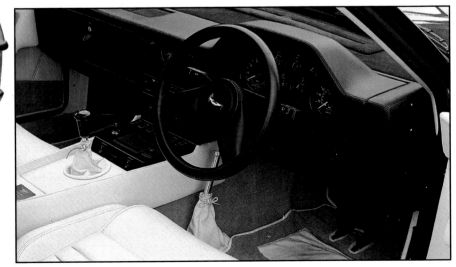

For the car to attain its projected 187mph (300km/h) top speed, weight had to be removed from its chassis, while the original coupé body was replaced by a lighter more aerodynamically efficient Zagato one. Engine modifications were in line with those optionally available in the Series 3 Vantage of the 1987 season.

The model began life at Newport Pagnell where the completed chassis was rolling-road-tested and then dispatched to Zagato's Milan factory for the body to be fitted. However, before this could be done, a section of chassis overhang, from behind the rear wheels, was removed. The car thus retained the V8's 8ft 6¾in (2610mm) wheelbase but, when the body was fitted, it was 11¼in (286mm) shorter overall than the production car.

The aluminium coupé body was the work of Zagato's chief stylist, Giuseppe Mittino, and at 3638lb (1650kg), the car was 370lb (168kg) less than the standard Vantage V8. Each body was handbuilt in the traditional manner which meant that the panels were beaten out over an old tree stump and the dimensions were then checked on a wooden styling buck. Each car took between two and three months to com-plete and, eventually, 52 examples were built.

An unusual feature of the design was that, for aerodynamic considerations, the windscreen, sides and rear window fitted flush with the body, This was achieved by glueing them directly to it. This could not, of course, apply to the door glasses but they were fixed in position and each contained a smaller opening window which was raised and lowered in the usual way.

Engine Refinements

Refinements were also made to the 5.3 litre V8 engine. Aston Martin's policy was not to declare the power developed by the unit but it made an exception with the Zagato's. It produced 432bhp, some 32 bhp more than the Series 3 Vantage modifications announced in October 1986, although they could be specified if required on the British-built car. The Zagato's engine was fitted with new pistons which raised the compression ratio from the customary 9 to 9.5:1. There were revised high-lift camshafts and four 48 1DF Weber carburettors specified. However, the air-box had to be redesigned because the original made too much of a bulge in the bonnet and although this was re-duced, it did to some extent mar the appearance of the finished product.

With an extremely good drag coefficient of 0.29, the factory claimed that the Vantage Zagato was capable of 186mph (299km/h) and no doubt on a good day it could attain the extra 1mph (1.6km/h). Performance was, not un-naturally, electrifying. A five-speed ZF manual gearbox was employed and Aston Martin maintained a 0 to 60 mph (96km/h) figure of 4.8 seconds with the car really coming into its own above 120mph (193km/h).

Once all the coupés had been sold, a Volante (open) version of the design seemed to be a logical development of the theme and an example was duly displayed at the 1987 Geneva Motor Show. Its price, at £125,000, was considerably higher than the coupé's and a £25,000 deposit was required. Production was to be limited to 25 cars but this figure was subsequently extended to 35. By the time that the car entered production some styling changes had been made. The most significant of these was that the controversial and intrusive bonnet bulge was deleted, a refinement made possible by the carburettors being replaced by a Marelli-Weber fuel injection system.

This 305bhp engine was therefore less powerful than the coupé's and with a top speed of 165mph (265km/h), the Volante was somewhat slower. Unlike the closed car, a three-speed automatic gearbox could be specified. The Volante model remained in production until 1990.

By this time Ford had bought Aston Martin, and Gauntlett believes that the creation of the Vantage Zagato was a key factor in the 1987 purchase. It showed that, with great ingenuity and limited resources, Aston Martin had been able to take the ageing V8 and develop a derivative which was one of the fastest and most exclusive cars in the world.

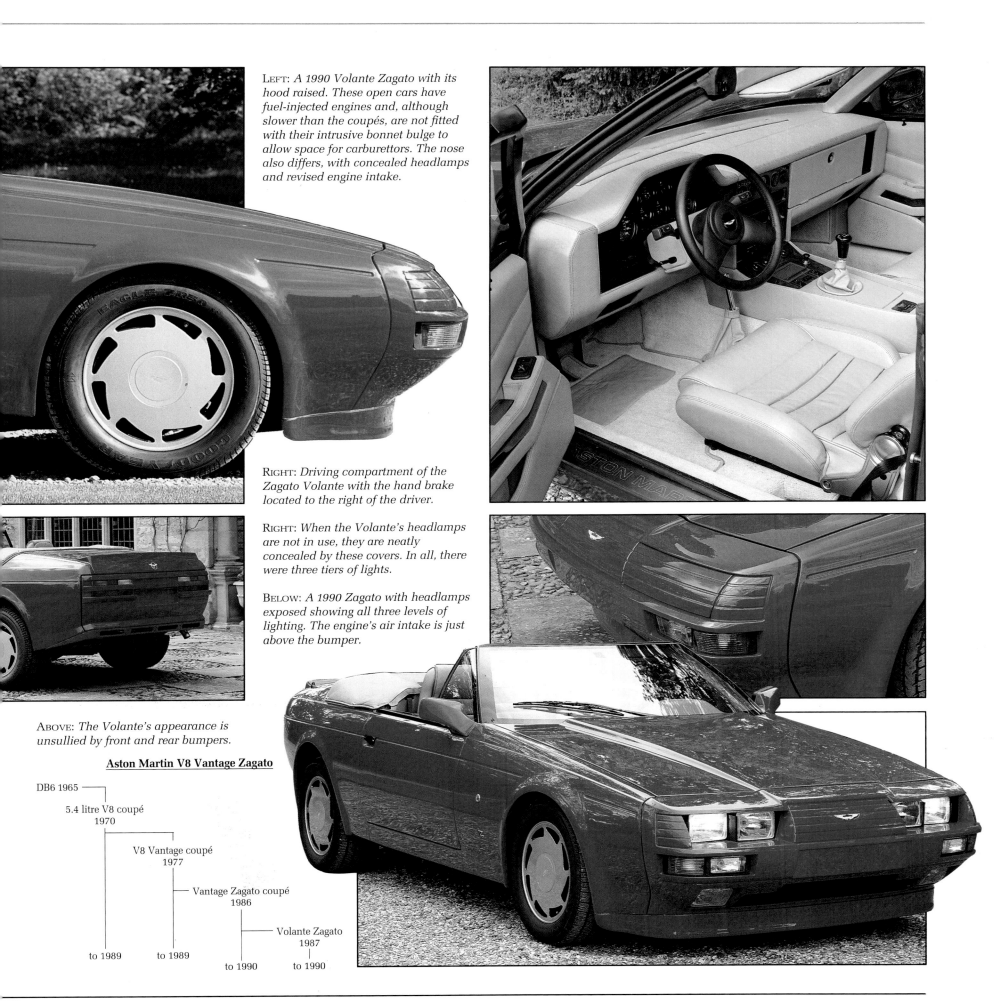

LEFT: *A 1990 Volante Zagato with its hood raised. These open cars have fuel-injected engines and, although slower than the coupés, are not fitted with their intrusive bonnet bulge to allow space for carburettors. The nose also differs, with concealed headlamps and revised engine intake.*

RIGHT: *Driving compartment of the Zagato Volante with the hand brake located to the right of the driver.*

RIGHT: *When the Volante's headlamps are not in use, they are neatly concealed by these covers. In all, there were three tiers of lights.*

BELOW: *A 1990 Zagato with headlamps exposed showing all three levels of lighting. The engine's air intake is just above the bumper.*

ABOVE: *The Volante's appearance is unsullied by front and rear bumpers.*

Aston Martin V8 Vantage Zagato

DB6 1965
5.4 litre V8 coupé 1970
V8 Vantage coupé 1977
Vantage Zagato coupé 1986
Volante Zagato 1987

to 1989   to 1989   to 1990   to 1990

FERRARI F40 (1987-1992)

In 1987 Ferrari celebrated 40 years as a car maker by unveiling the appropriately named F40, a wickedly impressive, sparsely furnished, mid-engined coupé capable of speeds in the region of 200mph (322km/h). This racer for the road was intended to wrest the mantle of the world's fastest car from the Porsche 959 and it succeeded in doing precisely that. Initially intended for a limited production of around 450 cars, eventually 1323 examples of this desirable car were built before manufacture ceased in 1992.

The origins of the F40 project are rooted in the limited production 288 GTO, unveiled in 1984. Named in memory of Ferrari's legendary sports racing GTO of 1950's, the latter-day version was intended for use as a Group B racer, but could not be so homologated until 200 examples had been built. Outwardly it resembled Ferrari's mid-engined 308 road car but its wheelbase was 4½in (114mm) longer because the 2.8 litre V8 engine was mounted longitudinally behind the seats in the manner of a grand prix car. The chassis was of the usual tubular steel design.

What about the engine? The twin turbocharged alloy 220bhp unit, with twin overhead camshafts per bank, bore some relationship to the 308's larger capacity 3.2 litre unit, but was in fact more closely related to the V8 engine which Ferrari had built for in-house Lancia's 1983 Group C sports racing LC2.

The Pininfarina body was mostly constructed of composite materials, which meant Kevlar and glass fibre. The GTO became an overnight collector's piece but Ferrari's plans for the model were seriously disrupted when, in 1986, Group B racing was banned following a spate of serious rallying accidents. As a result GTO production ceased in 1986 after a mere 273 examples had been built.

In addition to its Group B programme, Ferrari had created a racing version, the *Evoluzione*, which differed from it both bodily and mechanically. In retrospect, this can be seen as the stepping stone between the GTO and the F40. Ferrari's intention was to produce around 20 such cars to be sold to private car owners and the one-off *Evoluzione* became a mobile test bed for this programme. The chassis was dispensed with and replaced by a new one with a carbon fibre tub and tubular steel extensions. This and the revised body, complete with rear spoiler, were no less than 40 per cent lighter than the

GTO and, with the 2.8 litre turbocharged V8 boosted to 650bhp, it would have indeed been an impressive circuit performer.

The F40 proper was unveiled at Maranello in July 1987. The event was inevitably an emotional one as it was attended by the frail 89-year-old figure of Enzo Ferrari. There he revealed that he had wished to produce a car in memory of "the great days of Le Mans when you could drive a car on the streets or race it."

Faster Than A 959

With a claimed top speed of 201mph (323km/h), in theory the F40 would have the edge over the 197mph (317km/h) Porsche 959. The Ferrari would sell for £140,000 and the intention was to make five a week until 1990 with production limited to between 400 and 450 cars. In the event, it remained available for rather longer.

Specifications: Ferrari F40

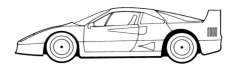

Length:	14ft 6in (4420mm)
Width:	6ft 6in (1981mm)
Height:	3ft 8½in (1130mm)
Wheelbase:	8ft 0½in (2451mm)
Track:	front 5ft 2⅘in (1595mm), rear 5ft 3⅖in (1610mm)
Unladen weight:	2425lb (1100kg)
Engine: V8 with twin overhead camshafts per bank, 82×69mm, 2936cc. Compression ratio, 7.8:1. Fuel injection. Twin turbochargers. Max power, 478bhp at 7000rpm. Max torque, 425lb/ft at 4000rpm.	
Transmission:	Five-speed manual
Drive:	Rear
Suspension (front):	Independent, coil springs and wishbones
Suspension (rear):	Independent, coil springs and wishbones
Top speed:	201mph (323km/h)
0-60mph (96km/h):	4.7 seconds
Production:	1310

ABOVE: *Engine accessibility is excellent on the F40. The 3 litre in-line V8 is fitted with twin IHI turbochargers with intercoolers and a boost pressure of 15.6 psi. There is a Marelli electronic ignition system.*

ABOVE: *Ferrari's 40th anniversary gift to the world was the mid-engined F40 with its Pininfarina-styled body built entirely of glass fibre, Kevlar and carbon fibre.*

LEFT: *The F40 was, in effect, a racer for the road which was intended to revive the days when drivers drove their cars on the public highways to the circuits. The fastest Ferrari of its day, it was capable of over 200mph (322km/h).*

BELOW: *The rear wing arrived late in the F40's development programme. Rear wheel spats were also contemplated and then, as can be seen, discarded. The transparent engine cover tantalizingly reveals the 478bhp V8 power unit.*

FERRARI F40

While the GTO's Pininfarina body-work was clearly related to that of the 308 road car, there were no such pretensions with the F40 which had all the appearances of a sleek sports racing coupé with a rear dominated by a large spoiler. Styled, as ever, by Pininfarina and built by Ferrari, the body was made entirely from carbon fibre and Kevlar. In view of the top speed envisaged, wind tunnel testing was obligatory and great attention was also paid to make the underside of the car as smooth as possible. The chassis, which shared the same 8ft 0½in (2451mm) wheelbase as the GTO, was the usual Ferrari tubular steel affair although strengthened with Kevlar.

The all-independent suspension followed the usual Maranello principle of employing wishbones and coil springs. The car's ride height had three settings: normal, high speed, when the car was lowered by ¾in (20mm), and parking when the F40 was raised by a similar distance above the norm.

Substantial ventilated brake discs were fitted all round but there was no servo-assistance. Inside the F40 was a pure competition machine. It was stark and functional. The fixed seats with body hugging contours came complete with racing harnesses and were available in three sizes. Despite this no-nonsense specification, the F40 was fitted with air conditioning as standard, no doubt to satisfy the requirements of the important American market.

Bigger Than The GTO

The twin-turbocharged 478bhp engine was essentially an enlarged version of the GTO unit, an alloy 2.9 litre V8 with twin belt-driven overhead camshafts per bank and four valves a cylinder. In the GTO its internal dimensions were 80×71mm but for the F40 both bore and stroke were altered, respectively to 82×69mm. Twin IHI turbochargers blew, via a Beher intercooler, at the rate of 15.6psi.

The engine was fitted with a sophisticated Formula 1-derived fuel-injection system which also controlled the four-coil ignition. At the heart of this technology was a computer which also informed the driver of any potential problems.

With F40 production beginning in 1988, independent confirmation soon came that it was, indeed, the world's fastest car. An example was tested by the Japanese motoring magazine, *Car Graphic*, on the oval Yatabe circuit where its driver achieved a speed of

Ferrari F40

```
Ferrari 308
  1975
        ├─────────── Lancia Group C car
        │                      1983
        └──── 2.8 litre V8 GTO ───
                    1984
                     │
              GTO Evoluzione
                    1986
                     │
               2.9 litre F40
                    1987
```

199mph (320km/h) on the straight before he eased off for the banking. The Ferrari reached 60mph (96km/h) in 4.7 seconds and 100mph (161km/h) came up in a mere 8.7 seconds.

Despite Ferrari making strenuous efforts to prevent owners from speculating on their cars, in 1989 an F40 changed hands in Germany for DM 1.7 million (£550,000) which was around four times its original price. Inevitably, demand for the car outstripped supply. The upper target of 450 cars was soon breached and Ferrari then said that it would build 1000. At the end of 1991 the company revealed that it was finishing off a batch for the American

ABOVE: *A 1991 F40. The model is fitted with adjustable dampers to provide three possible ride heights. Ferrari also went to great lengths to make the underside of the car as smooth as possible to improve roadholding.*

RIGHT: *Accessibility is the keynote of the F40's dry sump engine and rear upper and lower wishbone/telescopic damper suspension. The rear wheels are wider than those at the front and are shod with Pirelli P700 tyres.*

market and the final tally had increased to 1310 cars, the last of which was built in 1992.

Incredibly by this time the F40's top speed was being eclipsed by the Bugatti EB110 and Lamborghini Diablo but this should not detract, for a moment, from the F40's stature. If this 40th anniversary car is anything to go by, Ferrari will have to produce something even more sensational when the firm celebrates its half century in 1997.

RIGHT: *Like its Maranello-built contemporaries, the F40's headlamps are retractable for good aerodynamics.*

ABOVE: *As with any mid-engined car, getting air into the power unit is critical. One of a number of NACA ducts on the car, this intake is located ahead of the rear wing. Construction follows pace car technology.*

RIGHT: *The F40's cockpit has the minimum of creature comforts and functional rubber matting. Note the cryptic* Slow Down *warning on the instrument panel to prevent the catalytic converter from overheating.*

ASTON MARTIN VIRAGE (1988 to date)

When Aston Martin introduced its V8 model in 1969, there were few who could have predicted that it would remain in production for no less than 20 years. However, the company's chequered financial history ensured that it would not be until 1988 that the Virage, its long-awaited replacement, appeared. It did not, alas, receive the unqualified acclaim that might have been expected. This was a reflection, perhaps, of the car's all-too-brief, cost-conscious two-year gestation. For 1993 the Virage was impressively uprated in twin-supercharged 550bhp Vantage form, which differed, both mechanically and bodily, from the original.

Ford purchased Aston Martin in 1987, a move which provided the company with a sense of financial stability that had been lacking since the heyday of David Brown's ownership in the mid-1960's. In reality Ford's stewardship only had a limited impact on the Virage which appeared, a year later, at the 1988 British Motor Show.

Despite its longevity, the William Towns-styled V8 model was, visually, a difficult car to follow. Aston Martin's chairman, Victor Gauntlett, commissioned five British studios, Towns included, to submit designs for the new car. The lines chosen were the work of Royal College of Arts tutors, John Heffernan and Ken Greenley, who had previously been jointly responsible for styling the exclusive Panther Solo sports coupé.

The design had to be right first time because of the tight time schedule and the body had to progress from a quarter-scale model to full-sized car without any significant changes. The model was wind-tunnel-tested at Southampton University and some modifications accordingly were made to the tail, which raised the drag coefficient from 0.30 to a higher figure of 0.35, but represented a visual improvement on the original.

While it was hoped that the Virage would have a new chassis, in the event, in the interests of rationalization, the one adopted actually used much of the Lagonda saloon's substructure which contributed the front bulkhead, chassis and crossmember. These were then added to a newly designed platform and rear structure.

Suspension was by Aston Martin's established coil spring and wishbones system while Ford's takeover of Aston Martin meant that the Sierra Cosworth's steering was now an in-house component and this unit, in power-assisted form, was duly adopted.

The earlier V8 model had employed a de Dion rear axle. This was perpetuated but redesigned and, above all, lightened. One significant difference was that the massive rear disc brakes were moved from inboard to outboard which ensured better cooling.

A 32-Valve Engine

The new car could only be powered by the company's ever young V8 engine, but it had to conform to American and European emissions regulations. Already employing twin overhead camshafts per cylinder bank, the way clearly pointed to four valves per cylinder. Work had begun on this task in April 1986. Entrusted to an American company, Callaway Engineering of Connecticut, it was completed by the end of 1987. The engine's 5.3 litre capacity was retained and the resulting unit developed 330bhp which compared with 305bhp for the current V8. A five-speed ZF manual gearbox was available with the option of three-speed automatic transmission.

The Virage's interior naturally reflected the Aston Martin pedigree and was beautifully upholstered in leather which was complemented by walnut veneers on the instrument panel and door fillets. Air conditioning, courtesy of Jaguar, was a standard fitment.

Two Virages were completed in time for its 1988 British Motor Show debut where the car was universally acclaimed. Above all, it generated considerable interest among Aston Martin aficionados. With manufacture anticipated at six cars per week, the first two years' production was immediately sold out. The Virage's price was subsequently fixed at £125,000 which was £13,000 more than a Ferrari Testarossa. It was, however, early 1990 before the first cars were delivered.

Aston Martin claimed a top speed of 155mph (250km/h) which meant that,

Specifications: Aston Martin Virage	

Length:	15ft 6in (4724mm)
Width:	6ft 1in (1854mm)
Height:	4ft 4in (1321mm)
Wheelbase:	8ft 6¾in (2610mm)
Track:	front 4ft 11½in (1511mm), rear 5ft (1524mm)

Unladen weight:	3946lb (1790kg)
Engine: V8 with twin overhead camshafts per bank, 85×100mm, 5340cc. Compression ratio, 9.5:1. Fuel injection. Max power, 310bhp at 6000rpm. Max torque, 340lb/ft at 3700rpm.	
Transmission:	Five-speed manual
Drive:	Rear
Suspension (front):	Independent, coil springs and wishbones
Suspension (rear):	De Dion axle, coil springs and radius arms
Top speed:	155mph (250km/h)
0-60mph (96km/h):	6.7 seconds
Production (to date, including Volante):	approx 560

ABOVE: *Although the Virage was displayed at the 1988 British Motor Show, it was 1990 before deliveries of the car began. This example dates from that year.*

LEFT: *This side elevation of the Virage coupé, pictured at Newport Pagnell, shows the lines of the Heffernan/Greenley-styled body to good effect.*

RIGHT AND BELOW: *The Volante version of the Virage followed in 1992 after important modifications had been made to the original 1990 rendering, which did not allow space for rear passengers. The definitive two-plus-two version was announced at the 1991 Geneva Show.*

flat out, the Virage was around 5mph (8km/h) faster than the V8. The factory said that the older car could reach 60mph (96km/h) in 6.7 seconds and the new car's acceleration proved to be about the same. When road tested by the motoring press, the model was praised for its long-legged qualities and standard of construction, but there was some concern voiced about the Virage's handling and steering. In short, there was a feeling that the car had not yet proved itself a true successor to the V8 which had been discontinued in late 1989.

A convertible version was established Aston Martin practice and the Virage Volante was duly announced in September 1990. To the disappointment of many, it was a two- rather than a four-seater. The company responded to this criticism by unveiling, at the 1991 Geneva Motor Show, a revised and more acceptable two-plus-two Volante which became available early in 1992.

Much More Power

In the same January of 1992 came a tacit recognition by the factory that the Virage required more acceleration. Aston Martin announced that, for £50,000, customers could uprate their Virage; this involved extending the engine's capacity to 6.3 litres, which increases power by some 40 per cent, to 465bhp. This resulted in a claimed top speed of 174mph (280km/h) which was nearly 20mph (32km/h) more than the standard Virage with the 0-60mph (96km/h) time correspondingly dropping to 5.4 seconds.

Three months later, at the Geneva Motor Show in March, came an estate version. This had been taken over by Walter Hayes, formerly vice chairman of Ford of Europe, who had replaced Gauntlett in 1991. With a claimed top speed of 152mph (245km/h), the three-door Virage was, inevitably, expensive and sold for £165,000. It could also be fitted with the optional 465bhp performance package.

As ever, Aston Martin was one of the first car makers to feel the chill of a world recession, and by the autumn of 1992, production had dropped to around two cars a week which wholly consisted of the Volante Virage; the coupé was only being built to order. But for 1993 came a long-awaited Vantage version of the Virage which, unlike its predecessors, offered a visual restatement of the design in addition to its uprated mechanicals. Outwardly

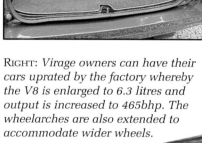

ABOVE AND RIGHT: *The world's fastest estate car, the 152mph (245km/h) Virage. It has a more spacious passenger compartment than the coupé and there is plenty of space for dogs, guns or golf clubs.*

Aston Martin Virage

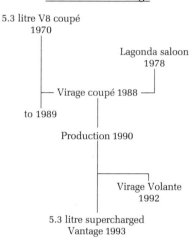

5.3 litre V8 coupé 1970

Lagonda saloon 1978

Virage coupé 1988

to 1989

Production 1990

Virage Volante 1992

5.3 litre supercharged Vantage 1993

RIGHT: *Virage owners can have their cars uprated by the factory whereby the V8 is enlarged to 6.3 litres and output is increased to 465bhp. The wheelarches are also extended to accommodate wider wheels.*

only the doors and roof panel were retained with the body lines being redrawn by Heffernan principally to accommodate new, wider wheels. The outcome is a more visually impressive car than the original. The engine retains its 5.3 litre capacity but has been extensively modified with power boosted to no less than 550bhp which is mostly achieved by the fitment of twin Eaton superchargers. Selling for £150,000, the company claims that the Vantage has a maximum speed of 185mph (298km/h) with 60mph (96km/h) spirited up in a mere 4.6 seconds.

In 1994 the Virage was joined by the cheaper six-cylinder DB7. For the first time for many years, there will be two modern Aston Martin sports cars available. This can only bode well for the company's long-term future.

LEFT: *A 1993 Aston Martin Vantage with 550bhp under its bonnet, pictured at the 1993 Goodwood Festival of Speed. The company used this car for development work that was undertaken by Jackie Stewart.*

ABOVE: *The Vantage is outwardly identifiable by its bonnet louvres to provide air intakes for the twin superchargers which so enhance the output of the 5.3 litre V8. In short, it is a real Aston Martin.*

ABOVE: *Rear view of the 465bhp Virage with rear wing and Virage 6.3 litres badge on the tail. Modifications were made to both the suspension and brakes.*

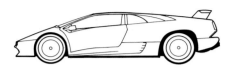

How do you replace a car like Lamborghini's Countach? The answer is with great difficulty; the Diablo has suffered a troubled period of gestation, birth and production. This was, in part, due to the collapse of the supercar market in 1990. On the plus side, the Diablo, which is also built in four-wheel-drive form, became the world's fastest road car before the Jaguar XJ220 claimed that accolade in 1993. Lamborghini responded with a more powerful version for 1994, but this coincided with Chrysler, which had owned Lamborghini since 1987, disposing of the business to an Indonesian-based group.

The man with overall responsibility for the Diablo was Luigi Marmiroli, who was appointed Lamborghini's technical director in 1985. A former Ferrari and Alfa Romeo engineer, he began work on the design, coded P132, early in 1986. The important styling commission was thrown open to a number of studios. Marcello Gandini, creator of the Miura and Countach who had left Bertone in 1979 to set up on his own account, was clearly a front runner and his was the design chosen. The scale model was completed in June 1988 and the first prototype was on the road by the spring of 1989. It was powered by the Countach's 5.2 litre engine but the car was not sufficiently fast, so the V12 was enlarged to 5.7 litres. In keeping with other Lamborghinis, the Diablo name – it is Spanish for devil – commemorates a famous fighting bull.

Chrysler had bought Lamborghini, in April 1987, and when it viewed the car, executives requested that Gandini make changes to its appearance. He duly responded but, dissatisfied with these modifications, Chrysler itself took a hand. The result of these dual influences is that, although visually impressive, the Diablo does lack the flair and impact of its predecessors. Chrysler was also responsible for creating the car's interior. These modifications were incorporated into the second prototype which was running by the middle of 1989.

Diablo Launch
The Diablo was launched at an extravagant party, staged in January 1990 at Monte Carlo, where it was officially unveiled, although it was not until January 1991 that deliveries of the £152,614 car began.

Outwardly and in respect of its in-line, mid-located engine the Diablo was clearly a Countach derivative, but it was bigger – the 8ft 8in (2642mm) wheelbase was 6in (152mm) greater and the coupé body was also slightly wider. It retained the Countach's famous upward-opening doors and while much of the hull was made of alloy, the bumpers, engine cover and bonnet were of a carbon fibre/glass fibre composite. It also had the virtue of a drag coefficient of a mere 0.31.

The 5.7 litre V12 was clearly related to the Countach's power unit with the enlargement in capacity being achieved by increasing both the bore and stroke. The unit was extensively re-engineered with the result that it developed 492bhp, compared with its predecessor's 455bhp. The drive passed, Countach-like, through the engine with the redesigned five-speed gearbox canted towards the driver.

The Diablo's chassis had also evolved from that of its legendary predecessor, but the space-frame employed square rather than round tubing because it was easier to attach components to it. The coil spring and wishbone, all-independent suspension was essentially carried over from the Countach. Steering, perhaps surprisingly, was not power-assisted nor were there anti-lock brakes.

As originally introduced, the Diablo was a rear-drive car but, at the time of its announcement, work was proceeding on the four-wheel-drive version, the Diablo VT, the suffix standing for Viscous Transmission. A notable feature of the system was that during acceleration in cornering, up to 17 per cent of power would be transferred automatically to the front wheels. One pre-production example was displayed at the model's Monte Carlo launch.

Inside, the two-seater cockpit was beautifully upholstered in leather. The Diablo enjoyed more headroom than the Countach because, at 3ft 7½in (1105mm), it was 1½in (35mm) higher.

But luggage space was, inevitably, limited to the small front compartment; a fitted four-piece luggage set was available at extra cost.

Lamborghini claimed that the car could reach 62mph (100km/h) in just 4.9 seconds and that it had a maximum speed of 202mph (325km/h). This was subsequently confirmed by *Road and Track* magazine which achieved 202.33mph (325.6km/h) in a Diablo, making it marginally quicker than the Ferrari F40. For a time, it was the world's fastest road car.

Good And Bad Points
On the road, the car's handling was found to be excellent, and the V12 engine did everything required of it, the Lamborghini being eager and formidably fast although tractable at low speeds. However, the unassisted steering and absence of anti-lock brakes came in for press criticism.

Once the Diablo had entered production, at the rate of 1.8 cars a day, work was concentrated on the four-wheel-drive VT version. However, that was not the derivative which Lamborghini unveiled at the 1992 Geneva Motor Show. It was a convertible with the shallowest of windscreens and, audaciously, no roof, be it a hard or soft top. The company intended to have this impractical confection in production by mid-1993 with the hope of building 300 cars over a four year period.

Specifications: Lamborghini Diablo VT	
Length:	14ft 7in (4445mm)
Width:	6ft 8in (2032mm)
Height:	3ft 7½in (1105mm)
Wheelbase:	8ft 8in (2642mm)
Track:	front 5ft 0½in (1540mm), rear 5ft 4½in (1640mm)
Unladen weight:	3640lb (1651kg)
Engine: Mid-located V12 with twin overhead camshafts per bank, 87×80mm, 5729cc. Compression ratio, 10:1. Fuel injection. Max power, 392bhp at 7000rpm. Max torque, 328lb/ft at 5200rpm.	
Transmission:	Five-speed manual
Drive:	Four-wheel
Suspension (front):	Independent, coil springs and wishbones
Suspension (rear):	Independent, coil springs and wishbones
Top speed:	202mph (325km/h)
0-60mph (96km/h):	4.9 seconds
Production (to date, total):	approx 1100

ABOVE: *The Diablo's body is full of visual surprises and (as in the Countach) the front-hinged scissor doors are of an irregular shape.*

BELOW: *The twin exhausts make their contribution to the car's rear and they produce all the right noises!*

RIGHT: *The Diablo's lines are the work of Marcello Gandini with some input from Chrysler.*

ABOVE: *Back to the future, the Diablo's impressive tail. As with the Countach, Gandini has placed the mass of the Diablo's structure at the rear to create a distinctive wedge shape.*

LAMBORGHINI DIABLO

This prediction proved to be wildly optimistic for, by the autumn of 1992, Lamborghini was in trouble. The lack of demand for the Diablo, caused, in part, by the depth of the world's recession, resulted in its manufacture ceasing in September. The firm's intention was to reduce a backlog of 55 cars and, when production restarted in November, cars would only be built to dealer order. By this time the Diablo was Lamborghini's sole product, the two-plus-two Jalpa having ceased production in 1989, and the cross-country LM002 in 1991. The firm manufactured 300 Diablos in 1992, which compared with 571 examples built in 1991. The factory was capable of building 650 cars a year.

Up For Sale

At the 1992 Paris Motor Show, Chrysler revealed that it wished to sell Lamborghini. Only a few cars were built in December 1992 and January 1993. But in March, at long last, the four-wheel-drive Diablo VT, which employs a semi-automatic gearbox, went on sale.

The 213mph (343km/h) Jaguar XJ220 had entered production in mid-1992 and, in September 1993, Lamborghini responded with the Diablo 30SE. This Special Edition car has a claimed top speed of 220mph (354 km/h) although McLaren's F1, then waiting in the wings, would be even faster. Produced to celebrate the 30th anniversary of Lamborghini's creation in 1994, the engine retained the 5.7 litres capacity but the fitment of a lighter crankshaft and changes to the valve timing, injection and ignition meant that power was boosted to 525bhp. External changes to the car included a new front air dam and a movable rear wing, both of which served to improve the aerodynamics.

The hope was to have the 30SE in production by mid-1994, along with the long heralded open version. But by then Lamborghini had a new owner in the shape of the Indonesian SETDCO Group, this company having bought the firm, in January 1994, from Chrysler for £20 million.

The firm claims that the 1994 Diablos have some 1500 modifications, of which the most significant are power-steering, anti-lock brakes and improvements to interior ventilation. The car clearly has plenty more mileage left in it and the 1000th example was built in February 1994. The Lamborghini Countach ran for 16 years and its successor, which is getting better as its gets older, could well do the same.

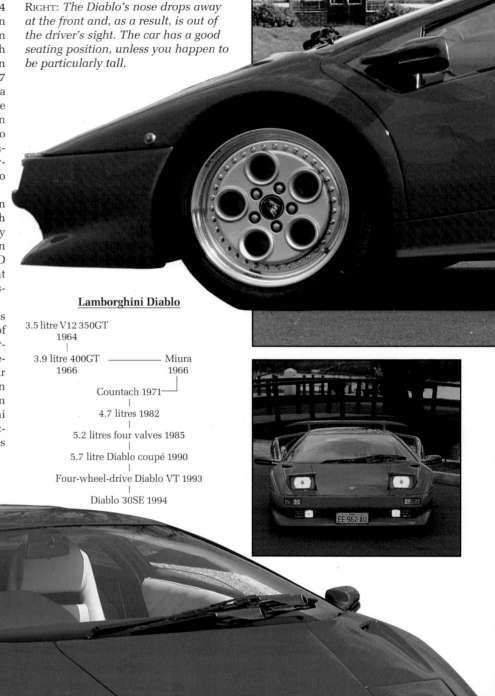

RIGHT: *The Diablo's nose drops away at the front and, as a result, is out of the driver's sight. The car has a good seating position, unless you happen to be particularly tall.*

Lamborghini Diablo

3.5 litre V12 350GT
1964

3.9 litre 400GT ———— Miura
1966   1966

Countach 1971

4.7 litres 1982

5.2 litres four valves 1985

5.7 litre Diablo coupé 1990

Four-wheel-drive Diablo VT 1993

Diablo 30SE 1994

LEFT: *The Lamborghini's cockpit is positioned well to the fore. The front-located boot is very small, but can accommodate a purpose-designed luggage set.*

BELOW LEFT: *A Diablo complete with a rear wing which was not originally on offer. Visibility is an improvement on that of the Countach and there is more headroom, which is an undoubted plus. Entry is, therefore, easier but ladies still find taking their seats a trifle undignified.*

RIGHT: *The Lamborghini's insect-like doors, which rise on dampers, with the massive engine cover also open to reveal the mighty V12.*

BELOW: *The bewinged rear prospect of a Diablo. The lack of front and rear bumpers makes parking something of a challenge.*

JAGUAR XJ220 (1991-1994)

The XJ220 is not only very fast – its claimed 213mph (343km/h) top speed is rivalled only by the McLaren F1 and Lamborghini Diablo SE, but at £403,000 it is also very expensive! This magnificent Jaguar suffered from a protracted seven-year gestation. Having been conceived late in 1984, it was unveiled in definitive form, to great acclaim, at the 1991 Tokyo Motor Show. In the interim, the 220 had evolved from being a mid-engined, V12-powered, four-wheel-drive supercar, displayed at the 1988 British Motor Show, to a no less impressive but simplified vehicle driven by a twin-turbocharged V6 unit. Announced in this revised form in 1989, its price was set at £361,000 but, by 1991, the index-linked figure had soared by over £40,000, which caused problems for some of the subscribers. As a result, despite 350 cars having been ordered, by the time that production ceased in the spring of 1994, this had dropped to 275.

The driving force behind the XJ220 was Jaguar's director of vehicle and concepts engineering, Jim Randle. It was in December 1984 that he set down the parameters for a 500bhp supercar to take on the likes of the Porsche 959. The go-ahead was given for a project to proceed on a semi-official status. Work on the single development car was undertaken after normal working hours and at weekends with its participants being accordingly dubbed members of The Saturday Club. Crucially, support was received from the company's suppliers.

At the heart of the car was Jaguar's V12 engine, mid-located and longitudinally mounted. Unlike the 5.3 litre, 291bhp unit with single cam, two valve heads which powered the XJ12 saloon, this was a 6.2 litre one with hitherto unseen twin overhead camshafts per bank and four valves per cylinder. This mighty engine developed over 500bhp which was greater than any other production road car of the day. Interestingly, the XJR-9 with which Jaguar won Le Mans in 1988 used a 6.9 litre V12 though still with single cam heads.

The XJ220 featured an FF Developments four-wheel-drive system with the five-speed gearbox mounted at the rear of the unit and the drive, ingeniously, taken through the V of the engine. The adaptive suspension was by double wishbones and rocker-oper- ated twin-spring damper units with provision made for the fitment of four-wheel-steering, although it was not employed. By contrast, anti-lock brakes were.

Helfet Style

The design of the all-important unstressed aluminium body passed through two phases. The first, styled by Cliff Rudell, was subsequently replaced, in 1987, by a new creation essayed by Keith Helfet. His were the lines adopted and the shell cloaked by a chassis constructed of sheet aluminium alloy that used Alcan's bonding and rivetting technology. The XJ220 was conceived as a road car, so Randle was determined that the cockpit should emphasise this identity. It was beautifully upholstered in Connolly hides; there was air conditioning and electric windows were fitted all round.

The Jaguar was unveiled at the 1988 British Motor Show, staged at Birmingham, where it was one of the principal

BELOW: *The XJ220 as displayed at the 1988 British Motor Show. Unlike the production cars, it was V12-powered and four-wheel-driven.*

Specifications: Jaguar XJ220

Length:	16ft 2in (4928mm)
Width:	6ft 7in (2007mm)
Height:	3ft 9in (1143mm)
Wheelbase:	8ft 8in (2642mm)
Track:	front 5ft 7⅓in (1709mm), rear 5ft 2½in (1587mm)
Unladen weight:	3031lb (1375kg)
Engine:	V6 with twin overhead camshafts per bank, 94×84mm, 3498cc. Compression ratio, 8.3:1. Fuel injection. Twin turbochargers. Max power, 542bhp at 7200rpm. Max torque, 475lb/ft at 4500rpm.
Transmission:	Five-speed manual
Drive:	Rear
Suspension (front):	Independent, coil springs and wishbones
Suspension (rear):	Independent, coil springs and wishbones
Top speed:	213mph (343km/h)
0-60mph (96km/h):	4 seconds
Production:	275

ABOVE: *The XJ220, as it appeared in 1991, with the essentials of the styling retained although slightly smaller than the original. It was V6-powered and with two-wheel-drive.*

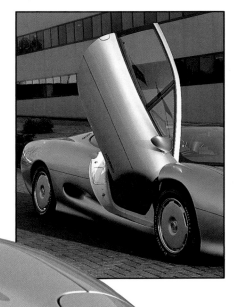

RIGHT: *The 1988 car's scissor doors were not perpetuated on the production version of the XJ220.*

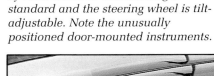

ABOVE: *The XJ220's cockpit, designed by Nick Hull. Air conditioning is standard and the steering wheel is tilt-adjustable. Note the unusually positioned door-mounted instruments.*

BELOW: *The 1988 XJ220's longitudinally mounted V12 48 valve engine, which developed in excess of 500bhp but was not carried over for the production version.*

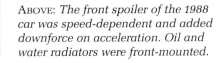

ABOVE: *The front spoiler of the 1988 car was speed-dependent and added downforce on acceleration. Oil and water radiators were front-mounted.*

Jaguar XJ220

attractions; the other was Aston Martin's new Virage. For its part, the 220 proclaimed that the recently privatized Jaguar company was ready to take on the best that the Italian and German opposition could offer.

At the Show there were suggestions that the car might enter production and that 200 could be built. Following the closure of the event, the car was taken over by JaguarSport, the business jointly set up earlier in 1988 by the car company and Tom Walkinshaw Racing, which had hitherto been responsible for the design and preparation of the marque's highly successful generation of sports racing cars. Once at its premises, located at Kidlington, near Banbury, Oxfordshire, the XJ220 was evaluated with a view to putting it into production.

No such decision had been made by September 1989 when Jaguar's chairman, Sir John Egan, revealed that if the 220 was built, the task would be undertaken by JaguarSport and that, instead of being V12-engined, it would use the turbocharged V6 unit and rear wheel driveline developed for Jaguar's new XJR-10 sports racer. Then, in November, Ford successfully obtained control of Jaguar and, in December, came news that the project would proceed although, in addition to the new engine, it would be slightly smaller, in overall terms, than the original.

Expensive And Exclusive

At £361,000, the 220 was about twice the price of the newly introduced Ferrari F40 and, even then, its price was index linked to the delivery date. A £50,000 deposit would be required to secure an order and a minimum of 220 examples, to echo the car's title, would be built. If there was sufficient demand, it was disclosed that as many as 350 could be produced and, in February 1990, the latter figure was confirmed, when it was stated that, of these, 90 cars would remain in Britain.

The XJ220 was finally unveiled at the 1991 Tokyo Motor Show, no doubt because JaguarSport hoped to secure potential customers in the Far East. There was, in theory, a full order book but a dramatic change in the financial climate meant that some potential customers were unable to complete their orders.

This looming problem did nothing to detract from the excellence of the product. Although there was a family resemblance to the 1988 Show car, its wheelbase was 8in (203mm) shorter,

while the overall length still remained at a little over 16ft (4877mm). Mechanically, the XJ220 was greatly simplified: the four-wheel drive, anti-lock brakes and adaptive suspension were all dispensed with. The twin-turbocharged 3.5 litre V6, with twin overhead camshafts per bank and four valves per cylinder, developed no less than 542bhp which was significantly more than the Ferrari F40's 487bhp and the Lamborghini Diablo's 492bhp. Top speed was claimed to be 213mph (343km/h) and 0-60mph (96km/h) came up in just four seconds and 100mph (161km/h) in eight.

The outcome was a car which proved to be deceptively easy to drive, had magnificent roadholding, superlative good looks and shattering performance. But the price had risen to £403,000.

Deliveries of the XJ220 began in mid-1992 and early in 1993 came the XJ220-C which was a lightweight racing version. At Le Mans, three examples were entered in the new GT class and one of the trio won. Regrettably, it was later disqualified because none of the cars was fitted with catalytic converters.

There was also trouble brewing for the XJ220 when, in April 1993, it had emerged that JaguarSport was preparing to sue a number of its customers who had not paid a £50,000 instalment due on their contracts. The matter was not resolved until September when the company announced that it was allowing any individuals who wished to do so to buy out their contracts.

As a result, the projected figure of 350 cars was reduced to the 275 mark. Those lucky and exclusive individuals who own one of them can pride themselves on possessing one of the world's truly great cars.

LEFT: This is the first production XJ220 of 1992, chassis 001, with appropriate number plate.

Jaguar XJ220

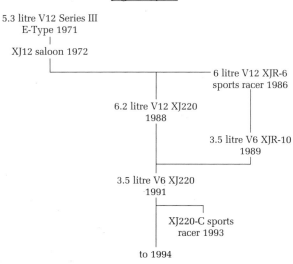

5.3 litre V12 Series III E-Type 1971
XJ12 saloon 1972
6 litre V12 XJR-6 sports racer 1986
6.2 litre V12 XJ220 1988
3.5 litre V6 XJR-10 1989
3.5 litre V6 XJ220 1991
XJ220-C sports racer 1993
to 1994

ABOVE: Ready for the road, the first XJ220 has been retained by Tom Walkinshaw, whose TWR Group was assigned the task of productionizing the one-off 1988 show car. Some changes came courtesy of the XJR-10 sports racer.

BELOW: The XJ220's side elevation which, in true Jaguar style, looks like no other car. The distinctive air scoop is for the radiator.

LEFT: *Even the petrol filler cap has a special feel to it and has its own built-in pressure relief valve. The engine can just be seen through the quarter light.*

RIGHT: *The 220's mid-located, longitudinally mounted, aluminium, 3.5 litre V6 engine which has twin Garret T3 turbochargers. Zytek multi-point fuel injection with electronic boost control is fitted.*

BENTLEY CONTINENTAL R (1991 to date)

Rolls-Royce's commitment to revitalizing the Bentley marque was further emphasized with the unveiling, at the 1991 Geneva Motor Show, of the Continental R. The key ingredient of its creation was that this magnificently equipped luxury coupé was specifically designed as a Bentley. In recent years the make had shared a commonized body with its Rolls-Royce stablemate; the new car rekindled the spirit of the fastback R-Type Continental of the 1950's.

It was in 1986 that Rolls-Royce's chief executive, Peter Ward, decided that the firm must build what he described as "the finest sporting coupé in the world". This came after the company had displayed a styling exercise at the 1985 Geneva Show which took the form of a handsome coupé, designated Project 90, commissioned from International Automotive Design of Worthing, Sussex. Styling was by Royal College of Art lecturers, John Heffernan and Ken Greenley, who were also responsible for the lines of Aston Martin's Virage. It was, maintained Rolls-Royce, "an exhibition mock-up ... with the specific intention of assessing general reaction and opinions." These were sufficiently encouraging for Rolls-Royce to press ahead with a production version. This again displayed its increasing commitment to the Bentley name, that had previously been shown by the Mulsanne Turbo of 1982, which was followed in 1985 by its better-handling R derivative.

Project 90 officially became Nepal in April 1989. This choice of code name harked back to the 1930's when Rolls-Royce allotted Far Eastern names to its models – the Silver Cloud, for instance, was Siam and the Silver Shadow started life as the Tibet. With its body lines requiring only the minimum of refinement, a prototype car was running by the summer of 1990.

Outpacing The Turbo R

The brief presented to Rolls-Royce's engineering department was to attain a 10 per cent improvement in the performance of the already rapid Turbo R. This meant a top speed approaching 150mph (241km/h) and acceleration to 60mph (96km/h) needed to be whittled down to a little over six seconds. This represented a formidable challenge for a large car with no pretensions to a low drag coefficient and which turned the scales at a substantial 5340lb (2422kg).

Some thought was given to fitting the long running 6.7 litre V8 with four valve heads developed by Cosworth Engineering which, coincidentally, Vickers, Rolls-Royce's parent company, had bought in 1990. As it happened, no such radical enhancement reached the production version for, when the Continental R was unveiled at Geneva in 1991, the minimum of modifications had been made to the turbocharged eight.

Traditionally, Rolls-Royce does not disclose the horse power developed by its engines but, in 1982, it had been forced to publish the 333bhp produced by the Mulsanne Turbo when that model went on sale in Germany. It was estimated that the Continental R's engine produced in the order of 363bhp. This was achieved by the fitment of a new Bosch K-Motronic fuel injection system, while the greater underbonnet space made it possible to design a more efficient inlet system. The Turbo R employed a three-speed automatic gearbox but this was replaced by a new General Motors four-speed unit with a choice of sports and economy settings.

The chassis otherwise followed that of the Turbo R saloon and the Continental shared its 10ft 0½in (3061mm) wheelbase along with the sophisticated suspension system and three-stage electrically controlled dampers. Power steering and brakes also followed the established pattern.

It was, of course, the coupé body which made the Continental so special and, despite its traditional lines and retention of the famous Bentley radiator grill, a very acceptable drag coefficient of 0.36 was attained. Inside, the car differed radically from its saloon counterpart. The customary dashboard had been replaced by a completely new layout in which the majority of dials were placed directly in front of the driver. An unprecedented refinement for the marque was the introduction of an instrument console between the seats. In addition, it housed the lever for the automatic gear change, transferred from the steering column which

Specifications: Bentley Continental R

Length:	17ft 6in (5334mm)
Width:	6ft 8½in (2045mm)
Height:	4ft 8in (1422mm)
Wheelbase:	10ft 0½in (3061mm)
Track:	front and rear 5ft 0½in (1537mm)
Unladen weight:	5340lb (2422kg)

Engine: V8, overhead valve, 104×99mm, 6750cc. Compression ratio, 8:1. Fuel injection. Turbocharged. Max power (estimated), 360bhp. Max torque, not disclosed

Transmission:	Four-speed automatic
Drive:	Rear
Suspension (front):	Independent, coil springs and wishbones
Suspension (rear):	Independent, coil springs and semi-trailing arms
Top speed:	145mph (233km/h)
0-60mph (96km/h):	6.6 seconds
Production (to date):	approx 500

LEFT: *The Continental R of 1991 was the first Bentley since the 1952 Continental to have its own purpose-designed body. The work of the Heffernan/Greenley partnership, the car evolved from Project 90, a styling exercise which Rolls-Royce displayed at the 1985 Geneva Motor Show.*

LEFT: *New inside and out. The Continental R benefitted from a revised interior with updated fascia and full length console between the seats, although the rear section can be detached. Note that the selector for the automatic transmission has been transferred from the steering column to the console.*

RIGHT: *How it looks as it passes you – the Continental R's sporting pedigree is readily apparent and is intended to appeal to the younger Bentley customer. It possesses all the style and performance associated with the famous name.*

BENTLEY CONTINENTAL R

had been a less convenient location. Unusually, it incorporated the control for the driver to switch from the standard to sport setting. When sport was selected, the gearbox was made to work harder and the suspension also tightened up. Top speed, in all modes, was limited to 145mph (233km/h), and 60mph (96km/h) arrived in a claimed 6.6 seconds when the performance programme was selected.

Smart Seats

The console was extended to the rear seats and also included a stereo unit and CD player. The rear section could be detached to transform the separate back seats into a bench-type unit. As might be expected on a car of this price, each front squab possessed its own memory which retained settings for height, rake and tilt. The seats also contained heating elements for cold conditions. Rolls-Royce's proven air-conditioning system was, similarly, a welcome and obligatory fitment.

This lavishly equipped coupé, which sold for £175,000, was in production by early in 1992. Rolls-Royce intended to build 70 such cars per annum. The first two years' allocation was sold even before manufacture began, and the first lucky owners were resident in Rolls-Royce's four principal markets of Britain, America, Europe and the Far East.

On the road the Continental R provided an environment unique to Rolls-Royce's products. Superb but re-

strained comfort, and an enviable level of silence all constituted the ingredients of a powerful, long-legged intercontinental tourer. However, on the debit side, when compared with the Turbo R saloon, was the inevitable loss of room at the rear. The motoring press also criticized a disappointing ride quality. The Continental R also seemed less happy on wet roads which suggested the need for some form of traction control.

The car continued to be produced in this form but improvements were ongoing. The 1994 cars were easily distinguishable by their new alloy wheels.

An airbag, hitherto only available on the driver's side, was extended to the front passenger position. Also standardized was an ingenious seat belt "presenter" which automatically proffered a belt as soon as anyone sat down in the car.

A convertible version, designed and engineered by Pininfarina, made its debut at the 1994 Geneva Show. Intended for sale in the summer, the painted and trimmed Italian bodies are dispatched to Britain to receive their mechanicals at Rolls-Royce's Crewe factory, so endowing the car with a truly continental dimension.

ABOVE: *The Continental R's chassis is similar to that of the Turbo R and its wheelbase is thus related.*

RIGHT: *The R, as it appeared in 1992, able to carry four people in considerable comfort.*

Bentley Continental R

6.2 litre V8 Bentley
S2/Rolls-Royce Silver
Cloud II 1959
|
Bentley S3/Silver
Cloud III 1962
|
Bentley T Series/Rolls-
Royce Silver Shadow 1965
|
6.7 litres 1970
|
Bentley Mulsanne/Rolls-
Royce Silver Spirit 1980
|
Mulsanne Turbo
1982
|
Turbo R 1985
|
Project 90
1985
|
Continental R
1991
|
to date   to date   to date

RIGHT: *A 1994 Continental R which is distinguished by new alloy wheels. Below the bonnet the 6.7 litre turbocharged V8 has been revised to permit high boost for short periods, such as when overtaking. Other refinements include the automatic transmission fitted with SEM, standing for shift energy management, in other words, a smoother gear change.*

3500 TU

BUGATTI EB110 GT (1991 to date)

One of the legendary marques of automobile history, Bugatti was dramatically revived with the 1991 appearance of the four-wheel-drive EB110 which is one of the world's fastest cars. It was early in 1988 that, to the astonishment of the motoring world, news broke that the make was to reappear on the road after an absence of nearly 40 years. The £100 million project involved the construction of a purpose-built factory in northern Italy and the outcome is a distinctive, mid-engined coupé aimed at the same wealthy clientele that would have bought Bugattis in pre-war days.

These were built at Molsheim, France from 1910 until 1939. The Italian Ettore Bugatti died in 1947, and the make made a final, flickering appearance at the 1951 Paris Motor Show, although the model displayed there was, essentially, of pre-war origin. The firm did survive, but no further cars were made, save for an abortive Grand Prix project in 1956. It undertook mostly subcontracted work for the aviation industry. Since 1968 the Bugatti company has been owned by SNECMA, the nationalized French aircraft engine concern.

Then, late in 1987, Bugatti Automobili SpA was registered in Italy, being 65 per cent owned by the Luxembourg-based Bugatti International SA. Who actually owns that was not known then and is still a mystery. Chairman of the Italian company is Romano Artioli, who initially stayed out of the limelight and, at the time, held the Ferrari concession for northern Italy and southern Germany. By contrast, Paolo Stanzani, the firm's then managing and technical director, played a high profile role and was responsible for the overall layout of the new Bugatti. Formerly of Lamborghini, Stanzani has the legendary Countach to his credit.

Details of the mid-engined, four-wheel-drive design emerged early in 1989 by which time work had begun on the new Bugatti factory at Campogalliano on the outskirts of Modena. Work proceeded apace on the project and, by early 1990, the first engine was running and developed an astounding 700bhp even though "only" 550bhp was required. The power unit in question was a 3.5 litre V12 with twin overhead camshafts per bank activating, unusually, five valves per cylinder. No less than four water-cooled turbochargers were employed.

The finished car was unveiled, 18 months later, in the autumn of 1991 but

the intervening period was not without incident. In July 1990, Stanzani, who held a substantial holding in the Italian company, was sacked by Artioli who accused him of wanting to take the business over. The Bugatti chairman also decided that the car's body, designed by Marcello Gandini of Lamborghini Miura and Countach fame, was not sufficiently distinctive and, early in 1991, he revealed that the coupé's lines were to be reworked.

Curtain Up
It was against this turbulent background that the car was launched in Paris, on 14th September 1991, the eve of the 110th anniversary of Ettore Bugatti's birth. This is why the car is called the EB110. Despite the emotion of the occasion, the car's appearance did not meet with universal acclaim, despite the in-house rethink by a team led by Giampaolo Benedini, the man responsible for the design of the new Bugatti factory.

The EB110 revealed modest changes to its bodywork when it appeared at the 1992 Geneva Motor Show, where it was said to have also benefitted from a more "torquey" engine. However, it was not until early in 1993 that the £220,000 coupé, which is only available in left-hand-drive form, entered production. It certainly looked like no other car with its distinctive squat nose incorporating a miniature representation of the famous Bugatti horseshoe-shaped radiator. At its heart was a light, rigid but costly carbon fibre substructure produced for Bugatti Automobili by Aérospatiale in France. The car was also extremely fast!

The mid-located, quadruple turbocharged V12 engine was mounted in-line between the two seats and drove all four wheels via a six-speed gearbox. The adaptive suspension system was produced by the original Bugatti factory at Molsheim.

RIGHT: *A NACA duct for the 3.5 litre V12 turbocharged engine. There are two of them, located on either side of the car on top of the rear wings.*

Specifications: Bugatti EB110 GT

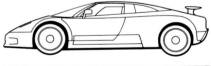

Length:	14ft 5¼in (4400mm)
Width:	6ft 5⅛in (1960mm)
Height:	3ft 8¼in (1125mm)
Wheelbase:	8ft 4in (2550mm)
Track:	front 5ft 1in (1550mm), rear 5ft 3¾in (1618mm)
Unladen weight:	3234lb (1467kg)

Engine: Mid-located V12 with twin overhead camshafts per bank, 81×57mm, 3500cc. Compression ratio, 7.5:1. Fuel injection. Four turbochargers. Max power, 553bhp at 8000rpm. Max torque, 451lb/ft at 3750rpm,

Transmission:	Six-speed manual
Drive:	Four-wheel
Suspension (front):	Independent, coil springs and wishbones
Suspension (rear):	Independent, coil springs and wishbones
Top speed:	212mph (341km/h)
0-60mph (96km/h):	3.7 seconds
Production (to date):	approx 120

ABOVE: *A 1992 EB110 GT, this particular example is Bugatti chairman Romano Artioli's own car. Note the miniature representation of the famous Bugatti horseshoe-shaped radiator at the front of the car.*

RIGHT: *The Bugatti's detail design is impressive and the neat rear end contains these flush-fitting back lights.*

BELOW: *The 110 in profile. The automatic rear wing is standard.*

Bugatti EB110 GT

In May 1992 a pre-production EB110 was timed at the Nardo test track in Italy at 212.5mph (342km/h) which made it a modicum slower than the Jaguar XJ220's 213mph (343km/h). It could also reach 60mph (96km/h) in an unprecedented 3.7 seconds and the Bugatti had an equally sensational 0 to 200km/h (124mph) time of 11.4 seconds. Whether lucky 110 owners would ever be able fully to extend their cars at such speeds on the road must be open to question.

By the end of 1993, the Campogalliano factory had completed 98 examples of the 110 and a lightweight version, titled the EB110 SS for Sport Stradale, or road racer, which had been launched at the 1992 Geneva Show. When it entered production in the summer of 1993, the original car was renamed the EB110 GT. The SS weighed 3127lb (1418kg) which was 440lb (200kg) less than the 110. This saving was achieved by stripping out many of the cockpit refinements. Although the engine's capacity remained unchanged, its management systems were revised for it to produce a stupendous 600bhp. Top speed was a claimed 217mph (349km/h), the 0-60mph (96km/h) figure was a staggering 3.4 seconds and the SS was priced at £304,000.

Superfast Saloon

Bugatti had more surprises in store at the 1993 Geneva event where it revealed what was claimed to be the world's fastest saloon, the EB112. Capable of 186mph (300km/h), it is a front-engined variation on the 110 theme. The V12's capacity is increased to 6 litres, which is attained by upping the stroke from 56 to 86mm, although turbochargers were not fitted. The body, by Ital Design, contains distinct echoes of the Bugattis of the past yet is, nevertheless, a thoroughly modern interpretation of a four-door saloon.

Also employing a carbon fibre underframe, the car has an overall length of 16ft 8in (5070mm), which is 2ft 2⅓in (670mm) greater than the two-seater. Bugatti Automobili's stated intention is to have the EB112 in production by the end of 1994.

In mid-1993 Bugatti, surprisingly, became the new owner of Group Lotus which it bought from General Motors for a reputed price of £20 million. As far as its own car line is concerned, a spider (open) version of the EB110 cannot be far off, and an anti-lock braking system, tailored to the demanding requirements of four-wheel-drive, is also promised. If the experience of the past six years is anything to go by, there must be plenty more surprises to come from that lavishly funded factory at Campogalliano.

Below: The car's oval badge, designed by Ettore Bugatti, dates from the marque's 1910 origins.

Below: The EB110 head-on. There is not much room beneath the nose except for the battery.

ABOVE: *The 110's distinctive upward opening doors and engine cover.*

TOP RIGHT: *The longitudinally mounted quadruple turbocharged V12 is available for all to see. Unusually, it is fitted with five valves per cylinder.*

RIGHT: *The 110 is left-hand-drive only. The quality of the air conditioning has been praised.*

BELOW: *The 110 is a very stable car, aided by the presence of low skirts and four-wheel-drive.*

McLaren F1 (1993 to date)

It comes as no surprise to find that the world's fastest production car, which is capable of nearly 240mph (386km/h), has more in common with a Formula 1 racer than a road car. The bodywork incorporates the twin attributes of race-bred carbon fibre technology and ground effect, with Grand Prix associations further underpinned by the fact that this car is a McLaren.

However, the appropriately named F1 has been specifically designed for the road, not the race track, and is unquestionably the most technologically sophisticated supercar ever built. To

Specifications: McLaren F1

Length:	14ft (4288mm)
Width:	5ft 11in (1820mm)
Height:	3ft 8in (1140mm)
Wheelbase:	8ft 11in (2718mm)
Track:	front, 5ft 1in (1568mm); rear, 4ft 9in (1472mm)
Unladen weight:	2244lb (1018kg)
Engine: V12, twin overhead camshafts per bank, 86×86mm, 6064cc. Compression ratio, 10.5:1. Max power, 550bhp plus at 7000rpm. Max torque, 442lb/ft at 4000rpm.	
Transmission:	Six-speed manual
Drive:	Rear
Suspension (front):	Independent, coil springs and wishbones
Suspension (rear):	Independent, coil springs and wishbones
Top speed:	c.240mph (386km/h)
0-60mph (96km/h):	3.9 seconds
Production:	300 total projected.

its creator, the quietly spoken, South African-born racing car designer, Gordon Murray, it is, quite simply, "the ultimate road car".

Murray, who arrived in the United Kingdom in 1969, had designed 34 racing cars with 41 Grand Prix victories to their credit when he left Brabham and joined McLaren late in 1987. The year after he arrived at the Woking-based company, McLaren won the Formula 1 Constructor's Championship and would repeat the feat for the following three years until its run of triumphs was successfully challenged, in 1992, by Williams.

It was against this upbeat background that in 1988 Murray, who had been nurturing his supercar idea since the 1960's, took the concept to McLaren's chief, Ron Dennis, who was, in due course, won over. The out-

come was the creation, on 17th March 1989, of McLaren Cars Ltd, formed to turn Murray's dream into a reality.

The car was to be created in a separate manufacturing facility to the Formula 1 cars and, while Murray was to be technical supremo, there was the all important matter of styling to be re-

solved. McLaren was fortunate to recruit as head of styling Peter Stevens who already had the lines of the 1989 Lotus Elan and Jaguar XJR-15 supercar to his credit.

Work on the project began in earnest in March 1990. The design was completed in a breathtaking 11 months and

ABOVE: *The F1's sensational lines, by Peter Stevens, are a marvel of packaging. Like many supercars, the magnesium wheels are wider at the rear than the front.*

RIGHT: *Scissor doors ease entry, which is best from the left, otherwise the gearlever intrudes.*

BELOW: *The F1's occupants are protected by a safety cell. The body structure is made from 94 parts.*

ABOVE: *Looking down on the F1, a view which, in particular, reveals the car's forward driving position. The McLaren is available in a choice of eight body colours.*

approved by the board of the TAG McLaren Group in June 1991. Trials immediately started on a mobile testbed, christened Albert, because McLaren Cars is based in Albert Drive of Woking's Genesis Business Park.

The F1 was officially, and appropriately, unveiled in the opulent atmosphere of the Sporting Club at Monaco, on 28th May 1992, on the eve of the Principality's Grand Prix. There it was announced that the McLaren would cost an eyebrow-raising £530,000. No less than 10 people handed over deposits of £106,000 apiece. Just 300 cars would be built.

So what are the mouth-watering specifications of the F1? All of its major components have been purpose-designed from scratch. The dramatic looking coupé body is functional, futuristic and made from light but immensely strong carbon fibre which is used extensively in racing cars. Little attempt has been made to make the car look fashionable. It is squat, stubby, above all, aerodynamically efficient, and a triumph of packaging. The two doors hinge, distinctively, forwards and upwards.

The handling of the F1 has been designed to benefit from ground effect

which creates downforce between the car and the road surface. In addition there are two fans designed to remove undesirable "boundary air" before it hits the defuser section at the rear of the car which, at high speed, would otherwise be tail light. The arrangement has some echoes of a system which Murray briefly used in his Brabham BT46 Formula 1 car of 1978.

The heart of the F1 is a central monocoque, a composite made up of 94 pieces of Dyneema carbon fibre, aluminium and Nomex honeycomb structures which is baked in McLaren's own massive vacuum oven. This hull makes an immeasurable contribution to the fact that the F1 has the highest power-to-weight ratio of any car yet built. Tipping the scales at 2244lb (1018kg) which is just 4lb (1.8kg) over a ton, the coupé's purpose-built BMW 6.1 litre V12 engine develops in excess of 550bhp.

BMW's New V12

This longitudinally mounted S70/2 aluminium unit, created by BMW Motorsport exclusively for the F1, bears no relation to that company's current V12 road car engines and will never power a BMW. Each six cylinder bank possesses its own twin chain-driven overhead camshafts that actuate four valves per cylinder, each of which is fired by its own transistorized coil. The V12 employs in-house TAG fuel injection and engine management systems.

Murray has eschewed weighty four-wheel-drive, and power is only applied to the back wheels via a rear-mounted six-speed gearbox. The first five are close ratio cogs for speeds up to 160mph (257km/h) while top is for 200mph (321km/h) plus motoring . . .

The handsome five-spoke OZ magnesium wheels are shod with specially developed Goodyear treads and, as they are asymmetric and unidirectional and front and rear tyres are differently sized, this precludes the use of a spare wheel. The F1 carries a puncture sealant cannister instead.

All-round disc brakes are arrested by racing-type four-piston calipers. At the rear they are cooled via small flaps on the trailing edges of the rear bodywork which also play an important role in the car's sophisticated underbody aerodynamics.

Innovation permeates the F1's fine, air-conditioned interior. It is, unexpectedly, a *three*-seater with the driver sitting centrally forward of the passengers who are positioned on either side. The seats are upholstered in black Connolly leather although the driver's is finished in a vivid red. The engine is started by its occupant raising a small flap on the dashboard and pressing (what else) but a large red button.

Should the unlucky F1 driver have the misfortune to break down in this McLaren F1, he or she would be well advised to ensure that it occurs near to a telephone. This is because the car has a pair of onboard computers which can communicate with McLaren's own database, via a modem. The system will, accordingly, work from anywhere in the world.

The first F1 was completed late in 1993 and delivered early in 1994. With manufacture now under way, for once Jaguar XJ220, Bugatti EB110 and Lamborghini Diablo owners will have to beware!

LEFT: The F1's unique seating arrangement with the driver sitting well forward in the middle and passengers on either side. The revolution counter reads to 8000rpm with a warning at 7500rpm while the speedometer stops at 240mph (386km/h). Air conditioning is fitted.

BELOW: The F1 with its doors raised. During the build process, they are some of the last components to be added. It takes a formidable 3000 or so hours to make the F1's complex body structure and car assembly a projected 750. Note the distinctive forward-mounted driving seat.

LEFT: *Not only is the McLaren F1 the world's fastest road car, at £540,000 it is also the most expensive. But then its performance is nearly on a par with that of a genuine Formula 1 racing car. Production of this supercar began in earnest in 1994, the first example having been completed on Christmas Eve 1993.*

BELOW: *Efficient brakes are an essential ingredient of the F1. They are the work of the Italian Brembo company. The four-piston caliper is a one-piece alloy unit.*

ABOVE: *The longitudinally mounted 6.1 litre BMW dry sump engine is purpose-designed and unique to the F1. Drive is conveyed, via a six-speed gearbox, to the rear wheels only.*

LEFT: *The cambox says McLaren while the BMW name also appears but is here obscured. There are twin overhead camshafts per bank, four valves per cylinder and variable inlet valve timing.*

SALOONS

Since the 1920's there have been more saloons built than any other automobile body style. This still applies today even though the shape of the motor car and the layout of its mechanical components have changed radically in recent years. Up until the 1970's most saloons perpetuated the "three box" look of the family car with a rear-located boot. Although this trend continues, it tends now to be more confined to the exclusive specialist sector.

Nowadays the mass market is dominated by the "two box" approach or what we know as the hatchback, with its functional opening tailgate, which was a theme pioneered back in 1965 by Renault's R16. Also, under the bonnet, most engines are now transversely located which permits more passenger space and indicates that the majority of popular cars are pulled along by their front wheels.

In view of these changes in the saloon's specification, it may come as some surprise to find that the best selling car in the history of the automobile does not conform to either of these parameters. Perversely, the Volkswagen Beetle is driven by its back wheels and powered by a rear-mounted, air- (as opposed to water-) cooled, four cylinder, horizontally opposed engine. This reflects a design that was finalized in 1938 and, to date, over 21 million examples of this automotive phenomenon have been built.

Having said that, some manufacturers have followed VW's philosophy, namely Fiat with its diminutive 500 of 1957 and, across the Atlantic, General Motors surprisingly opted for the rear-engined, air-

cooled approach with its Chevrolet Corvair. But today both firms are firmly wedded to the concept of the front-wheel-drive.

So what models have brought about this revolution? The pioneer of the layout is Citroën which, in 1934, introduced its legendary Traction Avant model that was built until 1957. Not only was it driven by its front wheels but it featured a host of other revolutionary features, all of which combined to make it the world's first truly modern saloon. Citroën pursued this theme with its utilitarian 2CV of 1948 and the DS model of 1955-75 vintage but it was the Traction Avant which fired the interest in front-wheel-drive technology of the British Motor Corporation's Alec Issigonis.

Already the creator of the much loved Morris Minor, in 1959, BMC unveiled his front-wheel-drive Mini with its revolutionary transversely located engine. Since then, the rest of the world has gradually decided to follow the Issigonis approach but it was nearly 20 years before the idea truly caught on amongst the industry's Big Battalions.

One of those which remained faithful to the traditional in-line front engine/rear drive configuration was Ford with its Cortina of 1962. This was destined to be the fastest selling car in the British industry's history. There were also a number of specialist manufacturers of more expensive, larger capacity saloons which, for technical reasons, do not lend themselves to front-wheel-drive and they continue to produce highly successful rear-driven cars.

In Britain this description has always applied to Rolls-Royce, the makers of "The Best Car in the World". After many years of building its automobiles

at a loss, in 1965 Rolls-Royce introduced the Silver Shadow which was profitable. Similarly, there has never been a front-wheel-drive Jaguar. Its best selling Mark II saloon of the 1960's combined the usual Jaguar formula of looks and performance and this, in turn, paved the way for the superlative XJ6 models, a design that attained levels of refinement and comfort that bore comparison with those of Rolls-Royce itself.

From the early 1960's onwards, Jaguar received an unexpected challenge in the shape of the products of a revitalized BMW company that, after a decade of vacillation, introduced its 1500, a car on which its present day reputation for excellence is built. Not only could BMW be regarded as challenging Jaguar but also Mercedes-Benz. The latter company achieved great success with its medium-sized 190 model, although its hugely impressive but complex S-Class cars of the 1990's have been less successful in a chilly economic climate of recent times.

This area of the market has also, in recent years, been challenged by the Japanese, with Toyota's highly praised Lexus marque making significant inroads both in America and Europe. Further Japanese influence is to be found in Rover's Honda-based 600 model, while in France the success of Renault's wacky Twingo has been a triumph of the unconventional over the norm. Sadly, there will be no right-hand-drive version of this characterful car.

The opposite is true of Ford's award-winning Mondeo of 1993 which is to be built in both Europe and America. It is Ford's first world car since the demise, in 1927, of the Model T, a car that truly put the world on wheels.

CITROËN TRACTION AVANT (1934-1957)

The world's first significant front-wheel-drive car was introduced in 1934, but so advanced was the concept of the Traction Avant Citroën that it survived for no less than 23 years. As such, the model was in production for longer after the war than before it, and the rest of the motoring community has now followed in its sure-footed drive tracks.

Work on the design, which bore no relation to any previous Citroën model, began in 1933. Unlike practically all its contemporaries, which possessed separate chassis frames, the new model had a unitary hull, much like today's cars. At its heart was a front-wheel-drive prototype saloon developed by the American Budd Corporation with which Citroën already had associations. Styling was undertaken in-house and was the work of Flaminio Bertoni, whose elegant four door saloon was enhanced by the presence of a handsome sloping radiator. The use of front-wheel-drive ensured that the car was lower than its rear-driven competitors because there was no propeller shaft tunnel to intrude into the rear passenger compartment.

Under the bonnet was an advanced four cylinder power unit employing, unusually for a mass-produced European car, overhead valves, while the pistons ran in detachable wet cylinder liners. Drive was via a three-speed gearbox, hastily designed in a matter of weeks when a revolutionary type of automatic transmission proved ineffective.

The suspension was similarly advanced with wishbones at the front and Porsche-patented, longitudinally located torsion bars which were similarly though transversely applied to the dead rear axle. Progressively, hydraulic brakes were fitted.

The new model was announced in April 1934 and later displayed at that year's Paris Motor Show. As introduced, the car was available in 7A (which only survived for one year) and B forms having engine capacities of 1303 and 1529cc respectively, and it was also listed in two-door open and closed forms. There was a more powerful 1.9 litre version, designated the 7S. Later, for 1935, this was renamed the Legère 11 (Light 11). The same year came the 7C which represented a combination of A and S themes and this 1.6 litre model replaced the 7B. With the car's front wheels pulling it along, the Traction's roadholding was outstanding. The low capacity models could attain 65mph (105km/h), while the larger engined versions were about 10mph (16km/h) faster.

So here, unquestionably, was the world's most advanced saloon, but for André Citroën the car represented a personal tragedy because his financially unstable company was overextended by the cost of developing such a radically new model. The banks foreclosed on him and in 1935 he was forced to sell out to Michelin, his wheel and tyre supplier and largest creditor. A broken hearted Citroën, by then suffering from cancer, died later in the year, aged only 57.

Meanwhile the Traction Avant continued to sell strongly. In 1938 came a six cylinder version of the design. The 15-6G was powered by a 2.8 litre engine related to that of the 11, and was capable of speeds approaching 80mph (129km/h), so combining looks with performance.

The Traction Avant was not only built in France but also by Citroën factories at Forest, Belgium and Slough in Britain. Production at all these centres was interrupted by World War II. Manufacture restarted in 1945 but the cars were only available in black until 1954. Output was concentrated on the 11 and 15 models. In the same year of 1954 the six was renamed the 15-6H, the suffix standing for *hydropneumatique*, which reflected the fitment of pressurized independent rear suspension that was to appear in a more extended form in Citroën's front-wheel-drive DS19 saloon of 1955.

The Traction Avant remained in production until 1957 with the last car being built on 18th July. Twenty three years on, the car had achieved everything expected of it, but it was a success which André Citroën, alas, never lived to see.

BELOW: *The Traction Avant was also produced in cabriolet form but it did not survive the war. This is a 1.9 litre 11CV, 15hp in Britain, with Michelin Pilote wheels.*

Length:	14ft (4267mm)
Width:	5ft 5in (1651mm)
Height:	4ft 11in (1499mm)
Wheelbase:	9ft 6in (2896mm)
Track:	4ft 4¾in (1340mm), rear 4ft 4¼in (1327mm)
Unladen weight:	2465lb (1118kg)
Engine: Four cylinder, overhead valve, 78x100mm, 1911cc. Compression ratio, 6.5:1. Max power, 55 bhp at 4250rpm. Max torque, 90lb/ft at 2200rpm	
Transmission:	Three-speed manual
Drive:	Front
Suspension (front):	Independent, torsion bars and wishbones
Suspension (rear):	Dead axle, trailing arms and torsion bars
Top speed:	75mph (121km/h)
0-60mph (96km/h):	22.1 seconds
Production (total):	759,123

LEFT: *A British-registered 1938 11CV cabriolet with its hood raised. This and the right-hand-drive car shown on the opposite page were assembled at Citroën's Slough factory.*

BELOW: *A 1956 left-hand-drive 11CV finished in traditional Citroën black, and still looking very much as it did in 1934. Bonnet louvres arrived in 1946.*

Citroën Traction Avant

Traction Avant 1934

1.3 litres 1.6 litres 1.9 litres

to 1934

2.8 litre 15-6G 1938

to 1940

to 1941 to 1941

1945 1945

to 1946

15-6D 1947

15-6H 1954

to 1957 to 1955

- - - - - out of production

VOLKSWAGEN BEETLE (1945 to date)

The most popular car in the history of the automobile is the Volkswagen Beetle and, to date, over 21 million have been built. Today this car, with its rear-mounted, air-cooled engine, that looks and sounds like no other, is still in production in Mexico having, incredibly, been designed back in 1938. The idea of a German "People's Car" is in fact even older than this; it originated with Adolf Hitler who, in 1933, became chancellor.

Soon after his election, Hitler commissioned the respected Austrian engineer, Ferdinand Porsche, to design a car which had to have a selling price of under RM1000, that at the time was the equivalent of £86. Hitler specified cheap air cooling and for similar cost considerations, the resulting car had a rear-mounted, horizontally opposed, 985cc, four cylinder engine. Suspension was all-independent by Porsche's own torsion bars and the distinctive two-door saloon body was wind tunnel tested to improve its aerodynamics.

The car was to be manufactured at a state-funded, purpose-built factory close to the village of Fallersleben, near Hanover, and the first stage of the plant was completed by 1939. It was intended to mass produce from 1940 what the Nazis called the *Kdf-Wagen*, an abbreviation for *Kraft durch Freude Wagen* (Strength through Joy car), but by this time Germany had invaded Poland. World War II began, but nevertheless limited manufacture of the car started in 1941. A mere 630 examples were built during hostilities, which was when the engine's capacity was enlarged to 1131cc.

Production Gets Going

After the war the factory fell within the British military sector and, under the auspices of the Royal Electrical and Mechanical Engineers, production restarted, the car having been renamed the Volkswagen and its manufacturing location became Wolfsburg. However, in 1948, a German manager, Heinz Nordhoff, was appointed and the Volkswagen company reverted to state ownership. Nordhoff decided on a one model policy and opted to retain the car's unusual appearance but he also embarked on a policy to refine and constantly improve the product. In 1949 came a better equipped Export model, an early example of which was shipped to America and, after a hesitant start, the Beetle attained great popularity there with sales peaking in 1968. The Export car of 1949 was joined by two cabriolet (open) versions of the design, a two- and four-seater, built by Hebmüller and Karmann respectively, although the former model only lasted until 1953.

In its original 1131cc form, the Beetle was capable of a mere 56mph (90km/h) but, as build quality improved, so did performance and, by the early 1950's, the car was capable of well over 60mph (96km/h). In 1954 engine capacity was upped to 1192cc but this had little effect on acceleration and it was not until 1961 that the flat four unit was extensively redesigned. This resulted in a 13 per cent increase in power even though the 1192cc capacity was retained. However, top speed went up to 72mph (116km/h). It is this 1200 Beetle that is still being built in Mexico.

The 1966 model year saw the introduction of a supplementary 1300 version and for 1967 came yet another, the 1500, which was notably faster than its predecessors and capable of 80mph (129km/h). This was replaced in 1970 by the 1302 which represented the first departure from the pre-war Porsche design. In a bid to counter criticism of the small front boot, the transverse torsion bars were replaced by MacPherson struts and semi-trailing arms were introduced at the rear. Engine size was upped once again, to 1584cc. For 1973 the concept was refined in 1303 form with similar mechanicals but a new curved windscreen and shorter bonnet, although this model was only built until 1975.

A World-Beater

Demand for the car was, nevertheless, phenomenal. The first million Beetle year was 1965 when Germany produced 1,008,983 cars and it repeated the feat in 1968, 1969 when output peaked, 1970 and 1971. In 1972 the car's total production figure exceeded the 15 million mark, so beating the

RIGHT: *A 1200 Beetle dating from 1976. Such right-hand-drive examples for the British market were built in Germany and also assembled at VW's Belgium factory.*

Specifications: Volkswagen Beetle 1200

Length:	13ft 4in (4064mm)
Width:	5ft 1in (1549mm)
Height:	4ft 11in (1499mm)
Wheelbase:	7ft 10½in (2400mm)
Track:	front and rear, 4ft 2⅛in (1290mm)
Unladen weight:	1645lb (746kg)

Engine: Rear mounted, horizontally opposed, air cooled, four cylinder, overhead valve, 77x64mm, 1992cc. Compression ratio, 7:1. Max power, 34bhp at 3900rpm. Max torque, 61lb/ft at 2000rpm.

Transmission:	Four-speed manual
Drive:	Rear
Suspension (front):	Independent, torsion bar with trailing arms
Suspension (rear):	Independent, swing axle, radius arms and torsion bars
Top speed:	72mph (116km/h)
0-60mph (96km/h):	32.1 seconds
Production (total):	21.2 million

Model T Ford's 45 year old record. Although Ford subsequently "found" a further 1.6 million Ts, Volkswagen overhauled that figure in 1973. But demand fell thereafter, and in the following year the impossible happened when, for the first time in its history, Volkswagen declared a loss. Thankfully that year saw the arrival of the Golf which proved to be the Beetle's true successor and, as it moved centre stage, Beetle output fell still further. German saloon production ceased in 1978, to be followed in 1980 by the end of production of the Karmann-made cabriolet.

However, the car was still being built by VW subsidiaries around the world, with Brazil as the largest facility outside Germany. It had started production in 1953 but this ceased in 1986, which left Mexico, opened in 1964, as the sole manufacturer of the car. Its Pueblo plant built the 20 millionth Beetle in 1981 and today demand shows no signs of abating. This automotive phenomenon has already been in production for longer than any other car, and is still instantly recognizable as the model which was unveiled in 1938, an incredible 56 years ago.

Volkswagen Beetle

985cc VW38 pre-production
saloon 1938
|
Productions begins 1941
|
1131cc engine 1943
|
Cabriolet
|
Two-seater   Four-seater
Hebmüller   Karmann
|
to 1953
|
1192cc engine 1954
|
1.3 litre 1300 1966
|
1.5 litre 1500 1967
|
1.6 litre 1302 1970
|
1.6 litre 1303 1973
|
to 1975
|
German saloon production
ends 1978
                          to 1980
|
20 millionth Beetle built
in Mexico 1981
|
to date

BELOW: *The Beetle's rear window was divided until 1953 when the central rib was deleted to improve visibility. These pre '53 cars are thus favoured by collectors.*

ABOVE: *A 1956 model year, left-hand-drive, British registered 1200 Beetle. The small oval rear window was retained until the 1958 season when it was enlarged.*

MORRIS MINOR (1948-1971)

Britain's best loved post-war car and the first in its industry to exceed one million units, the Minor was essentially the creation of one man, Alec Issigonis, who later gave the world the Mini. The most advanced small car of its day, regrettably Morris Motors failed to see its potential as a world beater, and that accolade passed to Volkswagen's Beetle.

Alec Issigonis began work on the Minor during World War II and the famous lines first existed as a scale model created in 1942. The original intention was to use a horizontally opposed, water-cooled, four cylinder engine to power what was coded Mosquito, but it was eventually designed to use the 918cc side valve four from the pre-war Morris Eight. Also, at a late stage in the model's pre-production life, Issigonis decided that the car needed to be wider, so a prototype was cut in half to gauge the new width which was 4in (102mm) greater than hitherto.

An Immediate Success

Morris introduced the Minor at the 1948 Motor Show and it soon became the firm's best selling model, with not only its distinctive appearance but its impressive roadholding attracting universal praise. The car was capable of 60mph (96km/h) and Issigonis had specified 14in (356mm) diameter wheels which were then much smaller than the norm. Torsion bars were used for the front suspension in conjunction with rack-and-pinion steering. The car was originally built in two-door saloon form but this was joined by a four-door version in 1951. A tourer model was also available from the outset.

In 1952 Morris merged with Austin to form the British Motor Corporation and that year the four-door Minor was fitted with Austin's superior 803cc overhead valve engine. The unit was subsequently extended to the two-door saloon and tourer in 1953.

The 1954 season saw the arrival of yet another body style in the form of the Traveller estate car with a distinctive composite wood-framed and metal body. The Minor remained outwardly unchanged until 1957 when the original divided windscreen was replaced by a new single piece curved one. The model also benefitted from an enlarged 948cc engine in the same year, which pushed the top speed up to 70mph (113km/h). It was accordingly named the Morris 1000.

A landmark for the Minor came in December 1960 when the millionth

example was built, which also took account of a van version that had appeared in 1953. A batch of 349 commemorative saloons, finished in a rather alarming shade of lilac and bearing the *Morris 1000000* legend, were built.

For 1963 the model was once again re-engined with a 1098cc version of the faithful four, which was destined to be the last capacity increase. The Minor continued to be built in this form until the end which came for the Tourer in 1969, and the last saloons followed in 1970. However, Traveller manufacture lingered on until 1971. By this time a total of 1.2 million Morris Minor cars had been produced.

Despite its demise, the Minor's mechanical layout was incorporated in the Marina saloon of 1971 which was destined to be the last Morris and that endured until 1984.

ABOVE: *A 1949 Morris Minor Series MM. The headlamps were repositioned in the wings from the 1951 season, although the divided windscreen survived until 1956.*

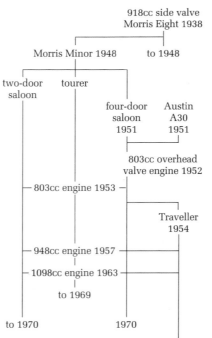

Morris Minor

```
                        918cc side valve
                        Morris Eight 1938
                    ┌───────────────┴──────────┐
            Morris Minor 1948              to 1948
        ┌─────────────┐
    two-door      tourer
    saloon                    ┌──────────┬──────────┐
                          four-door    Austin
                          saloon        A30
                          1951          1951
                              └──────────┴──────────┐
                                    803cc overhead
                                    valve engine 1952
    ├── 803cc engine 1953 ──┤
                                              Traveller
                                              1954
    ├── 948cc engine 1957 ──┤
    ├── 1098cc engine 1963 ─┤
         to 1969
    to 1970              1970
                              to 1971
```

Specifications: Morris Minor Series MM

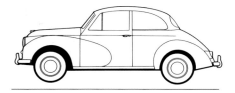

Length:	12ft 4in (3759mm)
Width:	5ft 1in (1549mm)
Height:	5ft (1524mm)
Wheelbase:	7ft 2in (2184mm)
Track:	front and rear, 4ft 2in (1270mm)
Unladen weight:	1680lb (762kg)
Engine: Four cylinder, side valve, 57x90mm, 918cc. Compression ratio, 6.6:1. Max power, 27.5bhp at 4400rpm. Max torque, 39lb/ft at 2400rpm	
Transmission:	Four-speed manual
Drive:	Rear
Suspension (front):	Independent, torsion bars and wishbones
Suspension (rear):	Live axle, half-elliptic springs
Top speed:	60mph (96km/h)
0-50mph (80km/h):	36.8 seconds
Production (total):	1,293,331

ABOVE: *The Minor Traveller estate car, with its distinctive wood-framed body, was produced from 1954 until 1971, which was a year after the saloon's demise.*

BELOW: *A 1967 Minor 1000 tourer, still with provision for a starting handle, which had been part of the model line since the car's arrival in 1948. It endured until 1969.*

CITROËN 2CV (1948-1990)

The distinctive and utilitarian front-wheel-drive 2CV enjoyed an impressive 42-year production life, and it comes as no surprise to find that its design dates back to the pre-war years. After a protracted gestation, which was interrupted by World War II, the car finally appeared in 1948 and has since become a Gallic, not to mention an international, institution. With over five million examples manufactured, the 2CV is, numerically, the most successful Citroën ever built.

Work on the project began in 1936 when Pierre Boulanger, Citroën's managing director, approached chief engineer, Maurice Bogly, with a brief for him to design "an umbrella on four wheels". This was a reflection of the fact that Boulanger wanted a cheap car aimed at members of the rural community who would previously have never aspired to car ownership.

Because of its intended market, he specified that the car should be capable of carrying two French peasants in their working clothes, along with 110lb (50kg) of potatoes, and have a top speed of 37.3mph (60km/h). But, above all, it should be able to cope with the rough roads of rural France. Boulanger argued that if a carton of eggs was placed on the rear seat, and the Citroën was then driven over a ploughed field, not one egg should be broken!

The project was designated the TPV, for *très petite voiture* (very small car). Like the company's legendary Traction Avant model, it espoused front-wheel-

drive and much the same design team was responsible for its creation. The first prototype was on the road in 1937 with production destined to start in 1939. In its original form, the TPV was powered by a water-cooled, 375cc, two cylinder, horizontally opposed, overhead valve engine but the car was never produced in this form because of the outbreak of World War II.

Nevertheless, work on the project continued during hostilities, with the most significant modification being made to the chassis. It was to have been made from aluminium, but this was replaced by steel. Another crucial change was applied to the engine,

which was converted to air cooling, although its 350cc capacity and two cylinder configuration was retained.

The 2CV or Deux Chevaux (two horsepower) was finally introduced at the 1948 Paris Motor Show. Its cost-conscious, four-door body lines made no concessions to fashion. The roll-back canvas roof had been a feature of the design from the outset. The ingenious interconnected all-independent suspension system featured front leading and rear trailing arms. Inevitably performance was pedestrian, with the car having a top speed of only 40mph (64km/h) but this was offset by a fuel consumption figure of 55mpg (19litres/100km). The model could carry a family of four and was exactly the type of vehicle to appeal to a Europe which was being rebuilt after six years of conflict.

A Bigger Engine

The 2CV was produced in its original form until 1954 when the engine capacity was increased to 425cc, which ensured that it was capable of over 50mph (80km/h). Demand for the model remained high and, in 1957, annual production exceeded the 100,000 mark for the first time in the car's history.

In 1961 came the first variation on the theme in the shape of the bodily updated and better equipped Ami with a 602cc twin. This was built until 1978. Then, in 1967, came the Dyane which used the 2CV chassis and engine, and had a more closely related body. It was viewed at the time as the successor to the 2CV but it ceased production in 1982. Despite the appearance of these outwardly more modern derivatives, demand for the basic 2CV remained constant. For 1971 the engine was enlarged to 435cc and the 602cc unit became available at the same time.

The model was particularly popular between 1973 and 1979 when the world was reeling from a rise in petrol prices and the public returned to more economy conscious models.

However, from 1980 onwards the 2CV went into a slow decline and it was unable to conform with impending European safety and emissions regulations. The car was still being made at Citroën's Paris factory at this time, but when it was decided to rebuild the ageing plant, 2CV production was transferred to Mangualde, Portugal. Its manufacture was destined to survive for a further two years. The last 2CV was built in July 1990 by which time the car had made friends all over the world, the vast majority of whom were not French peasants!

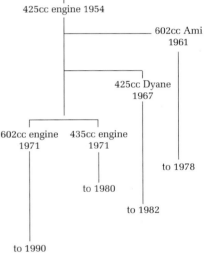

Citroën 2CV

```
375cc 2CV 1948
      |
425cc engine 1954
      |                          602cc Ami
      |                               1961
      |                                |
      |              425cc Dyane
      |                   1967
      |                    |
602cc engine   435cc engine
     1971          1971
      |             |                 to 1978
      |          to 1980
      |                    
      |             to 1982
   to 1990
```

LEFT: *This 2CV dates from 1990 which was the final year of production. The 602cc Dolly special appeared in 1985 and was available in a choice of "dolly mixture" colours.*

ABOVE: *Left, a 1956 right-hand-drive, Slough-assembled 2CV distinguished by a bonnet motif, semaphore indicators, split side windows, chromed hub caps and a steel boot lid (from 1953) which did not reach French cars until the 1958 season. Right, a traditional grey 1953 French 2CV. The badge's oval surround disappeared on the 1955 models.*

Specifications: Citroën 2CV Type A

Length:	12ft 6¾in (3829mm)
Width:	4ft 10in (1473mm)
Height:	5ft 3in (1600mm)
Wheelbase:	7ft 10½in (2400mm)
Track:	front and rear, 4ft 1½in (1257mm)
Unladen weight:	1120lb (508kg)
Engine: Air cooled, horizontally opposed, two cylinder, overhead valve, 62x62mm, 375cc. Compression ratio, 6.2:1. Max power, 9bhp at 3500rpm. Max torque, 17lb/ft at 3500rpm.	
Transmission:	Four-speed manual
Drive:	Front
Suspension (front): Independent, leading arms interconnected with central coil springs	
Suspension (rear):	Independent, trailing arms
Top speed:	40mph (64km/h)
0-40mph (64km/h):	42.6 seconds
Production (total):	5,114,966

There can be little doubt that the dominating American stylistic feature of the 1950's was the tail fin, which memorably made its first appearance in 1948 on General Motors' prestigious Cadillac marque. Destined for a brief but spectacular life, the fin was soon extended to other corporate products and was also taken up by rivals. Ten years on, it had grown to such absurd proportions that as a concept it was played out and, by the 1960's, had all but disappeared.

It was Harley Earl, General Motors' styling supremo, who had overall responsibility for the tail fin. The seeds of the idea were sown back in 1939 at the Detroit Army Airfield, where Earl and his staff were taken to see the still secret Lockheed P-38 Lightning high altitude interceptor aircraft with its distinctive twin tail booms. The 'plane triggered a crop of aeronautical themes in the GM studios and a number of experimental scale models, which incorporated such features as propeller boss-like front ends, wrap-around windscreens and aircraft-style cockpits, as well as tail fins, were completed.

A Fashion For Fins

Although, America's involvement in World War II put paid to private car production, a skeleton staff continued to develop these ideas and, after hostilities ceased, Earl wasted little time in reactivating the P-38-inspired designs. The most enduring of these was the tail fin which, he believed, would imbue the rear of the car with a sense of purpose that it had previously lacked. Having decided to apply the fin to one of General Motors' products, it was Cadillac, as the corporate flagship, which was the chosen vehicle for the innovation.

The 1948 model year Cadillacs, which had not changed outwardly since 1941, were therefore the first recipients of a stylistic update. As followed established marque precedent, the range was broken down in a number of Series which that year consisted of four model lines. These were, in price order, the Series 61, 62, 60 Special and 75. All were fitted with the new bodies, with the exception of the Series 75 Fleetwood range which perpetuated its pre-war lines.

Of these variations, the 61 and 62 shared the same 10ft 6in (3200mm) wheelbase. Both were produced in what was described as club coupé and four-door sedan forms. The 62 version was that year's best-selling Cadillac, and that series was completed by the

option of a convertible coupé body. The saloon could also be specified in 11ft 1in (3378mm) Series 60 Special guise.

Cadillac's new short stroke, overhead valve V8 would not appear until the 1949 model year, so the '48 line had to rely on the existing 150bhp, side valve, 346cid (5.7 litres) V8 which dated back in concept to 1936. There was four-speed Hydramatic automatic transmission and the option of a three-speed manual gearbox. Suspension was little changed from the pre-war cars with the established "knee action" system at the front, and a semi-elliptic sprung live axle.

These well-equipped, commodious cars could be wound up to around 95mph (154km/h) and demand was brisk. In 1948 the division built 52,706 cars; by 1950 this figure had doubled, an achievement which heralded a new era of growth for Cadillac. But it was the tail fin which, in the short term, really caught the public's imagination. Ironically these '48 examples were modest, almost understated offerings, but by then the genie was out of the bottle . . .

Specifications: Cadillac Series 62

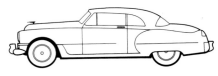

Length:	17ft 11in (5461mm)
Width:	6ft 7in (2006mm)
Height:	5ft 3in (1600mm)
Wheelbase:	10ft 6in (3200mm)
Track:	front 4ft 11in (1499mm), rear 5ft 3in (1600mm)
Unladen weight:	4100lb (1860kg)
Engine: Side valve 3.5x4.5in, 346cid (5669cc) V8. Compression ratio, 7.25:1. Max power, 150bhp at 3600rpm. Max torque, 275lb/ft at 1600rpm	
Transmission:	Four-speed automatic or three-speed manual
Drive:	Rear
Suspension (front):	Independent, coil springs and wishbones
Suspension (rear):	Live axle and half-elliptic springs
Top speed:	95mph (153km/h)
0-60mph (96km/h):	14 seconds
Production (60, 61, 62):	49,374

ABOVE: *A 1949 Series 62 convertible which accounted for no less than 8000 cars in that year. By contrast, the best-selling four-door saloon found nearly 38,000 buyers.*

RIGHT: *A Series 62 Coupe de Ville hardtop coupé, which was a new body style for 1949. This was, in fact, the rarest of the Series with just 2150 examples produced. That year Cadillac's long-running side valve V8 was replaced by a new 331cid (5.4 litres) overhead valve unit, which was built in that form until 1956. The all-important characteristic rear fins first appeared in 1948.*

1948 Cadillac Series 60, 61, 62

346 cid V8, 126in (3200mm)
wheelbase 1941

Series 61	Series 62	Series 63	Series 60 Special
to 1942	to 1942	discontinued 1942	133in (3378mm) wheelbase 1942
production restarted			
	1946		1946

General Motors' first post-war restyle 1948

to 1949 ——————— 331cid ohv V8 ——————— to 1949

to 1953

– – – – out of production

Jaguar Marks VII, VIII, IX (1950-1961)

Jaguar's famous twin-overhead-camshaft, 3.4 litre engine first appeared in the XK120 sports car of 1948, although it had originally been designed to power the company's big, thirsty Mark VII saloon which found popularity in America. Later for 1957 came the more powerful Mark VIII, while the ultimate version was the 1959 Mark IX with a 3.8 litre engine, all-round disc brakes and power steering.

Although Jaguar is always remembered for its sensational sports cars, the reality is that it has always, first and foremost, been a manufacturer of saloon cars. Before the war, what was then SS Cars relied on Standard-based engines. These were carried over from 1945 and employed in the firm's stop gap Mark V saloon of 1948. However, its Mark VII successor of 1950 (VI was skipped because of Bentley's saloon of the same name), was powered by Jaguar's new twin-cam six.

Big And Powerful

The Mark VII Jaguar was a large car, comfortably capable of carrying five to six people and weighing a substantial 3864lb (1752kg), which reflected its retention of a separate chassis carried over from the Mark V. The 160bhp six ensured that the Mark VII could attain 100mph (161km/h), even though this was at the expense of a 17mpg (16 litres/100km) fuel consumption, although this was less of a problem on the other side of the Atlantic which was where the majority of cars were sold. However, this figure was improved by the fitment of overdrive, which was available on the Mark VII from 1954. A further option was two-speed automatic transmission which was listed from 1953.

Extending The Range

For 1955 the model was updated with the arrival of the Mark VIIM, which was outwardly similar to its predecessor although engine output was boosted to 190bhp by the use of high lift camshafts. This was destined for a two-year production life. Then, in 1957, came the more refined Mark VIII, identifiable by its single piece curved windscreen which replaced the earlier divided one. Engine power was once again increased, this time to 210bhp, which pushed the top speed to around 105mph (169km/h). The Mark VIII remained available until late 1958 which was when the Mark IX appeared.

This was by far and away the best model of a by-then ageing range. It was

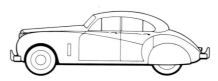

Length:	16ft 4in (4978mm)
Width:	6ft 1in (1854mm)
Height:	5ft 3in (1600mm)
Wheelbase:	10ft (3048mm)
Track:	front 4ft 8in (1422mm), rear 4ft 9in (1448mm)
Unladen weight:	3808lb (1727kg)

Engine: Six cylinder, twin overhead camshafts, 83x106mm, 3442cc. Compression ratio, 8:1. Max power, 160bhp at 5200rpm. Max torque, 195lb/ft at 2500rpm.

Transmission:	Four-speed manual
Drive:	Rear
Suspension (front):	Independent, torsion bars and wishbones
Suspension (rear):	Live axle, half-elliptic springs
Top speed:	100mph (161km/h)
0-60mph (96km/h):	13.8 seconds
Production (Mark VII, VIII and IX):	47,190

powered by a race-proven 220bhp, 3.8 litre engine, the Mark IX being the first Jaguar saloon to employ this enlarged unit. Another welcome fitment was the use of all-round disc brakes to arrest the car's top speed which was in excess of 110mph (177km/h). Less happily, weight went up to 3976lb (1803kg) and so fuel consumption fell to around 13mpg (21 litres/100km). Power-assisted steering was particularly welcome on such a big car and it became a standard fitment on the model that was mostly offered with automatic transmission. This Jaguar endured until 1961. However, it was the first of the line, the Mark VII, which proved to be the most popular with 20,908 built. The VIIM and Mark IX sold about the same quantities, of 10,061 and 10,009 respectively, with the VIII accounting for a mere 6212 examples. The Mark IX eventually made way for the less-than-memorable Mark X and with its 1970 demise in 420G form, Jaguar's big saloon line came to an end.

BELOW: *A 1953 left-hand-drive (as most were) Mark VII saloon; the big, powerful car came into its own in America. It was produced in this form until the autumn of 1954.*

ABOVE: *The interior of a right-hand-drive VIIM. It was similar to the Mark VII and is identifiable by the flat hornpush; previously a more pronounced one had been used.*

Jaguar Marks VII, VIII and IX

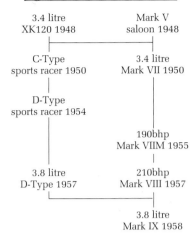

3.4 litre XK120 1948	Mark V saloon 1948
C-Type sports racer 1950	3.4 litre Mark VII 1950
D-Type sports racer 1954	
	190bhp Mark VIIM 1955
3.8 litre D-Type 1957	210bhp Mark VIII 1957
	3.8 litre Mark IX 1958

RIGHT: *A left-hand-drive Mark IX of 1960. It was externally similar to its Mark VIII predecessor and, unlike the VII series, was fitted with a distinctive Jaguar mascot.*

ROLLS-ROYCE SILVER CLOUD (1955-1965)

The Rolls-Royce and Bentley marques were drawn ever closer with the arrival in 1955 of their respective Silver Cloud and S1 models which shared the same standardized bodywork. This represented a major departure for the manufacturer of "The Best Car in the World" as, before World War II, every Rolls-Royce had been different because the company only built its cars in chassis form. Customers were then able to specify a body of their choice, the construction of which was the responsibility of a specialist coachbuilder.

During the war the firm recognized that its survival as a car maker depended on the adoption of standardized bodywork. Rolls-Royce had bought Bentley in 1931 and the first model to be manufactured in this way was its Mark VI saloon of 1946 powered by a new 4.2 litre, six cylinder, overhead inlet/side exhaust valve engine. This power unit was also used in the Silver Wraith, which was the first Rolls-Royce model of the post-War years but, unlike the Bentley, it was only available with bespoke coachwork. The car was built, in long wheelbase form, until 1959, having been joined in 1955 by the Silver Cloud.

Like the Bentley, this used a four-door saloon body, though of updated design and built by Pressed Steel, which was mounted on a new box-section cruciform chassis with trailing wishbone and coil spring front suspension and a live rear axle sprung by half-elliptic springs. The engine was a 4.9 litre version of the proven six, improved by the fitment of a new six port cylinder head. Unusually, the brakes used a dual system of actuation, with hydraulics at the front while the rears were operated by a mechanical servo unit which had been a feature of Rolls-Royce cars since 1924. Automatic transmission was standardized though a manual unit was available at special request by the customer.

The only outward difference between the two models was to be found in their radiators and badged wheel hubs but, at £4796, the Rolls-Royce cost £127 more than the Bentley. Inside, they had sumptuous leather upholstery with walnut veneer featuring on the dashboard and door cappings. In this form the Silver Cloud was able to reach a smooth, quiet and apparently effortless 100mph (161km/h) but at the expense of fuel economy — consumption was some 12mpg (23 litres/100km).

For 1957 the Cloud was offered with power steering as an optional extra on export cars. This was later listed for the home market and, subsequently, air conditioning became available. A long wheelbase version appeared in 1957 and was built throughout the Cloud's production life. At 10ft 7in (3226mm), this was 4in (102mm) longer than the mainstream model. It permitted the introduction of a central division for those owners who retained the services of a chauffeur.

A V8 Engine

In 1959 came the Silver Cloud II. This outwardly differed little from its predecessor, but under the bonnet was a new 6.2 litre V8 engine. It was also noticeably faster, being able to reach 60mph (96km/h) in a mere 11 or so seconds, which was around 2 seconds quicker than the six. Top speed was over 110mph (177km/h). The Cloud II

Specifications: Rolls-Royce Silver Cloud I

Length:	17ft 8in (5385mm)
Width:	6ft 2in (1880mm)
Height:	5ft 4in (1626mm)
Wheelbase:	10ft 3in (3124mm)
Track:	front 4ft 10in (1473mm), rear 5ft (1524mm)
Unladen weight:	4228lb (1918kg)
Engine: Six cylinder, overhead valve, 95x114mm, 4887cc. Compression ratio, 6.6:1. Max power, not disclosed. Max torque, not disclosed.	
Transmission:	Four-speed automatic
Drive:	Rear
Suspension (front):	Independent, coil springs and wishbones
Suspension (rear):	Live axle, half-elliptic springs
Top speed:	100mph (161km/h)
0-60mph (96km/h):	13.5 seconds
Production (total, all versions):	7365

also differed in having power steering and automatic transmission as standard fitments, while air conditioning was retained as an optional extra.

The Silver Cloud II was replaced in 1962 by the Silver Cloud III, which was mechanically similar but outwardly identifiable by the fitment of quadruple headlamps. It remained in production until 1965.

As the Silver Cloud retained a separate chassis it was also made available to coachbuilders. In this category, the offerings by in-house coachbuilders Mulliner Park Ward and also James Young were the best known. Such activity ceased with the arrival of the Cloud's Silver Shadow replacement in 1965. This was of unitary construction and heralded the beginning of a new chapter in Rolls-Royce history.

ABOVE: *A 1963 Silver Cloud III, identifiable by its horizontally positioned twin headlamps. The 6.2 litre V8 was essentially carried over from the Cloud II.*

LEFT: *The Silver Cloud in its original form was powered by a 4.9 litre six cylinder engine. The body, shared with the Bentley S1, was produced by Pressed Steel.*

BELOW: *In-house Park Ward produced both drop and fixed head bodies in its "straight through" style on the Silver Cloud chassis. This is a Silver Cloud III version.*

Rolls-Royce Silver Cloud

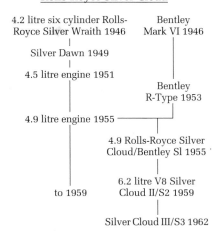

4.2 litre six cylinder Rolls-Royce Silver Wraith 1946
|
Silver Dawn 1949
|
4.5 litre engine 1951
|
4.9 litre engine 1955
|
to 1959

Bentley Mark VI 1946
|
Bentley R-Type 1953
|
4.9 Rolls-Royce Silver Cloud/Bentley Sl 1955
|
6.2 litre V8 Silver Cloud II/S2 1959
|
Silver Cloud III/S3 1962

Jaguar Marks I and II (1955-1969)

Jaguar's best seller of its day, this well-equipped, fast and distinctive medium-sized saloon is best remembered in its greatly refined Mark II form, which, impressively, outsold the original version by more than two to one. Initially produced as a 2.4 litre motor car, it was soon offered with 3.4 litre power and, ultimately, could be obtained with the 3.8 litre, twin-cam six which delivered a top speed of 125mph (201km/h).

Specifications: Jaguar Mark I

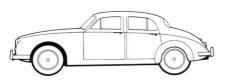

Length:	15ft (4572mm)
Width:	5ft 6in (1676mm)
Height:	4ft 9in (1448mm)
Wheelbase:	11ft (3353mm)
Track:	front 4ft 6in (1372mm), rear 4ft 2in (1270mm)
Unladen weight:	2800lb (1270kg)

Engine: Six cylinder, twin overhead camshaft, 83x76mm, 2483cc. Compression ratio, 8:1. Max power, 112bhp at 5750rpm. Max torque 140lb/ft at 5750rpm.

Transmission:	Four-speed manual
Drive:	Rear
Suspension (front):	Independent, coil springs and wishbones
Suspension (rear):	Live axle, cantilever springs and radius arms
Top speed:	95mph (153km/h)
0-60mph (96km/h):	14.6 seconds
Production (Marks I and II):	129,910

What was retrospectively titled the Mark I was launched at the 1955 London Motor Show. It was Jaguar's first unitary construction model, a handsome four-door saloon powered by a new short stroke 2.4 litre version of the firm's twin-overhead-camshaft, six cylinder XK engine. Another innovation for Jaguar was in the front suspension which, unlike its Mark VIIM and XK 140 stablemates that used torsion bars, featured coil springs and wishbones. Unusually, full cantilever springs were fitted at the rear with the live axle located by radius arms and a Panhard rod. Inside, these Jaguars were impressively furnished and finished with seats upholstered in leather and a walnut veneered dashboard and door cappings.

In this form the Mark I was capable of 95mph (153km/h), but performance was improved in 1957 with the optional fitment of the existing 3.4 litre engine which pushed the car's top speed well into three figures, to 120mph (193km/h). This version was identifiable by a new, wider radiator grille. Automatic transmission was introduced as an optional extra on all 1958 models at the same time as disc brakes could be specified all-round. Customers could also opt for wire wheels in place of the usual discs, which not only looked appropriately sporty, but also allowed welcome cooling air to reach the brakes more easily.

A Sleeker Mark II

The Mark II version of the design was introduced at the 1959 London Motor Show and was a notable visual and mechanical improvement on the original car. It greatly benefitted from a larger area of glass than in the Mark I, along with new, slimmer window pillars which much improved visibility. There was also a new radiator grille and partly recessed fog lamps. The interior was also improved with a redesigned dashboard and deeper, more comfortable seats. Servo-assisted disc brakes were fitted all-round and the rear axle was widened to improve roadholding. The Mark II was available with three engine options: in addition to the existing 2.4 and 3.4 litre units,

Below: A 1956 3.4 litre Mark I. Compared with its Mark II derivative, the windows are smaller and door pillars thicker. The wire wheels were available at extra cost.

there was a top line 3.8 litre version which was often fitted with the optional wire wheels. It could attain 125mph (201km/h) with 60mph (96km/h) coming up in under nine seconds. Power steering became available for the 1961 season and a much needed all-synchromesh gearbox arrived, in common with other Jaguar models, for 1966.

The 1968 season saw the cars' specifications downgraded, with Ambla upholstery replacing leather and cheaper carpeting fitted. These models were known as the 240 and 340 to indicate engine capacity, the 3.8 litre engine having been discontinued. The latter model ceased production in September 1968, but the 2.4 continued until April 1969. In all, 129,910 of these Jaguars were built, of which 37,350 were Mark Is and 93,560 Mark IIs.

In 1960 Jaguar took over Daimler and this association spawned the first variation on the Mark II theme. The Daimler V8 250 of 1963-69 was the Mark II body shell fitted with the 2.5 litre V8 from Daimler's SP250 sports car. In 1964 came the Jaguar Mark II-related S-Type with rear end and independent suspension courtesy of the Mark X saloon, which lasted until 1968.

Below: End of the line, 1968 Mark II 240 in company with its first cousin, a 1967 Daimler V8 250 automatic, so called because it was powered by a 2.5 litre V8 engine.

RIGHT: *A 1962 Mark II with its sleeker windscreen pillars readily apparent. This popular model was available with a choice of 2.4, 3.4 and 3.8 engines. This example has also been fitted with optional and eminently desirable wire-spoked wheels.*

Jaguar Marks I and II

3.4 litre Jaguar
XX120 1948

Mark VII
saloon 1950

Mark VIIM 1955

2.4 litre Mark I
saloon 1955

3.4 litre Mark I 1957

3.8 litre
Mark IX 1958

2.4, 3.4, 3.8 litre   Daimler
Mark II 1959   SP250
1959

Mark X 1961

2.5 litre V8
Daimler 250
1963

S-Type 1964

CITROËN DS (1955-1975)

Citroën differed from most of its competitors in that it designed advanced cars, which were destined for long production runs, unlike the majority of other manufacturers who opted for more conventional models, that were cheaper to develop but were changed more regularly. The first of these revolutionary Citroëns was the legendary front-wheel-drive Traction Avant of 1934-57 vintage, and it was followed by the DS, which shared the same drive configuration, and enjoyed a 20-year production life.

The arrival of a new Citroën used to be a rare occurrence which would dominate the Paris Motor Show at which it was unveiled, and this certainly applied at the 1955 event where the DS19 was revealed. Like the Traction Avant, the new model was masterminded by André Lefebvre and styled by Flaminio Bertoni. The bodywork was particularly striking for, in the interests of aerodynamic efficiency, there was no radiator grille. Instead, the bonnet dramatically descended to the bumper line and the engine's air intake was tucked in below it. This design approach would not be adopted by the rest of the motor industry until the 1970's. The body construction was similarly advanced and employed a base frame structure on to which the individual panels were attached.

The all-independent suspension was formidably ingenious, being self levelling and interconnected. It used front twin leading arms and rear trailing ones, each wheel having its own gas-filled oleopneumatic strut which was pressurized by hydraulic fluid from an engine-driven pump. This unit was similarly responsible for the steering and also the clutch for the semi-automatic gearbox. In addition, the brakes were power assisted and at the front featured inboard discs; the DS was thus the first road car in the world to be fitted with them.

None of these features had previously appeared on any Citroën and the only carry-over from the Traction Avant was the 1.9 litre four cylinder engine, which was fitted with a new aluminium cylinder head with hemispherical combustion chambers.

Riding In Comfort

Not only did this Citroën handle well, on account of its front-wheel drive, the advanced suspension system also made it an extremely comfortable car, while the wind-cheating body played its part in making the DS capable of 85mph (137km/h).

In 1956 came a cheaper and simplified version of the design in the shape of ID19 powered by the Traction's engine in unmodified form. The hydraulics accordingly only related to the suspension.

The DS19 continued essentially unchanged until the 1966 season, when it was fitted with a choice of two new short-stroke engines of 2 and 2.2 litres capacity, the cars being respectively designated the DS19 and DS21, the luxury versions of which were given the Pallas name. For its part, the ID received the DS's old long-stroke 1.9 litre unit and remained in production until 1969. The ID was also built in cabriolet form between 1961 and 1965 and then as a DS21 variant until 1971.

So advanced were the DS's body lines, few changes were made until the 1968 cars when, for better aerodynamics, their headlamps were contained behind transparent covers. On the Pallas, the inner pair of lights turned in conjunction with the power-

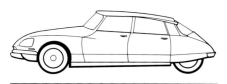

Specifications: Citroën DS19

Length:	15ft 9in (4801mm)
Width:	5ft 10in (1778mm)
Height:	4ft 10in (1473mm)
Wheelbase:	10ft 3in (3124mm)
Track:	front 4ft 11in (1499mm), rear 4ft 3in (1295mm)
Unladen weight:	2465lb (1118kg)

Engine: Four cylinder, overhead valve, 78x100mm, 1911cc. Compression ratio, 7.5:1. Max power, 75bhp at 4500rpm. Max torque, 101lb/ft at 3000rpm.

Transmission:	Four-speed semi-automatic
Drive:	Front
Suspension (front):	Independent, twin leading arm, oleopneumatic interconnected
Suspension (rear):	Independent, trailing arms, oleopneumatic
Top speed:	85mph (137km/h)
0-60mph (96km/h):	22.6 seconds
Production (total):	1,415,719

ABOVE: *In the foreground, a rare right-hand-drive DS19 cabriolet of 1962. This variant, converted by Henri Chapron, was produced from 1961 until 1971. Left background, the DS/ID range's headlamps were faired in from 1968 and, right background, the commodious estate car version, introduced in 1959. Known in Britain as the Safari, like its saloon counterparts, the model remained in production until 1975.*

assisted steering. The engines of 1971 models were available with fuel injection, along with automatic transmission. 1972 saw the arrival of the DS23 with a 2.3 litre engine and an optional five-speed manual gearbox.

The DS was also assembled at Citroën's factory at Slough, Berkshire between 1956 and 1966 and was the last model to be built there. However, French production continued until April 1975, by which time 1.4 million examples of this clever but complicated car had been built.

ABOVE: *Open wide! These front-wheel-drive Citroëns have an appropriately unconventional location for the spare wheel. Note aerodynamically faired front apron.*

LEFT: *A Slough-assembled 1960 DS19. The wing vents featured on some early cars. Owned by the same enthusiast since 1969, it has covered over 170,000 miles (273,700km).*

Citroën DS

1.9 litre Traction
Avant 1935

DS19 1955

ID19 1956

Cabriolet
1961

2 litre DS19 ‑ 2.2 litre
1966   DS21

to 1969

to 1971

2.3 litre
DS23 1972

to 1975   to 1975

FIAT 500 (1957-1975)

The original Fiat 500 of 1936 was one of the landmark designs of motoring history. In 1957 its spiritual successor appeared in the shape of the *Nuova* (new) 500 powered by an apparently unburstable, rear-mounted, 479cc two cylinder, air-cooled engine. In 1960 this deceptively tough little car evolved into the 500D with a slightly enlarged 499cc twin, and it was followed by the improved 500F of 1965. The final manifestation of the theme arrived in 1972 in the form of the 500R with a 594cc power unit, courtesy of its 126 successor.

Masterminded by Fiat's talented engineering supremo, Dante Giacosa, although the *Nuova* 500 followed his earlier model of the same name, it bore no mechanical relationship to it. The diminutive two-door saloon, into which two adults could be prised while children sat on a ledge behind, was created with the heat of the Italian summer in mind and accordingly featured a roll-back canvas roof that incorporated the rear window. After lengthy experiments with various power units, Giacosa opted for a twin located at the car's rear, in the manner of his 600 model of 1955. The aluminium overhead valve engine was Fiat's first to incorporate air cooling and developed just 13hp. This was mated to a four-speed, non-synchromesh gear-

box. Suspension was all-independent with wishbones and a leaf spring at the front and semi-trailing arms and coil springs at the rear. Introduced at the 1957 Turin Motor Show and priced a reasonable 465,000 lire (£265), in truth the earliest examples were horribly gutless. At this point Fiat looked again and unleashed a further 2bhp which gave the little car a top speed of 53mph (85km/h) and returned a miserly 50mpg (5.6 litres/100km).

In 1958 Fiat introduced a variant with the unlikely name of the 500 Sport, in which the engine's capacity was increased to 499cc achieved by upping the bore size from 66 to 67.4mm. Power soared to 21bhp; on a good day it could attain 65mph (105km/h). It was available until 1960.

The basic 500 also continued in its original form to 1960 when it was redesignated the 500D and fitted with the Sport's enlarged 499cc capacity engine, detuned to 17.5bhp. Rather than perching on a ledge, children now had a fold-down seat on which to sit. The D was easily identifiable by its smaller roll-back roof that no longer contained the rear window which was now conventionally incorporated into the car's bodywork.

In the same year of 1960 came the Giardiniera, a station wagon variant with improved carrying capacity and the wheelbase extended by 3.9in (100mm) to 6ft 4in (1930mm). A third door was introduced at the rear and, to provide access, the engine was laid on its side, although mechanicals were otherwise unchanged. The model received the in-house Autobianchi badge in 1968 and was built until 1977, two years after the 500 itself had ceased production.

In March of 1965 the D was replaced by the 500F with rear- rather than front-opening doors. The engine itself remained essentially unchanged although stronger drive shafts, differential and clutch were fitted. This continued in production until 1972.

That year came the final version of the model in the shape of the 500R, R standing for revised. Its 126 successor also appeared in 1972 and the R was powered by the new model's 594cc, two cylinder air-cooled engine although it developed only 18bhp in the 500 as opposed to 23bhp in the 126. Maximum speed was now nudging 60mph (96km/h), The 500R remained in production until 1975 although, after that, the theme was perpetuated in the styling of the 126. A great numerical triumph for Fiat, the grand total of 500s built stands at over four million.

Specifications: Fiat 500	
Length:	9ft 9in (2972mm)
Width:	4ft 4in (1321mm)
Height:	4ft 4in (1321mm)
Wheelbase:	7ft (2134mm)
Track:	front and rear 3ft 8in (1118mm)
Unladen weight:	1036lb (470kg)
Engine: Two cylinder, air-cooled, overhead valve, 66x70mm, 479cc. Compression ratio, 6.5:1. Max power, 13bhp at 4000rpm. Max torque, 20lb/ft at 2500rpm.	
Transmission:	Four-speed manual
Drive:	Rear
Suspension (front):	Independent, transverse leaf spring and wishbones
Suspension (rear):	Independent, semi-trailing arms, coil springs
Top speed:	53mph (85km/h)
0-50mph (80km/h):	32.1 seconds
Production (total):	approx 4,000,000

LEFT: *A Fiat 500-based Jolly, a beach car developed by the Ghia styling house. Introduced in 1957, it was produced in a variety of guises: on the Fiat 600, 4CV Renault and even the Lambretta scooter!*

Fiat 500

479cc Fiat 500 1957
|
499cc 500 Sport 1958
                        Giardiniera
                        station wagon
                        1960
500F 1965
|
594cc 500R ——— Fiat 126
1972   1972
|
to 1975
                        to 1977

BELOW: *A right-hand-drive 500L. The front-hingeing doors arrived with the 500F of 1965 and the roll-back roof featured throughout the model's production life.*

ABOVE: *The 500's air-cooled vertical twin engine was, for cost considerations, tucked away in the model's tail. Rear accommodation was a trifle cramped as a consequence.*

CADILLAC ELDORADO SEVILLE (1958-1959)

Cadillac, which gave the world tail fins in 1948, also provided their most extreme manifestation on its 1959 model year cars. Not only were these fins the most grotesquely elevated in the industry, they were embellished with bullet-shaped tail lights which contributed a further bizarre and somewhat incongruous element to a once ingenious styling feature.

As flagship of the General Motors conglomerate, Cadillac was a recipient of the unalloyed resources of the Corporation's famous Art and Color section, presided over since its 1927 inception by the legendary Harley Earl, who retired at the end of 1959.

Unlike 1958, when the Eldorado Seville hardtop and Biarritz convertible were considered as part of Cadillac's mainstream Series 62 line, for 1959 Eldorado emerged as its own, more exclusive sub-division. These existing models were retained and joined in the stable by the low production, costly and unrelated Eldorado Brougham.

The Eldorados, along with the Series 60 and 62 models, had their wheelbases lengthened from 129.5 to 130in (3289 to 3302mm) for 1959, but this modest extension paled in the wake of the fins that dominated much of the rear of the cars. Having said that, their fronts did not lack attention. The quadruple headlamps were carried over from the previous year, as were elements of the radiator grille which consisted of rows of tiny chromium plated bullets, that complemented the projectile-like rear lights, and were divided by a thick horizontal bar.

All-American Grille
A panoramic, compound curve windscreen was extended into the roof and there was similar but less extravagantly shaped glass at the rear. As if that part of the car had not received sufficient attention, the bullet-bedecked front grille was echoed on the back of the vehicle just above the bumper. The Seville shown here has no intrusive door pillar and is therefore a hardtop, this stylistic feature having been introduced to the motoring world in GM's 1949 range. However, all Cadillac's '59 sedans were so styled.

Mechanically, all versions benefitted from more powerful engines. Capacity was upped from 365cid (6 litres) in 1958 to a longer stroked 390cid (6.4 litres) V8 running in 325bhp form, but boosted to 345bhp with triple carburettors on the Eldorados. Petrol consump-

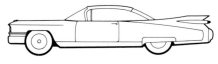

Specifications: Cadillac Eldorado Seville (1959)

Length:	18ft 9in (5715mm)
Width:	6ft 8in (2032mm)
Height:	4ft 10in (1473mm)
Wheelbase:	10ft 10in (3302mm)
Track:	front/rear, 5ft 1in (1549mm)
Unladen weight:	4921lb (2232kg)
Engine:	V8, pushrod, 4x3.88in (101x98mm), 390cid (6390cc). Compression ratio: 10.5:1. Max power, 345bhp at 4800rpm.
Transmission:	Four-speed automatic
Drive:	Rear
Suspension (front):	Independent, air springs and wishbones
Suspension (rear):	Live axle, air springs and trailing arms
Top speed:	110mph (177km/h)
0-60mph (96km/h):	11.2 seconds
Production:	975

tion was consequently prodigious: a mere 12 to 14 miles per gallon (23.5 to 20.1 litres/100km). Air suspension, optional on other models, was a standard fitment. The obligatory GM four speed Hydra-Matic automatic transmission was employed, as were power steering and brakes.

As befitted the gadget-orientated 1950's, the Seville was fitted with "power vent windows and six way power seat" and electric door locks.

Both the Seville and the open Biarritz sold for the same price of $7401; the Brougham, by contrast, retailed for an astronomical $13,075. However, despite all the razzmatazz, Eldorado division sales were relatively modest. Just 975 of these Sevilles were sold although the convertible was slightly more popular and found 1320 buyers. The following year's cars benefitted from less ostentatious fins and these features had disappeared altogether by 1965, having peaked so memorably and dramatically in 1959.

RIGHT: *The rubbing strip along the body distinguishes this 1958 Series 62 convertible from its more exclusive relation, the Eldorado Seville.*

Cadillac Eldorado Seville

```
                Series 62
                    |
    Coupe de Ville hardtop coupé 1949
                    |
    Eldorado Seville hardtop coupé 1956
                    |
         +----------+----------+
         |                     |
       1959          Eldorado sub-division
         |                     |
     Series 62        +--------+--------+
                      |                 |
                   Seville          Biarritz
                   hardtop         convertible
```

LEFT: *$7,400-worth of finned beauty! The extravagant lines of the Seville mark the extreme point of '50's styling.*

RIGHT: *Under the hood is a 6.4 litre, fuel-guzzling V8 engine; 14 miles to the gallon (20lit/100km) is good going!*

MINI (1959 to date)

Today the vast majority of the world's saloon cars are driven by their front wheels by engines that are transversely located to provide the maximum amount of space for the occupants. It has not always been so. For the first 80 or so years of the passenger car's history, most were pushed along by their rear wheels driven from front-mounted, in-line engines. The vehicle that brought about the design revolution is Alec Issigonis's Mini, introduced by the British Motor Corporation in 1959 and still in production today.

Issigonis began work in 1957 on the design, coded ADO15 in corporate parlance, after having been commissioned by BMC's chairman, Sir Leonard Lord, to produce a small car to compete with the swarms of bubble cars that were then invading Britain. Many of these German imports were attracted by the petrol rationing that followed the 1956 Suez Crisis.

Announced in Austin and Morris forms at the 1959 London Motor Show, the Mini was the most technically significant car in the history of the British motor industry. A triumph of space saving, it was possible to squeeze four people into the box-like, twin-door saloon, because the 848cc four cylinder engine was transversely rather than longitudinally mounted, while the gearbox was, ingeniously, located in its sump. The wheels were small – only 10in (254mm) in diameter – a factor which also saved interior space. Suspension was all-independent and, unusually, compressed rubber cones were used as the medium. Roadholding was good on account of the front-driven wheels, and the original cars were capable of over 70mph (113km/h).

The Super Cooper

In 1961 came a faster version in the shape of the Mini Cooper, which derived from a version created by the Cooper company, World Motor Racing Champions in 1959 and 1960. Introduced in tuned twin carburettored 997cc form, it was a 85mph (113km/h) car and benefitted from front disc brakes, an improved remote control gear lever and better interior trim. The model lasted in this form until 1969, and was built from 1964 with a 998cc engine.

In addition, the faster 1071cc Mini Cooper S was introduced in 1963. In 1964 the cars were offered with additional 970 and 1275cc units, but the latter size became the definitive version and the model was produced with

this engine until 1967. In this state the S was capable of over 100mph (161km/h) and it provided BMC with no less than three Monte Carlo Rally wins, in 1964, 1965 and 1967.

The more basic Mini continued to evolve with Hydrolastic interconnected suspension, courtesy of its 1100 derivative, arriving for 1965, while the 1966 cars were available with automatic transmission. The Mark II version appeared in the 1968 season with a new grille and enlarged rear window, and the Coopers were similarly updated. However, in 1968 BMC was

absorbed into British Leyland and the new management decided to discontinue the Cooper, which ceased production in 1969 with the S following it in 1971. The Cooper proper was replaced by the larger capacity but less potent 1.3 litre 1275GT of 1969 with a new squared front which lasted until 1980. The new, supplementary body style was also shared with the 998cc Clubman, which was engined with a 1098cc power unit for 1976. The model was built in this form until 1982.

For 1970, the original Mini was offered with the option of 848 and 998cc engines and, at the same time, the Hydrolastic suspension was discontinued and the car reverted to its original rubber system. Simultaneously, the marque names were dropped and all versions were solely known by the Mini name.

British Leyland was nationalized in 1965, the business became Leyland Cars and, in 1977, Michael Edwardes

became chairman. The company was once again renamed, this time as BL Cars. In 1980 the Austin Metro was launched, this being, ostensibly, the Mini's replacement. But demand for the standard model continued in 998cc form (the 848cc car having been discontinued in 1980) and it is produced in this variant to this day.

BL Cars became the Rover Group in 1986, and in 1990 it was decided to revive the concept of the rally winning 1275cc Mini Cooper S. The new Cooper is capable of 92mph (148km/h), which is slightly slower than the original, but as it fitted with catalysts as standard, it is much "cleaner".

A further variation on the Mini's body style arrived in 1993 with the appearance of a cabriolet (open) version. This underlined the fact that there is still plenty of life left in this great little design, which is a lasting tribute to the extraordinary talents of Alec Arnold Constantine Issigonis.

Mini

```
                                        848cc Mini
                                          1959
                                            |
                                    997cc Mini Cooper
                                          1961
                                            |
                                            |————————————————————
                                            |                   970cc, 1071cc, 1275cc
                                            |                   Mini Cooper S 1963
                              998cc engine 1964                        |
                                         to 1969                       |
                                      Clubman 1969                     |
          Optional                          |                          |
          998cc 1970                        |————————————             |
              |                             |           1275GT      to 1971
              |                             |            1971          |
           to 1980                          |          to 1980         |
                                         to 1982                       |
                                                                       |
                                                             1275cc Mini
                                                             Cooper 1990

          to date                  - - - - - out of production
```

LEFT: *In 1990 the Rover Group revived the concept of the 1960's Mini Cooper. Identifiable by its white roof and alloy wheels, the Cooper badge is on the rear wing of this 1991 car.*

ABOVE: *The Mini Clubman, with its angular front, was produced from its 1969 introduction in estate car form. It was so-built until the variant ceased manufacture in 1980.*

RIGHT: *That sideways look. The transversely located BMC A Series engine which made such a major contribution to the Mini's space-saving reputation.*

Specifications: Mini 850

Length:	10ft (3048mm)
Width:	4ft 7in (1397mm)
Height:	4ft 5in (1346mm)
Wheelbase:	6ft 8in (2032mm)
Track:	front 3ft 11¾in (1212mm), rear 3ft 9⅓in (1163mm)
Unladen weight:	1260lb (571kg)
Engine: Transversely mounted, four cylinder, overhead valve, 62x68mm, 848cc. Compression ratio, 8.3:1. Max power, 37bhp at 5500rpm. Max torque, 44lb/ft at 2900rpm.	
Transmission:	Four-speed manual
Drive:	Front
Suspension (front):	Independent, wishbones and rubber cones
Suspension (rear):	Independent, trailing arms and rubber cones
Top speed:	70mph (113km/h)
0-60mph (96km/h):	26.8 seconds
Production (to date):	5,280,000

CHEVROLET CORVAIR (1959-1969)

Ever since Henry Ford put the world on wheels in the 1920's, with his water-cooled, front-engined, rear-driven Model T, American cars had, until the recent front-wheel-drive revolution, followed this traditional layout. So there were many raised eyebrows when, in 1959, General Motors unveiled its thoroughly unconventional Corvair that was powered by, of all things, a rear-mounted, air-cooled, flat-six engine.

The Corvair was General Motors' response to the small engined European imports, such as the Volkswagen Beetle, which by the late 1950's were beginning to make a modest though noticeable impact on the American public. Chrysler responded with its downsized Plymouth Valiant and Ford came up with the Falcon, but Chevrolet's Corvair was by far and away the most radical of the trio.

Its overall concept sprang from GM engineer, Edward Cole, who in 1956 became general manager of its top selling Chevrolet division. One of his interests was aviation, which may account for the car's unusual engine, the configuration of which was shared by some aircraft units, not to say that of the Beetle. The capacity of this new, small Chevrolet was 140cid (2.3 litres) and the pushrod six was available in two forms; the standard unit developed 80bhp, and there was also an optional 95bhp version. A three-speed manual gearbox was employed. Suspension was all-independent, with the usual coils and wishbones at the front and a swing axle, with semi-trailing box section wishbones, at the rear.

The car's "push me, pull you" body lines were equally unorthodox by being almost symmetrical with the commodious front boot balancing the rear engine compartment.

The Corvair, which arrived for the 1960 model year, was available in three forms. There was the basic 500 with saloon and coupé bodies; these were retained in the better equipped 700, while there was a top line Monza coupé with bucket seats.

In its original form the Corvair was capable of over 85mph (137km/h) but controversy was to dog its handling, which suffered from a combination of factors – the rear-mounted and heavier-than-expected engine, cost-conscious rear suspension, plus undue sensitivity to anything other than correct tyre pressures.

Yet, suddenly, the Corvair caught on, but not quite in the way in which Chevrolet had imagined. A mostly youthful clientele showed a preference for the sporty, compact Monza coupé. In 1961 sales of the Monza, of which 109,945 were built that year, took off and stood at around 20,000 less than the rest of the entire range. This was a year in which the Corvair's engine was enlarged to 145cid (2.4 litres) and an optional four-speed gearbox introduced. In 1962, when Monza sales peaked, the division decided to expand the line to include, among other styles, a convertible, which was powered by a 150bhp version of the flat six engine, that was also available in turbocharged form.

Revisions And Changes

The Corvair's body lines were impressively revised and lowered for 1965 and substantial changes were made below the surface, above all to the controversial rear suspension. This was now a fully independent system incorporating coil-sprung half shafts, doubling as upper control arms with unequal length lowers and trailing radius arms. The engine had been enlarged to 164cid (2.7 litres) in 1964 and was carried over with the addition of a popular 140bhp unit. There was also a more powerful 180bhp version which was an optional fitment in the newly introduced top of the range Corsa.

However, the Monza continued to be the most popular version, although sales undoubtedly suffered with the publication, in 1965, of Ralph Nadar's book, *Unsafe at Any Speed*, which unmercifully pilloried the Corvair's handling. And by then many of the car's potential customers were flocking to Ford's new Mustang.

So the Corvair was left to fade away; 1969 production stood at just 6000 units. Needless to say, it was America's last rear-engined, air-cooled car. Ed Cole, however, went on to become, in 1967, president of General Motors.

RIGHT: *An example of the much-sought-after Corvette Monza Spyder of which a mere 4761 were built in 1964. Powered by 150bhp turbocharged engine, its rear location is not immediately apparent.*

LEFT: *A 1961 Corvair Monza. That year a four-door saloon Monza, of which this is one, was introduced, although it was overshadowed by the coupé. A total of 33,745 were built.*

Specifications: Chevrolet Corvair

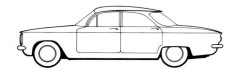

Length:	15ft (4572mm)
Width:	5ft 7in (1702mm)
Height:	4ft 3in (1295mm)
Wheelbase:	9ft (2743mm)
Track:	front and rear 4ft 6in (1372mm)
Unladen weight:	2408lb (1092kg)

Engine: Rear-mounted, horizontally opposed, air-cooled, six cylinder, overhead valve, 86x66mm, 140cid (2300cc). Compression ratio, 8:1. Max power, 80bhp at 4400rpm. Max torque, 124lb/ft at 2700rpm.

Transmission:	Three-speed manual or automatic
Drive:	Rear
Suspension (front):	Independent, coil springs and wishbones
Suspension (rear):	Independent, swing axle, semi-trailing wishbones
Top speed:	85mph (137km/h)
0-60mph (96km/h):	13.8 seconds
Production (total)	1,659,022

ABOVE: *Pininfarina built at least two special bodies on the Corvair floor pan. The first* coupé speciale *came in 1960 and this 2 + 2 variation of 1963 was the second. Paradoxically, the elongated nose suggested a front-engined car.*

BMW 1500, 1600, 1800 (1961-1968)

From the end of World War II until 1961, BMW was a company in search of an identity with its offerings lurching from the costly, V8-powered 502 saloon on the one hand to the Isetta bubble car on the other. All this changed with the appearance, in 1961, of the 1500, a model on which BMW's present prosperity is built. Ironically, sales were relatively small, but it presaged the arrival of the related 1800 saloon, which proved to be precisely the type of car required by company executives in West Germany's booming 1960's economy.

Because the 1500 bore little relationship to any previous BMW, there were virtually no carries-over from the models of the 1950's. This was a reflection of the fact that the loss-making company had, from 1960, new owners in the shape of industrialist Herbert Quandt and his half brother, Harald. They recruited a fresh management and engineering team, some of whom were involved in the creation of what the firm called its New Class car. Designed under the overall direction of BMW veteran, Fritz Fiedler, styling was the responsibility of Wilhelm Hofmeister, while the stalwart Alex von Falkenhausen's brief was the all-important power unit.

At the heart of the car was a 1.5 litre, four cylinder, single-overhead-camshaft engine which was the first BMW of this configuration to appear since the demise of the Austin Seven-based 3/20 in 1934. The 75bhp four was canted 30 degrees from the vertical to permit the use of a low bonnet line, which contributed to the four-door saloon's refreshingly modern appearance. It really looked like no other contemporary car with its spacious proportions and aggressively angled nose, although the interior was surprisingly stark. Suspension was all independent: by front MacPherson struts, which were new to BMW, while the concept of the rear semi-trailing arms was one of the few elements to be carried over from the past, in this instance from the 700 model of 1959.

The 1500 was unveiled at the 1961 Frankfurt Motor Show, staged in September. This was, in fact, a prototype and it would not be until over a year later, in October 1962, that production began, at the rate of 50 cars a week. By this time the engine's output had been increased to 80bhp, which gave the car a top speed of 92mph (148km/h). Production lasted until December 1964 and by then 23,807 examples of the 1500 had been built.

That model was replaced in 1964 by the outwardly similar 1600, the 1.6 litre capacity having been achieved by increasing the engine's bore size from 82 to 84mm. However, this model actually appeared after the 1500's 1800 derivative, which overshadowed it, and a mere 9728 1600s were built before it was withdrawn in 1966.

Success Story

What was BMW's really big success of the decade – the 1800 – had been introduced at the 1963 Frankfurt Show and put the company decisively into profit. Again the 1500's body and mechanicals were carried over but under the car's bonnet was a 1.8 litre 90bhp version of the four. This employed the as-yet-unannounced 1600's 84mm bore while the stroke was increased to 80mm. This 90bhp unit ensured that the 1800 was a 100mph (161km/h) car, and one destined for a five year production life with 102,090 examples having been built by 1968.

There was also a supplementary 109mph (175km/h) 1800 TI (for *Turismo Internazionale*) version with an 110bhp engine, and a top line TI/SA racer with twin-Weber-carburettored 130bhp engine and five-speed gearbox.

BMW 1500, 1600, 1800

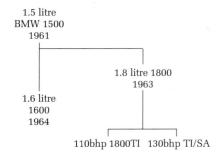

1.5 litre
BMW 1500
1961

1.8 litre 1800
1963

1.6 litre
1600
1964

110bhp 1800TI   130bhp TI/SA

Specifications: BMW 1500

Specifications: BMW 1500	
Length:	14ft 9in (4496mm)
Width:	5ft 7in (1702mm)
Height:	4ft 9in (1448mm)
Wheelbase:	8ft 4in (2540mm)
Track:	front 4ft 4 in (1320mm), rear 4ft 5in (1346mm)
Unladen weight:	2408lb (1092kg)
Engine:	Four cylinder, single overhead camshaft, 82x71mm, 1499cc. Compression ratio, 8.2:1. Max power, 80bhp at 5700rpm. Max torque, 86lb/ft at 3000rpm.
Transmission:	Four-speed manual
Drive:	Rear
Suspension (front):	Independent, MacPherson strut
Suspension (rear):	Independent, semi-trailing arms and coil spring
Top speed:	92mph (148km/h)
0-60mph (96km/h):	11.6 seconds
Production (1500, 1600, 1800):	155,288

LEFT: *The start of a new era; a pre-production 1500 which was displayed at the 1962 Geneva Show. The model's manufacture began in October of that year and continued until 1964.*

RIGHT: *The 1.6 litre four-door 1600 followed the 1500 in 1964. In 1966 came a two-door version, the 1600-2, which was revised as the 1602 in 1971. This is a 1974 car.*

BELOW: *The popular 1800 followed the 1500 in 1963. In 1968 the model received a new engine based on the block of the 1966 2000 and the crankshaft of the 1600. It was built in this revised form until 1972, and this is a 1969 example.*

FORD CORTINA (1962-1966)

The fastest selling car in the history of the British motor industry – over a million were built in four and a half years – the deceptively orthodox Cortina was the first of a line that endured until 1982. Outwardly a lively, well mannered family saloon, it spawned two potent derivatives, both of which appeared in 1963. The GT was mechanically closely related to the standard car, but the exciting Cortina Lotus was powered by a Ford-based, 1.6-litre, twin-overhead-camshaft engine and was capable of speeds in excess of 105mph (169km/h).

Created by Ford of Britain in response to its German counterpart's front-wheel-drive, V4-engined Taunus, the Cortina is regarded as a copybook exercise in engineering and, above all, product planning. This is a discipline that is commonplace today among car makers, but in the 1960's it was one which Ford alone practised within Britain's motor industry. Product planning was intended to remove the process of creating new models from being the exclusive domain of the chief executive, a system in which hunch and personal whim inevitably played their parts. The vital work was devolved to a separate department, headed in this instance by Terence Beckett, which, working in close conjunction with the engineers, also meticulously scrutinized costs and overall expenditure. An example of the vigour of these disciplines is that the Cortina's steering wheel was redesigned on no less than four occasions because the first renderings exceeded the planners estimates by a halfpenny (0.25p).

With the American/German-designed Taunus in the offing, Ford's chairman, Sir Patrick Hennessy, was determined to produce a rival and, in the spring of 1960, work began on what was coded project Archbishop. The starting point was Ford's substantial Classic saloon, due to appear in 1961, from which the structural engineers were directed to remove about 250lb (113kg) of weight. This was achieved by adopting aircraft stressing techniques in the car's sub-structure and further precious pounds were saved by dispensing with the boot floor so that the top of the petrol tank did double duty as such.

Styling was the work of Roy Brown, who had been responsible for the lines of the ill-fated American Ford Edsel of 1958 and who, after its failure, had been transferred to the company's British operations. Brown more than redeemed himself with the Cortina's body, which was to be built in two- and four-door saloon and estate car forms.

Engineering was the responsibility of Fred Hart, executive engineer, light cars. The Archbishop followed the company's well proven approach of using a four cylinder, overhead valve engine, in this instance of 1.2 litres, to drive the half-elliptic-sprung live rear axle. Ford's trusted MacPherson struts were used at the front.

Olympic Echoes

Very late in the model's evolution, the car became the Cortina, on account of the 1960 Winter Olympics having been held at Cortina d'Ampezzo in the Italian Alps. This was a reflection of the fact that Ford was also looking to export it to Europe.

As introduced at the 1962 London Motor Show, the light Cortina proved to be capable of around 75mph (121km/h). If offered good value for money, and was soon selling strongly.

It attracted private customers, and also fleet buyers who liked its conservative mechanicals.

Rally-Proven GT

The Cortina's performance was pepped up, in January 1963, with the introduction of an optional 1.5 litre engine. This power unit was also used, in Weber carburettored state in the 90mph (149km/h) Cortina GT. It sported front disc brakes, and was only built in two-door form, also appearing in 1963. The GT was not only a sales success for the company, but proved to be a successful rally car.

Lighter, faster but initially less reliable was the Cortina Lotus which similarly appeared in 1963. It had aluminium doors, bonnet and boot lid. It was powered by the Cortina-based, 1.6 litre, twin-overhead-camshaft engine used in Lotus's own Elan. it was only pro-duced in two-door form and was solely available in cream with a distinctive green side stripe. Completed by Lotus rather than Ford, the original rear suspension was dispensed with and replaced by a Lotus-designed system of trailing radius arm, coil springs and A brackets. However, this proved unsatisfactory and, in October 1965, the original layout was reinstated. Triumphant on both road and track, the Cortina Lotus crowned the launch of Ford Britain's most successful model line. The Cortina name was destined to endure for twenty years of consistent and highly profitable production.

Specifications: Ford Cortina 1200

Length:	14ft (4267mm)
Width:	5ft 2in (1575mm)
Height:	4ft 8in (1422mm)
Wheelbase:	8ft 2in (2489mm)
Track:	front and rear 4ft 1½in (1257mm)
Unladen weight:	1763lb (800kg)
Engine: Four cylinder, overhead valve, 80x58mm, 1198cc. Compression ration, 8.7:1. Max power, 48bhp at 4800rpm. Max torque, 63lb.ft at 2700rpm.	
Transmission:	Four-speed manual
Drive:	Rear
Suspension (front):	Independent, MacPherson strut
Suspension (rear):	Live axle, half-elliptic springs
Top speed:	75mph (121km/h)
0-60mph (96km/h):	22.6 seconds
Production (total):	1,014,102

Ford Cortina

1.3 litre Classic 1961

1.5 litre engine 1962

1.5 litre twin ohc
Lotus Elan 1962

1.2 litre Cortina 1962

two-door saloon   four-door saloon

optional 1.5 litre estate
engine 1963

Lotus Cortina
1963

GT
1963

BELOW: *A 1966 Lotus Cortina finished in its traditional livery. The Lotus badge is on the left of the radiator grille. The doors, bonnet and boot lid are made of aluminium.*

ABOVE: *The Cortina Estate Car which arrived in 1963. This Super version is identified by the Di-Nok imitation wood grain finish, an American import, on its body sides.*

NAR 362D

RENAULT R16 (1965-1979)

Nowadays the hatchback is relatively commonplace but in the 1960's an opening rear door was almost exclusively confined to estate cars. One of the first successful hatchback saloons, which had a profound impact on the rest of the motoring world, was Renault's front-wheel-drive R16. Destined for a 14-year production life, over 1.8 million examples of this spacious family car were built.

This was a brand new design with no carries-over from earlier Renaults and it was manufactured at a new factory, established at Le Harvre-Sandouville. The high five-door saloon body, styled by Yves George, was imbued with an almost awkward but, it transpired, timeless quality. It incorporated a strong unitary hull because of the loss of rigidity caused by the rear-opening door. The 16 was built in Standard, Luxe and Grand Luxe forms that were respectively fitted with a bench, separate and fully reclining front seats. The rear seat was also movable and there were no less than seven permutations of the various squabs to permit the maximum carrying capacity.

The 16's 1.5 litre 58bhp engine was an advanced concept and followed a theme, established with the R8-1100 of 1964, of a pushrod four with five bearing crankshaft. The principal departure from previous practice was the weight-saving aluminium, pressure diecast block used in conjunction with wet cylinder liners. Unusually, the 16 dispensed with the traditional dynamo and was equipped with an alternator which is now the norm. The nylon cooling fan was not operated by the usual belt but was activated by a thermostatic switch, today a familiar feature but then rather a novelty.

Although this was a front-wheel-drive car, Renault did not adopt the British Motor Corporation/Issigonis approach of a transversely mounted engine. Instead it remained in the usual in-line position driving the wheels via a forward-mounted, four-speed, all-synchromesh, aluminium cased gearbox. Unusually, for its year, the R16 perversely used a steering column gear change, a feature that the rest of the European motoring world had dispensed with in the 1950's.

Suspension was, inevitably, all-independent with wishbones at the front and rear trailing arms. The suspension medium was provided by torsion bars, in the manner of the R4 of 1962, which were longitudinally located at the front and transversely at the rear. A curious result of this layout was the fact that the R16 had an asymmetrical wheelbase with the right hand side about 2in (50mm) shorter than the left.

Little wonder that such an advanced model should be voted Car of the Year in 1965. The R16 performed as well as it looked and was capable of over 80mph (129km/h) with plenty of low speed torque; in other words, it was a real puller. Visibility was enhanced by the deeply sloping bonnet and the car was comfortable and softly sprung. A very real bonus was the excellent carrying capacity which made it a firm favourite among European families, for it could digest an apparently inexhaustible amount of people and luggage.

In 1968 came the 16TS with enlarged 1.6 litre 88bhp engine, while an automatic option arrived in 1969. This power unit was extended to all R16s for 1971 and in 1973 came the 93bhp TX, with five-speed gearbox and capable of over 100mph (161km/h). By the time that the R16 ceased production in 1979, there were many more hatchbacks on the road than had been in 1965. Imitation, as they say, is the sincerest form of flattery.

Specifications: Renault R16

Length:	13ft 10in (4216mm)
Width:	5ft 4in (1626mm)
Height:	4ft 7in (1397mm)
Wheelbase:	right, 8ft 8in (2642mm); left, 8ft 10in (2692mm)
Track:	front 4ft 4in (1320mm), rear 4ft 2in (1270mm)
Unladen weight:	2161lb (980kg)
Engine: Four cylinder, overhead valve, 76x81mm, 1470cc. Compression ratio, 8.5:1. Max power, 58bhp at 5000rpm. Max torque, 78lb/ft at 2800rpm.	
Transmission:	Four-speed manual
Drive:	Front
Suspension (front):	Independent, torsion bars and wishbones
Suspension (rear):	Independent, torsion bars and trailing arms
Top speed:	82mph (132km/h)
0-60mph (96km/h):	16.9 seconds
Production:	1,846,000

BELOW: *The R16's spacious interior displayed to good effect. The 16 popularized the concept of the hatchback with its ease of loading and good carrying capacity.*

ABOVE: *Looking like no other car, the high, roomy 16 was identified with outdoor pursuits as this picture, used in a manufacturer's brochure dating from 1974, emphasizes.*

BELOW: *Head-on view of a 1974 right-hand-drive 16TX with enlarged 1647cc engine and five-speed gearbox. It is identifiable by the rectangular headlights and revised grille.*

ROLLS-ROYCE SILVER SHADOW (1965-1980)

The most significant model in Rolls-Royce's post-war history, the Shadow incorporated three notable innovations for the company. The separate chassis, a feature of the marque from the outset, was dispensed with and replaced by unitary body construction. Another departure from previous practice was the fitment of independent rear suspension, while the long running, servo-assisted, mechanical rear brakes were dispensed with and replaced by all-round discs.

Created under the direction of chief engineer, Harry Grylls, the model was also available in T-Series Bentley guise, and was significant for being the first Rolls-Royce since the Silver Ghost, which had ceased production in 1925, actually to make money for its makers. Since the 1920's Rolls-Royce had balanced its books through revenues received from the sale of aero engines, but the Shadow was financially viable on its own account. This was fortuitous because in 1971 Rolls-Royce announced its bankruptcy; the car division was subsequently hived off and it was able profitably to manufacture the model until 1980.

Beyond The Cloud

The car was both shorter and lower than the Silver Cloud III it replaced which meant that the famous Rolls-Royce radiator returned to its more elegant pre-war proportions. The 6.2 litre V8 engine had first appeared in the Cloud II of 1959 but it was fitted with new cylinder heads, so that the hitherto almost inaccessible sparking plugs were more conveniently located above the exhaust manifolds, rather than below them. Four-speed automatic transmission was standardized as was power-assisted steering. The most radical mechanical departure was the fitment of independent rear suspension with trailing arms and coil springs. Also new was a high pressure hydraulic system serving the self-levelling suspension and the brakes.

The four-door saloon body was, like the Silver Cloud, produced by Pressed Steel, but the absence of a chassis meant that there were no more truly coachbuilt options. The interior was, however, beautifully trimmed in leather and featured specially selected walnut veneers.

On the road the Shadow provided the refined, comfortable motoring for which the marque is famous. The car was capable of 115mph (185km/h) with 60mph (96km/h) creditably coming up in a shade under 11 seconds. But on the debit side was excessive road noise and a slow response from the power-assisted steering.

The following year of 1966 saw the arrival of a two-door version, adapted by the in-house Mulliner Park Ward division, and it became available in convertible form in the following year. These two-door cars were known as Silver Shadows until 1971, when they were allotted the Corniche name.

Rolls-Royce pursued a policy of continual refinement of its cars, but the first major change to the Shadow's specifications came in mid-1968 with the arrival of three-speed automatic transmission; hitherto optional air conditioning was standardized for 1970. In mid-1970 the V8 was enlarged for the first time, to 6.7 litres, by lengthening the stroke from 91 to 99mm.

The greatly improved Silver Shadow II arrived early in 1977. Outwardly identifiable by a front air dam, it benefitted from the introduction of rack-and-pinion steering and inside there was a new fascia and sophisticated split level air conditioning. A long wheelbase version of the Shadow had appeared in 1969 and it was renamed Silver Wraith II in 1977. This second generation of cars was destined for a four-year production life. Finally, in 1980, these best-selling Rolls-Royces for over 40 years were replaced, with one exception, by the Silver Spirit. The survivor was the Corniche convertible and this two-door model remains in production at the time of writing, 13 years after the demise of its saloon parent.

ABOVE: *The Shadow II's facia: its instruments were concentrated more in front of the driver than previously. Outlets for the new split-level air conditioning are in the middle.*

RIGHT: *A 1979 Silver Shadow II. It was outwardly identical to its predecessor with the exception of black polyurethane-faced bumpers and air dam below. Note the presence of the wash and wipe headlamp facility.*

Specifications: Rolls-Royce Silver Shadow I

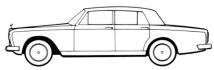

Length:	16ft 11in (5156mm)
Width:	5ft 11in (1803mm)
Height:	4ft 11in (1499mm)
Wheelbase:	9ft 11in (3023mm)
Track:	front and rear, 4ft 9in (1448mm)
Unladen weight:	4660lb (2113kg)
Engine: V8, overhead valve, 104x91mm, 6230cc. Compression ratio, 9:1. Max power, not disclosed. Max torque, not disclosed	
Transmission:	Four-speed automatic
Drive:	Rear
Suspension (front):	Independent, coil springs and wishbones
Suspension (rear):	Independent, coil springs and trailing arms
Top speed:	115mph (185km/h)
0-60mph (96km/h):	10.9 seconds
Production (total):	27,915

ABOVE: *The Corniche, a two-door version of the Shadow which was so named in 1971. The convertible, this is a 1975 car, remains in production at the time of writing.*

BELOW: *The chrome-bumpered Silver Shadow I changed little outwardly over the years. This is a 1976 car although, in 1970, the long running V8 was increased to 6.7 litres.*

Rolls-Royce Silver Shadow

6.2 litre V8 Silver Cloud II 1959

Silver Shadow/Bentley T Series 1965

four-door saloon   two-door saloon 1966

long wheelbase 1967   convertible 1967

6.7 litre V8 1970

Silver Shadow II/T2 1977   Silver Wraith II   Corniche 1971

to 1980   to 1980   to 1980   to date

NSU Ro80 (1967-1977)

Since the motor car first appeared in 1886, the reciprocating engine has been its driving force, but in the 1960's this status quo was challenged by a seemingly more efficient rotary engine created by the German inventor, Felix Wankel. Undoubtedly the most impressive Wankel-driven car of its day was NSU's Ro80, but, sadly, technical problems with the unconventional power unit were never wholly resolved, and the financial strain it placed on the small company resulted in NSU being absorbed by Volkswagen in 1969. The Neckarsulm-based business persisted with the idea, but eventually ceased trading in 1977.

ABOVE: *The Ro80's compact twin rotor Wankel engine which embodied the car's strengths and weaknesses. Smooth running and flexible, its unreliability kept the public away.*

BELOW: *A 1973 Ro80 with its distinctive aerodynamically refined body lines shown to advantage. Tinted windows, head restraints and reclining seats were standard.*

NSU had manufactured motor cycles prior to producing its first car in 1905 and, over 40 years later, in 1951 it built its first Wankel engine for use in a two-wheeler. The concept was then extended to cars and, in 1958, NSU introduced its Sport Prinz coupé. The open version of 1963 was the world's first rotary engined production car. Appropriately named the Wankel Spyder, it had a 497cc single rotor engine; just 2375 were built.

The Ro80 was, by contrast, a much more ambitious project. It was an impressive front-wheel-drive, four-door saloon with contours honed for aerodynamic refinement. Its appearance was greatly enhanced by a low bonnet line made possible by the use of the compact twin-rotor Wankel engine, with a capacity equivalent to 1990cc, located ahead of the three-speed semi-automatic gearbox. Disc brakes were fitted all round, being inboard at the front, and the rack-and-pinion steering was power-assisted. Suspension was all-independent.

Good Points And Bad Points

The element which excited the most interest was, of course, the unconventional power unit. One of the advantages of the Wankel is that it employs far less components than a conventional engine, which inefficiently converts the reciprocating action of its pistons to the rotary power of a crankshaft. Less happy was the fact that the petrol had to be mixed with oil to lubricate the combustion chambers which meant that the car's emissions levels were high. But the real problem concerned the important cast-iron seals at the tips of the three-cornered rotors. These were vulnerable to excessive wear and, despite ongoing research, this weakness dogged the car throughout its ten-year production life. Nevertheless, the overall excellence of the vehicle was recognized when the Ro80 was awarded the 1967 Car of the Year accolade.

On the road, the handsome five-seater saloon more than lived up to its good looks, possessing excellent road-holding and stability, while the smooth running engine endowed the car with a top speed of over 105mph (169km/h). Steering and brakes were deemed excellent. However, at best, the NSU could only return a fuel consumption of around 20mpg (14 lires/100km) with a pint (0.56 litres) of oil being consumed by the engine every 300 miles (483km).

A Mark II version of the Ro80 appeared for 1970, outwardly identifiable by twin headlamps. The engine benefitted from an improved lubrication system in this model, while single spark plugs per rotor replaced the original two. The 1971 cars were fitted with additional emissions controls but, despite the most generous of warranty-agreements, the public was still wary of the revolutionary engine and, by the time that production ceased in 1977, a mere 37,204 examples of this last NSU car had been built.

RIGHT: *Rear view of a 1977 Ro80 with its high tail and modern lines which do not appear out of place today. Alloy wheels were standard.*

BELOW: *This 1977 Ro80 is said to be the last example to have been imported into Britain and, since then, has covered well over 70,000 miles (112,700km).*

UGY 985M

Specifications: NSU Ro80

Length:	15ft 8in (4775mm)
Width:	5ft 9in (1753mm)
Height:	4ft 7in (1397mm)
Wheelbase:	9ft 4in (2845mm)
Track:	front 4ft 10in (1473mm), rear 4ft 8in (1422mm)
Unladen weight:	2668lb (1210kg)
Engine: Two chamber Wankel, 995cc per revolution, 1990cc. Max power, 115bhp at 5500rpm. Max torque, 117lb/ft at 4500rpm.	
Transmission:	Three-speed semi-automatic
Drive:	Front
Suspension (front):	Independent, MacPherson strut
Suspension (rear):	Independent, coil springs and trailing links
Top speed:	106mph (170km/h)
0-60mph (96km/h):	14.2 seconds
Production:	37,204

Jaguar XJ6, XJ (1968-1986)

Jaguar's large and medium-sized saloon lines merged in 1968 with the arrival of the low, lithe XJ6 model. Styled by chairman, Sir William Lyons, it was his favourite Jaguar. The model attained levels of refinement which were compared with those of Rolls-Royce cars and, in some respects, were superior to them. But because Jaguar was part of the turmoil that engulfed the British-owned sector of the motor industry in the 1970's, although the XJ6 was destined for a prolonged 18-year production life, for some of this time, its build quality left much to be desired.

The team that created the XJ6 was led by chief development engineer, Robert Knight. The finished product combined many of the best features of its predecessors; it was lower and slightly longer than the S-Type but shared similar interior dimensions to its big 420G stablemate.

Much work was expended on the suspension, which was a new coil spring and trailing wishbones system at the front, while at the rear it was essentially the same independent layout of upper drive shafts, lower wishbones and coil springs that had been introduced on the Mark X saloon and E-Type sports car in 1961.

The car was offered with two version of Jaguar's long-running, twin-over-head-camshaft, six cylinder XK engine. The 4.2 litre unit had first appeared in the Mark X in 1964 but its 2.8 litre alternative was a new capacity. A four-speed manual gearbox was fitted along with a three-speed auto-matic option which was selected for the majority of examples, many of which were sold in America.

The 4.2 litre car, which was capable of 120mph (193km/h), was by far and away the most popular model of the range and it soon became apparent that the XJ6 set new standards in ride, handling, smoothness and general refinement. It represented excellent value at £2687; in other words, Jaguar had done it again and there were few surprises when it became Car of the Year in 1968.

Options Available

The XJ6 was also available in more expensive Daimler form and, in July 1972, both versions were offered with the 5.3 litre V12 engine which had first appeared in the Series III E-Type of 1971. The Daimler was also produced in long wheelbase form, from September 1972, and this option was soon extended to the six- and V12-engined Jaguars.

The original XJ6 continued to be built until the 1974 season, when the Series II car appeared with a new, higher bumper line and accordingly a shallower radiator grille. The choice of wheelbases was retained initially but the shorter of the two was discontinued at the end of 1974 and the longer 9ft 4in (2845mm) version, which provided rear passengers with more legroom, standardized. The 2.8 and 4.2 options continued but the smaller capacity engine was only built for export for a year, and in 1975 the established 3.4 litre engine arrived as an alternative. Later in 1975 the 6 suffix was dropped from the model's title, the cars becoming the XJ3.4 and XJ4.2.

An attractive, though low production, two-door, pillarless, 4.2 litre coupé was announced in the autumn of 1973, although the first of these cars was not built until 1975. Only 6505 examples were made before production ceased in 1977.

By 1979 the lines of the XJ6 had outwardly changed little since its introduction but, in that year, Jaguar unveiled its Series III version of the design. The body was skilfully refined by the famous Italian coachbuilders Pininfarina with the rear roof line raised, deeper side windows introduced and the attendant wing lines enhanced. Further improvements were made to the interior and the 4.2 litre car was fitted with fuel injection, while a five-speed gearbox became optional. This was standardized in 1981.

In theory this was a greatly improved car but, at this time, the company's BL Cars parent was in the throes of yet another reorganization. The XJs suffered accordingly, although a turning point for Jaguar came in 1980 with the appointment of John Egan as its chairman. From there on the cars' quality gradually improved and the Series III became a desirable and sought-after car. It was replaced in 1986 by a new XJ6 (see page 300) although the V12-powered version continued in production until 1992. Still competitive at the time it bowed out, the model remains as a lasting tribute to the stylistic genius of Jaguar's then chairman Sir William Lyons and his outstanding engineering team.

Specifications: Jaguar XJ6 Series I 4.2

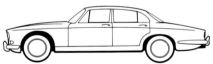

Length:	15ft 9in (4801mm)
Width:	5ft 9in (1753mm)
Height:	4ft 4in (1321mm)
Wheelbase:	9ft (2743mm)
Track:	front 4ft 10in (1473mm), rear 4ft 10⅓in (1482mm)
Unladen weight:	3524lb (1598kg)
Engine:	Six cylinder, twin overhead camshaft, 92x106mm, 4235cc. Compression ratio, 8:1. Max power, 245bhp at 5500rpm. Max torque, 283lb/ft at 5500rpm
Transmission:	Four-speed manual or three-speed automatic
Drive:	Rear
Suspension (front):	Independent, coil springs and wishbones
Suspension (rear):	Independent, upper drive shafts, coil springs and lower wishbones
Top speed:	120mph (193km/h)
0-60mph (96km/h):	10.4 seconds
Production (total, Series I-III):	278,344

LEFT: *Head-on view of a Series I XJ6. This type of radiator grille endured until late in 1973 which was when the Series II cars, with a higher bumper line, were introduced.*

ABOVE: *The Series III XJ which appeared in 1979, was subtly refined by Pininfarina. It was built in six cylinder form until the model ceased production in 1986.*

BELOW: *Jaguar's legendary XK twin-overhead-camshaft engine in a 1986 XJ, the final year of the model's production. It was available in 3.4 and 4.2 litre forms.*

Jaguar XJ6

```
E-Type 1961 ─ Mark X saloon 1961
    |                 |
4.2 litre engine ── 4.2 litre engine
    1964              1964
                       |
                   420G 1967
                       |
                Series I XJ6 1968
                       |
              ┌────────┴────────┐
           2.8 litres      4.2 litres
5.3 litres V12
    1971
              └────────┐
   XJ12 1972       Series II
                     1974
                       |
                  3.4 litres
                     1975
                       |
  to 1975         Series III
                     1979
                       |
                   to 1986      to 1986
  to 1992
```

ALFA ROMEO ALFASUD (1972-1983)

Alfa Romeo's brave bid for the mass market, the Alfasud, produced at a purpose-built factory near Naples, was the firm's first front-wheel-drive model. Ingenious in design, its roadholding was particularly impressive but the car suffered from build quality problems and production ceased in 1983, although a handsome Sprint version continued to be manufactured until 1989.

Alfa Romeo was established in Milan – indeed its badge incorporated the city's coat of arms – in the prosperous north of Italy. It was nationalized in 1933 and in the 1960's, in a bid to generate employment in the poverty stricken south, the government encouraged the firm to establish a factory at Pomigliano d'Arco. The resulting Alfa*sud* (for south) was its first product and a very impressive piece of design.

The car's overall conception was the work of an Austrian-born former Porsche engineer, Rudolph Hruska, who had joined Alfa Romeo in 1950. There were no carries-over from former models. The Alfasud had a distinctive fastback, four-door saloon body by Ital Design which cloaked some appropriately adventurous mechanicals. The 1.2 litre, flat-four, 63bhp engine was positioned ahead of the front wheel axis and each cylinder bank employed a single overhead camshaft, progressively driven by a toothed rubber belt. This was mated to a transmission unit incorporating the differential, with drive shafts arrested by inboard disc brakes, and the four-speed gearbox. Suspension was by front MacPherson struts, while the dead, disc-braked rear axle was also coil-sprung and located by a Watts linkage and Panhard rod.

In this form the Alfasud was capable of over 90mph (149km/h), and the low centre of gravity of the engine and drive unit, coupled with front wheel drive, endowed the car with extraordinarily impressive handling, even if this smooth-running, quiet model lacked accelerative sparkle. Capacity was therefore progressively increased, first to 1286cc allied to a five-speed gearbox in 1977, and for 1979 came two alternative capacities of 1350 and 1490cc. The model was built in these forms until 1983 but, sadly, by this time it had developed a reputation for rusting. However, the Alfasud's engines found a home in the Alfa Romeo 33.

The Two-Door Ti

So much for the basic saloon. In 1974 the potent Alfasud Ti, standing for *turismo internazionale*, appeared. This was a two-door version of the design, with four rather than the customary twin headlamps and rear spoiler. Originally it had the same 1186cc engine boosted to 68bhp and a standard five-speed gearbox, which

pushed the model's top speed to 100mph (161km/h). Capacity increases were thereafter similar to those of the four door model. Production continued until 1981.

In 1976 came a third variation of the theme in the shape of the Alfasud Sprint. This was based on the model's standard floorpan fitted with an impressive coupé hatchback body, also by Ital Design, which was similar in appearance to its larger Alfetta contemporary. Mechanicals were closely related to those of the Ti. The top line version was the 90bhp Veloce Sprint with a 1490cc engine. The coupé remained in production until 1989, six years after the saloon had been discontinued, its potential perhaps sadly unrealized.

LEFT: *The Alfasud as it originally appeared in Britain in 1973. It was an all new front-wheel-drive car with 1.2 litre, flat-four engine and body styled by Ital Design.*

ABOVE: *The Alfasud Sprint Veloce 1.5 hatchback coupé; its body, like the saloon, was by Ital Design. This is a 1981 car; the model outproduced the saloon and continued until 1989.*

BELOW: *An Alfasud Ti, with its twin rather than single headlamps, displaying the excellent roadholding for which all versions of the model were rightly renowned.*

Specifications: Alfa Romeo Alfasud 1.2 litres

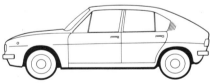

Length:	12ft 9in (3886mm)
Width:	5ft 2in (1575mm)
Height:	4ft 5in (1346mm)
Wheelbase:	8ft 1in (2464mm)
Track:	front 4ft 6in (1372mm), rear 4ft 5in (1346mm)
Unladen weight:	1900lb (862kg)

Engine: Four cylinder, horizontally opposed, single overhead camshaft per bank, 80x59mm, 1186cc. Compression ratio, 8.8:1. Max power, 63bhp at 6000rpm. Max torque, 63lb/ft at 3500rpm.

Transmission:	Four-speed manual
Drive:	Front
Suspension (front):	Independent, MacPherson struts
Suspension (rear):	Dead axle, coil springs and Watts linkage
Top speed:	91mph (146km/h)
0-60mph (96km/h):	15.5 seconds
Production (total):	156,001

RENAULT 5 (1972 to date)

One of the great French designs of the post-war years, this small front-wheel-drive car's mechanicals were deceptively orthodox, but cloaked in a two-door hatchback body of such distinct and enduring style that its lines were perpetuated when the 5 was updated in 1984. The model was produced with a wide variety of engine options throughout its life ranging from a modest 782cc to 1.7 litres.

The 5's original dimensions were similar to those of Renault's front-wheel-drive Renault 4, which was then 11 years' old. Its suspension also followed that model, and that of the Renault 16, with longitudinal torsion bars at the front and transversely located ones at the rear, these being respectively used in conjunction with wishbones and trailing arms.

The beautifully packaged and elegant body, the brainchild of Renault's Michel Boue, was a masterpiece of industrial design. The lines were sketched in a mere two days and accepted, without modification, by the management. The intention was to appeal, in particular, to young people and to women, sectors of the buying public who had hitherto scorned Renault's products. This objective was triumphantly achieved and, in consequence, no sheet metal changes were made to the 5 until its mechanicals were extensively revised twelve years later in 1984.

A Choice Of Engines
The car was initially offered with a choice of three engines which, like the 16, were mounted in-line rather than in the increasingly practical transverse location. The four-speed, all-synchromesh gearbox was therefore positioned ahead of the engine with the front disc brakes mounted outboard. The lowest capacity unit, of 782cc, was courtesy of the R4 and, for taxation reasons, only sold in France. It lasted until 1976. For the rest of Europe the smallest overhead valve wet liner four was of 845cc which was the 4's other engine, tuned to 34bhp. The third option was a linered-down 956cc version of the unit fitted to the 5's contemporary, the Renault 6-1100.

In its 956cc form, the 5 was capable of 85mph (137km/h). It was roomy,

comfortable and quiet, and its sheer practicality and good manners made it plenty of friends, not only in France, but wherever it was marketed throughout the European community.

The 956cc engine survived until 1979 when it was replaced by a 1108cc unit. Prior to that, in 1976, a 1.3 litre GTL had arrived which was tuned to

enhance economy rather than performance. The same engine was also used to power an automatic version for the 1979 season.

In 1976 came the much faster 5 Alpine, which used a bored-out 1397cc version of the 1.3 litre unit. Developing 93bhp, it was fitted with a five-speed gearbox. This potent but noisy car was capable of over 110mph (177km/h). In 1979 it won the Group 5 section of the Monte Carlo Rally. In that year it was introduced into Britain, where it was known as the 5 Gordini so as not to be confused with the Chrysler Alpine. Built until 1981, it was replaced by a turbocharged version.

The mainstream model continued in production until 1984, when it was replaced by the New 5 which visually re-

sembled the old model but was longer, wider and lighter than its predecessor. The three-door option was continued, but there was also a longer wheelbase five-door version. The engines were now transversely mounted and spanned the 956/1721cc range, and because of the new layout, front MacPherson struts replaced the torsion bars. There was also a GT Turbo version, with external air dam and rear disc brakes, capable of 125mph (201km/h).

The 5 remains in production, in 1.4 litre Campus form, at the time of writing. It is tribute, in particular, to the talents of stylist Michel Boue, who sadly never lived to see the success of his design. Aged only 35, he died of cancer in 1971.

RIGHT: *The front-wheel-drive R5, with its enduring body style essayed by Michel Boue, looked very up to date on its arrival in 1972. Little wonder that it lasted for 22 years.*

Renault 5 (to 1984)

	Renault 4 1961		
	6-1100 1969		12 1969
	Renault 5 1972		
782cc — 845cc		956cc	
to 1976			1289cc 1976 · 1397cc Alpine
	to 1979 · 1108cc 1979		turbo 1981
to 1984		to 1984	to 1984

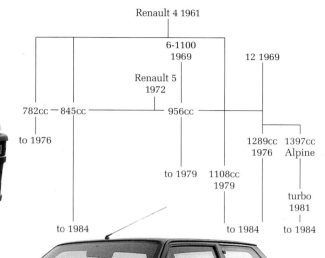

ABOVE: *Although outwardly resembling the 5, the Turbo was a 1.4 litre mid-engined design of 1980 for Group 3 competition. It was replaced in 1983 by the Turbo 2 shown here.*

RIGHT: *The New 5 appeared in 1984 and the Monaco arrived in 1988. Unlike its predecessors, the 1.7 or 1.4 litre engines were transversely mounted rather than being in-line.*

BELOW RIGHT: *The potent Alpine 5 arrived in 1976 and in 1981 was replaced by the Alpine Turbo which was called the Gordini in Britain. This example dates from 1983.*

Specifications: Renault 5 956cc

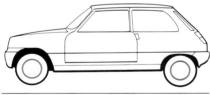

Length:	11ft 5in (3480mm)
Width:	5ft (1524mm)
Height:	4ft 7in (1397mm)
Wheelbase:	7ft 10in (2388mm)
Track:	front 4ft 2in (1270mm), rear 4ft 1in (1245mm)
Unladen weight:	1625lb (737kg)
Engine: Four cylinder, overhead valve, 65x72mm, 956cc. Compression ratio, 9.25:1. Max power, 43bhp at 5500rpm. Max torque 45lb/ft at 3500rpm.	
Transmission:	Four-speed manual
Drive:	Front
Suspension (front):	Independent, torsion bars and wishbones
Suspension (rear):	Independent, trailing arms, torsion bars
Top speed:	85mph (137km/h)
0-60mph (96km/h):	20.8 seconds
Production (to 1984):	5,471,709

The car for which Volkswagen, and Germany, had been waiting, the Golf was the long anticipated replacement for the Beetle, to which, perhaps significantly, it bore no resemblance. The crisply styled hatchback by Ital Design was powered by a choice of four cylinder, single-overhead-camshaft engines from in-house Audi. The front-wheel-drive Golf went on to become Europe's best-selling car. So successful was the theme that its proportions were retained for the enlarged New Golf of 1983. However, the third generation car of 1991 featured more rounded body lines. The model was also significant for spawning the GTI of 1975, which was the first of the "hot hatchbacks" that inspired a host of imitators.

In 1974 Volkswagen recorded its first loss ever, as demand for the distinctive but ageing rear-engined, air-cooled Beetle faltered. However, in that year the first of a new generation of VWs appeared in the shape of the Audi-engined, front-wheel-drive Passat saloon, styled by Ital Design. Next came the sporty Scirocco coupé, with a similar pedigree, and it was swiftly followed, in May 1974, by the long awaited Golf.

The car was closely related to the Scirocco and used its floor pan, suspension and 1.5 litre engine. The body, however, was completely different, being distinctive and well proportioned. Its lack of external decoration pointed towards a long production run. It was available in three- and five-door forms with two engine options; the second, a smaller 1.1 litre four, was to be shared with the Audi 50, announced later in 1974. These were transversely mounted and the larger capacity unit was available with three-speed automatic transmission. Suspension was all-independent with front MacPherson struts and trailing arms at the rear. Drums brakes were employed all round, but the 1.5 litre Golf was fitted with front discs.

Pedigree Performer

In its most basic form it was a 85mph (137km/h) car, while the 1500 was capable of an impressive 95mph (153km/h). From the very outset, Golfs were praised for their performance, handling and economy, while build quality was characteristically good.

Further engine options swiftly followed, a 1.6 litre version arrived in 1976 and then a 1.3 litre Golf for 1980. In 1977 the 1.5 litre car was offered in diesel form. Unusually, it shared the same block as the petrol unit and attained considerable popularity in view of its smooth running and general good manners. This engine was replaced by the 1.6 litre unit in 1980.

For 1976 came the lively Golf GTI which was powered by an uprated 1.6 litre, fuel-injected, 110bhp engine. Suspension was stiffer and lower, disc brakes were fitted all round and, externally, a front spoiler was employed. The GTI was a potent performer capable of over 110mph (177km/h) and the specification remained constant until 1982 when the engine was enlarged to 1.8 litres and a five-speed gearbox was introduced. This unit was also available in detuned form in the standard car.

The Golf was also produced with a cabriolet (open) body which arrived in 1979 as Karmann was ceasing to build the open Beetle. The Osnabrück company was also responsible for this open Golf, which was available in standard and GTI guises.

Creature Comforts

The Golf proper was produced in its original form until August 1983 when it was replaced by a car that outwardly resembled it, but was wider and longer and provided rear passengers with more leg room. Luggage space was also improved. Although these cars were heavier than their predecessors, better aerodynamics and different gearing saw fuel consumption improved. Engine options ranged from 1 litre to the 1.8 litre GTI, while the cabriolet was perpetuated in its lighter pre-1983 form. A further GTI variant appeared in 1985 with the fitment of a twin-overhead-camshaft 16-valve head, the 1.8 litre unit developing 139hbp. In 1989 came a supercharged four-wheel-drive Rallye G60, limited to 5000 cars, which were replicas of Volkswagen's fruitless bid to win the World Rally Championship. The Synchro, a four-wheel-drive Golf, had arrived in 1988.

A Mark III version of the Golf arrived for the 1992 season. Slightly larger than hitherto with more curved contours, it was styled at Volkswagen's own studios, and was offered with a range of six engines from a 1.4 four to a 2.8 litre V6. Volkswagen had done its work well and this latest Golf was voted Car of the Year for 1992. The GTI has also been upgunned with the eight- and 16-valve heads now grafted on to 2 litre engines, courtesy of the Passat. Thus reinvigorated, the latest Golf range is looking good, ready to take Volkswagen into the 21st century.

RIGHT: *The original Golf, styled by Ital Design, appeared in 1974 and became the Beetle's long-awaited successor. This is a 1978 GL version.*

Volkswagen Golf

```
                                              1.5 litre Scirocco 1974

                                              1.1, 1.5 litre Golf 1974

1.1 litre Audi 50
      1974
                                              1.5 litre engine 1976

                   1.6 litre GTI 1976

                                              1.5 litre diesel 1977
cabriolet 1979

                                              1.3 litre engine 1980

                   1.8 litre GTI 1982

                                              1.6, 1.8 litre New Golf
                                                     1983
                   1.8 litre 16 valve
                          1985

                                              Four-wheel-drive
                                              Synchro 1988

                                              1.4, 2.8 litre V6
                                              Mark III 1992

Mark III 1993

   to date             to date                     to date
```

LEFT: *A Golf GTI of 1987 powered by a twin-overhead-camshaft, 139bhp, 16 valve, 1.8 litre engine. Standard fitments were five-speed gearbox, alloy wheels, sports seats and sun roof. The suspension was also lowered and reinforced.*

Specifications: Volkswagen Golf Mark I 1.1 litres

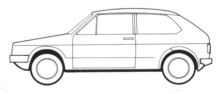

Length:	12ft 2in (3708mm)
Width:	5ft 3in (1600mm)
Height:	4ft 7in (1397mm)
Wheelbase:	7ft 10in (2388mm)
Track:	front 4ft 6in (1372mm), rear 4ft 5in (1346mm)
Unladen weight:	1808lb (820kg)
Engine: Transversely mounted, four cylinder, single overhead camshaft, 69x72mm, 1093cc. Compression ratio, 8:1. Max power, 50bhp at 6000rpm. Max torque, 67lb/ft at 3000rpm.	
Transmission:	Four-speed manual or three-speed automatic
Drive:	Front
Suspension (front):	Independent, MacPherson struts
Suspension (rear):	Independent, trailing arms and coil springs
Top speed:	85mph (137km/h)
0-60mph (96km/h):	15.9 seconds
Production (total to date):	14.1 million

CADILLAC SEVILLE (1980-1985)

As General Motors' flagship, Cadillac has long been in the vanguard of corporate innovation, be it stylistic or mechanical. The Seville offered both. It was fitted with a memorable saloon body which incorporated a blend of American and 1950's British styles. It also had the distinction of being the first Cadillac to be offered with a diesel engine as standard equipment. Regrettably this proved to be troublesome and was replaced, in 1982, by a petrol unit. So this is a car of extremes; some proved successful, others not so.

The 350cid (5.7 litres) Seville line, introduced in 1975, was the smallest Cadillac for 50 years which reflected a new, energy-conscious climate in America. The model endured, in essence, until the 1980 model year when it was replaced by the second generation Seville, which differed radically from its predecessor. The four-door saloon was, unusually, an amalgam of influences. The clipped, angular front was shared with its Eldo-rado stablemate but, at the rear, stylist Wayne Cady had adopted what was called a "trunkback" by grafting on a profile reminiscent of the Hooper- and Vanden Plas-bodied Rolls-Royces of the early 1950's. A blending of old and new themes was not unusual for General Motors; they had achieved precisely that with the original Buick Riviera of 1964.

Mechanically, unlike its predecessor, the new Seville espoused front wheel drive, which it shared with the Eldorado and the Buick Riviera and Oldsmobile Toronado. However, the Seville differed from them by being offered with a petrol-based Oldsmobile 350cid (5.7 litres) diesel V8 engine as standard. This had first been offered as an option by Cadillac in 1978. Apparently well mannered for a compression ignition unit, the diesel option represented a General Motors' challenge to Mercedes-Benz. The Seville was also available with 350 and 368cid (5.7 and 6 litres) petrol V8s. Drive was taken to the front wheels via a three-speed automatic gearbox. Suspension was by wishbones and torsion bars at the front and trailing arms and coil springs at the rear in conjunction with an electronic levelling control system. There were all-round disc brakes. The model was offered in two forms; the basic Seville and the more expensive limited edition Seville Elegante which featured sharper body lines and full-length beltline moulding.

Problems With The Diesel

In its diesel-engined form the Seville was capable of around 90mph (145km/h), while the petrol-engined cars could manage over 110mph (177km/h). As it happened, the majority of customers opted for the latter version, with over 63 per cent choosing one of the optional V8s. As if this was not discouraging enough, the Seville's diesel engine was soon plagued with reliability problems. Even so, it was retained in 1981 when the optional 350cid V8 was replaced by a 252cid (4.1 litres) V6.

It was not until the 1982 model year that the diesel was relegated to optional status, and the standard fitment became a new 250cid (4.1 litres), fuel-injected alloy V8. The Seville remained in production until 1985, when it was replaced by a new car of the same name. Seville sales were never high as a result of a combination of circumstances. The model's arrival coincided with the recession triggered by the 1979 oil price rise and, ironically, demand did not peak until 1985, which was the last year of production, when 39,755 cars were built. Earlier, the 1983 figure had stood at 34,115 of which the vast majority were Sevilles, plus a mere 3685 Elegantes.

LEFT: *The front-wheel-drive Seville with, curiously, the Cadillac name duplicated on the radiator surround and the grille! Mechanicals were shared with in-house Oldsmobile Toronado and Buick Riviera but the body was something different . . .*

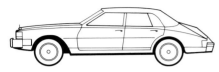

Length:	17ft (5182mm)
Width:	5ft 11in (1803mm)
Height:	4ft 6in (1372mm)
Wheelbase:	9ft 6in (2896mm)
Track:	front 4ft 11in (1499mm), rear 5ft (1524mm)
Unladen weight:	4195lb (1902kg)
Engine:	V8, overhead valve, 103x86mm, 350cid (5736cc). Compression ratio, 21.5:1. Max power, 105bhp at 3200rpm. Max torque, 205lb/ft at 1600rpm.
Transmission:	Three-speed automatic
Drive:	Front
Suspension (front):	Independent, torsion bars and wishbones
Suspension (rear):	Independent, coil springs and trailing arms
Top speed:	93mph (150km/h)
0-60mph (96km/h):	15.6 seconds
Production (total):	204,125

RIGHT: *The feature that made the Seville so memorable, its rear end which echoed coachbuilt British cars of the 1950's. This car dates from the introductory year of 1980.*

BELOW: *The Seville's body lines are beautifully revealed in this view. This is the standard car; the limited edition Elegante had sharper body lines and two-tone paintwork.*

MERCEDES-BENZ 190 (1982-1993)

The first small Mercedes-Benz since the demise of 1.9 litre 190 in 1961, the latter day 190 was, in effect, a scaled-down version of the company's large S-class saloon. Available with a choice of petrol and diesel engines, the model proved to be immensely popular and an impressive 1.9 million were built.

What Mercedes-Benz called the W201 took a lengthy eight years to evolve. Work began on the project in 1976 and a key factor in its creation was the fuel consumption legislation then pending in America, which was the firm's largest export market. This was the CAFE programme, standing for corporate average fuel economy, which took effect in the 1978 model year and required that any new model, either home-produced or imported, should have a fuel consumption of no less than 18mpg (15.7 litres/100km), with the figure rising in stages to 27.5mpg (10.3 litres/100km) by 1984. If this was not attained, the model's selling price would be inflated by fiscal sanction.

As the German company sold mostly large cars in America, CAFE was a powerful incentive for it to develop a smaller, more economical model. An added attraction was that such a car would appeal to young people who might not have previously contemplated Mercedes-Benz ownership. The 190 had a wheelbase of 8ft 9in (2667mm) which was 10in (254mm) less than that of its S-class brother. There was, as usual, a choice of engines – these had first appeared in the existing 200 model for 1981. They were a 2 litre, 90bhp, single-overhead-camshaft four which was available in the carburettored 190 and fuel-injected, 109bhp 190E form. However, for the American market the 190 was fitted with larger capacity engines: a 2.2 diesel and 2.3 litre petrol unit. Suspension was a departure from previous practice and was of MacPherson strut variety at the front with rear semi-trailing arms and coil springs.

Faster Versions
In its most basic form, the 190's top speed was approaching a leisurely 105mph (169km/h) although the fuel-injected 2 litre could attain 120mhp (193km/h). In 1984 came the 190E 2.3-16 which was powered by the enlarged 2.3 litre unit fitted with a twin-overhead-camshaft 16-valve cylinder head, developed by Britain's Cosworth Engineering. Capable of over 140mph (225km/h), 60mph (96km/h) came up in under nine seconds, making it the fastest in the Mercedes-Benz range.

In 1986 the 190 diesel range was joined by a 2.5 litre, turbocharged, five-cylinder unit; in the following year came a 2.6 litre petrol six – the 190E 2.6

having a claimed top speed of 134mph (216km/h). The 190 range was facelifted for 1989 as the original cars had been criticized for their rather basic interiors. In consequence, the seats were revised and improved. Outwardly these post-1989 cars are identifiable by the fitment of external mouldings which protect the lower area of the car's doors and wings. Simultaneously the 2.3-16 became the 2.5-16 on account of the engine's capacity being increased to 2.5 litres. This was achieved by upping the stroke, which took the top speed to beyond 145mph (233km/h),

The basic 2 litre carburettored model was replaced by a fuel-injected 1.8 litre engine in 1990. By now, the model was destined for only another three years' production. The 190 then bowed out in 1993 to make way for its C-Series replacement which sported a seven engine range essentially carried over from its predecessor. With sales of Mercedes-Benz's large and complex S-Class cars falling because of depressed markets at home and abroad, the 190's successor has now attained an importance which could never have been envisaged when the concept of a smaller, cheaper model was first conceived back in the 1970's.

BELOW: *Mercedes-Benz never produced a cabriolet version of the 190E so this 1984 car, complete with optional alloy wheels, would appear to be a private venture.*

Specifications: Mercedes-Benz 190 2 litre

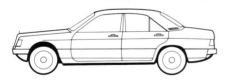

Length:	14ft 6in (4420mm)
Width:	5ft 6in (1676mm)
Height:	4ft 6in (1372mm)
Wheelbase:	8ft 9in (2667mm)
Track:	front 4ft 8in (1422mm), rear 4ft 7in (1397mm)
Unladen weight:	2381lb (1080kg)
Engine: Four cylinder, single overhead camshaft, 89x80mm, 1997cc. Compression ratio, 9:1. Max power, 90bhp at 5000rpm. Max torque, 122lb/ft at 2500rpm.	
Transmission:	Four-speed manual
Drive:	Rear
Suspension (front):	Independent, MacPherson struts
Suspension (rear):	Independent, coil springs and semi-trailing arms
Top speed:	105mph (169km/h)
0-60mph (96km/h):	13.6 seconds
Production (total):	1,879,629

ABOVE: *An American specification 190D powered by an economy-conscious diesel engine. The 1997cc four could return 35mpg (8 litres/ 100km).*

BELOW: *The 190E 2.3-16 of 1984 was the fastest car of the range and identifiable by its air dam and rear spoiler. The Cosworth-developed engine was a 16 valve twin-cam unit.*

BENTLEY TURBO R (1985 to date)

In the 1970's Bentley, as a marque name, was in severe danger of being axed by its Rolls-Royce parent. Since 1955, with the arrival of the outwardly similar Silver Cloud and S Series Bentley, its identity had been progressively subordinated to that of its illustrious owner. However, a turning point came in 1980 when the Bentley version of the Rolls-Royce Silver Spirit was given the model name of Mulsanne, rather than the customary identifying letter. Significantly, its potent Turbo derivative of 1982, which led to the greatly improved R, was only available in Bentley form. It came as a timely reminder of the make's illustrious racing history.

Bentley's finest hour arguably came when it won the Le Mans 24-hour race, on no less than five occasions, in the 1920's. The 1980 Mulsanne was named after the famous straight on the Sarthe racing circuit where the big green cars were once victorious. The model's origins were rooted in the Rolls-Royce Silver Shadow of 1965 (see page 282) and its T-Series Bentley equivalent. These were replaced in 1980 by the Silver Spirit, effectively a rebodied Shadow with revised independent rear suspension, in which the long-running V8 engine, of 6.7 litres, was retained.

The Mulsanne was, to all intents and purposes, a Rolls-Royce with a Bentley radiator. Sales prospects initially did not look encouraging for only 58 examples of its T2 predecessor had been sold in the three previous years, compared with 10,566 Shadows. But the Mulsanne name, rather than a simple identifying letter, clearly made some difference because Rolls-Royce produced 120 Bentleys in 1981 and this figure had quadrupled to 470 in 1985. This increase was, in no small part, due to the arrival, in 1982, of the Mulsanne Turbo.

Turbo Power

The car's underbonnet appearance was dominated by a Garret AiResearch turbocharger with the result that the engine developed approximately 398bhp. In its basic form the Mulsanne was capable of about 120mph (193km/h), but while the Turbo was potentially considerably faster, its top speed was limited to 135mph (217km/h) because of worries about possible tyre difficulties. However, this 4926lb (2234kg) Bentley could reach 60mph (96km/h) in under nine seconds. At £61,744 the Mulsanne Turbo cost £6504 more than the standard car, and outwardly differed from it as the radiator grille, instead of being chromed, was painted to match the body colour.

Customers undoubtedly responded to the car's performance, although some criticism was levelled at its handling because this was little changed from the standard saloon, the suspension of which was soft in the extreme. Rolls-Royce set about rectifying this shortcoming and the result, announced at the 1985 Geneva Motor Show, was the Bentley Turbo R, the R standing for roadholding. Its engine specifications were essentially the same as the Turbo's but the suspension had been stiffened up. The car was externally identifiable by its alloy wheels shod with low profile tyres. The instrument panel now sported a revolution counter. Performance was an improvement on the Mulsanne Turbo's with a top speed of over 140mph (225km/h) and if fuel was consumed at a mere 14mpg (20.1 litres/100km), for a car costing £79,397, who was pump watching?

The model got off to a flying start for, in September 1986, it took the national one-hour endurance title from a standing start at 140.91mph (226.76km/h) with a further 15 records falling at the same time.

Refinements continued and for 1987 came fuel injection, and anti-lock brakes. The interior was simultaneously improved with the car being fitted with special four-position seats which automatically retained a memory of the most suitable setting for each occupant. Today Bentley cars account for around 55 per cent of Rolls-Royce's total production, which is a significant measure of the key role played by the Turbo R in raising the marque's profile.

Bentley Turbo R

6.7 litre V8
Rolls-Royce Silver Shadow/
Bentley T Series
1965

Rolls-Royce Silver Spirit/
Bentley Mulsanne
1980

Mulsanne Turbo 1982

Bentley Turbo R 1985

Specifications: Bentley Turbo R

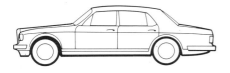

Length:	17ft 3in (5258mm)
Width:	6ft 2in (1880mm)
Height:	4ft 10in (1473mm)
Wheelbase:	10ft (3048mm)
Track:	front and rear, 5ft (1524mm)
Unladen weight:	4926lb (2234kg)

Engine: V8, overhead valve, 104x99mm, 6750cc. Fuel injection. Compression ratio, 8:1. Turbocharged. Max power, not disclosed (estimated 328bhp). Max torque, not disclosed

Transmission:	Three-speed automatic
Drive:	Rear
Suspension (front):	Independent, coil springs and wishbones
Suspension (rear):	Independent, coil springs and semi-trailing arms, automatic self levelling
Top speed:	140mph (225km/h)
0-60mph (96km/h):	8.6 seconds
Production (to date):	4200

ABOVE: *Like the Mulsanne Turbo, the R had a radiator shell painted in the body colour and was distinguished by the fitment of alloy wheels. The air dam was also revised.*

LEFT: *A 1991 Turbo R pictured against the background of the Member's Banking and Bridge at Brooklands, appropriately in company with a supercharged 4½ litre Bentley dating from 1930.*

RIGHT: *The instrumentation of the Turbo R differed from the Mulsanne by the presence of a centre console and leather-covered steering wheel.*

Jaguar XJ6 (1986 to date)

Making the second generation XJ6 a better car than its predecessor represented a considerable challenge for Jaguar. But when the new model arrived in 1986 it was universally praised for doing precisely that and today it is the company's sole saloon model.

When John Egan became Jaguar's chairman in 1980, his first priority was to instil some reliability into the then current XJ6 range. It was also the year that Jim Randle, Jaguar's director of product engineering, began work on its successor, which was coded XJ40. In the period between then and the model's launch, Jaguar eventually shook off, in 1986, its BL Cars parentage and became a publicly quoted company. It is one which, since 1988, has been owned by Ford.

The new car bore a family resemblance to its illustrious predecessor. It is a well proportioned four-door saloon, low and distinctive in the manner of the original, although there were actually few carries-over from it. Jaguar's replacement for its famous six-cylinder, twin-overhead-camshaft XK engine had first appeared in the XJ-S of 1983, and the AJ6 shared its cylinder configuration and valve layout. Produced in fuel-injected 3.6 litre form, it did suffer from some lack of refinement, and its valve gear was considerably reworked and quietened for its fitment in the new saloon. In addition, there was a new 2.9 version with a single overhead camshaft, which started life as half Jaguar's V12 engine.

Transmission was by a five-speed manual unit, while a four-speed automatic 'box was available at extra cost.

The all-independent suspension was also new with the wishbone and coil system reworked and lightened at the front. The excellent rear unit used on the original XJ6 dated back to 1961, so this was redesigned with wishbones, coil springs and fixed length drive shaft. Although not unlike the original, the new one had its rear brakes mounted outboard rather than inboard, as they previously had been.

The car's interior was in the traditional Jaguar style with the option of leather or cloth seats and the customary veneers applied to the instrument panel and door cappings.

Comfort And Class

On the road the new car more than lived up to its reputation, being capable of an extraordinarily refined 135mph (217km). It could reach 60mph (96km/h) in under eight seconds which made it faster, in every respect, than the original XJ6. Handling was also better and the new car was more economical.

In addition to the standard version, Jaguar borrowed the Sovereign name

from in-house Daimler and this model was fitted with air conditioning, an automatic braking system and more sophisticated suspension levelling as standard. As previously, the new Jaguar was produced in more expensive Daimler form, although only the 3.6 litre engine with automatic transmission was offered in this case.

For 1990 this larger capacity unit was replaced in all versions by a 4 litre derivative, and a new XJR 4.0 was also offered as a high performance saloon from Jaguar Sport. The 1991 season saw the 2.9 six similarly uprated, to a 3.2 litre unit.

When the XJ40 was first planned, the engineering team, fearing that Jaguar might subsequently be forced to accept the in-house Rover V8 engine as an alternative power unit, connived to design the car so that it could only receive the six. As a result, the previous generation of V12-engined Series III XJ6s had to be retained, and it was not until more than six years after the new XJ6's launch that – in late 1992 – it had been successfully modified to accept the V12 engine. The work required the replacement of no less than 60 body panels. The V12 was enlarged from 5.3 to 6 litres and the Daimler version is produced in long wheelbase form. With this, Jaguar now has a model, capable of an effortless 155mph (249km/h), which can rival the Mercedes-Benz 600SEL for the accolade of the finest four-door saloon currently available in the world.

BELOW: *The XJ6 as it appeared in its first year of production. This 1987 car certainly looks good from the rear. It was available in 2.9 and 3.6 litre six cylinder forms.*

Jaguar XJ6

```
                                                    5.3 litre V12
                                                    XJ12 1972

              3.6 litre
              six cylinder
              XJ-S 1983
                                    XJ6
                                    1986

              3.6 litre                  2.9 litre six
              engine


                         4 litre engine
                         1990

                                    3.2 litre engine
                                    1991


                                           6 litre V12
                                           1992
```

BELOW: *The origins of the XJ6's 3.2 litre engine, available from 1991, are to be found in Jaguar's V12. The six perpetuated its single-cam layout and appeared in 91×74mm, 2.9 litre form on the XJ6's 1986 arrival. When the stroke was lengthened to 83mm for the 1991 capacity increase, it acquired the twin-overhead-camshaft, 24 valve cylinder head shown here.*

ABOVE: *A 1994 XJ6 in high specification S guise with electronically controlled automatic transmission and a choice of 3.2 and 4 litre engines.*

Specifications: Jaguar XJ6 3.6 litres

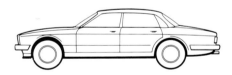

Length:	16ft 4in (4978mm)
Width:	6ft 6in (1981mm)
Height:	4ft 6in (1372mm)
Wheelbase:	9ft 5in (2870mm)
Track:	front and rear 4ft 11in (1499mm)
Unladen weight:	3903lb (1770kg)

Engine: Six cylinder, twin overhead camshaft, 91x92mm, 3590cc. Fuel injection. Compression ratio, 9.6:1. Max power, 221bhp at 5000rpm. Max torque, 248lb/ft at 4000rpm.

Transmission:	Five-speed manual or four-speed automatic
Drive:	Rear
Suspension (front):	Independent, coil springs and wishbones
Suspension (rear):	Independent, fixed length drive shafts, coil springs and lower wishbones
Top speed:	135mph (217km/h)
0-60mph (96km/h):	7.7 seconds
Production (total to date):	98,130

BMW's flagship saloon range, the 7 series cars, began life in six cylinder forms, which were soon joined by a V12. Later, in 1992, two capacities of V8 replaced the original sizes. Despite being introduced in 1986, these cars still possess levels of refinement, style and quality which have enhanced the Munich company's world-wide renown.

The lineage of these second generation 7 series cars reaches back to BMW's celebrated 1500 model of 1962. This was powered by a four-cylinder, single-overhead-camshaft engine; a six was the next logical development of the theme. The outcome, in 1968, was the 2.5 litre 2500 model, aimed four-square at the Mercedes-Benz market. Once again suspension was front Mac-Pherson struts and semi-trailing arms at the rear, while disc brakes were fitted throughout. Its 1977 replacement was designated the 7 series. This shared the same mechanical layout but had a new body and was offered in 2.8, 3 and 3.2 litre forms.

Improving Aerodynamics

This was succeeded, late in 1986, by the outwardly similar but improved new 7 series, the four-door body of which was skillfully reworked in the interests of aerodynamic efficiency. It was wider and slightly lower than its predecessor, and further wind-cheating improvements contributed to a drag coefficient of 0.32, better than the figure of 0.42 for the car it replaced. Changes included modifying the inclined radiator grille, which was reduced in height, and in the cabin area the roof pillars were more generously radiused than on the old model.

Mechanically the new cars followed the layout of the earlier ones although, in every instance, improvements were made. The series was initially available with two engine options, the 730i was a 3 litre, while the 735i was a 3.5 version – the *i* suffix indicated the presence of fuel injection. BMW claimed modest improvements in combustion with the smaller unit developing 197bhp, as opposed to 184bhp, while the 3.5 produced 220bhp instead of 218. Transmission was by five-speed manual gearbox or a four-speed automatic. The all-independent suspension and brakes followed earlier and well-established BMW practice.

In its larger capacity 3.5 litre form, the BMW offered 145mph (233km/h) motoring and 60mph (96km/h) came up in a little over nine seconds. Above all, roadholding was a great improve-ment on the previous series, but that was only the beginning of the story.

Soon afterwards, at the 1987 Geneva Motor Show, BMW revealed full details of its long awaited alloy, 300bhp, 5 litre, V12 engine with 32 valves and single overhead camshafts per cylinder bank. This was produced in standard 750i and long wheelbase 750iL forms. Both were capable of 155mph (249km/h) and able to reach 60mph (96km/h) in seven seconds. Four-speed automatic transmission was standardized, and these V12-powered cars were also fitted with air conditioning as standard, and trimmed in leather throughout. Suspension benefitted from automatic stability control and electronic damping.

Then, early in 1992, BMW announced two new V8 engines, of 3 and 4 litres capacities. In fact, they bore no design relationship nor shared components with the V12. They were all-alloy, 32-valve units, with twin overhead camshafts per bank. When fitted to the 7 Series cars they replaced the sizes which were accordingly phased out during 1992. The new 145mph (233km/h) 730i came with a five-speed manual gearbox, while the 740i, which was capable of speeds nudging 150mph (241km/h), had a new five-speed automatic one. This was also an optional fitment on the smaller capacity car. The 4 litre was also available in long wheelbase form.

This generation of 7 Series cars must be nearing the end of its life and the replacement will undoubtedly greatly benefit from this new generation of engines, which have been created to take on the best in the world.

BELOW: *BMW's flagship, the long wheelbase 750iL with 5 litre V12 engine. Refinements are "thinking" automatic transmission and adjustable suspension damping.*

RIGHT: *In 1992 the 7 Series sixes were replaced by V8 power units. These are of 3 and 4 litre capacities, and consequently are designated 730i and 740i respectively.*

Specifications: BMW735i

Length:	16ft 1in (4902mm)
Width:	6ft (1829mm)
Height:	4ft 7in (1397mm)
Wheelbase:	9ft 3in (2819mm)
Track:	front 5ft (1524mm), rear 5ft 1in (1549mm)
Unladen weight:	3883lb (1761kg)
Engine: Six cylinder, single overhead camshaft, 92x86mm, 3430cc. Fuel injection. Compression ratio, 9.2:1. Max power, 217bhp at 5700rpm. Max torque, 232lb/ft at 4000rpm.	
Transmission:	Five-speed manual or four-speed automatic
Drive:	Rear
Suspension (front):	Independent, MacPherson struts
Suspension (rear):	Independent, coil springs and semi-trailing arms
Top speed:	145mph (233km/h)
0-60mph (96km/h):	9.3 seconds
Production (7 Series, to end of 1992):	272,564

BMW 7 Series

1.5 litre four cylinder
1500 1962

1.8 litre 1800 1963

1.6 litre 1600 1964

2.5 litre six cylinder
2500 1968

7 Series 1977

2.8 litres   3 litres   3.2 litres

7 Series
1986

5 litre V12
1987

to 1992   to 1992   V8 1992

3 litres   4 litres

ABOVE: *Driving compartment of a 750iL with leather-upholstered seats which adjust electrically to accommodate every possible shape. Instrumentation is a model of clarity. The steering column is adjustable for length and the interior is, of course, air conditioned.*

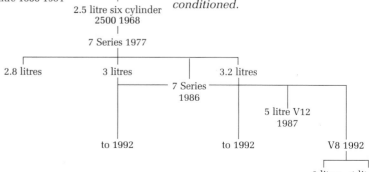

ALFA ROMEO 164 (1987 to date)

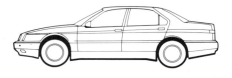

This is a car that Alfa Romeo desperately needed to re-establish its international reputation for, by the 1980's, the state-owned car company appeared to be badly out of touch with its potential customers. Not only did its products lack the usual Italian vitality, the cars were also badly built. So, the front-wheel-drive 164 was a model that *had* to be right. To a great extent, it has lived up to its expectations.

It was the last of a clutch of designs in which a quartet of manufacturers pooled their resources to develop four new models, all of which shared a common chassis/floorpan. The first of these so-called Type Four cars, the Lancia Thema, arrived in the autumn of 1984; it was followed by the Saab 9000 in 1985 with the Fiat Croma then appearing for 1986. The last of the series, the 164, was not completed until three years after the Lancia.

Thankfully for the Milan company, it had been worth the wait. In any event, Alfa Romeo's status had changed in January 1987, when it was taken over from state ownership by Fiat, its great rival. Although the 164's design had been completed by this time, its new owners delayed the car's introduction, so that changes could be made to its interior.

The Pininfarina Touch
Intended to take Alfa Romeo into BMW and Mercedes-Benz territory, the 164 represented a great visual improvement over its predecessors, being a four-door saloon with real flair. Not only did it look right, it was also aero-dynamically honed to produce a drag coefficient of just 0.30. Significantly, it was the work of the Turin-based Pininfarina styling house.

The car was available with a choice of transversely mounted engines. Because Italian cars are penalized by a 2 litre tax threshold in the home market, the smallest capacity unit was a 1962cc four with twin overhead camshafts, courtesy of the 75 model, with twin spark integrated ignition and output boosted to 148bhp for the 164.

Next came a 2 litre turbocharged petrol unit, a 2.5 litre turbocharged diesel, also a four, while the top line model was a 3 litre version of Alfa Romeo's proven V6 engine with a single overhead camshaft per cylinder bank. This had first appeared in 2.5 litre form in the GTV of 1981. The five-speed manual gearbox was a modified version of that used in the Lancia Thema, another Type Four vehicle.

MacPherson struts were used at the front, while the Thema-derived rear suspension employed struts in conjunction with transverse arms. The car's interior was also an improvement on past experience with Fiat input evident in the form of better ergonomics.

As the fastest version of the range, the V6-engined car was the most popular 164 sold outside Italy. This smooth, torquey power unit endowed the car with a 0-60mph (96km/h) figure of around 8.5 seconds and, impressively, it was capable of flat-out speeds approaching 140mph (225km/h). The only significant criticism of this 164 was that the steering suffered to some extent through 192bhp being put on to the road through the front wheels. There was, consequently, too much torque steer – that is, power developed by the engine adversely affected the feel of the steering.

An automatic version of the 164 was introduced in 1989 and a 200bhp car, named Cloverleaf, followed in 1990. In this, the steering problem was, to some extent, alleviated. Late in 1992 came the 210bhp Super with the V6 now fitted with twin-cam 24-valve heads, and producing an impressive claimed 0-60mph (96km/h) figure of 7.7 seconds and a top speed nearing 150mph (241km/h). The Cloverleaf's engine benefitted similarly and was boosted to 230bhp. A four-wheel-drive car, the 164 Q4, arrived in 1993.

The 164 range has done much to enhance Alfa Romeo's once tarnished image and it is also, unquestionably, the best car of the Type Four quartet.

Specifications: Alfa Romeo 164 3 litres

Length:	14ft 11in (4547mm)
Width:	5ft 9in (1753mm)
Height:	4ft 7in (1397mm)
Wheelbase:	8ft 8in (2642mm)
Track:	front 4ft 11in (1499mm), rear 4ft 10in (1473mm)
Unladen weight:	3583lb (1625kg)
Engine: Transversely mounted V6, single overhead camshaft per bank, 90x72mm, 2959cc. Fuel injection. Compression ratio, 9.5:1. Max power, 192bhp at 5600rpm. Max torque, 180lb/ft at 3000rpm	
Transmission:	Five-speed manual
Drive:	Front
Suspension (front):	Independent, MacPherson struts
Suspension (rear):	Independent, transverse arms, coil springs and trailing links
Top speed:	140mph (225km/h)
0-60mph (96km/h):	8.5 seconds
Production (total to date):	260,000

Alfa Romeo 164

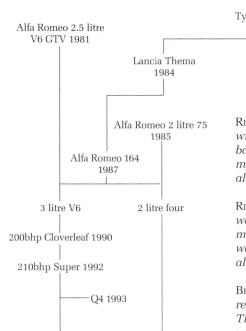

Alfa Romeo 2.5 litre
V6 GTV 1981

Type Four cars

Lancia Thema
1984

Saab 9000
1985

Fiat Croma
1985

Alfa Romeo 2 litre 75
1985

Alfa Romeo 164
1987

3 litre V6

2 litre four

200bhp Cloverleaf 1990

210bhp Super 1992

Q4 1993

to date

to date

RIGHT: *The 3 litre, 24 valve engine, with twin overhead camshafts per bank, of a 1993 164 Cloverleaf. Like many Alfa Romeos of the past, this is also a visually impressive unit.*

RIGHT BELOW: *The Cloverleaf's interior was revised in 1993 with changes made to the instrumentation, which was larger and clearer than hitherto along with better controls.*

BELOW: *The 164 is one of the best-received Alfa Romeos of recent years. The impeccable body lines are the work of Pininfarina. This is a 1993 164 Cloverleaf.*

K864 SLB

CITROËN XM (1989 to date)

A stunning aerodynamic body, front-wheel drive and the most advanced suspension system of its day spells out just one manufacturer, and that is Citroën. In 1989 it replaced its 15-year-old CX with the XM, which followed in the distinguished wheel tracks of its predecessor by being voted European Car of the Year for 1990 – an important accolade.

Stylistically the XM was a *tour de force* with the Italian Bertone concern essaying a sensational dart-like, five-door saloon with a low nose and flush-fitting double curvature glass. All this contributed to a drag coefficient of 0.28, although this rose, depending on the model, to a still respectable 0.30. A wheelbase of 112in (2850mm) resulted in a roomy five-seater car, and Citroën went to great lengths to keep rust at bay by zinc plating about half and galvanizing around a quarter of the body panels. The model was offered with a five-year anti-corrosion guarantee.

Choose Your Engine

The XM was available with five different transversely mounted engine options, all of which evolved from existing models. Bottom of the range was in-house Peugeot's XU engine with a 115bhp, carburettored, 2 litre, single-overhead-camshaft four, courtesy of the Citroën's best-selling BX. The same unit was also available in 130bhp fuel-injected form. Next came the familiar 3 litre alloy V6, developed by Peugeot, Renault and Volvo, with a single overhead camshaft per bank and 170bhp on tap. Diesel versions of both engines were also specified. One was XU-based although of 2.1 litres, and the emissions-conscious, three-valves-per-cylinder head set-up was a world first. The same configuration was extended to the heads of the V6 which, in this diesel form, was turbocharged. Two five-speed gearboxes were on offer – the fours used one, and the more powerful V6 the other. A four-speed automatic option followed in 1990.

Hydropneumatic, all-independent suspension had been a feature of Citroën cars since the celebrated DS of 1955 and the XM was also equipped in this way. It employed essentially the same system as that used on the CX and BX models with front MacPherson struts and rear trailing arms. The basic layout sufficed on the cheaper XMs but the top line cars employed what Citroën called its Hydractive computer-controlled spring and damping rates that adjusted the suspension relative to speed and cornering.

When the time came for critics to evaluate the XM, both ride and handling, as befitted its sophisticated mechanicals, were found to be outstanding. However, the consensus was that the 2 litre four cylinder versions were underpowered, and although the fuel-injected cars were capable of 120mph (193km/h), 60mph (96km/h) came up in a lethargic 11 or so seconds. As might be expected, the 3 litre performed better; it was capable of over 135mph (217km/h) with 60mph arriving in around nine seconds.

In mid-1990 came a supplementary 200bhp version of the V6, with 24 valve heads, which pushed the model's top speed to beyond the 145mph (233km/h) mark. For 1993 turbocharging was extended to the 2 litre petrol engines which pepped up their performance. With such an advanced specification, the XM bears witness to a design philosophy that began with the Traction Avant model back in 1934. Like its legendary predecessor it should run and run.

Specifications: Citroën XM 3 litres

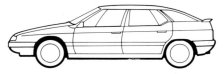

Length:	15ft 5in (4699mm)
Width:	5ft 10in (1778mm)
Height:	4ft 6in (1372mm)
Wheelbase:	9ft 4in (2845mm)
Track:	front 5ft (1524mm), rear 4ft 9in (1448mm)
Unladen weight:	2829lb (1283kg)

Engine: Transversely mounted V6, single overhead camshaft per bank, 93x73mm, 2975cc. Fuel injection. Compression ratio, 9.5:1. Max power, 170bhp at 5600rpm. Max torque, 180lb/ft at 3000rpm.

Transmission:	Five-speed manual or four-speed automatic
Drive:	Front

Suspension (front): Independent, MacPherson struts, interconnected hydropneumatic spring/damper units

Suspension (rear): Independent, trailing arms, hydropneumatic spring/damper units

Top speed:	137mph (220km/h)
0-60mph (96km/h):	9.1 seconds
Production (total to date):	255,999

LEFT: *The SM's front-wheel-drive configuration and transversely mounted V6 engine revealed for display purposes. Note the front MacPherson struts.*

RIGHT: *The driving compartment of an XM 2.0 Turbo which has a good seating position with plenty of leg room at the front as well as the back. Five individuals can be carried.*

BELOW: *A 1989 XM 2.0Si which is powered by a four cylinder engine of Peugeot/Citroën parentage. The Bertone-styled hatchback body is both stylish and roomy, with the model providing an outstanding ride but sluggish performance.*

Lexus LS400 (1988 to date)

When in the 1960's Japanese car makers began to make a significant impact on world markets, they concentrated on the low cost, high volume sector. By the 1980's such cars were setting new engineering standards that the rest of the motoring community was striving to emulate. This was the decade in which the Japanese manufacturers turned their attentions to the luxury saloon sector dominated by Mercedes-Benz, BMW and Jaguar. The most significant example of this new, more expensive generation of cars came from the largest of Japan's Big Five in the shape of the Lexus from Toyota. Such has been the success of the LS400 that it has become the world's best selling car in its class.

Lexus, it should be made clear, is not a model but a marque name, and the cars are sold through their own dealer network. There were initially two lines in the range; the ES250, based on Toyota's front-wheel-drive, V6-powered Camry and the all-new 150mph (241km/h) LS400 powered by a purpose-designed, 4-litre, 32-valve V8 engine with twin overhead camshafts per cylinder bank.

A factor in the car being capable of this speed was its aerodynamics – the four-door saloon body had a drag coefficient of 0.29, which is one of the best in its class. The somewhat anonymous lines were the work of Toyota's California design centre with the final touches applied by Japan.

The smooth and extraordinarily quiet 250bhp alloy V8 engine drove the rear wheels via an electronically controlled four-speed automatic gearbox.

An instance of the extraordinary degree of refinement built into this Lexus was that the 'box was fitted with a choice of economy and sport settings linked to an electronic engine management system, which retarded the ignition to ensure that gearchanges were as smooth as possible.

Suspension was by coil springs with double wishbones at the front and upper wishbones and twin parallel lower links at the rear. Air suspension was available as an optional extra. An electronic high speed ride control was employed.

Upholstery was in cloth or optional leather and the driver's seat had its own memory which could call up one of seven electronically activated settings. Wood trim was in evidence and for this Toyota turned to Yamaha's piano making division, which was responsible for crafting it in Californian

walnut. A novel feature was the steering wheel which slid out of the way when the ignition key was removed.

Ride and handling were judged to be on a par with the best that Europe could provide and complaints were generally confined to the incidence of excessive body roll during high speed cornering. Toyota claimed that this 3755lb (1703kg) car could reach 62mph (100km/h) in just 7.9 seconds.

American sales began in August 1989, and the Lexus reached Europe in the following May. The LS400 sold in Britain for £34,250 which was more expensive than the Jaguar XJ6, but less than the equivalent 7 Series BMW.

Good as the LS400 was, Toyota wasted little time in responding to criticisms of the car and changes were applied to the 1993 models, which were identifiable by a new matt black radiator grille. Most significantly, the damper settings were changed and bigger brakes and larger diameter wheels fitted. Inside, the specification of the body hugging driver's seat was extended to the front passenger seat, and twin airbags were introduced. Clearly Toyota means business and it is sobering to reflect that the Lexus name, at the time of writing (1994), is a mere six years old.

BELOW: *The LS400's steering wheel is electrically adjustable. The instrument panel is crisply presented and activated with the ignition. Automatic transmission is employed.*

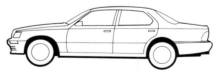

Specifications: Lexus LS400

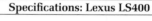

Length:	16ft 4in (4978mm)
Width:	5ft 11in (1803mm)
Height:	4ft 7in (1397mm)
Wheelbase:	9ft 2in (2794mm)
Track:	front 5ft 1½in (1565mm), rear 5ft 1¼in (1554mm)
Unladen weight:	3726lb (1690kg)

Engine: V8, twin overhead camshafts per bank, 87x82mm, 3969cc. Fuel injection. Compression ratio, 10:1. Max power 250bhp at 5600rpm. Max torque, 260lb/ft at 4400rpm.

Transmission:	Four-speed automatic
Drive:	Rear
Suspension (front):	Independent, double wishbones, air springs
Suspension (rear):	Independent, upper wishbones, air springs, twin lower links
Top speed:	150mph (241km/h)
0-60mph (96km/h):	7.5 seconds
Production (to date):	272,694

ABOVE: *The 400's styling does appear to be rather bland and lacking the flair of its rivals, but this four-door saloon possesses an impressive drag coefficient of a mere 0.29.*

BELOW: *An American specification 400. The car was launched there prior to it arriving in Europe in 1990. It is targetted at Mercedes-Benz, BMW and Jaguar territory.*

The first generation of S-Class models appeared in 1979 and endured for 12 years before being replaced by the current range, which is powered by six cylinder, V8 and V12 engines. These were undoubtedly the most mechanically complex, heavy cars ever to be offered by the Stuttgart-based company. Unfortunately, their arrival coincided with a deepening world recession, that was particularly apparent in Germany, and sales have suffered accordingly.

These extraordinarily impressive cars followed Mercedes-Benz's proven front engine/rear drive philosophy, while the understated but enlarged four-door saloon body perpetuated, in general terms, the outline of its predecessors. Similarly, all versions were produced in two wheelbases, but in this instance they were both longer than previous versions; they measured 9ft 11in (3023mm) and 10ft 3in (3124mm), and were respectively designated by the SE and L suffixes.

The bottom line S300 series was powered by a 3.2 litre six cylinder engine essentially carried over from the previous 300 SE/L. Originally a 3 litre, it was revised with the emphasis on greater torque rather than power, the bore and stroke were increased and the unit fitted with a new 24-valve, twin-overhead-camshaft cylinder head, courtesy of the top of the range V12. Next came a V8, of 4.2 and 5 litres, for the S400 and S500 series cars which was inherited from the earlier 500E. Both were specified with new V12-related four-valve heads. The larger capacity unit shared the internal dimensions of its predecessor, while the 4.2 litre was a small-bored version.

The Great V12

Top of the range was a fabulous 6 litre, 402bhp V12 which endowed the S600 series cars with a top speed limited to 155mph (249km/h). Ironically when work began on the design of what the company called its W140 range, a V12 engine was never contemplated. It was thought that a 5.6 litre V8, enhanced by twin cam heads, would be more than capable of propelling the 4400lb (1995kg) saloon to 155mph (249km/h), as indeed it could. But then came BMW with its 5 litre V12, destined for its 7 Series saloon, and caused Mercedes-Benz to think again. The firm even briefly toyed with the idea of creating an 8 litre V16 but, thankfully, wiser counsels prevailed. The starting point for its V12 was the work already completed on the revised six. The project began in 1987 and was completed

in a remarkably short four year period, even though the engine did delay the arrival of the big saloon by over a year. The 6 litre alloy V12, which is replete with electronic refinement, has twin overhead camshafts per bank, weighs 638lb (289kg) and develops 402bhp at 5200rpm. Mercedes-Benz's new five-speed automatic gearbox could not cope with that sort of power, so it used a strengthened four-speed unit which is also shared with the V8.

These S-Class cars retained the company's proven multi-link, coil-sprung, independent rear suspension while, at the front, was a new double wishbone system with its own subframe. But there is, of course, much more to it all than that in the form of adaptive damping that works in conjunction

with a rear self-levelling system, both of which operate with the effortless efficiency associated with the marque.

Simply entering one of these cars is something of an experience. Each of the wide, heavy doors has its own electric motor to pull it shut. The windows are double glazed which adds weight but prevents misting up in cold weather and excludes exterior noise. The windscreen wipers even have their own hot water bottle to prevent them freezing to the 'screen in extreme low temperatures. Inside, the air conditioning filter excludes dust, pollen spores and odours, and even the mirrors have their own three position memories.

Behind the wheel the big car concept disappears, as the V12 is able to reach 60mph (96km/h) in under six seconds. The 5 litre V8 shares its same (limited) 155mph (249km/h) top speed. The 4

litre version is able to exceed 150mph (241km/h) and even the 3.2 litre six can attain 140mph (225km/h).

The top-line long wheelbase 600 SEL sold for nearly £90,000 on its introduction to the British market, but in 1993 Mercedes-Benz's total sales fell by a massive 27 per cent and the S-Class cars were proving particularly hard to sell. The company responded by introducing for 1994 the S280, which entered the market at a new level. It was a £37,500 model powered by a 2.8 litre six courtesy of its E-class stablemates, which undercut the S300 by some £7000. While demand for the range may well rise as the world economy improves, it seems unlikely that Mercedes-Benz will ever again commit itself so wholeheartedly to such large, costly and over-complicated cars, however impressive they turn out to be.

RIGHT: *The understated luxury of the S-Class offering the ultimate in comfort and refinement, regardless of the quality of road surface. This is the 500SEL version.*

LEFT: *The 2.8 litre six cylinder S280 which arrived for 1994 was the cheapest model in the S-Class range and well geared to the European recession.*

Specifications: Mercedes-Benz S600 SEL

Length:	17ft 1in (5207mm)
Width:	6ft 2in (1880mm)
Height:	4ft 10in (1473mm)
Wheelbase:	9ft 11in (3023mm)
Track:	front 5ft 3in (1600mm), rear 5ft 1in (1549mm)
Unladen weight:	4818lb (2185kg)
Engine: V12, twin overhead camshafts per bank, 89x80mm, 5987cc. Fuel injection. Compression ratio, 10:1. Max power, 408bhp at 5200rpm. Max torque, 428lb/ft at 3800rpm	
Transmission:	Four-speed automatic
Drive:	Rear
Suspension (front):	Independent, coil springs and double wishbones
Suspension (rear):	Independent, coil springs and multi-link
Top speed:	155mph (249km/h)
0-62mph (100km/h):	6.1 seconds
Production (total to date, including SEC coupé):	180,955

FORD MONDEO (1993 to date)

Ford's first world car was the legendary Model T of 1908-1927 vintage. There was a 66 year hiatus before the arrival of its second, the highly acclaimed, Belgian-built, front-wheel-drive Mondeo which, from the autumn of 1994, will also be produced in America. European sales began in March 1993, and the model became an instant best seller. Public acclaim was endorsed by the experts as it was voted European Car of the Year for 1994.

The Mondeo was conceived as a replacement for Ford of Europe's rear-wheel-drive Sierra of 1982, which was distinguished by its radical aerodynamic styling. Work on the new car began immediately after the Sierra's launch and the Detroit-based Ford company soon decided that this would be a true world car. Once America had completed the advanced and pre-programme work, from 1987 the bulk of the design was undertaken by Ford's European facility at Dunton, Essex. Five years and nearly £3 billion later, initial optimism has been more than justified by the public's response to this advanced, visually attractive, well equipped model.

Built at Ford's plant at Ghenk, Belgium, the Mondeo comes in three body styles: a four-door saloon, five-door hatchback and estate car. Its slippery lines have a creditable drag coefficient of 0.31. Safety is a key element of the design and the body structure has been created to meet or exceed the demands of all existing American and European crash test regulations.

The specifications of the Mondeo's Zeta engines have more in common with a performance car of 20 years ago than a family saloon. Manufactured in Cologne, Germany and Bridgend, Wales, they are transversely mounted, fuel-injected, 16-valve, twin-overhead-camshaft fours which first appeared in 1.6 and 1.8 litre forms, in the 1992 Ford Escorts. They were joined by a 2 litre version, which was unique to the Mondeo. The engines respectively produce 90, 113 and 134bhp and there is also a 1.8 litre turbocharged diesel unit.

Stateside Specifications

The North American versions of the car will be powered by a US Ford-designed 2.5 litre, 24-valve V6 engine, also with twin overhead camshafts per cylinder bank, and may well be used for a future four-wheel-drive Mondeo. The V6 will simultaneously become available in Europe. As they are being shipped to the Old World, they will cross with batches of the five-speed MTX75 manual gearbox that are destined for America but which are manufactured in Europe. All this underlines the international jigsaw that is the Mondeo. There is also a newly designed optional four-speed automatic gearbox.

Great attention has been lavished on the all-independent suspension. Each system possesses its individual subframe, which adds to the overall weight of the car but greatly improves driveline and noise levels. At the front are MacPherson struts with offset coil springs, while there is a so-called quadralink design at the rear with strut-type coil springs and transverse and trailing arms. However, the estate cars have a more compact long/short arm layout which come close to double wishbones in concept. More expensive versions of the car can be fitted with an

BELOW: *Ford's Mondeo is a front-wheel-drive world car which was initially offered with a range of transversely mounted, twin-overhead-camshaft, four cylinder engines.*

optional traction control system which shuts down the throttle in the event of wheelspin. It is offered in conjunction with a sophisticated adaptive damping system. When it comes to the steering, all Mondeos are fitted with a power-assisted rack-and-pinion unit. Brakes are front discs with rear drums.

Although the Mondeo is smaller overall than the Sierra, the passenger accommodation is about the same because of the space saved by the adoption of a transversely located engine and front-wheel drive. Safety is a constant theme in the car's design: all examples are fitted with a driver's air-bag as standard equipment and the costlier variants have an electrically adjustable seat.

Ford claim that the basic 1.6 litre model is capable of 110mph (177km/h), that the 1.8 litre is a 120mph (195km/h) car, and that the top-line 2 litre model is able to reach 60mph (96km/h) in 9.1 seconds and attain 126mph (203km/h). Not only are the Mondeos fast, their handling and ride characteristics, noise levels, and brakes are equal to, and in most instances, better than those of their rivals.

The Model T Ford enjoyed a 19-year production life. While it is built in very different times, Ford's second world car looks like becoming one of the great international automotive success stories of recent years, and a worthy successor to such a renowned forebear.

ABOVE: *The Mondeo is also produced in Ghia Estate form. Powered by a 2 litre engine, it has a claimed top speed of 126mph (203km/h) with 60mph (96km/h) arriving in 9.1 seconds.*

RIGHT: *The hatchback version of the Mondeo; there is also a notchback body. Its styling, while not radically advanced, is intended for a long production life.*

Specifications: Ford Mondeo 2 litre

Length:	15ft 2in (4623mm)
Width:	6ft 8in (2032mm)
Height:	4ft 6in (1372mm)
Wheelbase:	8ft 10in (2692mm)
Track:	front and rear, 4ft 5in (1397mm)
Unladen weight:	2930lb (1330kg)

Engine: Transversely mounted, four cylinder, twin overhead camshaft, 84x88mm, 1989cc. Fuel injection. Compression ratio, 10:1. Max power, 134bhp at 6000rpm. Max torque, 133lb/ft at 4000rpm

Transmission:	Four-speed automatic
Drive:	Front
Suspension (front):	Independent, MacPherson struts
Suspension (rear):	Independent, strut type with transverse and trailing arms
Top speed:	126mph (203km/h)
0-60mph (96km/h):	9.1 seconds
Production (total to date):	348,205

RENAULT TWINGO (1993 to date)

A strong personality is not a characteristic usually associated with the automobile, but few would deny that Renault's new small car, the Twingo, possesses oodles of character. This comfortable four seater with its cheeky body lines seems to raise smiles wherever it goes. Initially produced for the French home market, a right-hand-drive version was anticipated but then ruled out on grounds of cost.

The brainchild of Renault's chief of design, Patrick Le Quement, the Twingo existed as a concept in 1988. Its three-door hatchback body shares a family resemblance with Renault's multipurpose Espace people carrier. However, at consumer clinics staged that year throughout Europe, the public's response to the design was decidedly mixed with only 50 per cent of its potential customers liking it. Nevertheless, Renault decided to gamble on the car's appeal and it was unveiled, to universal acclaim, at the 1992 Paris Motor Show. Built at Flins, France and Valladolid, Spain, the Twingo was officially launched in March 1993.

The model's front-wheel-drive mechanicals are rooted in Renault's small car, the Clio, that replaced the R5 in 1990. But only a handful of components have been carried over for it. As befits its no frills approach, only one engine is specified – it is powered by the Clio's transversely mounted, 1.2 litre, fuel-injected, single-overhead-camshaft four. It has, however, been re-engineered so that practically all the 66lb/ft of torque come in at 2000rpm and the 55bhp unit just keeps on pulling. Suspension is by front MacPherson struts with a coil-spring torsion beam axle at the rear. Brakes are front discs with drums at the rear.

RIGHT: *Cheeky, commodious and, above all, different, the Twingo is only built for Continental Europe with no plans for a right-hand-drive version.*

Based on a shortened version of the Clio's floorpan, the Twingo has an overall length of 11ft 3in (3422mm) which is about 1ft (300mm) less than the Clio. But the masterstroke of the design is the car's interior packaging. With the rear seat pushed right back, four six-foot (1.83m) tall occupants can be comfortably accommodated. Part of the reason for this is the height of the body which, at 4ft 8in (1422mm), is taller than anything else in its class. A width of 5ft 4in (1626mm) is similarly pioneering.

Come On In

The wide doors make access to the rear seats relatively easy. These are mounted on rollers and can be moved backwards and forwards to vary the amount of luggage accommodation. They also fold down flat, either singly or together, and in the latter instance, when the rear door is opened, access is provided to a luggage platform which is a usable 3ft 8in (1118mm) deep.

The Twingo's interior is a combination of the utilitarian and the cheerful. There is no instrument panel, as such, just a line of warning lights with such vital information as speed and fuel level digitally displayed in the centre of the fascia. Seats are upholstered in blues and reds which adds to the Twingo's image as a fun car, although this should not conceal the fact that it is a highly professional concept in terms of its design. Options are currently confined to a full length canvas roof and, perhaps perversely, air conditioning.

Despite its unconventional appearance, the Twingo is deceptively fast, being capable of 93mph (150km/h), although it takes around 14 seconds to reach 60mph (96km/h). Visibility is excellent, the car is unpretentious and, like the Mini, has a broad-based social appeal. It has also proved to be, at the end of its first year of production, a great sales success. At the time of writing (1994) it is France's best selling car, after the Clio. This is, after all, the country that gave the world the equally distinctive Citroën 2CV, and that survived for 42 years!

LEFT: *Apart from its wacky styling, the Twingo's carrying capacity is its other main attribute. Four tall individuals can be accommodated.*

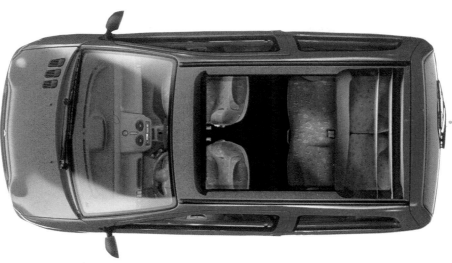

Specifications: Renault Twingo

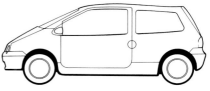

Length:	11ft 3in (3429mm)
Width:	5ft 4in (1626mm)
Height:	4ft 8in (1422mm)
Wheelbase:	7ft 8in (2337mm)
Track:	front 4ft 7in (1397mm), rear 4ft 5in (1346mm)
Unladen weight:	1742lb (790kg)
Engine: Transversely mounted, four cylinder, single overhead camshaft, 74x72mm, 1239cc. Fuel injection. Compression ratio, 9.2:1. Max power, 55bhp at 5300rpm. Max torque, 66lb/ft at 2800rpm	
Transmission:	Five-speed manual
Drive:	Front
Suspension (front):	Independent, MacPherson struts
Suspension (rear):	Torsion beam axle and coil springs
Top speed:	93mph (150km/h)
0-60mph (96km/h):	14.3 seconds
Production (to date):	125,420

ABOVE: *Bird's eye view of the Twingo revealing its cheerful upholstery and substantial rear passenger leg room. The back seat is movable, so varying the amount of luggage carried. The large windscreen echoes that of Renault's MPV people carrier.*

BELOW: *The front-wheel-drive Twingo is as radical in its way as the Mini was back in 1959. This three-door hatchback is imbued with plenty of personality which has pleased the public and helped to make it one of France's best-selling cars.*

ROVER 600 (1993 to date)

The most impressive manifestation, to date, of Rover's association with the Japanese Honda concern, the 600 is mechanically related to the new Honda Accord but, outwardly, the two cars could not be more dissimilar. Rover has cloaked the shared mechanics with an impressive body which, stylistically, has echoes of its saloons of 1950's. With this well received front-wheel-drive model, the British firm is consolidating its inroads into a market sector that hitherto had been almost exclusively occupied by BMW. The 600 has accordingly been favourably compared with the German company's 3 series cars.

It was back in 1979 that Michael Edwardes, then chairman of Rover's predecessor, BL Cars, recognized that its survival could only be assured by an association with another car company of approximately the same size, so that one firm could not dominate the other. As a result, an approach was made to Honda and the first fruits of the association came in 1981 with the arrival of the Acclaim. This was the last car to be badged a Triumph. It was, in fact, a Honda Ballade. The Rover 200 of 1984 had a similar pedigree. The Rover 800 and Honda Legend of 1986 differed by being a joint development mutually undertaken by the British and Japanese concerns, and it was the first large car to be produced by Honda.

Distinctively Rover
All these vehicles shared, with minor modifications, the same body styles. However, Rover then decided that, instead of simply rebadging Honda products, its cars should differ outwardly from those of Honda and the first model to exemplify this approach was the revised version of the 800, introduced in 1992. Back came the traditional Rover radiator grille, while the new body was unrelated to that of its Japanese stablemate, all of which contributed to the 800 being a great commercial success for the company.

The same approach has been applied to the 600, the body of which is the work of Rover's product design director, Gordon Sked. He was limited by the constraints of the Accord's floorpan, doors and roof but the outcome is a four-door saloon of great elegance which, above all, looks like a Rover. This is because Sked has, quite deliberately, been stylistically influenced by the company's past products, in particular the famous P4 range of 1949-1964 vintage. As a result the 600 possesses its own very British identity, which is complemented by a well equipped interior available in three trim options. The Rover is, however, more expensive than the Honda and, at £21,995, the top line 600 is a substantial £3520 more than the most exclusive Accord.

Mechanically the 600 is pure Japanese and is, at present, powered by a choice of two petrol engines in three stages of tune. There is the basic 2 litre, fuel-injected, transversely mounted, single-overhead-camshaft, 16-valve Honda unit in 114bhp form and a more potent 129bhp derivative. Top of the range is a 2.3 litre, twin-overhead-camshaft four developing an impressive 156bhp. A five-speed manual gearbox is employed. Suspension is by Honda's familiar short top link wishbones used in conjunction with coil springs and struts. There are all-round disc brakes and power-assisted, speed-sensitive steering.

The accent for the Rover 600 is very much on refinement and the car has been praised for its low noise levels, comfort and excellent build quality. Performance is on a par with most of its competitors, the 129bhp 2 litre being capable of around 125mph (201km/h). However, the critical consensus is that such rivals as the BMW 318 and Ford Mondeo have the edge on handling.

This is only the start of the 600 model line. There is said to be a Rover-designed 2.5 litre diesel engine waiting in the wings and, if the other models are anything to go by, a coupé version cannot be far off. With such models as the 600, Rover has shown that it can challenge the world's best, both at home and abroad.

RIGHT: The Honda Accord-based 623GSi has its own distinct body which incorporates echoes of Rovers of the past. Aimed foursquare at the BMW market, in 1994 the German company bought Rover.

Specifications: Rover 620

Length:	15ft 3in (4648mm)
Width:	5ft 7in (1702mm)
Height:	4ft 6in (1372mm)
Wheelbase:	8ft 11in (2718mm)
Track:	front 4ft 10in (1473mm), rear 4ft 10⅓in (1480mm)
Unladen weight:	2866lb (1300kg)
Engine: Transversely mounted, four cylinder, single overhead camshaft, 85x88mm, 1997cc. Fuel injection. Compression ratio, 9.5:1. Max power, 129bhp at 5400rpm. Max torque, 131lb/ft at 4800rpm	
Transmission:	Five-speed manual
Drive:	Front
Suspension (front):	Independent, coil springs and double wishbones
Suspension (rear):	Independent, coil springs and double wishbones
Top speed:	125mph (201km/h)
0-60mph (96km/h):	9.8 seconds
Production (total to date):	32,000

ABOVE: *Rear view of a 623iS. The car has not only been applauded for its design but also for the quality of its construction. Note the boot lid-mounted rear spoiler.*

BELOW: *The front-wheel-drive GSi's transversely mounted Honda engine, a 2.3 litre, fuel-injected, alloy, twin-overhead-camshaft four, which develops 156bhp at 5800rpm.*

Page numbers set in **bold** type denote the main references to the subject.
Page numbers in *italics* indicate captions to illustrations.

A

Abarth (*see* Fiat)
Abbey Panels, Coventry 16
Abbott body *77*
AC 10, **42-43**, *42. 43*. 68. 116.
 118-119, *118. 119*. 182
Ace 42, *43*. 118
Cobra series 10, 42, *42. 43*. 118
 428 **118-119**
Accord (*see* Honda)
Ace (*see* AC)
Adaptive Damping System 152
Aerovette (*see* General Motors)
AFN Ltd 47
Ahrens, Don **172**
Aldington, A J **80**
Aldington, Donald **80**
Alfasud (*see* Alfa Romeo)
Alfa Romeo **48-49**, *48. 49*. 86.
 88. **96-97**, *96. 97*. 176, 216.
 228, **288-289**, *288. 289*. **304-
 305**, *304. 305*
Alfasud 288. *288. 289. 289*
Alfasud Sprint 289, *289*
Alfasud Ti 288, *289*
Alfetta 216, 289
BAT 5/7/8/9 96
Cloverleaf 304, *305*
Duetto 48
Giulia 48, 96
Giulia TZ 1/2, 96, *97*
Giulietta 48. 96
Giulietta SS 96, *96. 97*
Giulietta Sprint 96
GTV 304
Spider 48, *48. 49*
Spider Veloce 48, *48. 49*
Alfetta (*see* Alfa Romeo)
Alfieri, Giulio **98**, **130**, **194**
Altman, Nathan D **108**
Alpine (*see* Renault)
America (*see* Ferrari)
Ami (*see* Citroën)
Anderson, Spike 55
Arkus-Duntov, Zora **44**
Artioli, Romano **240**, **241**
Ash, David 116
Aston Martin 74, **84-85**, *84. 85*.
 102-103, *102. 103*. **126-127**,
 126. 127. **158-159**, *158. 159*.
 162. **176-179**, *176. 177. 178*.
 179. 180, **204-207**, *204. 205*.
 206. 207. **216-219**, *216. 217*.
 218. 219. **224-227**, *224. 225*.
 226. 227. 236
DB1 84
DB2 74, 84, *84. 85*
DB2S 85
DB4 74, 85, 102, *102*. 126, 158,
 159. 176, *178*. 204
DB4GT 102, *102*. 176, *177. 178*
DB4GT Zagato 162, 176, *176*.
 177. 178. 178. 179. 216, *216*.
 217. 218, *218. 219*
DB5 102, *103*. 126, 158, *159*
DB6 74, 102, 126, 158, *159*
DB7 158, *158. 159*. 226
DBS 102, 204
Lagonda 84, 85. 162, 204, *204*.
 205. 206, *206. 207*. 216, 224
V8 126, *126. 127*. 206, 224, 226,
 226
Virage 126, 158, 224, *224. 225*.
 226, *226. 227*. 234, 236
Atlantic (*see* Austin Healey)
Audi 74, 122, **146-147**, *146. 147*.
 290
50 292
GT 146
Quattro 74, **146-147**, *146. 146*.
 147
200 146
Aurelia (*see* Lancia)
Austin 32, 40, *41*. 254
1800 40
3000 *41*
Metro 272
Seven Nippy 32
Austin-Healey 10, 12, **22-23**, *22.
 23*. 24, 28, **32-33**, *32. 33*. 54
100/4 22
100/6 22
Sprite series 32, *32. 33*
3000 22, *22. 23*. 32
Autenrieth (*see* BMW)
Auto Union 82
Avanti (*see* Studebaker)

B

Beattie, Kevin **122**
Beckett, Terence **278**
Beetle (*see* Volkswagen)
Beher intercooler 222
Benedini, Giampaolo **240**
Bensinger, Jorg, **146**
Bentley 84, 162, **164-167**, *164.
 165. 166. 167*. 200, *202*. **236-
 239**, *236. 237. 238. 239*. 260,
 262, 263, 282, **298-299**, *298.
 299*
Continental 162, 164, *164. 165*.
 166. 166. 167. 236, *237*
Continental R 162, 236, *236.
 237*. 238, *238. 239*
Corniche 164
Mulsanne Turbo 236, 298, *298.
 299*
S1 262, *263*
Turbo R 236, 298, *298. 299*
Berlinetta Lusso (*see* Ferrari)
Bertone 74, 96, 162, 176, 184,
 185. 192, 196, *197*. 198, 228,
 306, *307*
Bertoni, Flaminio 250, **266**
Bez, Ultrich **62**
Biarritz (*see* Cadillac)
Bishop, David **70**
Bizzarrini, Giotto **114**
BL Cars 272, 286, 300, 316 (*see
 also* British Leyland/Leyland
 Cars)
Black, Sir John **20**
Blatchley, John **164**
Bluebird (*see* Datsun)
BMW 54, **62-63**, *62. 63*. 80, *80*.
 132-133, *132. 133*. 246, *247*.
 248, **276-277**, *276. 277*. **302-
 303**, *302. 303*. 308, *309*. 310,
 316, *316*
Autenrieth 80, *80*
CS 132, *132*
CSi 132
CSL 132, *132. 133*
502 276
503 54
507 54
Isetta 276
1500 248, 276, *276. 277*. 302
1600 276, *277*
1800 276, *277*
7 series 302, *302. 303*. 308, 310
700 276
3 series 62, 316
318 316
325i 62
326 80
2000C 132
2500 302
2800C 132
Z1 62, *62. 63*
BMW Motorsport 246
BMW Technik 62
Boano **94**
Boano (*see* Ferrari)
Bogly, Maurice **256**
Borrani wheels 92, 190
Bosch fuel injection 136, *137*.
 202
Bosch K-Motronic fuel injection
 system 236

Boue, Michel **290**, *290*
Boulanger, Pierre **256**
Bowden, Ben **76**, *77*
Boxer, (*see* Ferrari)
Brabham 244, 245
BT46 245
Brasseur 92
Braungart, Martin **132**
Bristol (*see* Bristol Aeroplane
 Company)
Bristol Aeroplane Company 74,
 80-81, *80. 81*
Bristol 400 74, 80, *80*
Bristol 401 80
Bristol 403 80
Bristol 404 80, *81*
Bristol 405 80
Bristol 406 80, *81*
Bristol 407 80
British Leyland Motor
 Corporation 22, 36, 70, 272
British Motor Corporation 10,
 12, 22, 28, 30, 32, 40, 248,
 254, **272-273**, *272. 273*. 280
Mini 184, *185*. 248, 272, *272.
 273*. 314, 315
Mini Clubman 272, *273*
Mini Cooper 272, *272. 273*
Mini Cooper S 272
1275GT 272
British Motor Heritage 70
Broadley, Eric **180**, **182**
Brown, David 84, 85, 102, 126,
 127. **158**, **204**, **224**
Brown, Roy **278**
Budd Corporation 250
Bugatti 140. 162. 222, **240-243**,
 240. 241. 242. 243. 246
EB110 162. 222. 240. *240. 241*.
 242, *242. 243*. 246
EB112 242
Bugatti, Ettore *242*
Buick **110-111**, *110. 111*. 294, *294*
Riviera 110, *110. 111*. 294, *294*

C

Cadillac 162, **172-175**, *172. 173.
 174. 175*. **270-271**, *270. 271*
Biarritz 270
Eldorado Brougham 162, 172,
 172. 173. 174, *174. 175*. 270
Eldorado Seville 270, *270. 271*.
 294
Seville 294, *294. 295*
Seville Elegante 294, *295*
Cadillac (*see* General Motors)
Cady, Wayne **294**
Callaway Engineering,
 Connecticut 224
Callum, Ian **158**, *159*
Camry (*see* Toyota)
Campagnolo wheels 194
Canley, Coventry 20
Capri (*see* Ford)
Carrera (*see* Porsche)
Carter carburettor *174*
Caterham Cars 30
Caterham Seven (*see* Lotus
 Seven)
Chapman, Colin **10**, **38**, **66**, **100**,
 140
Chapman struts 38, 100
Chevrolet 10, **24-25**, *24. 25*.
 44-45, *44. 45*. **52-53**, *52. 53*.
 58-59, *58. 59*. 160, 248, **274-
 275**, *274. 275*
Corsa 274
Corvair 248, 274, *274. 275*
Corvair Monza 274, *274. 275*
Corvette 10, 24, *24, 25. 25*. 58,
 58. 59, *59*. 116, 160
Corvette Sting Ray 24, *25*. 44,
 44. 45. 52, *52. 53*. 108
XP-720 44
ZR-1 58, *59*

Chevrolet Corvette V8 engine
 108
Chrysler 68, *68*. 74, 80, 126, 194.
 228, *228*. 230, 274
 Plymouth Valiant 274
Chrysler Firedome V8 engine 92
Chrysler V8 engine 74, 80, *81*.
 122
Cibie headlights 130, *130*
Cisitalia 18, 74, **78-79**, *78. 79*
 202 Gran Sport 78. *78. 79*
Citroën 108, **130-131**, *130. 131*.
 248, **250-251**, *250. 251*. **256-
 257**, *256. 257*. **266-267**, *266.
 267*. **306-307**, *306. 307*
Ami 257
BX 306
CX 306
DS 108, 130, 248, 250, 266,
 266. 267. 306
Dyane 257
SM 130, *130. 131*. 140, *306. 307*
Traction Avant 248, 250, *250.
 251*. 256, 266, 306
2CV 248, 256, *256. 257. 257*.
 314
XM 306, *306. 307*
Citroën, André **250**
City (*see* Honda)
Clio (*see* Renault)
Cloverleaf (*see* Alfa Romeo)
Cobra (*see* AC Cobra)
Coker, Gerry **22**, **32**
Cole, Edward. **274**
Colombi, Gioacchino 82, 90, 94,
 136
Colotti gearbox 182
Continental (*see* Bentley)
Continental (*see* Lincoln)
Corniche (*see* Rolls-Royce)
Corolla (*see* Toyota)
Cortina (*see* Ford)
Cortina Lotus (*see* Ford)
Cortina GT engine 30
Costin, Frank 100
Cosworth Engineering 296, *297*
Countach (*see* Lamborghini)
Coventry Climax Four engine
 30, 100, *100*
CP Autokraft 42, *43*
Croma (*see* Fiat)
Cromadora wheels 190

D

Daimler 264, *264*. 300
 SP250 264
Dallara, Giampaolo **114**, **184**,
 192, **196**
Daninos, Jean **92**, **164**
Danny, Robert **134**
Datsun 10, **54-55**, *54. 55*. 144,
 150
240Z 10, 54, *54. 55*. 150
260Z 54
280Z 144, 150
510 Bluebird 54
Daytona (*see* Ferrari)
di Dion axle 86, 89, 126, 224
de Virgillio, Francesco **88**
Dennis, Ron **244**
Diablo (*see* Lamborghini)
Dino (*see* Ferrari)
Dodge **69-69**, *68. 69*
 Viper 68, *68. 69*
Dolomite (*see* Triumph)
Donald Healey Motor Company
 16
Duetto (*see* Alfa Romeo)
Dunlop disc wheels 28, *28*. 108
Dunlop Maxaret brakes 122
Dusio, Piero **78**
Dyane (*see* Citroën)

E

Earl, Harley, **24**, **172**, **258**, **270**

Eaton supercharger 226
Eclat (*see* Lotus)
Edsel (*see* Ford)
Edwardes, Michael **272**, **316**
Egan, Sir John **234**, **286**, **300**
Egbert, Sherwood H **108**
Eight (*see* Morris)
Elan (*see* Lotus)
Eldorado Brougham (*see*
 Cadillac)
Eldorado Seville (*see* Cadillac)
Eleven (*see* Lotus)
Elford (*see* Mazda)
Elite (*see* Lotus)
Ellena (*see* Ferrari)
Elliot (*see* Healey)
ENASA, Barcelona 86
Enever, Sydney **28**, **40**
Engellau, Gunnar **104**
Escort (*see* Ford)
Espace (*see* Renault)
Esprit (*see* Lotus)
Europa (*see* Ferrari)
Europa (*see* Lotus)
Evernden, Ivan **164**
Excel (*see* Lotus)
Excellence (*see* Facel)

F

Facel 74, **92-93**, *92. 93*. 164
Facellia 92
Vega 74. 92, *92. 93*. 164
Vega Excellence 92, *93*
Vega HK500 92, *92. 93*
Facel Metallon 164
Facellia (*see* Facel)
Falcon (*see* Ford)
Fangio, Juan 98
Feeley, Frank **84**
Ferrari, Dino 124
Ferrari, Enzo **74**, **82**, **94**, **124**,
 156, **220**
Ferrari 10, 20, 68, 74, **82-83**, *82.
 83*. **90-91**, *90. 91*. **94-95**, *94.
 95*. 98, 106, *106. 107*. 118.
 120-121, *120. 121*. 134, **136-137**,
 136. 137. 155. **156-157**, *156.
 157*. 162. 170, 178. 180. 184.
 186. **188-191**, *188. 189. 190.
 191*. 196. **208-211**, *208. 209*.
 210. 211. **220-221**, *220. 221*.
 222. 223. 224. 228. 234. 240
Boxer 208. 210
Daytona 156. *156*. 162. 188. *188.
 189*. 190. *190. 191*
Dino 206 124
Dino 246 124. *124. 125*. 196.
 198. *198*
F40 68. 162. 214. 220. *220. 221*.
 222. 222. 223. 238. 234
Mondial 210
Testarossa 156. 162. 208. *208.
 209*. 210. 210. 211. *211*. 224
125 Sport 82
166 Sport 82
166 Inter 82. *83. 83*. 90
195 Inter 82
212 Inter 90
250GT Ellena 94
250 Europa 94, *95*
250 Europa GT 94
250GT 94, *94. 95*. 106
250GRT *94*
250GTE 94. 106. 136
250GT Berlinetta Lusso 94.
 106. *106. 107*
250GT Boano 94, *95*
275GTB 120. 188
275GTS 120
288GTO 220
308 220
330GTC 120. *120. 121*
340 America 90. *91*
342 America 90
365GT4 136. *137*. 208

365GTC 120. *121. 136*
375 America 90. *90. 91*
400A 136. *137*
400i 136. *137*
400GT 136. *137*
412 136. *136. 137*
412i 156
456GT 156. *156. 157*
500 Superfast 120
512TR 208. *208. 210. 211*
FF Developments
 four-wheel drive 232
Fiat 18. 60. 78. *79*. 94. 124. 180.
 196. 199. 200. 248. **268-269**,
 268. 269. 304
Abarth 199
Croma 304
500 248. 268. *268. 269*
508 CMM 78
Giardiniera 268
130 200
Nuova 268
X 1/9 60
Fielder. Fritz **276**
Fiorio. Cesare **196**, **198**
Flying Nine chassis 20
Ford. Henry **274**
Ford Shelby (*see* AC Cobra)
Ford 10. 42. *43*. 72. 74. **116-117**,
 116. 117. 118. 126. **128-129**,
 128. 129. 158. 162. **180-183**,
 180. 181. 182. 183. 184. 206.
 218. 224. 226. 234. 248. 253.
 274. **278-279**, *289. 279*. 300.
 312-313, *312. 313*. 316
Capri 74. 116. 128. *128. 129*
Cortina 248. 278. *278. 279*
Cortina Lotus 278. *278. 279*
Edsel 278
Escort 128. 312
Falcon 274
GT40 42. 162. 180. *180. 181*.
 182. *182. 183*. 183. *184*
Model T 248. 253. 274. 312.
 313
Mondeo 248. 312. *312. 313*
Mustang *43*. 74. 116. *116. 117*.
 128. 180. 274
S 72
S3 72
Sierra 312. 313
Thunderbird 110
4-Rotor (*see* General Motors)
Franay. France (coachbuilders)
 166
Franco Brittanic Autos 164
Frayling. John **100**
Frazer Nash (*see* Bristol)
Fuhrmann. Dr Ernst **56**, **212**
Fulvia (*see* Lancia)

G

Gandini. Marcello **184**, **192**, **194**,
 196, **228**, *228. 229*. **240**
Garrett turbocharger *145*. 235.
 298
Gauntlett. Victor **178**, **216**, **218**,
 224, **226**
Gemini (*see* Isuzu)
General Motors 10. 24. 44. 52.
 64. 66. 110. 136. 140. 172. 236.
 242. 248. **258-259**, *258. 259*.
 270. 274
Aerovette 58
Cadillac 16. 258. *258. 259*
4-Rotor 58
Mako Shark II 52
Orleans 172
Park Avenue 172 (*see also*
 Buick. Chevrolet. Cadillac
 and Oldsmobile)
George. Yves **280**
Giacosa. Dante **78**, **268**
Giardiniera (*see* Fiat)
Giugiaro. Giorgetto **140**

Ginther, Richie **12**
Giulia (*see* Alfa Romeo)
Giulietta (*see* Alfa Romeo)
Glowacke, Ed **172**
Gobbato, Piero **196**
Goertz, Count Albrecht **54**
Golf (*see* Volkswagen)
Gordini (*see* Renault)
Graber, France (coachbuilders) 166
Gran Sport (*see* Cisitalia)
Greenley, Ken **224**, *225*, **236**, *237*
Griffith (*see* TVR)
Grylls, Harry **282**

H

Halibrand wheels 42
Hall, Bob **64**
Hamilton, Duncan **26**
Hampton, Peter *115*
Hart, Fred **278**
Hayes, Walter **158**, **226**
Hayter, Don **40**
Healey, Geoffrey **32**
Healey, Donald Mitchell **16**, **22**, **32**, **76**
Healey **16-17**, *16*, *17*, 74, **76-77**, *76*, *77*
D 16
E 16, *16*, *17*
Elliot 74, 76, *76*, *77*
Silverstone 16, *16*, *17*
Tickford 76, *77*
Westland 16, 76, *77*
Heffernan, John **224**, *225*, **226**, **236**, *237*
Helfet, Keith **232**
Hennessy, Sir Patrick **278**
Heynes, William **34**
Hill, Phil **12**
Hispano-Suiza 86
Hodges, Len **16**
Hoffman, Max **170**
Hofmeister, Wilhelm **276**
Holls, David **52**, *53*
Honda 74, **154-155**, *154*, *155*, 160, 248, 316, *316*, *317*
Accord 154, 316, *316*
City 154
CRX 154
Legend 316
NSX 74, 154, *154*, 155, *155*, 160
Hruska, Rudolph **288**
Hull, Nick *233*
Humber 76
Hurlock, Derek **118**
Hydra-Matic transmission 270
Hydramatic automatic transmission 258
Hydrolastic suspension 272

I

Iacocca, Lee **116**
IHI turbocharger *220*, 222
Iltris (*see* Volkswagen)
Inter (*see* Ferrari)
Interceptor (*see* Jensen)
International Automobile Design 236
Issigonis, Alec **184**, **248**, **254**, **272**, **280**
Isuzu 66, *67*
Gemini 66
Ital Design 288, *288*, 289, *289*, 292, *292*, *293*

J

Jabbeke, Belgium 14, 20, 76
Jaguar 10, **14-15**, *14*, *15*, 24, **26-27**, *26*, *27*, **34-35**, *34*, *35*, 68, 74, 118, **134-135**, *134*, *135*, **138-139**, *138*, *139*, 158, 162, 224, 228, **232-235**, *232*, *233*, *234*, *235*, 244, 246, 248, **260-261**, *260*, *261*, **264-265**, *264*, *265*, **286-287**, *286*, *287*, **300-301**, *300*, *301*, 308, *309*
C-Type 26, 34, 168
D-Type 26, *27*, *33*, 34
E-Type 10, 34, *35*, 44, 54, 74, 134, *134*, *135*, 138, 286
F-Type 158
S-Type 286
Mark I 264, *264*
Mark II 248, *261*, 264, *264*, *265*
Mark V 260
Mark VII 260, *260*, *261*, 264
Mark VIII 260, *261*
Mark IX 260
Mark X 34, 260, 264, 286
XJ5 134, 138, *138*, *139*
XJ6 138, 248, 286, *286*, *287*, 300, *300*, *301*, 308
XJ12 134, *139*, 232
XJ13 134
XJ220 158, 162, 228, 230, 232, *232*, *233*, 234, *234*, *235*, 242, 246
XJR-5 138
XJR-9 232
XJR-10 234
XJR-15 244
XJS 74, 158, 300
XK55 26, *26*, *27*
XK120 10, 14, *14*, *15*, 26, 260
XK140 *15*, 26, 264
XK150 *15*, 34
XKD540 *27*
420G 286
Jaguar Sport 234, 300
Jalpa (*see* Lamborghini)
Jano, Vittorio **88**
Jensen, 74, 104, 105, **122-123**, *122*, *123*, 146
FF 74, 122, 123, 146
Interceptor 74, 122, *122*, *123*, 146
Jordan, Chuck **64**, **110**
Jordan, Mark **64**
JW Automotive Engineering 183

K

Kamm tail 102, 106, *106*
Kar Kraft 182
Karmann, Germany 36, 105, 132, 292
Kerguen, Jean *177*
Kimbereley, Mike **66**
Kirwan-Taylor, Peter **100**, *101*
KKK turbocharger 56
Knight, Robert **286**
Kraus, Ludwig **168**

L

Lagonda (*see* Aston Martin)
Lamborghini 68, *68*, 74, **114-115**, *114*, *115*, 134, 162, **184-187**, *184*, *185*, *186*, *187*, **192-195**, *192*, *193*, *194*, *195*, 208, 210, 222, **228-231**, *228*, *229*, *230*, *231*, 232, 234, 240, 246
Countach 162, 186, 192, *192*, 193, *193*, 194, *194*, *195*, 196, 208, 210, 228, *229*, 230, *231*, 240
Diablo 162, 195, 210, 222, 228, *228*, *229*, 230, *230*, *231*, 232, 234, 246
Jalpa 230
LM002 230
Miura 114, 162, 184, *184*, 185, *185*, 186, *186*, *187*, 188, 192, 196, *197*, 228, 240
350GT 74, 114, *114*, *115*, 120, 162, 184, 186, 188
400GT 114, *114*, 184, 186
Lamborghini, Ferruccio **74**, **114**, **185**, **195**
Lampredi, Aurelio 90, 94
Lancia 74, **88-89**, *88*, *89*, 146, 172, 176, **196-199**, *196*, *197*, *198*, *199*, 220, 304
Aurelia B20 74, 88, *88*, 89, *89*
HV Fulvia 196
LC2 220
Stratos 196, *196*, *197*, 198, *198*, 199, *199*
Thema 304
2500GT 88, *88*, 89, *89*
Le Quement, Patrick **314**
Lefebvre, André **266**
Legend (*see* Honda)
Lexus (*see* Toyota)
Leyland Cars 272
(*see also* British Leyland)
Lincoln 172, 174
Continental 172, 174
Lilley, Arthur **72**
Lilley, Martin **72**
Livanos, Peter **178**, **216**
Loasby, Mike **204**
Lockheed 86
Loewy, Raymond **108**, *109*
Lola Cars 180, 182
Longbridge 22
Lord, Leonard **22**, **32**, **272**
Lorscheidt, Manfred **168**
Lotus 10, **30-31**, *30*, *31*, **38-39**, *38*, *39*, 58, 60, 64, **66-67**, *66*, *67*, **100-101**, *100*, *101*, **140-141**, *140*, *141*, 242, 244, 278
Eclat 66, 140
Elan 10, 38, *38*, *39*, 100, 244, 278
Elan SE 66, *66*, *67*
Eleven 100
Elite 66, 100, *100*, *101*, 140
Esprit 66, 140, *140*, *141*
Esprit Turbo 140, *140*, *141*
Europa *39*, 140
Excel 60, 140
Seven 30, *30*, *31*
Super Seven 30
Lutz, Bob **68**
Lyons, William ***14***, ***286***

M

MacPherson struts 54, 128, 132, 144, 148, 252, 276, 278, 288, 290, 292, 296, 302, 304, *306*, *307*, 312, 314
Marelli electronic ignition system *220*
Marelli-Weber fuel injection system 218
Marina (*see* Morris)
Marmiroli, Luigi **228**
Maserati 74, **98-99**, *98*, *99*, 130, *130*, *131*, 194
Mistral *99*
Sebring 98
350S 98
3500GT 74, 98, *98*, *99*
Matano, Tom **64**
May, Michael **138**
Mayflower suspension 20
Mazda 10, **64-65**, *64*, *65*, 68, 74, **144-145**, *144*, *145*
MX5 Miata 10, 64, *64*, *65*, 68
110S 144
R100 144
RX7 64, 74, 144, *144*, *145*
RX7 Elford *144*, *145*
787B *65*
323 64
McLaren 162, 230, 232, **244-247**, *244*, *245*, *246*, *247*
F1 162, 230, 232, 244, *244*, 245, *245*, 246, *246*, *247*
McLellan, Dave **58**
Mercedes-Benz 82, **112-113**, *112*, *113*, **152-153**, *152*, *153*, 162, **168-171**, *168*, *169*, *170*, *171*, 248, 294, **296-297**, *296*, *297*, 300, 302, 304, *309*, **310-311**, *310*, *311*
190 296, *296*, *297*
190SL 112, 248
200 296
220SE 112
230SL 112, *112*
250SL 112
280SL 112, *113*
SL300 152, *153*
SL500 152, *152*, *153*
SL600 152
300SL 162, 168, *168*, *169*, 170, *170*, *171*
300SLR 170
600SEL 300, 310
S-Class 310, *310*, *311*
MG 10, **12-13**, *12*, *13*, 24, **28-29**, *28*, *29*, 32, 33, 34, **40-41**, *40*, *41*, 54, **70-71**, *70*, *71*
EX175 28
EX182 28
MGA 10, 28, *28*, *29*, 40
MGB 10, 28, 40, *40*, *41*, 70
MGB GT V8 *40*, *41*, 70, *70*
MGC 40, *40*, 41
RV8 10, 40, 70, *70*, *71*
TA 12
TB 12
TC 12, *12*
TD 12, *13*
TF 12, *13*
Y 12
Miata (*see* Mazda)
Michelin 130, 250
Michelin Pilote wheels *250*
Mini (*see* British Motor Corporation)
Mistral (*see* Maserati)
Mitchell, Peter **70**
Mitchell, William **24**, *25*, **44**, **52**, **108**, **110**, *111*
Mittino, Giuseppe **218**
Miura (*see* Lamborghini)
Miura, Don Eduardo **185**
Mondeo (*see* Ford)
Mondial (*see* Ferrari)
Morgan 10, 20, **50-51**, *50*, *51*
Plus 4 50
Plus 8 50, *50*, 51, *51*
Morris 248, **254-255**, *254*, *255*
Eight 254
Marina 254
Minor 248, 254, *254*, *255*
Minor (*see* Morris)
Moss gearbox 34, 51
Moss, Stirling **170**
Moulded Glass Fiber Works, Ohio 312
MTX75 gearbox 312
Mulliner, H. J. coachbuilders 164, *165*, 166, *167*
Mulliner Park Ward coachbuilders 200, *200*, 202, 263, *263*, 282
Mulsanne (*see* Bentley)
Murray, Gordon **244**, **245**, **246**
Mustang (*see* Ford)

N

Nadar, Ralph **274**
Nash Healey 16
National Lorry Company, Spain **86-87**, *86*, *87*, 104
Pegaso Z102 86, *86*, *87*
Z103 86
Z102B *86*
Nearn, Graham **30**
Neerpasch, Jochen **132**
Newman, Leo **108**
Nickles, Ned **110**
Nissan 54, **150-151**, *150*, *151*, 154, 160
300ZX 74, 150, *150*, *151*, 154, 160
MID4 151
240SX Silvia **150**, 151, *151*
Nordhoff, Heinz **252**
NSU 74, 144, **284-285**, *284*, *285*
Ro80 284, *284*, *285*
Sport Prinz 284
Wankel Spyder 284
Nuova (*see* Fiat)

O

Ogier, David *177*, **178**
Oldsmobile 110, 294, *294*
Toronado 110, 294, *294*
Orleans (*see* General Motors)

P

Palmer, Jerry **58**
Park Avenue (*see* General Motors)
Park Ward (coachbuilders) 166, *166*
Paxton supercharger 108
Pegaso (*see* National Lorry Company)
Z102 **86-87**, *86*, *87*
Z103 86
Petterson, Helmer **104**
Petterson, Pelle **104**
Peugeot 16, 130, 306, *307*
402 16
XU engine 306, *307*
Piech, Ferdinand **46**, **146**
Pinin Farina, Battista **94**, **106**
Pinin Farina, Sergio **200**
Pinin Farina, **74**, **78**, *79*, **88**, *89*, **90**, *90*, *91*, **94**, *95*, **106**, **164**, **166**, **174**
Pininfarina **48**, **74**, *79*, **106**, *106*, *120*, *121*, **124**, *124*, *125*, **136**, *137*, **154**, **155**, **156**, *156*, **162**, **188**, *191*, **200**, *200*, **208**, *208*, **210**, **220**, *221*, **222**, **238**, *275*, **286**, *287*, **304**, *304*, *305*
Pirelli P700 tyres *222*
Porsche 10, **18-19**, *18*, *19*, **46-47**, *46*, *47*, **56-57**, *56*, *57*, **142-143**, *142*, *143*, 144, **148-149**, *148*, *149*, 155, 162, **212-215**, *212*, *213*, *214*, *215*, 220, 232, 252
Carrera 18, 46, *47*, 56
Carrera 2 46
Carrera 4 46, 56
Speedster 18, 46
Targa 36, 46, *46*, 52, *53*
356A 10, 18, *18*, *19*
356B 18, *18*
356C 18
550 18
911 46, *46*, *47*, 54, 142, 162
911 Turbo 10, 46, 56, *56*, *57*, 212, *212*, *213*, 214, *215*
924 142, 144, 148
928 142, *142*, *143*, 148
928GT 142, *143*
928S 142, *142*, *143*
935 56
936 56
944 148, *148*, *149*
944 Turbo 148, *148*
956 214
959 162, 212, *212*, *213*, 214, *214*, 215, 220, 232
961 214
962 214
968 148
Porsche, Butzi **46**
Porsche, Ferdinand **252**
Porsche, Ferry **18**, **46**, **212**
Powerglide transmission 24
Power Plant Frame 64

Q

Quandt, Harold **276**
Quandt, Herbert **276**
Quattro (*see* Audi)

R

Randle, Jim **232**, **300**
Ravenscroft, John **72**
Renault 248, **280-281**, *280*, *281*, **290-291**, *290*, *291*, 306, **314-315**, *314*, *315*
Alpine 290, *291*
Clio 314
Espace 314
Gordini 290, *290*
R4 280, 290
R5 290, *290*, *291*, 314
R8 280
R16 248, 280, *280*, *281*, 290
6-1100 290
Twingo 248, 314, *314*, *315*
Ricart, Wilfredo **86**
Richardson, Ken **20**
Riley engine 16, 76, *77*
Riviera (*see* Buick)
Rochester carburettor *174*
Roller, Franz **168**
Rolls-Royce 110, 162, 164, 166, *167*, **200-203**, *200*, *201*, *202*, *203*, 236, *237*, 238, 248, **262-263**, *262*, *263*, **282-283**, *282*, *283*, 286, 294, 298
Camargue 162, 200, *200*, *201*, 202, *202*, *203*
Corniche 200, 282, *283*
Silver Cloud 166, 236, 262, *262*, 263, *263*, 282
Silver Ghost 282
Silver Shadow 200, *200*, *201*, 202, 236, 248, 263, 282, *282*, 283, 298
Silver Spirit 202, 282
Silver Wraith 262, 282
Roots-style supercharger 60
Rostyle wheels 32, *33*, 40
Rover 51, 70, 72, *72*, *73*, 272, *272*, *273*, 300, **316-317**, *316*, *317*
200 316
600 248, 316, *316*, *317*
800 316
P4 range 316
Rudell, Cliff **232**

S

Saab 304
9000 304
Salisbury drive 114
Sampietro "Sammy" **76**
Samuel Elliott and Sons 76
Savonuzzi, Giovanni **78**
Sayer, Malcolm **34**, **138**
Scaglietti, Modena 106, 124
Scaglione, Franco **114**
Schultz, Peter W **212**
Scirocco (*see* Volkswagen)
Scragg, Phil *27*
Sebring (*see* Maserati)
Seven (*see* Lotus)
Seven Nippy (*see* Austin)
Seville (*see* Cadillac)
Seville Elegante (*see* Cadillac)
Shelby, Carroll **42**, **68**, **116**, *117*, **182**
Sierra (*see* Ford)
Silver Cloud (*see* Rolls-Royce)
Silver Ghost (*see* Rolls-Royce)
Silver Shadow (*see* Rolls-Royce)
Silver Spirit (*see* Rolls-Royce)
Silver Wraith (*see* Rolls-Royce)
Silverstone (*see* Healey)
Silvia (*see* Nissan)
Sked, Gordon **316**
Sleator, Walter **164**
Solex carburettor 168, 200
Sopwith, Tommy *93*
Spada, Ercole **176**
Speedster (*see* Porsche)
Spider (*see* Alfa Romeo)
Spider Veloce (*see* Alfa Romeo)

Spitfire (*see* Triumph)
Spooner, Colin **66**
Sportomatic gearbox 46
Sprite (*see* Austin-Healey)
Standard 20, *21*
Stanzani, Paolo **184**, **192**, **194**, **240**
Stevens, Peter **66**, *67*, **244**, *245*
Stratos (*see* Lancia)
Stromberg carburettor 36
Studebaker **108-109**, *108*, *109*
 Avanti 108, *108*, *109*
SU carburettor 22, *100*
Super Seven (*see* Lotus)
Supra (*see* Toyota)
Surrey hardtop 36

T

Targa (*see* Porsche)
Thema (*see* Lotus)
Tickford (*see* Healey)
Testarossa (*see* Ferrari)

Thunderbird (*see* Ford)
Tonti, Gianni **196**
Toronado (*see* Oldsmobile)
Touring, Milan 74, 80, 82, *86*, 98, *98*, 102, 114, 122, 176, 184
Towns, William **126**, **204**, *204*, **206**, **224**
Toyota 10, 54, **60-61**, *60*, *61*, 74, **160-161**, *160*, *161*, 248, **308-309**, *308*, 309
2000GT 54
Camry 308
Corolla 60
Lexus GS300 160
Lexus SC300 160, 248
Lexus LS400 308, *308*, *309*
MR2 10, 60
Supra 74, 160, *160*, *161*
Traction Avant (*see* Citroën)
Treser, Walter *146*
Trevcar Motors 72
Triumph 10, **20-21**, *20*, *21*, 32,

36-37, *36*, *27*, 54, 76
Dolomite 36
Spitfire 32, 64
2000 36
TR1 20
TR2 20, *21*
TR3 20, *20*, *36*
TR3A 20, *20*, 36
TR3B 20, 36
TR4 20, 36, *36*
TR4A 36, *36*
TR5 36
TR6 36, *37*, 54
TR7 36, *37*
TR8 36
TVR 10, **72-73**, *72*, *73*
 Griffith 10, *72*, *72*, *73*
Twingo (*see* Renault)
TWR Group 158, *159*, 234, *234*

U

Uhlenhaut, Rudolph **168**, **170**

V

Vauxhall engine *31*
Vega (*see* Facel)
Vega Excellence (*see* Facel)
Vignale, Turin 78, 90, 122
Viper (*see* Dodge)
Virage (*see* Aston Martin)
Volkswagen 10, 18, *19*, 146, 148, 248, **252-253**, *252*, *253*, 254, 274, **292-293**, *292*, *293*
 Beetle 10, 248, 252, *252*, 253, *253*, 254, 274, 292, *292*, *293*
 Golf 253, 292, *292*, *293*
 Golf GTI 292, *293*
 Iltris 146
 Passat 292
 Scirocco 292
Volvo **104-105**, *104*, *105*, 306
 P120 105
 P1800 104, *104*, *105*,*105*
 PV44 104
von Falkenhausen, Alex **276**

W

Wade supercharger 16
Walkinshaw, Tom **158**, **234**, *234*
Wallace, Bob **184**
Wankel engine 58, 74, 144, 284
 (*See also* NSU Ro80)
Wankel, Felix **284**
Ward, Peter **236**
Ward, Thomas **76**
Watt, James **76**
Watts linkage 288
Weber carburettor 30, 46, 96, *102*, 136, 168, 176, *177*, 188, *189*, 218, 276, 278
Weissach axle 142
Westland (*see* Healey)
Wheeler, Peter *72*
White, George **80**
Wilkinson, Trevor *72*
Williams, Richard *178*
Willment, John **183**
Wyer, John **180**, **183**

X

XK engine 264

Y

Young, James (coachbuilders) 166, 200, 263

Z

Z axle 62
Zagato (*see* Aston Martin)
Zagato, Elio **216**
Zagato, Gianni **216**
Zenith Stromberg carburettor 134
Zeta engine 312
ZF gearbox 58, 100, 102, 114, 126, 224
Zytek fuel injection *235*

PICTURE CREDITS

The publisher would like to thank the following photographers, picture libraries and motor manufacturers whose photographs are reproduced in this book. Pictures are credited by page number and position on the page: (B) bottom, (T) Top, (C) Centre and so on.

Aston Martin Lagonda Ltd:
8-9, 226-227(T)

Autocar and Motor:
54, 54-55, 55, 60, 60-61, 62-63, 63T, 77T, 77B, 78, 78-79, 79, 81B, 86-87B, 87, 92-93, 93T, 93B, 96-97B, 97, 98, 99T, 99B, 101, 104T, 104B, 104-105, 129T, 129B, 130-131T, 132, 151B, 212, 251, 253T, 253B, 257, 262-263, 263B, 266-267T, 266-267B, 267, 268, 273B, 280, 281B, 284T, 284B, 284-285, 285, 289B, 296, 297, 298-299T, 311

Basil Productions/Bengt Holm:
228TR, 228CR, 228-229, 229

BMW GB Ltd:
303T

Chris Brooks/Aviation Photographs International:
187TR

Neill Bruce Motoring Photolibrary:
6-7, 12, 17B (courtesy Midland Motor Museum), 20-21B, 22-23 (car courtesy Nigel Dawes), 26-27, 27T, 27B, 28-29B, 31, 32, 36, 37B, 38, 38-39 (car courtesy Nigel Dawes), 41T (car courtesy Nigel Dawes), 42-43T, 42-43B (courtesy Midland Motor Museum), 48-49, 49, 51T (Sven Eric Deler), 52-53T, 52-53B (courtesy Midland Motoring Museum), 56-57, 66-67, 67T, 67B, 70, 70-71, 71, 80, 81T, 84, 88, 89T, 89B, 90 (Bengt Holm), 94-95T, 96-97B (courtesy Brooks Auctioneers), 100-101, 102-103, 106-107T, 117T (Tobjorn Hansson), 118 (courtesy Midland Motor Museum), 118-119, 119, 120-121T, 123T, 126, 127, 131, 133T (courtesy Midland Motor Museum), 134-135T, 134-135B, 136-137T, 137, 140-141 (Peter Roberts Collection), 141, 143, 146-147, 152, 152-153, 155B, 156, 156-157, 158, 158-159, 159, 162-163, 164C, 164-165, 165, 167CR, 170T (courtesy Midland Motor Museum), 176-177, 177BR, 178, 178-179T, 178-179B, 179T, 180-181T, 180-181B, 181CR, 181BR (courtesy Midland Motor Museum), 182-183, 188-189T, 188-189B, 189, 190-191T, 190-191B, 196-197T, 196-197B, 197CR, 197BR, 198T, 198C, 198-199, 199, 204, 204-205B (courtesy the Marquis of Tavistock), 207C, 207BR, 208-209T, 210, 210-211T, 210-211B, 211, 213, 214, 214-215T, 215TR, 215CL, 215BR, 216-217, 217CL, 217CR, 217BR, 218-219T, 218-219C, 219T, 219C, 219B, 222-223T, 222-223B, 223BR, 224, 224-225T, 225B, 225CR, 226T, 226C, 226-227B, 227, 232-233, 233C, 233BR, 234, 234-235T, 235CL, 240, 240-241T, 240-241B, 241, 242, 242-243, 243TR, 243CR, 246BR, 246-247, 247BL, 247BC, 247BR, 252-253 (Peter Roberts Collection), 255, 264, 264-265, 268-269, 269, 272-273, 273T (Peter Roberts Collection), 288-289, 291BR, 292-293, 293 (Peter Roberts Collection), 303CR, 304-305, 305T, 305B, 306, 306-307, 316-317, 317B

Bugatti Automobili S.p.A.:
243B

Chrysler Corporation:
10-11, 68, 68-69T, 68-69B, 69T

Citroën UK Ltd:
307

Colour Library Books Archive:
13, 14, 15T, 15B, 18-19T, 18-19B, 24, 25T, 25B, 28-29T, 29, 30-31T, 30-31B, 33B, 34-35, 39, 40B, 41B, 44-45T, 44-45B, 46, 47B, 53, 56, 74-75, 85T, 85B, 90-91, 94-95B, 95, 110-111, 111, 113, 116-117, 117B, 124, 124-125, 125, 135, 142-143B, 148, 149, 162-163, 168, 168-169, 169, 170-171, 171TR, 171CR, 173T, 173C, 173B, 174T, 174C, 174-175T, 174-175B, 175BC, 175BR, 208-209B, 214-215B, 215C, 220, 221T, 223TR, 223BC, 248-249, 258-259T, 258-259B, 260, 260-261, 261, 265, 270-271T, 270-271B, 271, 274-275, 286-287T, 286-287B, 294, 295T, 295B, 296-297, 300

Ferrari S.p.A.:
157

Ford Motor Company Ltd:
313T, 313B

General Motors Corporation, Chevrolet Division:
59T

Jaguar:
138-139B, 233T, 233CR, 300-301, 301

McLaren Cars Ltd:
Front jacket, 244-245T, 244-245B, 245C, 245CR, 246BL

Morgan Motor Company:
51B

The National Motor Museum, Beaulieu:
12-13 (Nicky Wright), 16 (Nicky Wright), 17T (Nicky Wright), 19TR, 20-21T (Nicky Wright), 21T, 22, 23 (Nicky Wright), 33T (Nicky Wright), 35, 37T, 40T (Nicky Wright), 43 (Nicky Wright), 45, 47T (Nicky Wright), 48, 50-51, 57, 59B (Nicky Wright), 63B, 76, 82-83T, 82-83B, 83, 84-85, 86-87B (Nicky Wright), 91 (Nicky Wright), 100L, 100R, 102, 103, 106-107B (Nicky Wright), 107 (Nicky Wright), 108-109T (Nicky Wright), 108-109B (Nicky Wright), 112-113T, 112-113B, 114, 114-115 (Nicky Wright), 115, 120-121B (Nicky Wright), 121 (Nicky Wright), 122-123 (Nicky Wright), 123B, 126-127, 128, 130-131B, 133B, 136-137B, 138-139T, 142-143T, 144, 145T, 145B, 147T, 147B, 148-149, 150-151 (Nissan), 153, 154-155, 155T, 160, 160-161T, 164T, 166, 166-167, 167CL, 167B, 170C, 171TL, 172-173 (Nicky Wright), 176, 177T, 177C (Nicky Wright), 182, 183, 184 inset, 184B, 184-185, 185, 186-187T, 186-187B, 187CR, 191T (Nicky Wright), 191C (Nicky Wright), 192, 192-193T, 192-193B, 193, 194T, 194B, 195TL, 195TR, 195B, 196, 200-201T, 200-201B, 201, 204-205T, 205C, 205TR, 206-207T (Nicky Wright), 206-207B (Nicky Wright), 208-209C (Nicky Wright), 209TR, 209CR (Nicky Wright), 212-213, 217T, 220-221, 221B (Nicky Wright), 230CR, 230B, 230-231, 231BL, 231BR, 234-235B, 235CR, 236, 236-237, 237, 238, 250, 250-251, 254, 254-255, 256, 263T, 274, 275, 276-277T, 278-279, 279, 282-283T, 282-283B, 283T, 283C, 287, 289T, 291T, 298-299B, 299, 302-303, 309, 310-311, 312

Nissan Motor (GB) Ltd:
151T

Quadrant Picture Library (© Autocar):
276-277B, 277

Renarchive Service:
281T, 290-291, 291CR

Renault UK Ltd:
314, 314-315T, 314-315B, 315

Rolls-Royce Motor Cars:
202, 202-203T, 202-203B, 203CR, 203BR, 238-239, 239

Rover Group Ltd:
317T

Toyota GB Ltd:
61B, 160-161B, 308, 308-309

TVR Engineering Ltd:
72, 72-73, 73